D1029463

The

ORIGINAL
BLACK ELITE

The
ORIGINAL
BLACK ELITE

*Daniel Murray and the Story
of a Forgotten Era*

ELIZABETH DOWLING TAYLOR

Amistad

An Impint of HarperCollinsPublishers

HarperCollins books may be purchased for educational, business, or sales promotional use. For information, please email the Special Markets Department at SPsales@harpercollins.com.

FIRST EDITION

Designed by Suet Chong

Library of Congress Cataloging-in-Publication Data
has been applied for.

ISBN 978-0-06-234609-4

17 18 19 20 21   DIX/RRD   10 9 8 7 6 5 4 3 2

To Tim Berners-Lee

You do not know me, Sir Berners-Lee, but I know a lot more because of you, and I am grateful.

Contents

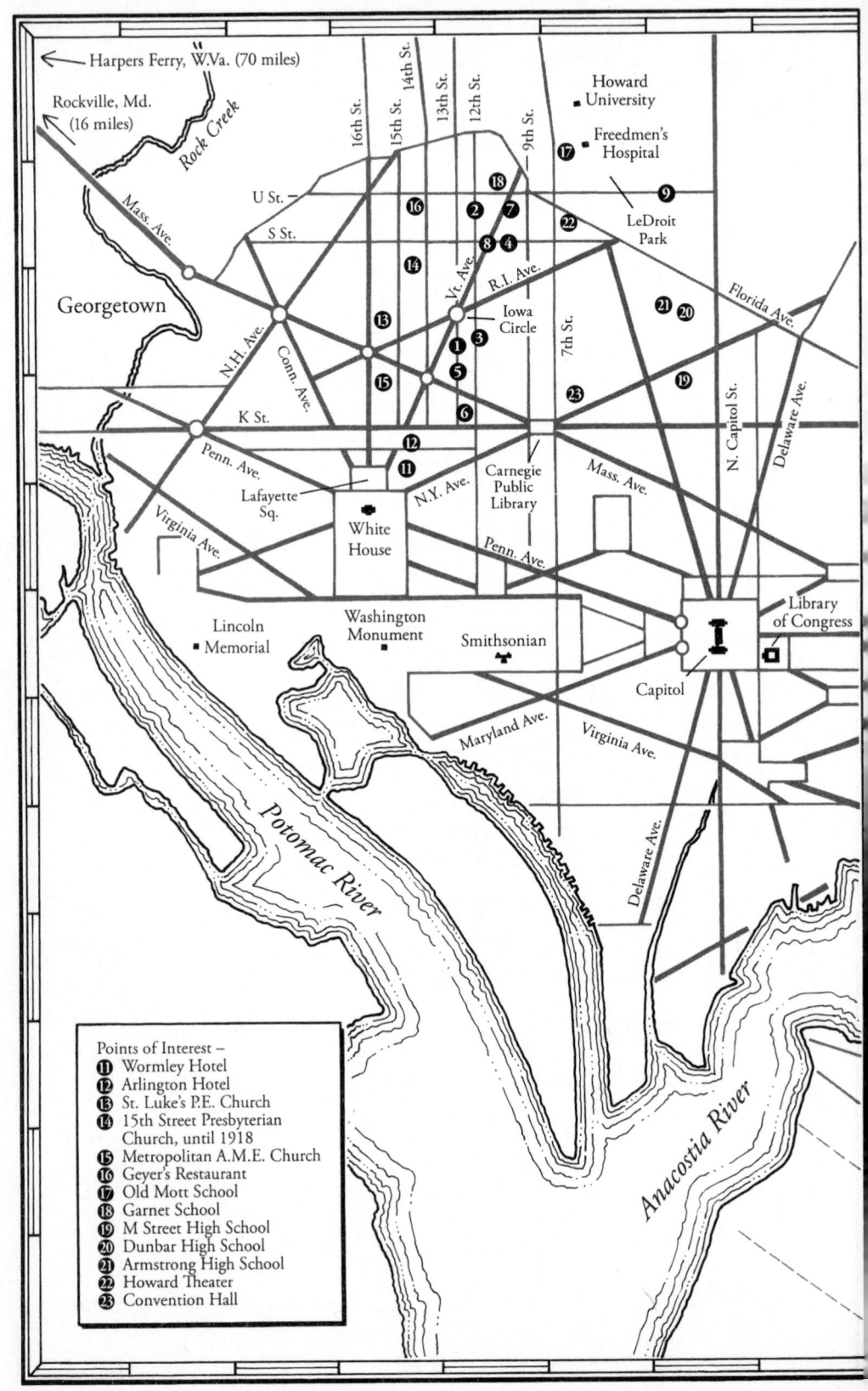

Harpers Ferry, W.Va. (70 miles)

Rockville, Md. (16 miles)

Rock Creek

Mass. Ave.

16th St.
15th St.
14th St.
13th St.
12th St.
9th St.

Howard University

Freedmen's Hospital

U St.

S St.

Georgetown

N.H. Ave.

Conn. Ave.

Vt. Ave.

R.I. Ave.

Iowa Circle

LeDroit Park

Florida Ave.

7th St.

N. Capitol St.

Delaware Ave.

K St.

Penn. Ave.

Virginia Ave.

Lafayette Sq.

N.Y. Ave.

Carnegie Public Library

Penn. Ave.

Mass. Ave.

White House

Lincoln Memorial

Washington Monument

Smithsonian

Maryland Ave.

Virginia Ave.

Capitol

Library of Congress

Delaware Ave.

Potomac River

Anacostia River

Points of Interest –
11 Wormley Hotel
12 Arlington Hotel
13 St. Luke's P.E. Church
14 15th Street Presbyterian Church, until 1918
15 Metropolitan A.M.E. Church
16 Geyer's Restaurant
17 Old Mott School
18 Garnet School
19 M Street High School
20 Dunbar High School
21 Armstrong High School
22 Howard Theater
23 Convention Hall

Daniel Murray's Washington

Places Daniel Murray Lived –

❶ With sister Ellen Butler (ca. 1869-79): 1216 13th Street
❷ With Henry & Henrietta Evans (1880-83): 1926 12th Street
❸ First house (1883-90): 1333 12th Street
❹ Second house (beginning 1890): 934 S Street

Relatives' Houses –

❺ Samuel Proctor: Three locations on 13th Street
❻ Charles Proctor: Two locations in close proximity, I Street and L Street
❼ Bruce Evans, Lillian Evanti: 1910 Vermont Avenue
❽ George Henry Murray: 928 S Street
❾ Nathaniel Murray: 150 U Street
❿ Catherine Proctor, Samuel Proctor, Kate Jordan: Barry Farm / Hillsdale in Southeast Washington

Florida Ave.

Graceland Cemetery

Baltimore, Md. (40 miles)

Maryland Ave.

Tenn. Ave.

Benning Rd.

Woodlawn Cemetery

N.C. Ave.

Mass. Ave.

S.C. Ave.

Kentucky Ave.

Penn. Ave.

Ga. Ave.

N

W   E

Navy Yard

S

Pennsylvania Ave.

Anacostia

Cedar Hill

❿

Barry Farm / Hillsdale

DISTRICT OF COLUMBIA

MARYLAND

Nichols Rd.

Saint Elizabeths Hospital

0   1

Scale of Miles

The

ORIGINAL
BLACK ELITE

Prologue

A T THE CRACK OF DAY DANIEL MURRAY, IN A SILK TOP HAT, moved along the city streets with purpose. He walked at a steady clip given the chilled air this second morning of October 1899. Though the temperature had dropped to freezing overnight, the forecast promised a warm-up for the special occasion ahead. The nation's capital was to receive the famed seaman Admiral George Dewey, who the year before had led the navy so fearlessly, so decisively at Manila Bay, routing the Spanish fleet and claiming the Philippines as war booty. President William McKinley was to present the hero with a $10,000 sword crafted of steel, gold, and diamonds by Tiffany & Company, a symbol of the country's gratitude. Prominent citizens were awarded the great honor of traveling to New Jersey in a specially outfitted train to escort the admiral back to Washington. The *Washington Post* reported that the roster of the select might be announced on the evening of September 30, but not until the next day, Sunday, would the names of the escort committee—Daniel Murray's among them—be released.

It was nearly 7 a.m. when Murray reached the train station near Pennsylvania Avenue and 6th Street. His three-story brick home was in a fashionable block of 12th Street NW, and no doubt he was excited when he checked, then clicked shut his gold pocket watch and bid his wife, Anna, good-bye. He was the proud father of five sons, his eldest a premier violinist in New York City, his second soon to be a Harvard freshman, the three youngest still at home. Any normal Monday, Murray would be taking the streetcar to the Library of Congress, where he was an assistant librarian. But now he joined the group of gentlemen gathered on the train platform who were dressed just as he was: striped trousers, Prince Albert coat, patent-leather shoes, silk hat, and gray gloves. A good number of them, like Murray (and the gallant Admiral Dewey himself), sported full mustaches that encroached more than a little over the upper lip. More than half the escort committee members had made the Elite List, a compilation of those in the District with "assured social position." There is no reason to think that Murray was uncomfortable: he knew many of the men from his full slate of business and civic activities. The flag-festooned train that hissed in waiting alongside the forty-some distinguished escorts was furnished by the Pennsylvania Railroad Company. Equipped with every modern convenience, the polished nickel-plated train was "one of the finest that ever ran on American tracks." And the fastest, up to ninety miles per hour.

Boarding for the 7:30 a.m. departure, Murray showed his ticket with pleasure: parlor car A, seat 21. He was ensconced in a plush upholstered easy chair when the train jolted out of the station. The ride smoothed out, and the men chatted about the two days of festivities in the nation's capital that would be let loose upon their return with the hero of Manila. From time to time some took advantage of the smoking car with its leather chairs, well-selected library, and fully supplied writing tables. Adjoining it was a completely outfitted barbershop. In the dining car a dozen tables were covered with fine linen and set with sparkling glass and silver. Waiters served broiled bluefish, sirloin steak, and mutton chops. Porters and waiters, "in spotless white," were the only black people aboard the train. Except for Daniel Murray.[1]

The recognition bestowed on Murray by Washington's leading citizens with his inclusion on the "famous committee" was the kind for which he had worked assiduously, traveling far from a humble start in life. Yes, he knew he was what later would be referred to as the "token black." No, he did not crave the company of white people. His lifelong objective was assimilation into mainstream culture and equal political footing and opportunity. The pronouncement "We are Americans in every fibre of our being, and we have the aspirations common to the citizens of this Republic" had issued from a political meeting of race activists that he had presided over earlier in 1899.

Daniel Murray was "a race man to the core." If he took any pride in being the first black man to join this organization or the only one to be invited to that social occasion, his greater goal, his long-range vision, was to be in the vanguard of merit-based recognition for every American of color. The rise of those in Murray's black elite circle was realized rather than potential. Its members had attained high levels of education, achievement, culture, and economic security and thus negated from the start a false line of reasoning that white supremacists gave against racial equality. They were living proof that African Americans did not lack the ability to become useful contributors to mainstream society. Though their race consciousness and identification were strong, they were ready to think of themselves as American citizens first, poised for assimilation into society at large. Though believing that they had earned the right to be evaluated as individuals rather than prejudged, much less dismissed, on account of color, many, including Murray and his wife, energetically took on the role of leaders of the race. They worked for the advancement of all people of color in the spirit of noblesse oblige, yes, but for other reasons, too. Though they identified with all blacks according to race, there was another "consciousness of kind" operating, and that was class. So long as others lumped all African Americans together, those in the upper class were embarrassed by some of their unschooled, low-class counterparts, and that generated some of the energy they put into "uplift" activities.[2]

Prospects rose for all African Americans following Emancipation, and progress was substantial through the Reconstruction period. But a backward slide commenced with the government's refusal to honor the US Constitution's Fourteenth and Fifteenth Amendments, granting all rights of citizenship to people of every color. In the name of reconciliation with the South, the new citizens were abandoned to renewed oppression by white supremacists. Not only did they lose ground in political influence, economic prospects, and access to public services; the government failed to protect them against lawlessness as extreme as murder. Jim Crow tactics—segregation, discrimination, intimidation, humiliation—confronted all black people. The elite, despite their achievements and gentility, were not excluded. Indeed, when the rug was pulled out from under African Americans following their government's betrayal, the elite had only further to fall. In the end not only would the example and activism of the upper class fail to lift the race as a whole in the eyes of most whites, but not even the select set would be allowed to assimilate as exceptional. The rude awakening that they were to be segregated and stigmatized with the rest of the race became increasingly clear through the 1890s, a period of reckoning and disillusionment for Washington's black elite.

Yet on the afternoon of October 2 in the last year of that decade, Daniel Murray found himself among the leading citizens of the nation's capital who, arriving at the Jersey City railroad station, pressed around Admiral Dewey as they welcomed him aboard the "triumphal train." Five hours later, the engine screeched into the Washington depot punctually at 6:50 p.m. The cheers of those who had seen the escort train off in the early morning dimmed in comparison to the boisterous ovation that accompanied its return with the war hero. At the signal every noisemaking entity in the vicinity—locomotives, steamships, churches, factories—held forth with clangs, toots, chimes, and whistles. An artillery squad fired a twenty-one-gun admiral's salute. A joyful mass of people, many from far and wide, joined in the din.

A procession of horse-drawn carriages carried the admiral and his escorts to the White House. The admiral's carriage was a magnificent Grand Daumont, identical to those favored by European royalty. Murray and the rest of the escort committee followed the admiral into the White House for a reception in the East Room. Once President McKinley had a brief private chat with the nation's guest, the entire company made its way to the reviewing stand for the "monstrous" parade. Planned for nighttime, it was a show of sound and light: "all that the combined efforts of tons of powder, thousands of voices, millions of lights, acres of illuminations, and scores of bands of music can produce." The Potomac River was set on fire, the Washington Monument painted vermilion. While Roman candles and other pyrotechnics exploded overhead, twelve giant searchlights roamed, illuminating the grand public buildings. Multitudes of tiny lights in trees created a fairyland effect. Down the broad avenue they marched: bands and drum and bugle corps interspersed with endless civic and military groups. The admiral did his best to show appreciation, but after a solid two hours of waving, then replacing, his elaborate chapeau-bras, weariness set in. All parties were due at the Capitol in the morning for the sword presentation ceremony followed by, yes, another parade.[3]

It had been a long day for Daniel Murray, too. A big day. All his life he saved as a souvenir the nontransferable ticket that had admitted him into the train's parlor car A. This gratifying experience was, symbolically at least, among the last of its kind—a rally, a throwback to more hopeful times rather than a taste of things to come. The overlap of such positive-leaning events with newer, harsher realities had become increasingly rare. For black elites the slide that had started a decade earlier was now, in the last years of the century, accelerating. More and more of the directional signs pointed backward.

In 1897, Daniel Murray's steady advancement at the Library of Congress had stalled following a demotion, due to "the friction incident to caste," and a drop in salary that never budged over an additional quarter century of service. A year later, in response to fresh atrocities in the South, Murray helped found the National Afro-American Council, a forerunner of the NAACP. He and the other executive committee members labored over a host of discriminatory issues, including disenfranchisement maneuvers and Jim Crow segregation on interstate railroad lines. There was an irony in Murray's first-class experience aboard the Dewey-escort train, given that in a few months' time he would be required to transfer to a Jim Crow car immediately upon venturing across the river into Virginia.

The story of Daniel Murray, father of black bibliography, race leader, and prominent member of Washington's "colored aristocracy," echoes and animates the larger narrative arc of the rise and disillusionment that African Americans experienced over his 1851–1925 life span. Though he was able and ambitious, primed for integration into society at large, his expectations were foiled by what he called "the virus of race madness." There was little about Murray's life that was not infected by race. He lived in a city and was employed by a government that was becoming more segregated with each decade. As he developed a specialty in black bibliography and biography, even his work at the Library of Congress often focused on race. Home was not altogether a refuge, either— it was the "office" of the National Afro-American Council bureau he headed and a meeting place for planning strategies to resist and reverse the second-class citizenship that was especially galling for those in the upper crust of black society.[4]

UP AND COMING

D ANIEL MURRAY WOULD MAKE HIS MARK IN THE NATION'S capital and come to pride himself on being among the oldest inhabitants there, but he likewise identified as an "Old Marylander." It was in Baltimore, Washington's sister city, that Murray was born, on March 3, 1851. Maryland was a slave-owning state, but 90 percent of black Baltimoreans were free. The city was home to the country's largest free black population, numbering more than 25,000 when Murray was a boy. Murray always emphasized the fact that he had been born to free parents, never directly referring to his father's history as a slave.[1]

George Murray was a "bright mulatto" from the Eastern Shore county of Queen Anne's, born in 1775 by his own reckoning. George's mother was a slave and his paternal progenitor a white man of Scottish ancestry. George was enslaved on the farm of William Hopper. A merchant as well as a farmer, Hopper was a prominent citizen in county affairs and served in the Maryland Legislature. In 1771, he built a large brick dwelling, which came to be called Wharf House, on his estate, located on high ground between the west and east branches of Corsica Creek. This was about two miles from what became Centreville, the county seat;

he was one of the original commissioners. In 1788, Hopper, the owner of fifty-nine slaves, was declared insolvent. He managed a financial recovery, and by 1803, three years before his death, had repurchased twenty-one of those slaves, George Murray included.

Murray was manumitted by Hopper's widow, Ann Cox Hopper, in 1810. She gave his age as forty-three—much inflated—and referred to him as "my negro man George (who calls himself George Murray)." His emancipation was contingent on payment of $100. If Murray raised the sum himself, he, in essence, bought his own freedom. He did not move to Baltimore for two decades. Employed by his former owners, he might have stayed because members of his family were still enslaved. In 1822, Ann Cox Hopper manumitted Bill Murray, age twenty-eight, and a William Hopper manumitted Tom Murray, age twenty-one, and his sister Mary, thirty-two. George Murray relocated to Baltimore by 1831. Working as a laborer at a lumberyard, his job was to inspect the timber as he stacked it. A devout believer in the Bible and a temperate man, he did not use tobacco and, except for a rare glass of wine, did not drink.[2]

Daniel Murray's mother was an octoroon with Indian predominating in the admixture, "a fact clearly discernible to everyone who saw her eyes, features and hair." Born Eliza Wilson in Frederick, Maryland, in 1804, she lived her life in Baltimore. There George and Eliza married on May 13 in 1847. It was the second marriage for both. The bride's first married name was Proctor, and she was mother to four children. George had a dozen children by his first wife; his surviving offspring were long grown and out on their own (nothing more is known of them). Eliza and her younger children moved into the house on Forrest Street that her husband had already called home for sixteen years. She worked as a laundress. The family's circumstances were limited but proved secure.

George and Eliza Murray were active members of the Bethel African Methodist Episcopal (AME) Church. George was a church leader, licensed as a local exhorter not long after joining the church upon his arrival in Baltimore. Exhorters—lay teachers of the Scriptures—served as spiritual overseers of church congregants, in particular those who might have wandered from the fold. "Sister Murray" was prominent in secret orders. Such societies provided ritual and community, while dues generated what amounted to an insurance fund, dipped into when misfortune struck individual members.[3]

The members of the African Methodist Bethel Church, as it was earlier incorporated, had been worshipping at the Saratoga Street site since 1815, when Reverend Daniel Coker was pastor. Coker was both preacher and teacher. The first black educator in Baltimore, Coker initially went to the city to conduct a school, recruited by local men who had raised the money to secure his free status. As a clergyman, Coker grew dissatisfied with the oppressive way the black ministry was treated by the Methodist Episcopal hierarchy. He and Philadelphia pastor Richard Allen withdrew their congregations from the white-controlled Methodist Episcopal Church and, in 1816, organized the African Methodist Episcopal Church, a separate and distinct body of Methodists.

At the time of George and Eliza's 1847 marriage, the congregation was preparing to build a new church. Reverend Daniel Alexander Payne served as pastor of Bethel AME Church from 1845 to 1850 and oversaw construction of its new edifice. Designed by the architect Robert Cary Long, Jr., who specialized in churches, and built at a cost of more than $15,000, it was dedicated in 1848. Payne's five-year ministry at Bethel was not without controversy. Raucous, emotion-laden singing and dancing were staples in many black churches, Bethel included. Services were interspersed with cries, wails, groans, and foot stomping. The new pastor, a man of pronounced civility and an advocate for an educated ministry, objected to such demonstrative behavior. Although a slight man weighing about 100 pounds, Payne expressed his opinions forcefully. "The time is at hand," he insisted, when we "must drive out this heathenish form of worship." Payne introduced instrumental and choral music at Bethel Church. To say that this did not sit well with the many parishioners who continued to prefer a physical and emotional letting-go experience at church is an understatement.[4]

George and Eliza had two children together. The first did not survive. The second, Daniel, was born when his mother was forty-seven and his father seventy-six. The delivery took place not at the family's Forrest Street home but on Little McElderry Street, where, for reasons not clear, the family lived for a few years, moving back to the house on Forrest Street when Daniel was two. The child's full name was Daniel Alexander Payne Murray after Bethel's strong-willed pastor, the "warm friend" of George Murray and Daniel's baptism sponsor. Reverend James A. Shorter was the officiating minister at the baptism. Both reverends would become AME bishops. Payne, elevated in 1852, may already have been Bishop Payne at the time of Daniel's baptism, given that Shorter's term as Bethel's pastor did not start until two years after his birth. A tireless promoter of education, Payne was an apt model for his namesake. He became the founding president of Wilberforce University in Ohio, the first black-owned and -operated institution of higher learning in the United States, and frequently spoke out on race-related issues.

As "the child of Godly and intelligent parents," Daniel experienced Christian training as one element of his upbringing, but it did not make for a rigid household steeped in religion alone. He ascribed much of his later success to the "tender care bestowed on him by his mother" and enjoyed looking back on his childhood in Old Town Baltimore. He recalled the neighborhood storyteller, Basil, "a man in age, stunted in growth and with the mind of a child." A playmate to Daniel and his friends, Basil shared stories of the Revolution and the War of 1812, as well as folklore and fairy tales. "The mothers in the neighborhood were quite willing to see their boys sitting in a group listening to Basil relate those wonderful stories of animal lore, battle incidents, and the adventures of Sinbad and Robinson Crusoe." Several of Murray's lifelong close friends grew up with him in Baltimore. One was George A. Myers, whose family also attended Bethel Church. When a father himself, Murray wrote to his old friend about his sons playing football and other field sports, and reminded him that sports of that kind had been in their infancy when they were boys. They ran not on a track but around the square. "Most of our running was done away from the police and in that way many of us became tolerably fair sprinters." By "square," he probably meant the open area around the Bel-Air Market that ran along Forrest Street. On market days, the stalls were stocked with fresh fish, game, fruits, vegetables, dairy products, and flowers, and it was a lively place where boys played marbles and sometimes got into trouble with local watchmen. In another letter to Myers, Murray nostalgically recalled childhood Christmases: "No Christmas nowadays seems like the time when I was a boy in Baltimore. The hearty good cheer of the old Maryland hospitality is not known among the people of Washington."[5]

Daniel's mother was illiterate while his father could read but not write, yet both were "fully alive to the benefits of education" and saw to the schooling of their youngest child. At about five, Daniel attended a segregated grammar school in the neighborhood. His study continued under a series of accomplished private tutors: Charles C. Fortie (a noted local schoolteacher), Alfred Ward Handy (a former sergeant in the Union Army and a Bethelite like the Murrays), Reverend James Lynch (a missionary educated by Daniel Payne and at Dartmouth College who later became Mississippi's secretary of state), and Reverend George T. Watkins (an AME minister and one of the first black men in the country to earn a doctorate of divinity).

Daniel's mother may not have been educated, but she was

"a thoughtful, shrewd and thrifty woman" and early on taught him to save money. "When young Murray was but ten years of age his mother gave him $5 and carried him to the savings bank and opened up an account in his name charging him to add to it diligently which he was eager to do, and by industry out of school hours and during vacation was able to accumulate several hundred dollars." The virtues of saving and frugality were thoroughly ingrained in Eliza's son, a characteristic noted by others throughout his life. His father passed on his remarkable gift for memory, a characteristic admired by his son. George Murray "probably knew the Bible by heart and could recite the remaining verses to any passage that was suggested to him . . . verbatim et literatim."

The Civil War began on April 12, 1861, when Confederates in South Carolina opened fire on the Union-held Fort Sumter in Charleston Bay. There were no fatalities. The war's "first blood" came a week later in Baltimore. Murray, all of ten years old, was present and witnessed a mob of Southern sympathizers attack Union troops who were en route from Boston to Washington. After Fort Sumter was taken, President Abraham Lincoln called for volunteers to put down the insurrection, and the Sixth Massachusetts Regiment, seven hundred men strong, responded immediately and enthusiastically. Arriving at Baltimore's President Street depot near noon on April 19, the soldiers disembarked in order to make their way a mile along Pratt Street to reach Camden Station, where they would board the Baltimore and Ohio Railroad heading south. Jeering prosecession rioters launched bricks and stones at the troops. Gunfire ensued on both sides, and the mayhem ended with the deaths of four soldiers and about a dozen civilians; many more were injured. Lincoln maneuvered to keep Maryland from following Virginia into the vortex of secession. Martial law was declared in May, and federal troops were garrisoned in the state. "Fired by a desire to assist the Union cause," Murray wanted to fold into a Union regiment as drummer boy, but his mother would not hear of it.

During the war years, young Murray spent time during school vacations visiting his half siblings who had moved to Washington. The B&O Railroad left from Camden Station for Washington four times a day for the forty-mile trip. He was thrilled by a special encounter that occurred on December 29, 1862, during one of his earliest trips to the nation's capital. James E. Murdoch, an eminent tragedian of the day, was participating in a benefit for sick and wounded soldiers in the House of Representatives hall that evening, reciting from Shakespeare, Byron, and Tennyson. Murray related the germ of the story, with "evident pride," many years later to Edward E. Cooper, the editor of the *Colored American*, who retold it in his newspaper:

> President Lincoln was expected to lend the aid of his presence to the cause but was late in arriving, so the reading began. Young Murray then about eleven years of age was standing in the door leading to the rear lobby when the President accompanied by Mrs. Lincoln . . . appeared in the lobby. Mr. Lincoln saw through the open door Senator Wilson of Massachusetts [Henry Wilson, chairman of the Senate Committee on Military Affairs] in the audience and requested young Murray to call him out. This he did and upon returning to the President, Mr. Lincoln caught him up in his arms, squeezed him slightly and kissed him on the forehead.

Murray was in Baltimore in early July 1864, when Confederates under General Jubal Early invaded Maryland. It was not clear initially if his forces were targeting Baltimore or Washington. Young Murray "joined the ranks to repel the invaders." Though the experience was relayed using phrases implying that Murray had an official role, in fact, his recruitment was ad hoc. (When later asked on a work form at the Library of Congress if he had served in the military, Murray responded in the negative.) The thirteen-year-old Murray could not handle a gun, but he could keep the soldiers supplied with water as they built up batteries around the city. While so engaged Murray rendered a solid contribution. He witnessed a rebel in the act of poisoning the spring that served as the men's water source. Fleeing when Murray sounded an alarm, the miscreant was caught in a nearby house, hidden among mattresses, and identified by his informant as the person who had emptied a white powder into the spring.

The crown in Murray's list of schooling was the "Unitarian Seminary in Baltimore of which Rev. John F.W. Ware was president." While no actual institution of this name has been confirmed, John F. W. Ware was certainly well known in Baltimore. A white Unitarian clergyman and the pastor at First Independent Church, Ware was devoted to African American education. Described as a "large-brained, large-hearted man," Ware was a Harvard graduate. Because his manner was not condescending or patronizing, Ware was esteemed by the city's black population, despite the many who considered Unitarians infidels. Daniel Murray completed his formal education under Ware in 1868 or 1869. One imagines him carrying away Ware's advice to young men: "The great attainments and great achievements of men have been not only won through sturdy struggle, but wrung of what men call an adverse fate, which is the best educator a man can have. A young man is not to seek a place made, but to make a place. Openings in life are things compelled, not things granted."

By this time, Murray's father had given up work at the lumberyard and devoted himself to church activities, visiting the sick, and officiating at funerals. George Murray, who would outlive all of his biological children except for Daniel, was well over ninety when his youngest son moved out of the Forrest Street house for good.

One by one, Eliza's four older children had relocated to Washington, DC. Now they welcomed their young half sibling.[6]

Daniel moved in with his sister Ellen Butler and her daughter Ella on the block of 13th Street NW between M and N streets. Ellen, the widow of James Butler, was in her late forties. Ella, eight, was the last of her four children still at home. Ellen owned the small house at 1216 13th Street and would live there until her death. Daniel's half brother Samuel Proctor resided on the same block. He was exactly twenty years older than Daniel and already living in the nation's capital when a baby brother was born back in Baltimore on his own birthday of March 3. Caterer, grocer, and restaurateur, Proctor was well established in the city. "The undersigned takes pleasure in announcing that he is prepared to serve dinner, parties and receptions," his advertisements ran. "He will also furnish separate dishes such as boned turkey, patties of birds, sallads, etc." Proctor was ready to cater all events from picnics and excursions to dinners and balls "at the shortest notice." Since Ellen's occupation was caterer, she probably assisted her brother. Proctor's client list was topped by President Lincoln himself.

Murray's other two siblings in the District were Charles W. Proctor and Catherine Proctor Sephus. Charley was the youngest of Daniel's half siblings, a bit over thirty when Daniel moved to the city. A sexton, he and his wife, Mary, lived on I Street between 12th and 13th streets, about four long blocks from the homes of Ellen and Samuel. Catherine resided east of the Anacostia River, in the new subdivision of Barry Farm (shortly to be referred to more commonly as Hillsdale), abutting the grounds of the Government Hospital for the Insane to its south. Barry Farm was a project of the Freedmen's Bureau, created in 1865 to assist black and white citizens in the transition to a society without slavery. The bureau commissioner, General Oliver Howard, sold most of the one-acre lots to former slaves but some to those, like Catherine Proctor (now separated from her husband, Solomon Sephus, and using

her maiden name), who were "fairly well off." In 1867, the same
year that Catherine bought lot 5, General Howard was involved in
another enterprise: the founding of Howard University. He steered
considerable Freedmen's Bureau resources to the construction and
development of this interracial institution, named in his honor.[7]

When Daniel Murray settled in the nation's capital, the Washington Monument was still a relative stub. The dome of the Capitol
was the city's beacon, its lantern illuminated at night, the standing statue of Freedom rising above. Little did Murray know that
his own career would be launched in that landmark. At this time
a third of the city's population was black, some 35,000 souls in
number. Though Washington remained a town with a primarily
southern outlook, prospects for its people of color had advanced
at a rapid rate, thanks to the Radical Republicans in Congress,
who were committed to equality and enfranchisement for black
Americans and harsh penalties for the former Confederate states.
Nine months before President Lincoln issued the Emancipation
Proclamation, releasing slaves in rebellious states from bondage,
Congress passed a bill freeing slaves in the District. On April 14,
1862, Bishop Daniel Payne was received by President Lincoln at
the White House and urged him to sign the bill. Though the President did not tip his hand to the bishop, two days later the bill
passed into law.

Lawmakers considered DC emancipation a kind of experimental run. Nationwide emancipation came in 1865 with ratification
of the Thirteenth Amendment to the Constitution, abolishing
slavery. Again looking to the federal city as a test case, Congress
granted unrestricted manhood suffrage in the District in 1866.
Many white Washingtonians had fought against this liberal measure even as their black counterparts agitated on its behalf. At a
strategizing meeting held in July 1865, Samuel Proctor presided
as chairman and John F. Cook, Jr., acted as secretary. Cook, an
established community leader, subsequently submitted a petition

from 2,500 African American residents to Congress. Victorious, approximately 8,200 black men (compared with 9,800 white) registered to vote in the 1867 municipal elections. Integrated Republican ward clubs formed, and though there was dissidence enough as the democratic process played out at club meetings, there was little discord along racial lines. Samuel Proctor was on the executive committee of the Second Ward Republican Club.

Black Washingtonians took pride in these "firsts." They commemorated the April 16 anniversary of District emancipation annually. For example, on that date in 1868, despite a spring rain, they staged an elaborate procession. The parade marshal was mounted on President Lincoln's horse, "Old Abe." His escorts included Samuel Proctor and another of the city's well-known caterers, John A. Gray. Drum corps and military units marched behind a banner with a portrait of the late President. Though "the rain still drizzled when not pouring, those in the delegations manfully stood the deluge."

Two more Reconstruction amendments to the Constitution followed: the Fourteenth Amendment, ratified in 1868, and the Fifteenth Amendment, ratified in 1870, extended civil rights and protections, including the franchise, to former slaves and all people of color.[8]

→ ←

DANIEL MURRAY BEGAN HIS WORKING LIFE AS A WAITER FOR his brother Samuel Proctor. By 1869, Proctor was keeper of one of the two restaurants on the ground floor of the Capitol. The grand edifice, situated on a commanding plateau ninety feet above the level of the Potomac River, covered more than three and a half acres. The original structure had become too small for the burgeoning needs of Congress, and the cornerstone for flanking extensions was laid in 1851. Constructed of white marble slightly variegated with blue, the extensions were considered complete in

1868, although the House and Senate had already been holding sessions in their respective new wings for years. Sculptural and other artistic embellishments were still under way when eighteen-year-old Murray started accompanying his brother to "the Hill." The old structure was now the center of the whole complex, and entrances to the principal floor were located under three porticoes spaced along the east front and reached by wide flights of stone steps. Vaulted carriageways beneath provided access to the ground floor where the restaurants were located.

The reputable restaurateur George T. Downing, "a gentleman of color" with "the most elegant manners to be seen in the Capitol" and a prominent race activist, had charge of Downing's Restaurant in the House wing when Proctor took over proprietorship of the restaurant in the Senate wing. He called it "The Senate Saloon," and his advertisements promised that patrons would find "all the luxuries of the season in the elegant saloon immediately under the Senate Chamber." It was open to visitors as well as lawmakers and staff and consisted of one large L-shaped dining room and a smaller refectory that was reserved for use by senators. Murray waited at the fourteen marble-topped tables (one less than the number of spittoons available) and served oysters, game, fruit, and ice cream; he also served as cashier.

The month after brothers Samuel and Daniel celebrated their thirty-ninth and nineteenth birthdays, respectively, Samuel finally took a bride. On April 21, 1870, he married a young woman named Eugenia Dukehart, whose family lived on the same 13th Street block. The bride's father hosted the home wedding, which was covered in the mainstream newspaper the *Evening Star.* "The leading colored people of the city were well represented," the article noted, singling out the new senator from Mississippi, Hiram Revels, and mentioning that several white friends of the bridegroom had come by to congratulate him. "The refreshment table, it need hardly be added, was beautifully supplied." The couple's two-story frame house at 1209 13th Street served as both home and catering establishment. Eugenia was a hairdresser like her father and kept a shop on 11th Street.

The presence of Revels at the Proctors' wedding was a distinct honor. Originally from Fayetteville, North Carolina, Revels was the first black citizen to serve in either chamber of Congress, filling a Mississippi Senate term vacated when that state seceded. Revels arrived in Washington at the end of January 1870. It was finally decided on February 25 that he would be seated. The heated debate came to a close with the stirring speech of Massachusetts Senator Charles Sumner. "Today we make the Declaration a reality," Sumner intoned, explaining, "The Declaration was only half established by Independence. The greatest duty remained behind. In assuring the equal rights of all we complete the work." When Revels entered the Senate Chamber to take his oath of office, visitors in the galleries, aware that they were witnessing a historic occasion, rose in applause.[9]

Samuel Proctor had the opportunity to make connections like Senator Revels through his work in the Capitol building, and now his younger brother would, too. At the Senate Saloon, as one chronicler of the day noted, "An excellent repast can be procured at any time during the session of the Senate," continuing, "Legislation seems to improve the appetite, and it is noticed that the chambers prove excellent customers." Daniel Murray met senators and other Capitol luminaries in the restaurant. One of them was Senator Timothy Howe of Wisconsin. On the ground floor near the restaurant were various Senate committee rooms, including one for the committee responsible for oversight of the Library of Congress. Senator Howe served on that committee.

The Library of Congress was located on the Capitol's main floor, and its librarian, Ainsworth Rand Spofford, also frequented the Senate Saloon. One imagines Murray encountering Spofford not only in the restaurant but in the library upstairs. Surely he had explored the Capitol early on. Marble stairways led from the ground to the main floor, and dealers sold guidebooks and diagrams. The library, which stretched across the entire projection of the central building on the west side, was open to the public, and visitor access to the entire building was liberal. Indeed, when Congress was not in session it was virtually absolute, including even to the House and Senate private apartments. The library was accessed by a short passage from the Rotunda, the heart of the Capitol (and the literal center of the capital city as it was laid out). First-time visitors usually looked up upon entering, in awe of the dome's height and grandeur. At the eye, 180 feet up, was the mural *The Apotheosis of Washington.*

Murray impressed both Howe and Spofford, and with their combined support, he procured a part-time, minor position at the library. His first day of work was January 1, 1871. He was nineteen years old. The library consisted of three handsome halls painted a delicate cream color with flourishes of gold leaf. The ceilings were made of iron and glass, the floors of black and white marble. Pilasters and architraves were decorated with consoles, shields, and grape clusters. The main hall was ninety-one feet long, thirty-four feet wide, and thirty-eight feet high. Two rows of galleries, constructed of ornamental ironwork and reached by spiral staircases, arose on all four sides. The north and south halls were situated at right angles to the main hall. The books composing the law library were housed in a semicircular room on the ground floor.

Though the library was part of the legislative branch of government, with its expenditures determined by the Joint Committee on the Library (comprising three senators and three representatives), the President appointed the Librarian of Congress. It was President Lincoln who had awarded Ainsworth Rand Spofford that title on December 31, 1864. Spofford had come to the library in 1861 and was well acquainted with its history, which included two disastrous fires. The first had occurred in 1814, when the British, in the course of the War of 1812, torched the Capitol. Thomas Jefferson, retired at Monticello, had offered to sell his private library of nearly 7,000 books, unequaled in the country, to the government. After some debate, Congress accepted the offer as providing "a most admirable substratum for a national library." By the end of 1851, the library's holdings had grown to 55,000 volumes. On Christmas Eve of that year, a fire caused by a defective flue broke out in the library, and 35,000 volumes were either consumed by flames or too charred for use (including two-thirds of Jefferson's books).[10]

The 20,000 volumes that were saved thus formed the new nucleus of the library. Impregnable fireproofing was a high priority in the reconstruction of the hall, and cast iron was used in rebuilding walls, ceiling, and shelving. The restored library was reopened to the public in August 1853. The new black walnut furniture included not only desks but sofas and cushioned chairs as well.

Spofford's appointment as Librarian of Congress followed the 1861–64 tenure of John G. Stephenson. The staff under Stephenson consisted of Spofford and two other assistant librarians, one messenger, and two laborers. Often absent, Stephenson had proved a most disengaged chief, in utter contrast to the new librarian's style. When Spofford took over, the library occupied one hall on the Capitol's main floor and the law book room on the ground floor.

It did not take long for Spofford to agitate for more space. "More space" would be his recurring mantra. "In 1865 and 1866 the library had so encroached upon the narrow space it occupied as to render an enlargement imperatively necessary," he recalled. Two flanking wings were duly added by reconfiguring space that had been used for offices, meeting rooms, and storage. Spofford cared more for book space than ornamentation, and each new hall was capable of holding 75,000 volumes because he made sure they accommodated three galleries above the floor-level book alcoves.

"Yet these spacious wings were no sooner completed than they were almost entirely filled by two great acquisitions of books brought to the Capitol in a single twelvemonth," he continued, referring to the transfer of the Smithsonian Institution's 40,000 volumes and the purchase of Peter Force's American history collection. In mid-1870, a new copyright law went into effect that made the Library of Congress responsible for all copyright registration and deposit activities. Two copies of all copyrighted items (books and pamphlets, musical and dramatic compositions, maps and charts, plus prints, engravings, and photographs) were required to be sent to the library henceforth. The pre-1870 copyright records and deposits arrived immediately.

Spofford envisioned the library as a "national repository of knowledge," and he had no intention of slowing down the rate of collecting. "Let all other libraries be exclusive," he declared, "but let the library of the nation be inclusive." To handle the increased workload and his future ambitions, Spofford was scaling up when he hired Daniel Murray, who joined a staff of twelve: eight assistant librarians, one messenger, and three laborers. Spofford himself, "a long, lean figure in scrupulous frock" and quaint in manner, might be found absorbed at his standing desk or in purposeful stride, as he attended to a myriad of tasks. Murray's role was no doubt custodial to begin with. The library was open to the public daily, except Sundays, throughout the year from 9 a.m. to 4 p.m. During congressional sessions the library did not close until the hour of adjournment. Anyone was allowed to consult the collections, but only members of Congress and the Supreme Court, the President, the Vice President, cabinet secretaries, and certain other officials could check out material. Books were delivered to the offices of those so privileged, sometimes directly to their homes. The library maintained a horse and wagon.

Murray began his job in the winter. The library's heating was inadequate, and Spofford complained of the "deficiency of warmth" and asked the library committee for additional radiators. In the summer the library grew stifling hot. Staff and visitors could step out onto the library's balcony, "a cool and refreshing place," for relief. And to take in the scenery. Though one might mount to the Capitol dome and survey "the city of magnificent distances," as it was dubbed, the view from the library balcony was almost as grand. It faced west, so the stretch of Pennsylvania Avenue leading to the White House and the rest of the principal part of the city was mapped out. (The Capitol entrances faced east because city planners had wrongly predicted that the area in that direction would be populated first.)

During Murray's first year at the library, the number of acquisitions was the second greatest in its history: 39,178 books and 9,075 pamphlets, adding up to grand totals of 236,846 books (28,302 of this number in the law library) and about 40,000 pamphlets. Lack of space for such growth meant that library operations were being carried out in parts of the library normally kept clear for patrons. As Spofford reported to the library committee:

> The constant and rapid growth of the Library under my charge renders it necessary to call the attention of the committee to the emergency which will soon compel the provision of more room for books. The large additional space provided by the construction of the two wings opened in 1866 was soon nearly filled. . . . Since the last session, I have had constructed and placed in the galleries about one hundred cases of shelving of light materials, as a necessary though temporary expedient, to accommodate the overflow of books in the alcoves, and to prevent their accumulation upon the floors. More than seven thousand linear feet of shelves have thus been added.[11]

This opportunity, or "opening" as his former teacher Reverend Ware might call it, would determine the course of Murray's life, but he was only part-time for now, and he probably continued to assist his brother on occasion. Like his catering for President Lincoln, Samuel Proctor would long be remembered for the plum assignment he secured for the celebration of George Washington's birthday in February 1871. The city went all out not only to honor the "immortal Washington" but to commemorate the newly completed paving of Pennsylvania Avenue with wooden blocks from 1st to 17th streets. This was the city's first attempt at such a large-scale celebration: two days of pomp and pageantry, spectacle and merrymaking. The culmination of the "grand carnival and fete" would be the Civic Ball at the Masonic Hall, attended by President Ulysses S. Grant and other officials, as well as the cream of Washington society. The *Evening Star* announced, "The supper [would be] prepared by Samuel Proctor, the caterer for the Senate Side in the Capitol, assisted by Mr. John A. Gray, and is to be *the* supper of the season."

Pennsylvania Avenue was cleared for the second day of festivities, Tuesday, February 21. Crowds in their Sunday best gathered along the sidewalks as the amusements began with races of every kind down the wide thoroughfare. Men raced on foot, in sacks, pedaling velocipedes, and pushing wheelbarrows. There was no distinction of color among contestants. Several black men were among those blindfolded for the wheelbarrow race, for example. Goats, mules, and horses each had their chance at "trials of speed" as well. In the afternoon a procession of masqueraders parading from 15th Street to the Capitol took over the avenue. Washingtonians felt they had outdone even New Orleans in their "variety and novelty of the costumes, the grotesque combinations, the successful caricatures of current topics, and the rollicking fun without grossness." Here came the Frost King in his horse-drawn chariot covered in wool and attended by foot-men in costumes representing snow and ice. There went a well-executed model of the Capitol in the form of an immense mask going around on two legs. One whole division of the parade was composed of men dressed as women: drum corps in skirts, brass band in nightgowns, and, in a send-up of Victoria C. Woodhull and "woman's righters," the first woman president with her female cavalry riding on broomsticks.

The Civic Ball, as anticipated, "was *the* feature of the evening." As the ticket holders entered the Masonic Hall's second-floor grand ballroom, they faced the Gilbert Stuart portrait of George Washington, borrowed from W. W. Corcoran for the occasion. An American eagle stood guard above the painting on a bracket draped with flags and banners. Overhead, flutelike music from suspended birdcages filled with canaries and other songbirds entranced the guests. The ball was well under way when President Grant, the First Lady, and their daughter Nellie arrived to the tune of "Hail to the Chief." The "magnificent" table, catered by Samuel Proctor, did not go unnoticed.

The menu for a dinner Proctor catered on February 12, 1873, shows the sophistication of his offerings.

POTAGES

Soup à la Paysanne

POISSON

Salmon à la Maintenou

ENTRÉES

Fillet de Boeuf à la Provençale
Poulet à la Florentine
Punch à la Romaine

REMOVES

Pheasants à la Dauphinaise
Turkey à la Perigueux

RÔTIS

Canvasbacks
Aspic de foie gras en Belle vece

ENTREMETS

Pudding Diplomade, sauce Sambayon
Charlottes Russe
Glaces, Fruitage
Ice cream
Nougats en Pyramids
Jellies &c.
Coffee

The occasion was a dinner for Pinckney Pinchback, senator-elect from Louisiana. It was held at the residence of Frederick Douglass, who had moved to Washington in 1872. The famous abolitionist was away on a lecture tour, so his sons Lewis and Charles filled in as hosts. The guests included John F. Cook, Jr., and James Wormley, Sr., representatives of two of the oldest, most successful, and most respected families of color in the District. Pinchback expected to be sworn in the next month, but his seat was contested and he would remain "Governor Pinchback," having briefly served as acting governor of Louisiana.[12]

In 1873, Daniel Murray was still working part-time at the Library of Congress. In April of that year, for example, he was paid $88.79 for sixteen days' work. Murray was not the only black man on the library staff. John F. N. Wilkinson was a native Washingtonian two decades Murray's senior, whose tenure had started prior to Spofford's own. He had begun working in the law library in 1857, dusting books and providing custodial care for the reading room. For doing "the chars," laborers at the time Spofford became librarian made about $500 a year. Wilkinson may have been "a figure of simple dignity," but his drive was not to be denied. He learned the law collection inside and out and developed a precise knowledge of its patrons such that he advanced steadily, earning a salary of $864 in 1869 and $1,000 two years later. His industry, concentration, and perseverance made up for his limited education, and he became "a walking cyclopedia of the thousands of reports and digests of decisions of the various appellate courts." Wilkinson was rewarded with the assistant librarian title about 1872 and was even considered for chief assistant librarian in the law library when the occupant of that position died.

Frederick Fowler was another of Murray's black coworkers, a laborer who started at the library about the same time he did. Fowler's duties would stay the same for the next forty years: sweeping the library and dusting the volumes, delivering and collecting books drawn by House and Senate members. Even by 1887, he made only $600 a year.

Wilkinson served as Murray's model. Both made themselves proficient at what was of paramount importance to Spofford: finding books fast. Spofford himself was the master, his sense of any given book's location "as keen as a retriever's scent." The classification scheme Spofford preferred, and would be called on to defend, was one that "produces a book in the shortest time to one who wants it." Wilkinson and Murray's cultivation of memory in regard not only to books and other library materials but to their users as well made them indispensable. Murray's abilities would eventually outstrip Wilkinson's. Said Spofford of the latter in 1896, "He is an expert book finder, but not competent to catalogue books."

In 1874, Spofford chose Murray to be his personal assistant, and Murray's employment went to full-time. Spofford trained him not only in retrieving books and aiding members of Congress in their research but in all aspects of the librarian's trade. He mentored him in historical inquiry and encouraged his study of foreign languages. Spofford had gotten to know Murray initially over the year or so that he had worked in the Senate restaurant and, in offering Murray a job, he had promised "to make a man of him." Thus, even when the forty-six-year-old Spofford hired Murray, he intended to take him under his wing.

Elements in Spofford's own background provide insight into why he might have favored Murray and assisted him in his self-cultivation. Spofford had grown up in New Hampshire, the son of a Presbyterian minister. His formal schooling had been limited to attending Williston Seminary. He had not been dismayed when ill health had prevented his going on to college, as he preferred informal education. He had left home at nineteen to pursue his ambitions in a new city, Cincinnati. He had a keen appetite for reading and was proud to call himself a self-educated man. Enthusiasm, especially in one's work, was the quality he valued above all others. It quickened the vital energy and provided a path to distinguishing achievement. Murray felt that same enthusiasm. He "burned the midnight oil to make of himself a man of no ordinary intelligence and of book learning." Both Spofford and Murray would eventually be awarded honorary doctorates of law.

In the federal government's Official Register of 1879, Murray is one of twenty-one staff members under Spofford, listed, for the first time, as an assistant librarian. His annual salary was $1,000. Murray naturally appreciated Spofford's patronage and, indeed, "warm friendship" and described him as "a man singularly free from the blight of color prejudice." Spofford, himself father to three children, took an active interest in his protégé's welfare, even outside work. He advised Murray to save his earnings and loaned him money to make a start in investing. The younger man's gratitude was deepened when on one occasion he lost $5,000 due to another person's ineptitude or treachery. Spofford came to his rescue and immediately provided him with $2,100, the only security being his faith in Murray's integrity.[13]

That crisis averted—with such a large sum risked—came later. Murray began on a smaller scale, opening an account at the Freedman's Savings Bank in 1872. Faithfully making monthly deposits, he accumulated $349 plus $1.72 in interest in just over a year's time (he kept his passbook all his life). The Freedman's Bank would fail, but most of Murray's financial transactions paid off handsomely. In 1875, an advertisement over Murray's name offered a house for rent at 1207 13th Street. Inquirers were instructed to call after five o'clock at number 1216, the house Murray shared with his sister. Though Murray would go on to rent houses he acquired, at this early date he was probably picking up a fee as the owner's agent. That same year he and several associates organized and incorporated the Progressive Building Association. Murray was vice president. The capital stock was fixed at $100,000. Before the decade was over, he was not only buying and selling properties but overseeing house construction, sometimes for speculation, sometimes for specific clients. In 1880, he invited three friends to purchase a property with him at 16th and M Streets for $2,500, convincing them that they would all make a profit. And so they did, selling it a year later for $4,500. "Being of a natural thrifty turn" and envisioning early on the lucrative possibilities of real estate investments in the nation's capital, Murray never had to depend on his library salary alone.[14]

Though Murray's virtue of thriftiness may have been inculcated by his mother, in matters of religion Murray strayed from parental influence when he joined the Episcopal Church. St. Mary's Chapel for Colored Episcopalians, located on 23rd Street NW between F and G streets, was established in 1867. One of the founding members was the church sexton, Charles W. Proctor. Daniel thus followed the lead of his brother Charley. Samuel eventually did the same, leaving the Metropolitan AME Church (their sister Ellen stayed behind). St. Mary's was an African American mission church under the control of St. John's Episcopal Church on Lafayette Square. The assigned ministers were white. Members bent on recruiting a black clergyman to take charge succeeded in bringing Reverend Alexander Crummell to St. Mary's in 1873. Crummell, born free in 1819, was not only a spiritual mentor but one of the preeminent black intellectuals of his day. His education included a degree from Queen's College, Oxford. "As much as anyone," according to one historical assessment, "Crummell was responsible for the precedent of putting scholarship to the service of Negro protest and advancement." This is the notion Daniel Murray would ultimately dedicate himself to.

At Crummell's initiative, many in the congregation became determined to build an independent Episcopal church. In 1875 three lots on 15th Street NW, above P Street, were purchased. A sinking fund association was formed, and Murray was among the ardent young people eager to raise money for it. He organized, conducted, and gave the opening address at the association's "grand musical, literary and art entertainment" that took place on June 7, 1876. The fund-raiser, well attended by "lovers of literature" despite the evening's heat, featured readings and recitations interspersed with music and complemented by an art exhibition. The following month ground was broken for St. Luke's Protestant Episcopal Church. Crummell requested that Murray act as marshal for the occasion of the laying of the cornerstone on November 9, 1876.

During the transition from St. Mary's to St. Luke's, brothers Samuel Proctor and Daniel Murray were elected vestrymen. In July 1874, Samuel's wife, just twenty-three, died, leaving him with a three-year-old daughter, Eugenia, her mother's namesake. Samuel sold the entire stock of his wife's hairdressing shop and moved in with his brother Charley's family (now living on L Street), presumably so that Charley's wife could help raise little Eugenia along with her own son.[15]

Spencer Murray was also elected a church vestryman at this time. Spencer Murray was three years older than Daniel Murray. They grew up in the same Baltimore neighborhood and may have been cousins. What is certain is that they became lifelong close friends. Daniel and Spencer, in their twenties and determined to construct "the good life" in the nation's capital, belonged to the Bachelors' Social Club. A "representative society body of our colored citizens, composed of young men of the highest social position and literary culture," the club rented Willard's Hall for a ball on April 9, 1874. Daniel was chairman of the invitations committee, and Spencer was on the arrangements committee. Other up-and-comers in the club were Calvin Brent, the District's first black architect and treasurer of the Progressive Building Association, and John R. Francis, who would earn his MD degree from the University of Michigan in 1878. Both were scions of old and admired Washington families.

Daniel accomplished his role splendidly. Members and guests together numbered nearly three hundred. The men were in full court dress, the women elegantly gowned with their jewelry kept to a tasteful minimum. Many eligible young ladies attended, some accompanied by one or both parents. The restaurateur George T. Downing escorted his daughter, for instance, and Christian Fleetwood did the same. Fleetwood, a recipient of the Congressional Medal of Honor for heroism in the Civil War, was a founding member of St. Luke's. Also present was Congressman John R. Lynch from Mississippi, who, unlike Hiram Revels, had been born into slavery.

"The dancing programme was minutely observed. . . . The music was the best in the market and the dancing was of the highest order for taste, simplicity and dignity. . . . The supper was simply *right*. Not only was it superb but the manner in which it was served added ten percent to the delicious taste of the boned turkey, pickled oysters, and fine sandwiches. There was no liquor, no wine; all was serene; all was what the dignity of the evening called for. It was an evening of pleasure, the first this season among the class in question." These remarks were contained in an article submitted to the *National Republican* (a city newspaper representing Republican Party philosophy) by one "Van Auken," who went on to poignantly comment:

> I do wish that all the people in Congress who oppose our having civil rights could have looked in on us last evening as we were to be seen at Willard hall. My word for it, if they had done so, the civil rights bill that Mr. Sumner [Senator Charles Sumner, who died a month earlier] left in the hands of the nation would pass without a murmur of opposition. . . . The *Republican* is read by all thinking people, and if you publish our reception, or something about it, you may change the opinion of some of our white friends, who don't know really why they hate us—still they hate us—and who certainly do not know of the "Bachelors' Club," an institution composed of colored citizens, whose forefathers were serfs.[16]

→ ←

DANIEL MURRAY PURSUED INTELLECTUAL INTERESTS ALONG with business and social ones. The three were linked for Murray as they were for many others in high-status circles. In 1877, he joined the Negro Society, forerunner of the better-known American Negro Academy. At a meeting at the residence of John W. Cromwell, a lawyer and newspaper editor, eleven committees were formed. Murray served on the Lectures Committee along with Alexander Crummell and T. Thomas Fortune. Fortune was a Howard University student who would, in a few years, establish the *New*

York Globe. Other committees included Education, Publication, Cooperation and Business, Charities, and Amusements. Richard Greener, Frederick G. Barbadoes, and John H. Smyth—like Cromwell, Crummell, and Fortune—were founding members of the organization. All six men were—or would become—influential intellectuals and activists, and all would be ongoing Murray associates. Greener had made history in 1870 as Harvard's first black graduate and was now a law professor at Howard University. Barbadoes and Smyth were both government clerks. Smyth would be appointed US minister to Liberia in a year's time.

A few months after this meeting, the Negro Society commemorated the 108th anniversary of the death of Crispus Attucks with an evening program at 15th Street Presbyterian Church. Murray presented an historical sketch of Attucks, the black patriot who had been killed in the Boston Massacre, the first man to die for the Revolutionary cause. Those seated on the platform included two national legislators, Joseph H. Rainey, the first black citizen to serve in the House of Representatives, and George B. Loring, a white congressman from Massachusetts. President Rutherford B. Hayes sent regrets that he was unable to attend. Had he done so, the mix of black and white dignitaries would have been even more striking.

Murray was one of the "prominent colored men," as described in the *Evening Star*, invited to the farewell banquet for John Mercer Langston held on October 24, 1877. Langston, the founder of Howard University's law school, had been named the new minister to Haiti and was preparing to leave on his mission in a few days. The banquet was presided over by Richard Greener, with John H. Smyth serving as master of toasts. Among the other gentlemen present were Christian Fleetwood, John Cromwell, Frederick Barbadoes, William E. Matthews, Wyatt Archer, and William Syphax. Matthews and Archer were government clerks and future cohorts of Murray. William Syphax was distinguished by virtue of his family lineage as well as his service as the first African American trustee of the District's black public schools. The raising of glasses began with Greener's toast to the honored guest and was followed by Langston's own remarks. Among the subsequent toasts was one offered by Murray: "To Our Country." [17]

Daniel Murray's rise was truly remarkable. In 1873, he might have helped cater a meal for many of these same gentlemen. Four years later, he was a guest at a noteworthy event, included among leading members of the capital city's black elite. By contrast, Samuel Proctor advanced to middle-class respectability over a matter of decades, never reaching the status his younger brother would. The boy kissed by Lincoln, clearly an auspicious encounter, was on his way.

2

THE GOOD WIFE

IF A FAMILY BACKGROUND OF ILLUSTRIOUS ABOLITIONISM WAS an asset for admittance into black elite society, Anna Evans, Daniel Murray's future wife, had that in abundance. Many of her family members were devoted and determined antislavery activists, in particular her father, Henry; uncle Wilson Evans, and first cousin John Copeland on the paternal side; and uncle Lewis Sheridan Leary on her mother's side. All four men were involved in the celebrated fugitive slave case known as the Oberlin-Wellington Rescue, and Copeland and Leary sacrificed their young lives as two of John Brown's raiders at Harpers Ferry.

Anna's mother, Henrietta Raglan Leary, was born in 1827, a free North Carolinian of complex racial mixture. She "looks like an Indian, not a negro," wrote an interviewer who met her late in life. Henrietta inherited Croatan Indian ancestry through her paternal grandparents. Her grandmother Sara Jane Revels was a triracial woman born in Robeson County, home to North Carolina's largest population of Croatans, later designated Lumbee Indians. She married Jeremiah Leary (or O'Leary), of Irish and Croatan descent, who was born in the nearby county of Sampson. According to Henrietta, her grandfather was able to legally marry her grandmother "even though she was of mixed negro and Croatan blood because she nevertheless came from stock which held entirely aloof from Negroes and was recognized as a Croatan." Indeed, the 1800 census listed the family as white.

The story of the Croatans in Robeson and Sampson counties entails the tradition that when white settlers first penetrated this part of North Carolina early in the eighteenth century, they discovered a tribe of Indians speaking broken English, many with gray or blue eyes, settled along the Lumbee River (later called Lumber River), seventy-five miles from the coast. The theory developed that these people were the descendants of intermixture between Croatan Indians and survivors from the "Lost Colony of Roanoke" who had been left behind in 1587 while others in their party had sailed back to England for supplies. The relief expedition had been delayed for three long years. When it had finally arrived, there was no trace of where the colonists had gone, save for a word carved into a tree post: "Croatoan." Croatoan, fifty miles south of the settlement, was home to the Croatan Indians (also called Hatteras Indians). Archaeological artifacts later excavated there revealed direct interactions between them and sixteenth-century Englishmen. Proponents of the theory contend that migrants descended from an admixture of this tribe and Lost Colony survivors can be traced westward to the Indians of Robeson and Sampson counties.

Some of the Croatans along the Lumbee River intermarried with mulattoes, the hues of their offspring varying from white to deep copper. Sara Jane and her father, Aaron Revels, were among those "tinctured with African blood." There is no record of any Revels ever being enslaved. They were "patriots and ardent supporters of the American cause." Aaron Revels fought in the Revolutionary War under General Nathanael Greene.[1]

In 1806, four years after Sara Jane and Jeremiah Leary's son, Matthew Nathaniel, was born, they moved to Fayetteville in Cumberland County, on the edge of Croatan territory. The family of their kinsman Hiram Revels did the same, and there the future US senator was born. As a boy, Matthew Leary was apprenticed to a local saddle- and harness-making shop and later purchased the business. In 1825, he married Juliette Anna Meimoriel, a mulatto woman. Juliette, also called Julia, had been a little girl when her mother, Mariette, dubbed "French Mary," had come to North Carolina from Guadeloupe in the French West Indies. The same year Juliette married Matthew Leary, the Marquis de Lafayette visited the town named in his honor. General Lafayette's secretary described Fayetteville as a "pretty little City . . . situated on the western bank of the Cape Fear River" with a population of nearly 4,000 and a prosperous commerce. As it happened, Juliette's mother had the opportunity to converse with Lafayette in his native language. As a longtime resident recalled many years later:

> There was a great dinner and ball on the occasion, and Gen. Lafayette, after reviewing the tables, asked who cooked the dinner. He was told "French Mary." He exclaimed, none but a French cook could get up such a dinner. And who was "French Mary?" . . . She was widely known as a great cook, and sought after to cook for weddings, etc. . . . She was a small woman, quite dark in color, with straight hair, and always wore a head-handkerchief, in turban style . . . her language was a mixture of French and English.[2]

Two years after this memorable event, Juliette and Matthew's first child, Henrietta, was born, followed in another two years by a second daughter, Sarah. The disastrous fire of 1831 that destroyed half of Fayetteville may have been one of four-year-old Henrietta's first memories. The Sunday-morning blaze engulfed more than six hundred buildings in the heart of town, including Leary's saddle- and harness-making shop. Many families were undone, but Leary, ever provident, recovered and prospered, growing his business into an extensive wholesale firm and eventually purchasing considerable farmland.

Two sons were soon added to the family: Matthew, Jr., in 1833 and Lewis Sheridan, who went by his middle name or his nickname, Shurd, in 1835. According to Henrietta, her mother named this infant after a former boyfriend, merchant Louis Sheridan, a mixed-race slaveholder who had emigrated to Liberia to be "freed from the tyranny of the white man." The Learys were described as "a family of as much respectability as any Colored family in the State" and lived comfortably in a large white house fronting Ramsey Street. Henrietta's sister, Sarah, remembered being raised in a strict environment where frugality was inculcated. There was a school for free black children in Fayetteville, but to provide the very best education for his offspring Leary hired private tutors. A singing master himself, he passed his interest in music on to his children.[3]

Matthew Leary was proud of his Croatan ancestry, yet he was an outlier. The Croatans claimed descent from American natives and English colonists and greatly resented when, as time went by, the entire tribe was classified as "Negro." Though Leary was "said to have been almost a double for Horace Greeley," he readily acknowledged all elements of his own triracial heritage and, in Juliette, married a woman of clear African descent. One of his granddaughters wrote of being "descended from an ancestry that was fired with patriotism and a firm belief in the equality of all. Grandfather Leary was a staunch abolitionist and philanthropist. He hated the system of slavery and gave freely of his time and money to help many slaves secure their freedom. . . . In his home, the children knew nothing of color lines." Henrietta and her siblings were accustomed to their father having friends and hiring employees of all races. The family's laundress was a white woman, some of the children's tutors were white, and Leary employed a white manager for his business.

Leary trained his sons in the saddle- and harness-making trade as they grew. Other young men working in the shop were bound as apprentices. Henrietta recalled that it was her father's custom to buy slaves offered in the market, have them work off their purchase price, and then emancipate them. Or he would advance money to slaves to buy their freedom from their masters, and they would pay back the loan in labor. But starting in 1830, the state superior court was given jurisdiction over manumissions so they were no longer perfunctory, as they had been under the Cumberland County court. Then, in 1835, the newly amended state constitution repealed the right of suffrage for "free persons of color" (and contended that the Croatans came under that category). It was a blow. The men in Leary's family line had been used to voting since Aaron Revels had first exercised the franchise.

Altogether, Henrietta Leary had six brothers and sisters. Her youngest sibling was born in 1843, the year she married and left home. She was barely sixteen. Her twenty-six-year-old bridegroom, Henry Evans, was a resident of Hillsborough, about seventy-five miles north as the crow flies.[4]

→ ←

THE FATHER OF THE FUTURE MRS. DANIEL MURRAY, HENRY Evans, was born in 1817 in Hillsborough, North Carolina, the seat of Orange County. His mother, Fanny Evans, had been born in Virginia thirty-two years before his birth. She was a free mulatto and the head of her Hillsborough household, as described in the 1820, 1830, and 1840 censuses. The paternity of her growing brood of children, eventually numbering seven, is a mystery. One can conclude from photographs and descriptions of Henry and his brother Wilson that they could easily pass for white (as Wilson eventually did temporarily while serving in a white regiment in the Civil War). Of all his siblings, Henry Evans was closest to this younger brother, seven years his junior. When Henry was fourteen, his older half sister Delilah married John A. Copeland, a house carpenter and former slave, and moved to his home in Raleigh; three years later their son, John, Jr., was born. Delilah's family would play a prominent role in Henry and Wilson's joint future.

Henry Evans grew to be a tall man of erect carriage. He learned the carpentry and cabinetmaking trade. His work must have taken him to Fayetteville, for there he met Henrietta Leary and there he married her on April 10, 1843. Evans undoubtedly got to know Henrietta through her father, given the network established among free black artisans in central North Carolina. It included the master mason John E. Patterson, who served as Henry's bondman at his wedding.[5]

The couple settled in Hillsborough, a hilly town on the north bank of the Eno River. Henrietta became mother to two daughters while still a teenager. She must have found living in Hillsborough, a mile square, markedly different from the more cosmopolitan Fayetteville, where in 1850 there were 576 free people of color out of a total population of 4,646 (1,542 of them slaves). In 1850 Hillsborough there were only about 75 free blacks. Included in that number were Henry, Henrietta, and their now four children, as well as Henry's sixty-five-year-old mother, Fanny. Also living with Henry's family on Union Street in downtown Hillsborough was a James Allison, sixty-seven, a white carpenter. His relationship to the family, if more than a boarder, is unknown.

Evans became a prosperous and accomplished cabinetmaker, employing workers at his shop, which adjoined his home, and, by 1850, owning property valued at $1,400. He made the lectern and altar at St. Matthew's Church and in 1847 was considered for the job of finishing interiors and making furniture at the university in Chapel Hill, ten miles south. He ran advertisements in the *Hillsborough Recorder* for his "Cabinet Ware-House," offering sofas, sideboards, bureaus, looking glasses, bookcases, bedsteads, and tables crafted of mahogany, maple, cherry, walnut, marble, and glass.

By 1849, he had diversified his business to include undertaking ("coffins at three hours' notice") and "Accommodation for Travelers." His driver was already delivering furniture to those living at a distance and now was prepared to convey passengers to and from Hillsborough by carriage, hack, or buggy. About that time Henry's brother Wilson completed his own apprenticeship in cabinetmaking. It must have delighted Henrietta when her brother-in-law began courting her sister, Sarah. In 1853, Wilson Evans and Sarah Leary were married in Fayetteville.[6]

Henry Evans was active in the Underground Railroad. According to his grandson Harold Murray, "By means of secreting them one by one in a laminated steel trunk, he was spiriting [fugitive slaves] up country and across the Ohio River to safety." After the Fugitive Slave Act of 1850 became federal law, no runaway slave was safe south of Canada, and those who assisted them were subject to imprisonment and extravagant fines. Evans began to worry that he was attracting too much attention and might be seized and jailed.

For this reason, as well as the ever-tightening restrictions on North Carolina free blacks generally, Henry decided to move to Ohio. On or shortly after April 22, 1854, he appeared before the governor in Raleigh with a letter from two officers of the Fayetteville Independent Light Infantry Company informing Governor David Reid that "the bearer, Henry Evans, a free man of color, his wife and children, are about to emigrate to Ohio and desire to make arrangements that will permit himself and family to pass by public conveyance from the Southern States without interruption. . . . We are pleased to say that the party are entitled to as much respect and regard as any Colored family in our state." Henry and Henrietta's children now numbered six, including a year-old daughter and an infant son. Wilson and Sarah Evans and their one-year-old son were part of the party, too. Their papers properly prepared, the Evanses (along with about seven others) set out on their journey, traveling by ox team, boat, stage, and train. After a stay in Cincinnati, the two Evans families finally reached Oberlin after a trip of some 750 miles.[7]

The journey may have been arduous, but choosing Oberlin, a village ten miles south of Lake Erie in Lorain County, as their destination was easy. The Evans brothers' sister Delilah and her family had migrated to Oberlin in 1843, the year Henry and Henrietta had married. The Copelands had left North Carolina because of the oppression they experienced there and settled in Oberlin, following up on a recommendation that it was a place safe from kidnapping, a fate even free people of color feared. They were surprised on the day they arrived to see a young black man and a young white man walking together with arms linked. Oberlin citizens of both races extended assistance to new immigrants. In addition to fair play and security from kidnapping, African American families went to Oberlin for the educational opportunities. The village and its college had been founded together in 1833. Oberlin College (called Oberlin Collegiate Institute until 1850) had pioneered coeducation and admitted African American students beginning in 1835. The village public school was open to black children. Oberlin, in a former student's words, represented the "phenomenon of the bi-racial town," a place whose racial makeup and practices attracted enterprising black men such as Henry and Wilson Evans. When they arrived in 1854, Delilah and her husband had seven children. Their eldest, John A. Copeland, Jr., twenty, was a student in the college's preparatory department (equivalent to high school). When not busy with his studies, he assisted his father as carpenter and joiner.

Henry Evans purchased Oberlin College's Walton Hall on South Main Street, and "Henry Evans and Brother" set up shop as cabinetmakers, upholsterers, and undertakers there. Formerly a men's dormitory, the two-story frame building of twelve rooms was transformed into a furniture warehouse. The brothers built a house for Wilson's family on East Mill Street (later renamed East Vine Street, where the house still stands) and one for Henry's around the corner on South Main Street, adjoining their business. There Anna Jane Evans was born on February 17, 1858. The family called her Annie.[8]

The 1850s was a period of growth and prosperity for Oberlin's African American community. Over that decade the black population grew substantially as economic opportunities, especially for skilled craftsmen, increased. By 1856, as a visitor reported, there were black "cabinet makers, house contractors and builders, carpenters, blacksmiths, stucco workers, masons, coach trimmers and harness makers, upholsterers, bootmakers, grocers, farmers." At the start of the decade there were 174 African American residents, representing 9.2 percent of the population, but by 1860 the count was 422, or 20 percent of Oberlinians. The town's total population that year was 2,115. Many of the whites were transplanted New Englanders and New Yorkers. Many of the blacks had come from North Carolina, including others from Fayetteville who were well known to the Evanses. Indeed, one of them was Sheridan Leary, Henrietta and Sarah's brother, who arrived a year or so before his niece Anna was born.

Back in Fayetteville, Juliette Leary had paid special attention to this always reflective son "because even in his earliest days he was subject to peculiar difficulties," often brought on by his unflinching will. No insult was ever given Sheridan Leary—or any person of color—that he did not manfully resent. He "was always going among the slaves on the plantations around Fayetteville and preaching to them insurrection," his sister Henrietta recalled, adding "Nothing could prevent him." One day he witnessed a master beating his slave, and, fearlessly following his instincts, he thrashed the white man. When a ruckus ensued in town, Matthew Leary advised his son to flee for his own safety, "the place having become too hot for him." Escorted by his younger brother to the far bank of the Cape Fear River, Sheridan disappeared into the dark as night fell. He resurfaced in Oberlin, welcomed by kin and other connections.

John H. Scott, a saddle and harness maker who had been bound to Matthew Leary as an apprentice, and John E. Patterson, the mason who had served as Henry Evans's bondman at his wedding, arrived from Fayetteville about the same time as Sheridan Leary. All three men settled into Oberlin's community of black artisans. Scott's shop was right next to the Evans brothers' furniture warehouse on South Main Street. Scott employed young Leary, his former boss's son. One of Leary's nieces recalled that "To stitch intricate and various designs upon a set of harness was a delight to him as he was an inveterate lover of horses and a rider of great skill." In May 1858, Sheridan Leary married John Patterson's daughter, Mary S. Patterson, a student in Oberlin College's preparatory department. The couple would have known each other back in Fayetteville. Leary participated in one of the town's debating societies and continued his own education with serious reading. His ardor for the antislavery cause never waned.[9]

The most distinguished of Oberlin's African American residents, John Mercer Langston, practiced law and held local elective office. Langston had already been familiar with Oberlin when he and his wife, the former Caroline Wall, had moved to their new home on East College Street in 1856, having resided there earlier for college. His older brothers, Gideon and Charles, had been among the first African Americans to enroll in the college's preparatory department back in 1835. John Mercer Langston not only had attended the preparatory school but had earned two degrees at Oberlin before being admitted to the Ohio bar in 1854. Caroline Langston's brother, O. S. B. (Orindatus Simon Bolivar) Wall, was a cobbler in town. Datus and Mercer, as they were known in casual circles, grew close, not only as brothers-in-law but in their common devotion to black advancement. The two of them, along with

Henry and Wilson Evans, John Scott, and John Patterson, were among the dozen most prominent social and political black leaders in town, citizens of integrity, intelligence, and industry who demonstrated the feasibility of race mixing when coupled with opportunity. It was a close-knit community that Anna Evans was born into in 1858. All these families lived within walking distance of one another and took advantage of access to the educational, social, political, economic, and religious culture of the town. Oberlin was not free of color prejudice, but by Langston's evaluation, it came "nearer to it than any other place in the United States."

Many people of color attended Oberlin's earliest house of worship, First Congregational Church. Only narrowly denominational and equally welcoming to both races, First Church was a focal point for all the town and college residents. John Mercer Langston rented a pew there (Gideon and Charles Langston had joined in 1836, among the first blacks to do so). Wilson Evans and Sheridan Leary were members, and we can presume that the Henry Evans family worshipped there as well. First Church was as much meeting place as sanctuary. It was, for example, where the Oberlin Anti-Slavery Society gathered.

John Mercer Langston called Oberlin "the most noted Abolition town in America." Antislavery activities there drew black and white, young and old, townspeople and college professors and students. Oberlin was an early and major station on the Underground Railroad. The mission of network participants, who were aware that although "talk was a national institution, it did not help the slave," was to "receive, forward, conceal, and protect fugitives." Six miles out of town a guidepost pointed to Oberlin by way of the image of a full-length figure in black silhouette sprinting in that direction. Runaway slaves were dispatched from Oberlin to departure sites along Lake Erie, where they were hidden aboard vessels bound for Canada. Some fugitives, instead of proceeding across the border, had the courage to remain in Oberlin, confident that the village would protect them. The prevailing attitude of those in surrounding counties was one of disdain for Oberlin abolitionists and their "niggers' heaven."[10]

Young John Copeland was one of the most faithful and prominent members of the Oberlin Anti-Slavery Society. The organization's goals included not only an end to slavery but "the emancipation of the free colored man from the oppression of public sentiment" and the elevation of his race "to an intellectual, moral, and political equality with the whites." Although most local residents held abolitionist sympathies, certainly many were not supportive of all of the society's liberal agenda. Copeland, skilled in debate, insisted that the nation's rights "be extended to all because we are men—because we are natives—because these rights are inseparable from us by nature." Meanwhile, he stayed mindful of slaves currently in bondage, and his immediate object was their freedom. He often attended night meetings at Oberlin's Liberty School, a forum for fugitive slaves to tell their stories. Engrossed, he revealed "by the deep scowl of his countenance, the moist condition of his eyes and the quivering of his lips, how deeply he was moved."

Not surprisingly, Copeland's kinsman Sheridan Leary joined the Oberlin Anti-Slavery Society. The two young men, just a year apart in age, had much in common. Reminiscent of Leary's actions in Fayetteville, Copeland was "determined and unyielding in all that he considered right and just. Impositions he would not tolerate in any form," but, true to his manhood, he defended his rights and intervened when those of others were violated. Copeland and Leary were both students of history and well aware of the roles that Crispus Attucks, Toussaint L'Ouverture, and others of their race had played in it. They related to and wanted to claim ownership in the country's founding ideals but felt that "our modern Democracy was all an ugly cheat, and that the principles of Washington and his compatriots were long since forgotten." Leary studied the Constitution with "much zeal." The 1857 Dred Scott decision "aroused anew the fires of indignation in his soul." He felt himself "proclaimed an outlaw" by the Supreme Court's declaration that black men had no rights that white men were bound to respect. Serious beyond their years, Copeland and Leary were preachy if not downright judgmental. Copeland "seemed not unconscious of his own infirmities, but would always reprove young colored men, delinquent as to duty . . . not so much by gentle persuasion as by ridicule . . . with that sarcasm peculiar to himself." Leary rebuked anyone not ready to defend "God's inalienable rights to man." Leary's advice to his peers: get an education, seek elevation, pursue trades and wealth, be industrious, be honest and friendly, care not for difficulties, and quit dancing and frolicking. Devoted Christians, both were well versed in the Bible. Copeland "would almost invariably quote passages from the Bible" to justify his opinions. Leary became convinced that God intended him to devote his life to the cause of his race.

Most Oberlin residents were proud of the town's reputation as "perhaps the most important station along the whole line of the Underground Railway" and "second only to Canada as an asylum for the hunted fugitive." Their concern over the threat posed by slave catchers grew once the federal government passed the 1850 Fugitive Slave Act and so did their degree of alertness. Oberlinians had never permitted a slave within their gates to be carried back to bondage. That point of honor was challenged on September 13, 1858.[11]

The event that became known to posterity as the Oberlin-Wellington Rescue began on a Monday afternoon when shopkeepers were just reopening their doors after the noon meal. Something was amiss, and soon the whole town was buzzing. Sheridan Leary, "all excited," interrupted a meeting at First Congregational Church to spread the news. John Price, one of approximately thirty fugitive slaves living in Oberlin at the time, had been picked up by slave catchers. His captors were taking him to Wellington to wait on a southbound train. The town reaction was automatic. When it was all over, Wilson Evans would say that John Price was not "wuth shucks," but that was not the point. The hated Fugitive Slave Law would not prevail; Oberlinians were responding to a higher law. Scores took off for Wellington, nine miles south, by any available conveyance or by shoe leather if necessary. Henry and Wilson Evans, Sheridan Leary, and John Copeland were in the mad rush. John Mercer Langston missed the action, having left town early that morning on business, but Charles Langston, on a visit to his brother, hurried to Wellington.

There, the Oberlinians discovered that John Price's kidnappers had him squirreled away in the attic at Wadsworth's Hotel. The crowd outside swelled, eventually reaching well into the hundreds. After hours of grandstanding, scheming, and stalling, a cluster of men, with John Copeland and the Evans brothers in the lead, overcame the back-door guards, surged up the stairs, and stormed the door to the garret. They grabbed Price and literally carried him downstairs and threw him into a waiting buggy, which then sped off in a cloud of dust toward Oberlin. Price was hidden in the home of one of the college professors by the time his rescuers returned to town in celebration. After a few days, Copeland secretly escorted Price to Canada.

A federal grand jury caught up with the lawbreakers on December 7, 1858, when a US marshal came to Oberlin to serve indictments. Of the total thirty-seven warrants, two dozen were issued to Oberlinians, half of them men of color, including Henry and Wilson Evans, John Scott, Charles Langston, O. S. B. Wall, and John Copeland. Of those six, only Copeland was not available to be served (and was never arrested). Sheridan Leary's name was not on the roll of the indicted, leading him to wonder why he was "overlooked by the marshal's vigilant spies." The twenty-seven men who were successfully served and subsequently arraigned in a Cleveland courtroom were released on their own recognizance when they refused to post bail. The trial date was set for March.

A lawyer, a professor, and several college students, in addition to craftsmen and shopkeepers, were among the Oberlinians charged with violating the Fugitive Slave Act, and on January 11 of the new year, they threw themselves a "Felon's Feast" at a local inn. The guest list was topped by the Wellington men distinguished by the same badge of honor. Wilson and Henry Evans were present, and Henrietta Evans was among the wives who attended. A "sumptuous repast" was followed by a "feast of reason and flow of soul," the overall event described as "a singular spectacle."

After a delay, the trials began in Cleveland, thirty-five miles northeast of Oberlin, on April 5, 1859. The first man tried, Simeon Bushnell, who had driven the buggy that had spirited Price back to Oberlin, was found guilty. The defendants had been staying at a Cleveland hotel during the week, and on Friday, April 15, they appeared in court with their valises, prepared to head home for the weekend. Instead, the twenty defendants on hand would spend the first of many nights to come in jail. Upon learning that the next man to be tried, Charles Langston, as well as the rest of the defendants, would face the same jury as Bushnell, with their fates thus predetermined, defense lawyers refused to proceed. In the course of the animated back-and-forth that ensued, the judge threatened the defendants with jail if they did not pay hefty bail sums after all. They chose jail.[12]

Soon the Rescuers, as they were dubbed with a capital *R*, were drawing attention beyond the local press and populace. They played such notice to their advantage and presented themselves as "political prisoners." The nationally prominent abolitionist William Lloyd Garrison predicted, "This very persecution will give a fresh impetus to our noble cause."

The sheriff and jail keeper were sympathetic to their plight, and life in jail was far from brutal. Not only were the Rescuers well fed and allowed all visitors, but the jailor and his wife gave up their own third-story sitting room and two bedrooms to them. Those spaces plus three cells made up their quarters. Still, the confinement grew wearisome as the weeks went by, and both their families and businesses suffered. Some prisoners were released on technicalities or by pleading *nolo contendere*. By the end of May, Henry and Wilson Evans were two of the fourteen men, all Oberlinians, still in jail. Charles Langston had been found guilty. He and Bushnell were serving their sentences, but the rest of the men had to wait until the court's July term for their trials to commence.

To fight the monotony, the prisoners converted the spacious jail yard into a workshop: "Our shoemaker makes shoes; our saddler, harness; our cabinet makers, furniture; our lawyers 'declarations;' and our ministers, sermons." With the expertise of two printers in the group, and employing the assorted skills of all, the men produced a newspaper, the *Rescuer*. Much of the writing was satirical but biting political commentary. The four-page rag, priced at three cents a copy and sold from the jail yard, included advertisements such as that for Henry Evans and Brother, "Upholsters and mattress makers, late of Oberlin, who have removed to the shed one door west of John Scott's saddle and harness shop."

Over those months, meanwhile, the legal maneuvering was playing itself out. The men who had initially seized John Price were themselves indicted on kidnapping charges under an Ohio personal liberty law, and trial was scheduled in the Lorain County Court of Common Pleas. With little chance of prevailing in the county court and fearing for their personal safety, the men had their lawyer propose that their cases be dropped in return for the untried Rescue cases being dismissed in federal court. The proposition was accepted and effected. On July 6, 1859, the Rescuers were free to go after eighty-three days in jail, thus concluding one of the nation's most decisive cases to undermine the Fugitive Slave

Law. That evening there was a jubilant public reception at First Congregational Church. "Amid showers of flowers and a swelling strain from the grand old organ," each Rescuer was presented with a wreath as he entered. "The pent-up feelings of all found expression in song, prayer and story." Henry Evans was among the speakers. Referring to his long months in prison, he claimed "that to suffer for humanity's sake has been to me a pleasure and not a pain." He also alluded to past personal afflictions—the deaths of a "darling child" and a "loved and loving mother." He had not been at home with his children for three months. Anna, now a toddler, had probably taken her first steps while her father was in jail.[13]

Meanwhile, a new infant had been born into the extended family circle. Sheridan and Mary Leary became parents to a baby girl, Louise, at the start of 1859. Sheridan's status as a family man did not deter him from antislavery affairs. In March, he went to Cleveland to hear John Brown speak. The seasoned abolitionist declared it the duty of every man to liberate the slaves but did not share with the audience the audacious plot he was hatching to incite a slave rebellion triggered by a raid on the US armory at Harpers Ferry, Virginia. Brown appreciated that the interracial aspect of the Oberlin-Wellington Rescue had enhanced its effect and was seeking a mixed army for his enterprise. His son, John Brown, Jr., and lieutenant, John Kagi, recruiters for the daring and dangerous raid, foresaw likely candidates among Oberlin blacks. Young men such as Sheridan Leary and John Copeland, fueled by the success of the Rescuers, were particularly susceptible. Believing that people were tired of talk, they were fired up for action.

The clandestine recruitment of Sheridan Leary and John Copeland was facilitated by Charles and John Mercer Langston. "Charlie goes to see Leary to-day," read the postscript in an August 22 letter to John Kagi from a fellow agent. About a week later, John Brown, Jr., appeared at John Mercer Langston's door in Oberlin. At some point that afternoon, Sheridan Leary and John

Copeland joined the prolonged conversation in the Langston parlor. The young men were receptive. Indeed, Leary exclaimed, "I am ready to die!" This sentiment would have pleased his namesake, Louis Sheridan, who had pronounced in 1836, "I would die tomorrow to be free today." Leary only asked "that when I have given my life to free others, my own wife and dear little daughter shall never know want."

Leary was assured that his family would be provided for if he did not return, enabling Brown to report to Kagi, "Friend L___y at Ob____ will be on hand soon." If there was any hesitation on Copeland's part, it was dispelled by September 8, when Leary wrote to Kagi, using the agreed-upon coded language, "Nothing delays me more than want of means. . . . I saw J.B. Jr. a week ago. . . . His statements to me were satisfactory. . . . I have a handy man who is willing and every way competent to dig coal, but, like myself, has no tools. If the company employs him they will have to furnish him tools. His address is John Copeland Jr., Oberlin, Ohio." Having raised $17.50, Sheridan Leary, twenty-four, a man of pronounced physical strength "with the fear of no man plainly written upon his face," and John Copeland, twenty-five, tall, muscular, and skilled with a gun, left Oberlin on October 6. The Langston brothers knew their destination, but their own families did not. Henrietta Evans recalled that neither her brother nor nephew "told their Errand to any of the family, when they left Oberlin. Leary merely came in one day with his saddlers' kit in his hand. He told them he was going off to where he could get higher wages." Leary told his wife that he was taking a trip south that he hoped would benefit his health. Mary believed he might be going to see family but thought the emotions he showed at his departure strange. "He wept like a child" as he took his infant daughter in his arms and paced the floor, "shaken with grief." Leary did confide in his employer, John Scott, acknowledging that he was going to join John

Brown in a raid on the South "to free the slaves" and asking him to explain this to his wife in case of his death.[14]

The kinsmen were the last of the recruits to reach the farmhouse outside Harpers Ferry from which the strike was staged. In the end, only twenty-one men answered John Brown's call, five of them African Americans. Brown decided to launch his operation on October 16, just a day after Leary and Copeland arrived. That Sunday night, cloaked in blanket shawls to protect their weapons from the drizzle, the men walked in silence on the road to their destiny. By the late afternoon of the next day it was clear that there would be no triumph, no wholesale liberation of slaves. Brown's band succeeded in seizing the armory's engine house, the arsenal, and the rifle works, but a state of siege resulted once those structures were assaulted by outside gunfire. Leary and Copeland, cornered with John Kagi at the rifle works, fled out by the back door and into the Shenandoah River. Pursued, Kagi was shot dead and Leary mortally wounded. As his sister Henrietta later told the story, "When he was shot in the river, and left for dead he crawled to the bank and into a blacksmith shop. He lived yet 8 hours. He told those who came to him who he was. He asked them to write to his people." Copeland, meanwhile, was apprehended and barely escaped lynching before being jailed.

Like John Brown, who rather miraculously survived his wounds, Copeland was sentenced to death. On December 16, fourteen days after Brown was executed, Copeland was hanged. Even as his body writhed below the gallows, there were vigils in Oberlin, one at the Copeland home and another in town. Not an hour before his death, Copeland exclaimed, "I had rather die than be a slave." His mother seemed to echo this sentiment when she revealed to those standing with bowed heads around her, "If it could be the means of destroying Slavery, I would willingly give up all my menfolk." Delilah Copeland badly wanted her son's body, and her brother Henry volunteered to go to Virginia for it, but since only a white man was acceptable, one of the college professors undertook the mission. He was not successful; Copeland's body had been stolen by medical students for dissection.

Leary's corpse was piled into a box with those of other raiders, buried somewhere along the banks of the Shenandoah River. Back in Fayetteville, the *Carolinian* described its former resident as "an infamous scoundrel who ran away from justice, and thereby cheated the rope of a deserving compliment." If the Oberlin-Wellington Rescue accelerated the process of sectional polarization, the strike at Harpers Ferry was a direct catalyst for the bloody Civil War to follow. Even though the raid had not succeeded in freeing the slaves, it was, as Copeland wrote to a friend from jail, "the prelude to that great event."[15]

➤ ◄

THE 1860 CENSUS TAKER REACHED THE HENRY EVANS HOME in June. Henry, forty-three, and Henrietta, thirty-three, were now parents to eight children, the newest a six-month-old son named Lewis Sheridan. Anna and her siblings grew up steeped in family history. It was a source of pride, as well as motivation for their own race activism. As the decades went by, nearly every family obituary referenced the abolitionism of generations past. Anna's own son Harold, profiled in a 1971 magazine article, boastfully retold family lore detailing his ancestors' antislavery action.

The Oberlin of Anna Evans's youth was a place where chickens and wandering livestock shared the unpaved streets and plank sidewalks. An ordinance limited the speed of teams in the village to four miles per hour. When they could move at all, that is: a farm wagon once sank to the wheel hubs in mud trying to travel along South Main Street. Just a half block north of the Evans residence on that thoroughfare was the grocery and confectionary of the leading black businessman John Watson, a former slave and one of the Oberlin-Wellington Rescuers. Surely Anna and her siblings took seats at one of the marble-topped tables in Watson's ice cream saloon on occasion and indulged in a cool treat. They also enjoyed outings to Aunt Delilah and Uncle John's farm, once they moved to the countryside.

Henry Evans seemed financially secure in 1860, the owner of $3,600 in real estate and $500 in personal property, but his livelihood was impacted the following year when he was seriously injured. "A heavy iron wrench, which had fallen upon the planer he was operating, was flung directly at him crushing the bones of his nose and upper face." He may also have lost the sight in one eye. The community held Evans, the town sexton, in high regard and "immediately gave his family assistance and then saw that the proceeds from a lecture were used for his benefit." Just three, Anna knew her father only as he looked after the accident. His hair was white even before she was born. Her uncle Wilson's hair and flowing beard also turned snow white. The transition to white hair early in life was an Evans family trait that Anna's generation, too, would manifest. Another setback to the cabinet factory of H. Evans and Company occurred in 1864, when the former Walton Hall, which the brothers had moved to East Mill Street, burned down.

That was the same year that forty-year-old Wilson Evans joined the Union Army. The Civil War had been under way since 1861. When word reached Oberlin on January 2, 1863, that President Abraham Lincoln had issued the Emancipation Proclamation, there was a spontaneous gathering of celebration in the college chapel. John Mercer Langston read the document aloud and then read it again. Langston and O. S. B. Wall were major recruiters of black men now that they were allowed to enlist. Thanks to their efforts, nearly a score of Oberlinians joined the soon-to-be-famous 54th Massachusetts all-black infantry regiment. Wall himself was the country's first African American to be commissioned a captain in the regular army. In March 1865, with the war drawing to a successful close for Union forces, Captain Wall's Oberlin neighbors honored him with the presentation of a ceremonial sword. When, two years earlier, the town residents had celebrated the Emancipation Proclamation, the local newspaper had exulted, "We doubt that Oberlin had ever been so genuinely happy." A very different mood characterized the town in April 1865 as its residents again gathered in the college chapel, this time to mourn the assassination of President Lincoln.[16]

Sheridan Leary's widow, Mary, who had moved back into the Patterson household with her little daughter, was cared for as promised. Funds were raised for her, as well as for a monument commemorating John Brown's "heroic associates" from Oberlin. In January 1869, Mary Leary married Charles Langston, twenty years her senior. Louise Leary was ten at the time. Langston took his new family back to Kansas, where he had lived for seven years past.

Changes were transpiring in the Henry Evans household as well. Henrietta had given birth to three more children, daughters Henrietta and Mary and son Wilson Bruce. With the October 1867 birth of this last baby, called Bruce in contrast to the uncle for whom he was named, the family was complete.

By 1870, Oberlin's population was nearing 3,000. Ladies had gone from bonnets to pasteboard hats, the new railroad depot was finished, and the first steam fire engine had arrived, as had the lighting of streets with gas lamps. Though there were plays and dances, parlor socials and sleigh rides, Oberlin was, by and large, a temperance town. Still, the village committee on temperance had to maintain ongoing vigilance to keep liquor traffic suppressed. Most of the town conservatives also opposed billiard halls and bowling alleys and frowned on the use of tobacco. Encouragement for churchgoing was hardly necessary. Second Congregational Church, an extension of First Congregational Church, was established to relieve the pressures of a burgeoning congregation. Its house of worship, located just two blocks from the Henry Evans home, was completed in 1870. Wilson Evans served as deacon there.[17]

Anna Evans turned twelve in February 1870. Her two oldest sisters had left home; three of her remaining siblings were working (two as teachers); the next three were, like Anna, attending public school; and the littlest, Mary and Bruce, were still under their mother's feet. Henrietta Evans placed a high value on education. Anna never forgot her mother's pronouncement: "Education is a pearl of great price by which you will be able to set yourself free in your environment, wherever that may be." The public school, built alongside the College Green in 1850–51, was later named Union School. By the time Anna became a pupil there, two-story flanking wings and a third floor for the original building had been added. All grades through high school were taught in the approximately dozen rooms. Following a community appeal, music was added to the curriculum, a welcome enhancement for Anna, who sang and played piano. In that she was hardly alone. There were 150 pianos among Oberlin residents, more than in any other small town in Ohio, according to the local newspaper.

By 1873, there were 820 white and 232 black children of school age in Oberlin, with 654 of them enrolled in the public school. A bond issue for a new school was approved that year. A striking structure in Gothic Revival style was built on South Main Street across from the Evans home. It opened in the fall of 1874, too late for Anna, a member of the last high school class to graduate from the old building. She was sixteen and on her way to college.

Several of Anna's siblings and cousins had attended Oberlin College, and now it was her turn. Anna was one of 170 women who enrolled in the Ladies Course in 1874. The curriculum was collegiate level but compared to the BA-granting course had less emphasis on mathematics and Greek and Latin and more on French.

While Anna was a student, the Ladies Course was renamed the Literary Course. She had opted for a two-year program and hoped to graduate with her class of 1876. But she made do with just a year of college once Henry Evans determined to relocate his family to Washington, DC.[18]

Henry himself had been living in Washington by 1871, working as a laborer in the Department of the Interior's land office. He had opened an account at Freedman's Bank, giving his address as Oberlin, "residing temporarily" in the District. After he decided the move would be permanent, he called for his family. Henrietta arrived in the nation's capital on the first day of 1875 with the younger children: Lewis, fifteen, Henrietta, eleven, Mary, nine, and Bruce, seven. Anna, about to turn seventeen, presumably waited until the school year closed to join them. Why did Henry relocate his family, who were so much at home in their Oberlin community? He had attained substantial financial recovery, but perhaps his earlier injury had impaired his skill as a cabinetmaker and accounted for his taking a departmental job in Washington. Government positions, government protections, and good education opportunities had led to an influx of aspiring middle-class black migrants. Some said Washington was a "colored man's paradise."

Certainly the Evans family had impressive connections in the District in John Mercer Langston and O. S. B. Wall, both of whom had moved to Washington after the war and prospered, and were prominent in black elite circles. Langston was the first dean of Howard University's law school, and when the Evans family came to town, he was acting president of the university, which was considered "the capstone of Negro education." Captain Wall had earned a law degree at Howard, set up a practice in the city, and twice been elected to municipal office by a majority white district. He was currently serving as a justice of the peace. The Langstons and the Walls maintained stately homes near the university. The

Evans family settled into a house on 12th Street NW between T and U streets. They joined the 15th Street Presbyterian Church. Anna and her sister Mary sang in the choir.

Members of Oberlin's extended Patterson family had moved to Washington as well. John E. Patterson's niece, Mary Jane Patterson, had graduated from Oberlin College in 1862, the first black woman in the country to earn a BA degree, and she and her several siblings were now working in the District's colored school system. When Anna secured a position in the public schools, Mary Jane Patterson was principal of the Preparatory High School for Colored Youth. While waiting for the school year to begin, Anna taught music at Howard University. But instructing young students was her calling, and starting in 1875 she was a third- and fourth-grade teacher at the grade school later named for Lucretia Mott. During part of that time, her sister Mary and brother Bruce were pupils at the wood-frame school situated near Howard University. When Anna married Daniel Murray in April 1879, Mary was thirteen and Bruce only eleven, yet it was these two youngest siblings with whom Anna remained closest.

On February 11, 1878, a concert featuring Miss Anna Evans as a soloist was presented at Lincoln Hall under the auspices of the sinking fund for St. Luke's. Daniel Murray, so much engaged in the sinking fund efforts, may well have been involved. The next month, on March 5, the Negro American Society presented a program at the 15th Street Presbyterian Church. Sitting on the platform was Daniel Murray from the Library of Congress. He rose to give a talk on Crispus Attucks. That was a meaningful topic for the Evans family, and the event took place at their church. One wonders if Anna was there.[19]

3

THE BLACK ELITE

Daniel Murray and Anna Evans likely met through church-sponsored programs or entertainments, or thanks to one of their mutual acquaintances. They married in the early spring of 1879. They were a good-looking couple. Daniel, twenty-eight, was five feet, eight inches tall, of medium build and fairly proportioned, with closely trimmed hair and a full mustache, and his twenty-one-year-old bride, tall and slender, had "alert brown eyes" and a "soft, musical voice." Both were light in complexion, Anna's color described as "about as dark as a Spaniard's." As was the custom in the public school system, Anna, as a married woman, planned to leave her teacher's position at the end of the academic year. St. Luke's, still under construction, was not an option for the April 2 wedding. The ceremony took place at 15th Street Presbyterian Church, officiated by its new pastor, Reverend Francis Grimké, ordained just the year before.

Besides St. Luke's and 15th Street Presbyterian, there were several other high-status African American churches in Washington, including Metropolitan AME and 19th Street Baptist, but according to a newspaper article headlined "Washington's Colored Aristocracy," 15th Street Presbyterian, established in 1841 by

John F. Cook, Sr., was the first among equals: "the focus or pole around which the high-toned colored society revolves." Features on the black elite usually ran in the black press (the *Washington Bee* or *People's Advocate*), but this one was carried by one of the city's mainstream newspapers, the *Evening Star*. Most of its white readers would be taken aback to learn that "There is an aristocracy among the colored people of Washington as well as among the white, and it is quite as exclusive. . . . These people have their own society, give balls, dinner parties, receptions, and other entertainments. . . . At a 'high tea' or ball given by this circle of the colored aristocracy one can find quite as much intelligence, quite as much beauty, and quite as much grace of manner as will be gathered at any of the swell receptions of white folks."[1]

At this time there were nearly 60,000 black Washingtonians, making up a full third of the population. They formed a pyramid of three strata. The lowest band of poor and uneducated was the largest by far. The middle class was small but growing. The pyramid's tiny tip represented those in the "colored aristocracy," never more than a hundred families. Well educated, refined, accomplished, and prosperous, these men and women followed politics and current events, engaged in the city's civic life, race-related issues in particular, and enjoyed socializing. With rare exceptions, they were significantly lighter in complexion than the black majority.

The *Evening Star* article identified leading men from this upper stratum who were associated with 15th Street Presbyterian Church, namely, George F. T. Cook and John F. Cook, Jr. (sons of the church founder, who had died in 1855), James Wormley, Hon. John Mercer Langston, Dr. Charles B. Purvis, Senator Blanche K. Bruce, and Professor Richard T. Greener. Taking a closer look at just these individuals up to the time of the Murrays' 1879 wedding reveals much about the history and characteristics of Washington's black elite society.[2]

The Cooks and Wormleys were long-established District families, pillars of the antebellum free black community. John F. Cook, Sr., had been a school and church leader, and his sons, educated at Oberlin College, had followed suit. George was the superintendent of the colored public school system. John pursued a career in municipal government and Republican politics. By this date, the elective city government that had previously allowed him to be voted in as alderman and city registrar had been replaced with a system of three district commissioners appointed by the President. Washington residents having thus lost the franchise, he was now appointed to office and was currently serving as district collector of taxes. He was one of the richest black men in Washington, most of his wealth held in real estate. He was married to Helen Appo, a daughter of one of Philadelphia's black elite families.

James Wormley had been born free in the nation's capital. An entrepreneur, he owned boardinghouses and stables, and became a celebrated hotelier. His luxurious Wormley Hotel, located near Lafayette Square, was one of the finest in the capital. The clientele was mostly, though not strictly, white, and included eminent men in government from across the United States and abroad. This was a time when many officials in Washington lived in hotels and a lot of government and financial business transpired in hotel settings. Wormley's enterprises were considered safe investments, and he himself was a judicious investor. Through acquiring valuable real estate in the District he had eventually become worth $150,000, placing him among the wealthiest Washingtonians of color.[3]

Employment with the Freedmen's Bureau had brought John Mercer Langston and Charles Purvis to the nation's capital. Langston was the son of a Virginia plantation owner and his former slave, Lucy Langston. His parents had lived together openly, but both had died when he was just four. His father had devised an arrangement for his youngest son's education before his death and by the terms of his will had bequeathed to him a considerable inheritance of land and other resources. Langston now had a national reputation and was US minister to Haiti.

Charles Purvis was born in Philadelphia into an affluent black elite family with notable abolitionists on the paternal and maternal sides of the family. His mother, Harriet, was the daughter of James Forten, a race activist and wealthy businessman. After attending Oberlin College, Purvis earned a medical degree from Wooster Medical College (later renamed Western Reserve Medical School). He enlisted in the Union Army as a surgeon and afterward worked at Freedmen's Hospital adjacent to Howard University (where he would be promoted to surgeon in chief in a few years' time). He was also on the medical faculty at Howard.

Like the Cook brothers and Wormley, Langston and Purvis were on-the-ground witnesses in the capital to the rapid changes Congress wrought in favor of their race. The 1866 Civil Rights Act, according black Americans the same rights of citizenship as their white counterparts, followed on the heels of the Thirteenth Amendment abolishing slavery. To oversee compliance with the new order, the Reconstruction Act the next year divided the former Confederate states into military districts and formulated conditions by which Southern states would be recognized by Congress. The Fourteenth Amendment, granting citizenship to all persons born or naturalized in the United States and guaranteeing them federal rights, was ratified in 1868, followed by the Fifteenth Amendment in 1870, certifying that the right to vote could not be denied because of "race, color, or previous condition of servitude." The Force Acts of 1870 and 1871 banned the use of terror or force to prevent blacks from voting. From 1869 to 1873, a series of public accommodation laws for hotels, restaurants, bars, and places of entertainment was enacted in the District of Columbia. The 1875 federal Civil Rights Act ensured that the same safeguards against race-based discrimination in public facilities applied in every state.[4]

A setback followed when, to resolve the disputed presidential election of 1876, Republican nominee Rutherford B. Hayes promised to remove the last of the federal troops from the South in exchange for Democrats' conceding a series of electoral votes that allowed Hayes to assume the presidency in 1877. Since some of the political strategizing had taken place at the Wormley Hotel, the compromise is referred to by historians—with unintended irony—as the Wormley Agreement. Despite the initiation of this "let alone" policy in the South, African Americans, looking back in 1879, could point to a "glorious harvest of good things," as one ex-slave (the brother of Blanche Bruce) expressed it, and believe that the overall momentum was on their side. No one could have foretold that the Civil Rights Act of 1875 would be the last civil rights legislation passed by Congress for eighty years.

Senator Blanche Bruce was born in slavery; his white father was the owner of his mother. He was occasionally tutored along with his father's legitimate son. Freed by the general emancipation at age twenty-two, Bruce took full advantage of political opportunities in Mississippi during Reconstruction. He also acquired a 3,000-acre Delta plantation. His term as a US senator from Mississippi, the second black man to attain that distinction, began in 1875. By 1879, sixteen black citizens had been seated in the US Senate and House of Representatives. Of the group of men named in the *Evening Star* article, Bruce was the closest to "self-made." Except for the early tutoring his father had provided, his education had been limited to a few months' study at Oberlin College. But he was a man of "unconquerable ambition." He developed an air of self-assurance and the polished "manners of a gentleman of the old school." And in 1878, he "married up." His bride was Josephine Willson, the daughter of Joseph Willson, the author of *Sketches of the Higher Classes Among the Colored Society in Philadelphia*. After Josephine's birth, the Willson family had moved to Cleveland, Ohio, and been key in establishing that city's black elite. Josephine Bruce, described as "fairer than many a Caucasian belle," was an accomplished linguist and a charming hostess. The Bruce home in Washington was a center of social life.[5]

Richard T. Greener went to preparatory school at Oberlin College and Phillips Academy Andover. In 1870, he distinguished himself as the first black graduate of Harvard University. After becoming the principal of Washington's Preparatory High School for Colored Youth in 1872–73, he next earned a law degree at the University of South Carolina. He was welcomed back upon his return to Washington in 1877, especially by the city's black intelligentsia, and was now the dean of Howard University's law school.

Francis Grimké was not an unknown quantity when he became a pastor in Washington. He and his brother Archibald were born slaves on a plantation near Charleston, South Carolina. Their father, a white lawyer named Henry Grimké, who had acknowledged his paternity, sent Francis and Archibald to private school, and in his will left instructions for their freedom. Francis suffered a period of reenslavement, but eventually, with the financial help of their white half sisters, the famous abolitionists Sarah Grimké and Angelina Grimké Weld, the brothers benefited from first-rate educations. Francis graduated as valedictorian from Lincoln University in Pennsylvania. Turning to the ministry, he completed graduate studies at Princeton Theological Seminary. He married in 1878, the same year he was ordained a minister. His wife was the former Charlotte Forten, a sister of Charles Purvis's mother.

The stories of these eight individuals illustrate their ability, ambition, drive, and desire. The advantage they had relative to the many freedmen to follow, who may have possessed equal ability and determination to get ahead, was a head start. They were either scions of free, established, well-to-do families or had a leg up because their white fathers acknowledged their paternity and provided at least some schooling, which was extremely rare (the miscegenation was not). They enjoyed a head start not only in acquiring education and refined manners but in landing respectable livelihoods in a competitive environment. Despite the allure of Washington, in truth there was opportunity for only so many African American entrepreneurs, federal and municipal officials and clerks, ministers, teachers, professors, doctors, dentists, and lawyers.[6]

The "colored aristocracy" of Washington was protective of their head start. Theirs was an exclusive club, hard to break into, especially from the middle class. With its unique advantages, Washington was a Mecca for upper-class blacks from other cities. They were attracted for the same reasons that made it a comparative colored man's paradise for the many: government jobs and protections and superior educational pathways for themselves and their children. "Would be's" who fancied inclusion in the District's black elite circles had to meet a combination of requirements. Being wealthy or light-skinned ("mulatto nobodies") or even both was not enough. The more important question was "Who are your people?" Was the aspirant known to those already secure in the city's "colored aristocracy" or introduced by one of its members? Did he stem from a family distinguished by virtue of including well-known abolitionists or war heroes? Did he have a first-class education or had he arrived in Washington to serve as a high official? One's package of qualities determined whether one would be admitted to the capital's black elite or not. As for money, without enough to buy a home worthy of being used for entertainment and the clothes and accoutrements that signaled a level of success and etiquette, one was done for. And although light skin was not enough, few were those folded in without it. One exception was Paul Laurence Dunbar; when the celebrated poet moved to DC, the smart set readily overlooked his very dark color.

Although class conscious and socially exclusive, the black elite never lost sight of the unifying goal of equality for all people of color. Dunbar employed his literary gift in articulating this: "In aims and hopes for our race, it is true, we are all at one, but it must be understood, when we come to consider the social life, that the girls who cook in your kitchens and the men who serve in your dining-rooms do not dance in our parlors."[7]

Those in the "colored aristocracy" were not works in progress. They had proved their worthiness and could offer their own success as exhibit number one to counter criticism that blacks were not ready for full participation in the social contract. They were primed to think of themselves as Americans first and foremost, with no apology for color. Assimilation was the logical next step if there were to be one society. Attempts to categorize by race frustrated Charles Purvis, who resented the expression "leading colored doctor or lawyer," averring, "We are all Americans, white, black, and colored."

In the 1870s, the possibilities seemed positive enough for the *New Era* (a black paper with a national reach) to predict that "in the newer and better life upon which we have now entered, the color of the skin will cease to be a bar to recognition of gentlemanly qualifications here in the United States." For instance, O. S. B. Wall joined the white First Congregational Church. When the pastor objected, the support of the parishioners was with Wall, and it was the reverend who had to go. The Walls, Langstons, and Bruces all had experience mingling in interracial society and occasionally entertained liberal whites in their Washington homes. Less occasionally they were entertained by them, as when the journalist and government official John Forney invited several prominent African Americans to a gentlemen's party also attended by the President of the United States and several cabinet members.[8]

But few whites were as progressive as Forney. Many were willing to interact courteously with the best class of African Americans in work or business settings but drew the line at social equality.

William S. Scarborough, a Wilberforce University professor, understood that "The white man does not know the Negro. . . . To know the Negro one must be with him, and of him, and see what he is doing and above all what he is thinking." The remedy, according to John Mercer Langston, depended "on the ability to place oneself among those with whom one would associate." That was easier said than done. As Scarborough pointed out, because of the sensitivity that came with the "growing refinement of the Negro . . . he naturally recoils from rebuff."

The drawback in not seeking full inclusion with whites was that when it came to advancement, business and social functions fundamentally overlapped. It was at after-work get-togethers over meals or drinks that contacts were made and deals were struck. Left out of such opportunities for interpersonal networking, including membership in professional societies such as the American Medical Association, markedly added to the black man's handicap.

For many upper-class citizens of color in Washington, progress depended on some kind of white patronage. That was certainly the case for positions in municipal and federal government. Being an independent business or professional man was not necessarily an exception. There were not enough well-to-do black clients to support the black lawyers in the capital, for example. Not only were wealthy white patrons the bread and butter of James Wormley's enterprises, but it was his associations with white men that facilitated the large loans he needed to construct his hotel. Like others in the black elite, Wormley skillfully cultivated relationships with influential whites that were characterized by gentility and respect on both sides (if not altogether evenly). Francis Grimké admired Wormley's style: "There was nothing obsequious about him in his contact with white people, as so many colored people are." Veering into "toadying" was not dignified.[9]

Even as aspiring elites of color had their hands full trying to make progress in a white world, they faced criticism from the black majority. A mix of truths, half-truths, and untruths came hurling forth: *You are snobbish show-offs and do not want to socialize with the rest of us. You decry prejudice by whites against yourselves but practice class and color prejudice against us. You want to run away from your race and wish you were white. You care only about your own advancement and do not want to help the down-and-out among us or raise the race as a whole.*

Though the elite strongly supported black causes, they did not deny their class-consciousness and claimed the prerogative to socialize with whomever they pleased, following the natural tendency to associate with like-minded people of similar habits and interests. They were not without criticisms of their low-class counterparts, of course, but insisted that they did not want to distance themselves from the race so much as distinguish themselves from those who might add to its unfair generalization as a worthless and vicious culture. Joseph Willson observed as early as 1841 that the public "have long been accustomed to regard the people of color as one consolidated mass, all huddled together, without any particular or general distinctions, social or otherwise. The sight of one colored man with them . . . is the sight of a community; and the errors and crimes of one, is adjudged as the criterion of character of the whole body." The black upper class has echoed this sentiment ever since. As Paul Laurence Dunbar admitted, "Some of us wince a wee bit when we are thrown into the lump as the peasant or serving class."[10]

Though the degree of effort expended to uplift the race varied among individuals, many black elites acted upon a sense of noblesse oblige to assist the downtrodden by organizing and contributing to charities or by agitating for political and educational advancements. They were convinced that they also aided the overall cause by personal example. They saw themselves as cultural brokers: their success and gentility would inspire the black masses while proving to whites that, given education and opportunity, all African Americans would follow in their footsteps.

Blacks with lighter skin color, more European features, proper English, and impeccable manners put whites at ease and opened more doors. It was useless for those in the black upper stratum to deny their own color bias. It was obvious in their selection of mates alone. Nevertheless, those who valued their status in black elite circles did not wish to run from their race. They identified wholeheartedly with people of color. Many could have passed for white. Daniel Murray's close friend Cyrus Field Adams lamented, "My trouble is, all my life I have been trying to pass for colored."

People of both races mocked and caricatured the black elite for "putting on airs" and "affectation of erudition." Their targets were sensitive to such barbs, by and large unfair exaggerations. They reacted by ensuring that their social events, though first class, were tasteful and elegant affairs, all signs of ostentation eschewed. They rejected the emotional displays prevalent in most black churches, for example. The services at high-toned churches were restrained and featured classical music. In their homes and dress they avoided gaudy finery. The precise manners of the upper class and the exemplary behavior they insisted on in their children were carefully cultivated.[11]

Daniel and Anna Murray were outstanding exemplars of this culture. Murray's hometown newspaper noted, "Baltimoreans naturally feel proud of Daniel Murray for he takes his place among men. . . . He is a cultured and refined gentleman. Nothing of the coarse or vulgar, or cheapness in Mr. Murray." Entering upon their married life, all signs were auspicious for an assured place in elite circles. Anna was not only related to former senator Hiram Revels, the first black citizen to serve in either house of Congress, but hailed from an impressive line of abolitionists who had played major roles in the Oberlin-Wellington Rescue and John Brown's Raid. Her education at Oberlin College provided an immediate connection to many of the top elites in Washington. Daniel held a distinguished professional position at the Library of Congress.

Part of the black intelligentsia, his acumen as a businessman in addition was already well established. Still, he would need to add to his real estate and construction ventures to cushion the nest egg that would allow him to pursue the upper-class lifestyle and purchase a house for entertaining. As hard as Murray worked, it did not keep him from the nonstop socializing that he and Anna indulged in during the first years of their marriage. The newlyweds were invited to one black elite occasion after another, including a number of weddings for which, unlike their own, much detail is available.

Daniel and Anna were among the guests at the matrimonial alliance of Spencer Murray and Margaret Myers on a September evening a few months after their own wedding. The "Misses Myers" present at the Bachelors Ball that Daniel and Spencer had helped organize five years earlier may well have referred to Maggie and her sister. The wedding of William Myers's "lovely and much-admired" daughter was highly anticipated. The *National Republican* effused, "The elite of our colored fashionable societies are on the qui vive about a marriage to take place in this city. . . . The high contracting parties move among and are much respected by the leading colored citizens of Washington and Baltimore."

St. Luke's was still not completed, so the ceremony was held, through the courtesy of its rector, at St. John's Episcopal Church, "the Church of Presidents" on Lafayette Square. Reverend Alexander Crummell officiated. The "various shades of complexion represented" in the audience impressed the commentator, who opined, "They drew a full house, of all classes of citizens regardless of race . . . and it was a beautiful sight to see." The prominent white guests included Joseph Nimmo, the chief of the Bureau of Statistics, where Spencer Murray was employed, two former mayors of the city, and two of the current district commissioners. The bridegroom wore the "regulation suit of black, relieved by a white tie and kid gloves." Maggie was costumed in white satin and tulle, decorated with orange blossoms. "A beautiful brunette," her hair *à la pompadour* was covered by a delicate veil. The catered reception was held at the Myerses' home, their parlors "thronged with many of the leading citizens of the community." Spencer and Maggie left the reception in time to catch a late train for their Niagara Falls honeymoon. Daniel and Anna's gift of a silver jewelry case lined with blue silk was one of the many valuable presents listed in the *People's Advocate* the next day.

When Maggie's sister Henrietta, described as "a Washington Belle," married a few years later, the ceremony, performed by Reverend Grimké, and the reception were held in the Myerses' parlors. It is telling to note that the *Washington Bee* pronounced that on this occasion "there was no unnecessary display of toilets or false demonstrations. It reminded one of the many fashionable weddings in the days gone by." Though the nuptials of both Myers sisters were tasteful affairs, this sentiment shows that the sensitivity of black elites to any ostentation that might make them vulnerable to criticism sometimes resulted in conservative understatement.[12]

On the last evening of October 1879, the Daniel Murrays attended the party that O. S. B. Wall and his wife, Amanda, held to celebrate their twenty-fifth wedding anniversary. The Wall home was next door to John Mercer Langston's chalet-inspired Hillside Cottage. Happy to step from the windy night into "the light and warmth of their beautiful parlors," the Murrays congratulated the Walls and added their gift of a silver butter knife to a table laden with presents. Captain Wall was a frequent host and sometimes reminisced about the Oberlin-Wellington Rescue and how he and his cohorts had been cast into jail. "It moves one to tears," recalled a listener. On that evening, Wall's sister Caroline Langston was present and so was Mrs. John H. Smyth, while their minister husbands were serving abroad in Haiti and Liberia, respectively. Senator and Josephine Bruce, John Cromwell, Christian Fleetwood, William E. Matthews, and several professors from

Howard University were in attendance, as were Milton Holland and his wife, Virginia, who lived nearby. Holland had been known to Langston and Wall since the time they had recruited him into the 5th Regiment, United States Colored Troops. Holland had distinguished himself at the Battle of New Market Heights, earning a Congressional Medal of Honor. He was now a rising clerk in the US Treasury Department. The anniversary party was characterized by stimulating conversation, a catered supper, and abundant wine and liquor. The evening was "enlivened further by music from the charming Mrs. Murray."

Anna Murray may have given up her role as music teacher in the public schools, but she sustained "her reputation as a singer whose sweetness of voice is only equaled by her easy manner of bearing herself." She presided at the piano at the Howard University commencement in May, one of her first public appearances as Mrs. Daniel Murray. Now she was slated to share the bill at a benefit concert in November with a famous headliner, Madame Marie Selika. The "wonderful colored Prima Donna" had entertained the President and Mrs. Hayes the November before, one of the first African American artists to perform at the White House. Christian Fleetwood directed the "Grand Concert" at Lincoln Hall, an auditorium available to all without regard to race, on November 3, 1879. There were about six hundred people in the racially mixed audience, "many of whom were whites of the most fashionable circles in the city." As a vocalist, Anna apparently commanded quite a vocal range, as she was variously described as singing soprano, alto, and contralto.[13]

Meanwhile, St. Luke's, according to one commentator, had moved "toward completion with all the rapidity of a chained snail." The congregation was determined to hold the first divine service on Thanksgiving Day, November 27, 1879, even though there was work left to do. The church was Gothic Revival in style, made of blue stone quarried from the Potomac River. The design choice was Reverend Crummell's, inspired by Anglican churches he had visited in England. He worked with the architect Calvin Brent to bring it to fruition. Evidence of excellent craftsmanship was everywhere. The finely proportioned building had a sharply pitched roof. The main entrance consisted of two pairs of lancet doors with a stone tympanum above. The large stained-glass window centered above the entrance, not quite finished, was composed of five narrow lancet windows surmounted by a tracery, giving the impression of a single pointed-arch window.

Anticipation was pronounced. Sneak peeks at ten cents each were allowed in the days leading up to the official debut. When the day finally arrived, worshippers began filling the pews two hours before the eleven o'clock service. Soon the seating for eight hundred was filled to capacity, "at least one-third of those in attendance being from the white membership of the several Episcopal Churches in the city." The nave was divided into six bays separated by columns with Gothic-inspired foliated capitals. The chancel, three feet above the level of the main floor, was decorated with evergreens and the gift of a cross of ferns and wheat. Christian Fleetwood led the choir in singing the processional as Reverend Crummell entered. Daniel Murray must have reflected on his blessings that Thanksgiving day. The congregation had elected him vestryman of this magnificent new church, and he and his wife were expecting their first child.[14]

Murray was in a lighthearted mood throughout the holiday season. In December he worked on an article for the *Evening Star* entitled "The Ladies Law of Leap Year." The feature ran a few days before the leap year of 1880 commenced—an interesting subject for one who had so recently surrendered his own bachelorhood. Murray reviewed the tradition that allows women to propose marriage during leap years, "a privilege which, during the other three years, is the sole prerogative of men." It was Murray's first published piece of writing, and it revealed a verbose style. He turned what should have been a puff piece into a ponderous read by including an erudite history of calendars.

The first day of 1880, Murray was out and about according to the New Year's custom. Families opened their homes to receive friends and offer libations. The "flowing punch bowl" added to the festive mood on the streets as well-wishers called at one household after another. Many couples were among those making the rounds, but a social chronicler noted seeing "Hon. Frederick Douglass and brother Daniel Murray, solus" at one reception.

Anna did step out with her husband the next evening. Pinckney Pinchback from New Orleans, former Louisiana governor, was in town, and hosted a party at the home of Mamie and Robert J. Harlan, Jr., he the son of the eminent Colonel Robert James Harlan. The senior Harlan (President Hayes had bestowed his colonel's commission), who was prominent in Ohio and national Republican Party politics, was visiting from Cincinnati. The extravagances of the holidays were in effect, and Governor Pinchback prepared eggnog spiked with so much alcohol that William Matthews insisted on "pouring in milk afterwards and bringing it down to the average." In recognition of leap year, many single ladies were invited. It was an animated scene, and "ever and anon the wondrously rich voice of Miss Mattie Lawrence [one of the Fisk Jubilee Singers] or Mrs. Daniel Murray would break on the company in sweetest song."

Not even a week later, another occasion took place at Harlan's house, this one a dinner for twelve hosted by the younger gentlemen to honor Governor Pinchback and Colonel Harlan. Murray and others present at the January 2 party were joined this evening by provisions merchant James T. Bradford. He was one of Baltimore's foremost businessmen and would, in a few years' time, acquire a house in Washington and become an active member of St. Luke's Church and a regular crony of Murray.[15]

Daniel (who had continued rooming with his sister Ellen until his marriage) and Anna were living in the 800 block of M Street when their son, Daniel Evans Murray—called Dannie by the family—was born on February 11, 1880. Soon thereafter, the family of three moved to Anna's parents' house at 1926 12th Street NW, presumably for help with the baby. Anna's siblings Henrietta, Mary, and Bruce were all attending school, while Lewis, having completed his studies at Howard University, was now a working teacher.

Daniel's brother Samuel Proctor had remarried in 1877 to Alice Harris of Baltimore, his junior by more than two decades, and moved back to 13th Street, right across the street from his siblings, Ellen and Daniel. By the birth of their son the following year, the Proctor family had relocated to the countryside near Rockville, Maryland. Samuel had bought a farm there and turned it into a summer resort. His daughter Eugenia was of course part of the household, and by the summer of 1880, when the Murrays came calling, the Proctors, like Daniel and Anna, had added an infant to their family.

Samuel and Alice Proctor received guests from the fifteenth of May until the close of the season in early September. Their large country house was situated on the crest of a hill. A wide veranda encircled the dwelling, and from the porch above one could view the village of Rockville below and the rolling blue-violet mountains in the distance. Some guests came for a prolonged stay, but, as the resort was only a sixteen-mile train ride from Washington, weekend or even day jaunts were also options. Proctor eventually added enough rooms to the house to accommodate thirty people. He provided all the comforts of home for "a class who are mutually agreeable."

In mid-July 1880, Daniel and Anna Murray were part of just such a class gathered for a weekend outing at Proctor's Resort, along with Charley and Mary Proctor, Christian and Sara Fleetwood, Bob and Mamie Harlan, Caroline Langston, and Virginia

Holland. Actually, the wives of Murray, Charley Proctor, Fleetwood, and Harlan were already there, enjoying a longer stay when
the others arrived by Saturday's train.

After supper some strolled the landscape, dotted with shade
and fruit trees and a cool spring. Others engaged in croquet or
archery on the front lawn. When evening shadows arrived, Chinese lanterns illuminated the lawn, but eventually all retired to the
parlor, where, to the strains of a Strauss waltz furnished by Anna,
those so inclined twirled in dance. The company next attempted
an amateur performance of *H.M.S. Pinafore* with Chris Fleetwood
in the major role and Bob Harlan and Dan Murray alternating between several characters and supplying the chorus. The musical
was fresh on their minds because the December before St. Luke's
had staged performances of the popular Gilbert and Sullivan oper-
etta at Lincoln Hall, a fund-raiser for the church.

Sunday started with a religious service and was followed by a
full day of amusements and fellowship, winding up with punch and
a light repast at 8 p.m., served in "Proctor's style." As one who sampled his hospitality noted, an excursion planned to Proctor's meant
"There is a good time coming, boys." Indeed, black-people-only
occasions were at once relaxing and invigorating; whites would
have poisoned the party. Come Monday morning, a six o'clock bell
announced breakfast. Daniel Murray and other male guests rushed
in the pink dawn to catch the train back to DC. These were working "aristocrats." The fortunes of the wealthiest among them never
compared to those accumulated by upper-class whites of the day.[16]

On August 6, Murray attended a Friday-evening stag party
honoring the diplomat John H. Smyth, in town for a brief period. Such gentlemen-only occasions followed a familiar format:
card playing, a late supper, then numerous toasts and responses,
all accompanied by drinks and cigars. Murray was out again the
next Friday night for a "truly grand scene" at Milton and Virginia
Holland's house. Like the Langstons and Walls, the Hollands had

a handsome home on Howard University Hill. Theirs was modeled after a French villa with a mansard roof and an ample portico. It stood on an eminence entirely surrounded by spacious lawns. The commodious interior, elegantly furnished, included a library stocked with "a choice selection of the best works of the best authors." On this occasion "men noted in literature, men of official station and of wealth" were gathered, "surrounded by charming ladies equally well known."

Daniel and Anna attended two notable weddings in 1881. The first, "a wedding which called out the elite of our colored society," took place the evening of April 8 at 15th Street Presbyterian Church, almost precisely two years after the Murrays had been married in the same church. The bride was Mamie Syphax. She sang soprano in the choir at St. Luke's, where her cousin Douglas Syphax and his wife, Abbie McKee Syphax, were active members. Mamie was the daughter of Charles Syphax and the granddaughter of Maria Syphax, herself the offspring of Martha Washington's grandson George Washington Parke Custis and his slave Ariana Carter. Custis had eventually freed Maria and given her fifteen acres on his Arlington, Virginia, estate.

Now eighty, the venerable matriarch came to the wedding from Arlington at the special request of the bride. "The spectacle of three generations being represented was as beautiful as it was rare," reported the *National Republican*, describing the overall audience as a "select company, representing the beauty, wealth, and culture among our colored citizens." (Compared to other mainstream newspapers, the politically oriented *National Republican* had a more inclusive tone in reporting on African American affairs, commonly using phrases such as "our colored citizens.") "The bride, with her fair and clear complexion . . . was a picture of loveliness." She wore white satin damasse—court en train—trimmed with old point lace and tulle, looped with a floral horseshoe composed of lilies of the valley. The groom was Albert K. Brodie, a Justice Department clerk and the son of Reverend George Brodie, the pastor at Metropolitan AME Church, who officiated at the ceremony along with Reverend Grimké.

December 28 brought the wedding of Dr. John R. Francis. Like the Syphaxes, Cooks, Wormleys, and Brents, the Francis family was prominent in Washington's exclusive group of respected "old citz." Dr. Francis, a surgeon and gynecologist, was growing a prosperous private practice. His bride, Bettie Cox, like Anna before her, was a grade school teacher expected to leave her position upon being married. "The 15th Street Presbyterian Church was the scene of one of the most fashionable marriages that have been here for years," claimed the *People's Advocate*, adding, "The audience room was filled with the elite of the city." Dressed in a gown of white satin and French grenadine garnished with orange blossoms, the bride was escorted up the aisle by her uncle, Milton Holland, to a wedding march composed for the occasion. The reception at the home of the Hollands was a "brilliant affair." Blanche and Josephine Bruce, she stunning in a canary silk dress designed by Worth, were among the impressive guests. The presents displayed in the second-floor library included an entire set of French china from best man William E. Matthews and a cream pitcher from the Murrays. This event closed a very active period of elite socializing for Daniel and Anna.[17]

4

THE GOOD LIFE

DANIEL MURRAY WAS A MAN OF "UNTIRING ENERGY." HIS history of service to the race went back to 1877, when he and some of his associates formed the Social Relief Association; Murray was elected president. Now, over the same period of steady socializing that followed his marriage, he remained active in black causes.

In early 1880, the US Treasury held a balance of $510,000 from the unclaimed pay and bounty of deceased African American soldiers. Congress announced that this sum would be allotted for the education of blacks and welcomed specific bids for its use. On February 5, in the first of his many appearances before Congress, Murray joined a delegation headed by Alexander Crummell to request that the entire amount be used for establishing a National Mechanical and Industrial Institute (with Frederick Douglass among the incorporators). Crummell, "regarded as the most learned colored man in the District," argued that employment was the greatest need for the race "just now," and that education for trades and crafts should take priority in the use of these funds.

In August 1881, a Washington correspondent noted that "Educated colored ladies and gentlemen find access to the public libraries and reading rooms of this city extremely difficult." The Library of Congress, for one, was not open in the evening, and its books did not circulate anyway. To remedy this situation, the article announced, "Prof. Greener, Mr. Henry Johnson, and Mr. Daniel Murray have inaugurated a movement looking to the acquisition of a first class library and reading rooms which shall be accessible to all."

In its issue of January 22, 1881, the *Evening Star* published an editorial by Daniel Murray entitled "Garfield's Administration and the Colored People." Murray contended that black support must not be taken for granted. "Too long the colored people have been held as the absolute property of the republican party," he wrote, its leaders assuming that "the negroes are with us always." He discredited the idea that a token appointment here and there "pays off the claims of the whole race." Black politicos deserved more positions, he insisted, especially the kind that came with "patronage and power."

Though Murray continued to assert political independence, specifics aimed at James Garfield became moot when, just months after the editorial ran, Garfield was struck down by an assassin's bullet. Efforts to establish an industrial education institution and a public library in Washington failed in the 1880s, but Murray would continue to push those pet concerns with diligence and determination until they were realities.[1]

Murray was devoted to his church. Besides serving as vestryman, he participated in efforts to extend the Episcopal belief among African Americans and volunteered to take charge of numerous church projects, from repairing the church's heating apparatus to raising funds for a memorial stained-glass window. At the Thanksgiving Day service of November 24, 1881, St. Luke's was honored by the presence of the new President, Chester Arthur. He normally attended St. John's Episcopal Church, a block from the White House. Those assembled there this Thanksgiving hoping to see him were "doomed to disappointment as that gentleman worshipped elsewhere to-day." At eleven o'clock the President's carriage pulled up to St. Luke's entrance. Several members of the cabinet and District Commissioner Josiah Dent attended as well. President Arthur, seated in a prominent pew near the chancel, "joined in the responses as earnestly as if he had been seated in his own pew at St. John's." Anna Murray sang in the choir, which performed Blumenbach's "Te Deum" among its offerings that Thursday.

As memorable as that occasion was, St. Luke's had been experiencing growing pains from the time of its first service on Thanksgiving Day 1879. The difficulties centered on the responsibilities and power of the rector versus the vestry. The precipitating issue was music, important at many churches and especially so at St. Luke's, where expectations were high. One manifestation involved responsibility for musical selections. The pastor objected to the piece the choir had been practicing for Easter Sunday 1880 and insisted at the eleventh hour that he had the prerogative to nix it. Even before that conflict, Crummell's controlling attitude toward the choir, and his imperious style in general, were resented. Choirmaster Christian Fleetwood and others in the vestry and congregation admitted that the pastor had ultimate authority but resisted the rigid way he exercised it. All that was covered in the local papers, including the *Evening Star* and *Washington Post*, with headlines such as "Trouble in St. Luke's Church" and "A First Class Riot," extremely embarrassing for an institution that had earned recognition in the larger society as a "a symbol of black bourgeoisie culture."

"The thermometer still rises" at St. Luke's, reported one newspaper a year later, and the "internal strife is having a very damaging effect upon the congregation." It was clear that Crummell's lack of tact in interacting with the vestry, especially over issues with the choir, was chronic. The Convocation of Washington, having already requested that Crummell harmonize with his vestry and choir, now called for his resignation. The vestry concurred except for the wavering Daniel Murray, who was finally coaxed into revealing that he favored whatever course would facilitate his securing a government job for a young man whose talented wife Murray wanted to recruit into the choir! Crummell managed to retain his office after all that, but, as if in a comedy of errors, two dueling sets of vestrymen were elected. Those embarrassments were exacerbated by the church debt, which had gotten to the point where the mortgage holder was threatening to put the building up for sale. Murray, having decided he was a Crummell partisan, and the other men serving in the vestry recognized by the pastor raised $1,000 in ten days' time to avoid that calamity.[2]

In June 1883, Alexander Crummell celebrated his ten-year anniversary in Washington, and Murray was on the Men's Guild committee that arranged an evening garden fete and strawberry festival. It took place in a private garden, "the spacious and beautiful grounds and elegant residence kindly tendered by the owner as a special favor to the church." The garden, "brilliantly illuminated by Chinese lanterns," was "well filled with a goodly class of people," who in turn were well filled with strawberries and ice cream as they listened to a lively band.

Not only were those in Washington's black elite working "aristocrats," most of them managed two streams of income. Certainly that was a necessity as a hedge against administrative changes for those whose positions depended on political patronage. Others sought extra income just to keep up with the expensive lifestyle. Some depended on three sources for funds—a practicing lawyer, for example, might also hold a government clerkship plus speculate in real estate. Real estate was a popular second source of income. Indeed, those in the black upper class who had achieved substantial wealth had done so not by earning their daily bread but through real estate, construction, and other financial ventures. This was another area in which elites established early on in the capital had a head start. Native Washingtonians such as the Cooks and Wormleys held cheaply acquired properties that had become prime city real estate. Those like Murray who came shortly after the war and realized that property in the nation's capital would only increase in value and thus was a winning investment also had early pickings.

By skillful speculation, Daniel Murray had acquired property holdings of substantial value and become one of the District's leading black men in the building trade. His father-in-law, Henry Evans, acted as his construction superintendent. Murray erected scores of city and suburban dwellings and became known for "houses of the higher order." He built residences for some of his friends, such as John H. Smyth and Wyatt Archer, and spec houses for others, including two for Pinckney Pinchback.[3]

One of Murray's projects in 1882–83 was the construction of three brick houses with basements and tin roofs on 12th Street between N and O streets NW. They were for Murray himself. He planned to live in one and rent out the other two. The three-story houses had pressed-brick fronts with Ohio stone trimmings, fancy belt courses and panels of molded brick, and bay windows with stained-glass transoms. The interiors, finished in natural woods, were Queen Anne–style, with patent cornices and slate mantels, alcoves, double parlors, and French plate glass. First class all the way, the houses were outfitted with modern conveniences: porcelain baths, gas ranges, hot and cold water, the latest Latrobe heating stoves, and bells and speaking tubes throughout.

The family moved into number 1331 in February 1883— Daniel, Anna, toddler Dannie, and a new baby, George Henry (called by his middle name), born at the Evanses' the September before. The house had ten rooms, and the Murrays rented out a few—not unusual, even for upper-class families, and Daniel Murray in particular could pinch pennies. By the end of 1883, having waited on its completion, the Murrays relocated to number 1333, the closest of the three houses to Iowa Circle (later renamed Logan Circle). This was a posh section of town, and the Murrays were now ready to entertain friends in their handsome new home.[4]

→ ←

IN 1883, MURRAY RECEIVED A RAISE AT THE LIBRARY OF CONgress, increasing his annual salary to $1,200 (this puts the $7,500 cost of building Murray's three houses into perspective). By the close of 1883, the library had 513,441 books and about 170,000 pamphlets. Ainsworth Spofford had cried for more space when the holdings were half as large. In 1882, a Washington physician, Dr. Joseph M. Toner, began donating his collection—rich in medical science and biography and local history—of nearly 50,000 books, pamphlets, scrapbooks, periodicals, manuscripts, and maps. Still, most of the library's growth came from copyright deposits: not only books but manuscripts, magazines, newspapers, maps, charts, dramatic compositions, and musical scores, plus photographs, engravings, and other graphic arts. The library rooms had been designed to hold books. There was no specialized shelving or containers for other kinds of material. Consequently they were stored in a more or less inaccessible state or sat in tottering heaps on the library's marble floor, where they kept company with piles and piles of books. Faced with more than half a million volumes when there was shelf space for less than 300,000, this was the option of last resort. Spofford finally succeeded in securing additional space—a couple of small, remote annexes plus the dark crypt of the Capitol, two flights of stairs below the library. The Toner Collection was carried to the crypt, where it languished year after year, unavailable to the public.

Then there was the safety issue. After all the effort to fireproof the library, books were being stored in various nooks and corners of the Capitol that were vulnerable to fire, and inflammable construction had been reintroduced in the library proper when the extensive wood shelving had been added. There was also a serious risk of fire in the library's dark upper loft, which held heaping piles of loose newspapers, documents, and maps. Gas had to be lit by the assistant librarians when their duties called them there. The dust of decomposing paper and the friction generated by constant handling of those materials increased their inflammability.

The library was a jam-packed, confused, ever-increasing mess. At least that was how outsiders saw it. Spofford, compelled to make do with the chaos, steadfastly continued his work amid the masses of materials growing around him. Information and publications for members of Congress were retrieved as requested. Acting on an inquiry, Spofford would make "a nervous burrow in some apparently futile heap" and "return triumphant, yet staidly triumphant, with the required volume." He maintained that even given the current wretched conditions, his subject system of classification, technical imperfections notwithstanding, allowed for the "promptitude of service" that remained his priority. Daniel Murray and the other experienced assistant librarians, "thoroughly familiar with the Library's subject scheme of arrangement, and nimble in movement from one location to another, might locate any volume without too great delay," claimed Spofford.

Thus, despite the disorderly state of things, the basic functions of the library—copyright, acquisitions, and "legislative reference"—were carried out. What bothered the Librarian was that they were, by necessity, carried out "under the eye and almost under the feet of members of Congress and other visitors." It was embarrassing that the library, given the commotion and noise, was no longer fit for the quiet pursuit of study. There was no place to separate process from results. All elements of the library craft, such as the receipt, cataloguing, and binding of books, were conducted in public areas.

The drawbacks of housing a monumental library in a space too crowded for proper care and arrangement of its collections grew daily. Accretion was steady and, as Spofford put it, "illimitable." He predicted that there would be two million books long before the close of the century. As early as 1871, he realized that a separate edifice of great scope would be required. Selling the idea to Congress was a long-term process. Numerous commissions, committees, and experts weighed in, but by 1884 the Librarian reported that "No progress whatever has been made toward the relief of the overcrowded rooms and piled-up floors. The bill matured in the last Congress for the construction of a fire-proof library building failed to pass." The urgent need for a new library, he continued, "demands prompt and decisive action on the part of Congress to provide the most ample, safe, and permanent accommodations for the accumulated stores of the nation's literature and art." Describing the situation as an emergency, he warned, "I hope a conflagration here in the Capitol may not be necessary to unite our minds in the discharge of a plain public duty."[5]

→ ←

WASHINGTON'S BLACK ELITES WERE WEALTHY ENOUGH TO GET out of town during the severe heat of summer. The John F. Cooks retreated to their "country seat." Others traveled to particular resorts where they were not only welcomed but catered to and where they rendezvoused with black elites from other cities. "Our exclusive smart set is naturally very circumscribed and the lines are strictly drawn and discreetly determined," noted one in the charmed circle. Some "summered" as far away as Saratoga, New York. Atlantic City, New Jersey, was a popular destination. The Murrays took occasional trips there and also sampled the countryside in nearby Loudon County, Virginia, with its beautiful Blue Ridge views. Harpers Ferry, West Virginia, just a two-hour train ride away, attracted many of Washington's elites.

Harpers Ferry was a town steeped in historical significance and scenic splendor. Though the ravages of war were still evident in the lower part of town, up on Camp Hill, surrounded by ragged mountains, one looked out on a breathtaking natural scene: the Shenandoah River on one side and the Potomac River on the other, the point of confluence providing the view with a picturesque consummation. In August 1883, Anna Murray, with her two sons, registered for a stay at Storer College's Lincoln Hall. The college, founded in 1867 and open to all without regard to gender or race, had recently begun renting its Camp Hill dormitories for white and black summer boarders. Though they were housed separately, the college "consciously sought to foster an atmosphere of interracial amity." Lincoln Hall was the principal dormitory that welcomed African American families. It was a three-story structure with thirty-four double rooms and a two-story porch at the east end. Newspaper advertisements for Lincoln Hall promised "pure waters, cool mountain breezes, pleasant shades, free from malaria and unmolested from mosquitoes" and a "table furnished from fresh country produce."[6]

At the end of 1883, the Murrays received a visit of a few days from Daniel's parents. It was covered in the *Evening Star* with the headline "A Baltimore Centenarian." George Murray was credited with being "one of the oldest, if not the oldest, man in Baltimore." The article went on to state that "Mr. Murray is active and enjoys excellent health, and has every evidence to justify the opinion that he will have many years yet." Surely Daniel and Anna were proud to show off their new home on 12th Street, not to mention their two growing boys. They may have revealed that Anna was expecting a third child. There was not-so-happy news in the extended family: Charley Proctor, having claimed that his wife had deserted him two years earlier, was freshly divorced.

Perhaps inspired by the *Evening Star* story, "A Chat with a Centenarian" appeared in the *Baltimore Sun* shortly after the senior Murrays' trip to Washington. The reporter visited with George and Eliza Murray at their Forrest Street home. "Uncle George

Murray is an Eastern Shore colored man of the quaint, genial old-time ways," the resultant article read, "a nice-looking darkey with an intelligent face, iron gray hair, and a hearty and respectful manner. He is a genuine specimen of the old-fashioned Eastern Shore darkey." George was quoted in "Negro dialect." Most of the piece was about his advanced age and memories of the historical times through which he passed. "The old man said he is not thinking about dying yet," the article concluded. As for Eliza, she "is still a vigorous woman, and was hard at work in the kitchen at the time of the Sun reporter's call."[7]

The rise of politicos of color continued under Republican administrations through the first half of the 1880s. Frederick Douglass was appointed recorder of deeds, and Blanche Bruce, his Senate term completed, landed the plum position of register of the Treasury, which carried the distinction of having his signature imprinted on every bill of US currency. There was serious consideration of an African American for the cabinet and Bruce as the next Republican vice presidential nominee. Black leaders continued to be elected to Congress. John R. Lynch and South Carolina's Robert Smalls began new terms in 1882, joined by James O'Hara from North Carolina the following year.

But the political winds shifted when Democrat Grover Cleveland became President in 1885, the first time in twenty-four years that the Republicans had lost the top office. Murray, for one, thought the new president was "willing to give the colored people an equal chance in the race of life." Political patronage being what it was, the Republican loyalists Douglass and Bruce were asked to relinquish their positions. Nevertheless, Murray was impressed by Cleveland's treatment of Frederick Douglass at White House receptions, "showing him every courtesy and making no distinction on account of color." Furthermore, maintained Murray, "Mr. Cleveland has been very liberal with the distribution of patronage among us, and we have no reason to complain on that score." Murray was mindful that "our people have been wedded to the republican party," but he continued to believe that "the time is coming when they will act for themselves, and become independents." It was with that attitude that he spearheaded the drive to collect 5,000 names for a petition promoting James C. Matthews, a black Democrat from New York (no relation to Murray's friend William E. Matthews from Baltimore), for recorder of deeds. When President Cleveland nominated Matthews, his supporters rejoiced, one remarking, "The young men of the city are especially proud and will give Mr. Matthews a royal greeting, as it introduces into public life one of their own class—young, ambitious, educated and fully qualified for public station." As it turned out, the Senate ultimately rejected Matthew's nomination and eventually confirmed James Monroe Trotter, another African American. Murray was pleased with Cleveland's second choice of Trotter, a Massachusetts Democrat, calling his appointment a "good stroke of policy."[8]

Signs of Murray's own growing leadership were evident in the newspapers. The *Critic-Record*, an exponent and advocate of Washington interests, characterized him as "a very intelligent colored man" who is "well up on all matters relating to the welfare of his race, social and political." In May 1884, Murray's name, for the first but not the last time, was suggested for school board trustee. Two years earlier it had been floated for a diplomatic post—"Daniel Murray is a young aspirant, and his knowledge of books, acquired in the office of the Librarian of Congress, would enable him to master the intricacies of diplomatic life." Murray even came to the notice of the black press outside of the District. The *Cleveland Gazette*, for example, in an April 1885 issue, identified Murray as one of four Washingtonians indispensable at their government posts. The article closed on a hopeful, if a bit fanciful, note: "That these four gentlemen . . . are colored, is but a passing remark."

Meanwhile, Daniel and Anna's ascendancy in black elite society continued apace. The *National Republican* identified the couple among the "prominent citizens both black and white" attending a Washington Cadet Corps program. The *Washington Bee* noted in its "Society Dots" section that "Mr. and Mrs. Daniel Murray live in the fashionable part of the city" and described how the prestigious Orpheus Glee Club called on Murray, "one of our popular gentlemen," hoping to render him a serenade: "Mr. Murray was not at home but his accomplished wife acted in his stead. The Club could not have honored a more worthy young man."[9]

The Murrays' third child was born in April 1884. Named Nathaniel Allison, he was casually known as Nat. With a four-year-old, a two-year-old, and an infant to care for, Anna advertised for help a few months later. "Wanted: a woman to cook, wash and iron for a small family. Also, a girl. Good wages. Bring reference." In December, Anna held a parlor social for the benefit of a new memorial window at St. Luke's. The following fall the Murrays welcomed Madame Marie Selika and her husband, Sampson Williams, back to Washington as their houseguests. Under Daniel Murray's management, the prima donna presented two concerts, and on November 6, 1885, she was "tendered a grand reception" at the Murray residence.

To celebrate turning thirty-five, Murray threw himself a birthday party on March 3, 1886. It was covered in the *New York Freeman* (the new name of T. Thomas Fortune's newspaper formerly called the *New York Globe*): "Mr. Daniel Murray gave a very pleasant tea party to a number of his gentlemen friends in honor of his birthday. Progressive euchre was the entertainment of the evening and six tables were kept until 11 p.m. when a fine supper was served." Euchre was a popular, fast-paced, trick-taking card game. In progressive euchre multiple tables of four engaged in tournament-style play. It would be surprising if tea had been the only libation served.

The first week in June came with a hair-raising scare for the Murrays. Nat, now an active two-year-old, fell from the second-story porch of their home to the concrete fifteen feet below, "cutting a frightful gash in his head." To the relief of all, his skull was not fractured and there were no ongoing repercussions.

In July 1886 the *Washington Bee* published an article on the "fight for supremacy" within the black elite. Recognizing that Washington "can boast of its colored society more so than any other city in the country," the *Bee* ascertained "a growing mania in this city among a certain class, for social recognition." Anna and Daniel Murray were named among those who had gained "social distinction." Assimilation into mainstream culture seemed promising when the 1888 Washington Elite List was published and included, among others adjudged to be of "assured social position," the Cook, Wormley, Purvis, Langston, Lynch, and Somerville families. Perhaps the Murrays would make the next edition.[10]

→ ←

August 5, 1886, was a very special date for Ainsworth Spofford. Fifteen years after he had first articulated the need, the construction of a new Library of Congress building was authorized on a site immediately east of the Capitol; $555,000 was allotted for purchase of the property. After the final hurdle had been cleared in Congress, the Librarian himself carried the bill to the President for his signature. "I am again the happiest man in Washington," he enthused, "the last obstacle in the way of the Library Building being removed."

Daniel Murray was one of twenty or so assistant librarians in 1886. Despite Spofford's requests, the number of new staff hired had not kept pace with the library's acquisitions; by the end of the year, it held 581,678 books and 193,000 pamphlets. An *Evening Star* reporter visiting the library observed "books stowed rank behind rank so that their titles are concealed instead of exhibited, in alcoves overflowing into every adjacent space and corridor, and in floors heaped high with books, pamphlets, musical compositions and newspapers, from the ground floors of the Capitol to the attic. Besides this, nine dark and unventilated rooms in the crypts below the Capitol have been filled." Given the utter exhaustion of space, Librarian Spofford was pleased to report that the passage of the act for a new building was "the most gratifying event of the year." He elaborated, "By the terms of this act a site immediately opposite the Capitol and adjoining the eastern park has been purchased, of ample dimensions to accommodate a building to contain over 3,000,000 volumes, with space in the rear adequate for the ultimate erection of an annex to hold 2,000,000 volumes additional. . . . The necessary excavations for the foundation are now in progress."

Continuing his self-improvement, Murray took a course in conversational German that began in March 1886, meeting at Lincoln Memorial Church three nights a week. The instructor was Cyrus Field Adams, who, having gained mastery of the tongue in Germany, had taught the language and its literature at Kentucky State University. Murray completed his study in 1887, adding the knowledge of another foreign language to his familiarity with French and Spanish.[11]

> ← ←

ANNA'S FATHER, HENRY EVANS, HAD RETAINED OWNERSHIP OF his Oberlin house. He was there, working on repairs for the current renters, when he was seriously injured in a fall in late August 1886, leading to his death. Henrietta and her son Bruce, just shy of nineteen, traveled to Oberlin and buried Henry in the town's Westwood Cemetery on September 2. The Washington branch of the family had been visiting with their Ohio relatives regularly over the years; Anna had made her first trip as Mrs. Daniel Murray just the summer after marrying. The Evanses were a family of teachers; all but one of Henrietta's eleven children pursued the profession. Bruce, her youngest, received his first appointment in the District school system the year before his father died.

July 1887 brought the birth of the Murrays' only daughter, Helene Ethel Murray. It was followed two months later by the demise
of Samuel Proctor. Although he was only fifty-six, his obituary notice carried the headline "Death of an Old Caterer." Two years
earlier, when he had begun to suffer from tuberculosis, Proctor
had moved his family to Nichols Avenue in Hillsdale.

Samuel Proctor's property in Southeast Washington was not
far from the one his sister Catherine had long owned on Howard
Avenue between Nichols Avenue and the Anacostia River. Catherine was particularly close to her niece Catherine, known as Kate,
one of Ellen's daughters. Kate was part of the Baltimore household
of this aunt and her husband at age twelve when the 1860 census was taken. She later married a Joshua Jordan but by 1879 was
widowed and living in her aunt's Hillsdale house. Kate, like her
younger sister Ella, told fortunes. She made a business of her clair-
voyance, welcoming customers to her home for consultations. She
read tea leaves and furnished charms, "conjuration powder," and
"sprinkling fluid" to her more superstitious patrons. Charley Proctor, who remarried the year after Samuel died, and Ellen Butler
continued to live in Northwest Washington. Daniel Murray, the
youngest sibling, was by far the most successful and sophisticated,
and he became the family go-to member, the one who could be
counted on for a loan or other support. Several years earlier he had
been appointed guardian to his niece Ella, and he had steered her
and her mother through an equity court case as their "next friend,"
winning them a handsome sum.[12]

✦ ✦

In 1888, two more black citizens were elected to the
US Congress, Henry P. Cheatham from North Carolina and
John Mercer Langston, representing Virginia. Benjamin Harri-
son won the presidential vote in the same election, returning the
Republicans to power in the executive branch. With Harrison's

inauguration on March 4, 1889, came "the most brilliant spell of gaiety and elegant entertainments ever known to Washington, and possibly the country." The main inaugural ball was scheduled for the evening of the swearing-in ceremony. The newspapers wondered aloud if citizens of color, "elated over the election of the candidate of their chosen party," would attend. "There is likely to be a considerable sprinkling of the colored people," speculated the *Washington Critic*. "They will be the very best of colored society, of course," the article continued. "Naturally they regard the ball as an occasion on which they should not be conspicuous by their absence, even if they didn't want to go. . . . It can be stated positively, though, that no attempt will be made to exclude anyone from the ball because of his or her color. . . . Anyone properly dressed and sober presenting a proper ticket will be admitted to the ballroom." As it turned out, a less-than-considerable "sprinkling" of black citizens attended the ball that rainy day; most preferred to wait for their own Welcome Ball two nights later, held at the new Grand Armory Hall. Organized by local African Americans for their out-of-town friends, it was lauded as "the most brilliant, the most representative, the largest and most fashionable gathering of the best elements of the race that ever assembled in the country."

With so many guests in the city to be entertained, the ball was just one of many events hosted by the black elite. Two took place at the Murrays' home on March 5. Anna held an afternoon reception. In the evening her sister Mary, now a twenty-three-year-old teacher, threw a soiree for the younger generation that lasted past midnight. "The lovely costumes on lovelier ladies harmonized admirably with conventional full dress of the gentlemen, and under the bright lights made a sight beautiful to look on," reported the *New York Age* (the *New York Freeman*'s new name). "The dancing, sparkling conversation, witty sallies and sharp repartee all united to make the party all that the most enthusiastic seeker after pleasure could desire."[13]

One way that Washington black elites separated themselves from those of lower social strata was through exclusive clubs. Some of those organizations reflected shared interests. For the musically inclined there was the aforementioned Orpheus Glee Club or the Carreno, a musical club composed of a dozen young women, including Mary Evans, "whose musical training had been of a superior order." For book lovers, there were literary clubs, foremost among them the Bethel Literary and Historical Association, first organized by Bishop Daniel Payne. Many clubs, even those primarily social in nature, included charitable functions or other activities aimed at racial uplift.

The Diamond Back Club, of which Daniel Murray was a member, was purely social and ultraexclusive, limited to twelve members. From its formation in 1884, the club was considered "one of the most conspicuous social factors" in black Washington, notable for the social and political standing of its members and their guests as well as the gourmet board, good cheer, and hearty fellowship that characterized its gatherings. The Diamond Back Club's celebrated reputation was not limited to the capital; the club maintained fraternal relationships with the well-known Ugly Club of New York and its Philadelphia annex and was included in multistate events with those and other similar exclusive clubs.

The Diamond Back Club met monthly at the residence of one of the members. On March 7, 1889, it was Murray's turn to host the club. Members present that evening included James Bradford, John Smyth, Chris Fleetwood, William Matthews, Wyatt Archer, Fred Barbadoes, John Francis, and Robert Terrell. Terrell was a fairly recent addition to Murray's circle. A magna cum laude Harvard graduate, he earned a law degree from Howard University in 1889 and accepted a chief clerk position in the Treasury Department. The members wore full evening dress, as did their guests, among them Congressman-elect Langston, Blanche Bruce, John R. Lynch, Governor Pinckney Pinchback, and Colonel Robert

Harlan. (Frederick Douglass had been invited but was kept away by a lecture in Alexandria. He would be the club's guest of honor at a future date.) A sophisticated meal featuring terrapin, freshwater snapping turtle, was served at each meeting. At Murray's "magnificent reception," the supper was "a marvel of excellence." The menu "was a most chosen one embracing terrapin cooked only as the Diamond Backs can," along with oyster patties, chicken salad, creams, and ices. Champagne, punch, whiskey, brandy, and sherry were offered, and with them "came magnificent bursts of eloquence" in the form of toasts and speeches. "It was quite 2 o'clock when the party broke up." [14]

Come March 14, yet another occasion was hosted by the Murrays, this one a reception for Governor Pinchback. It was the fourth event at the Murrays' home in the span of ten days. There was no rest for poor Anna—who was nearly nine months pregnant—even if help or a caterer was on hand. On April 25, she delivered a son whom they named Pinckney Pinchback in honor of their recent guest. The Murrays were now a family of seven.

In November 1889, Murray bought land on the 900 block of S Street NW (lot 74, square 363) and commenced building a three-story brick house with English basement for his family. This was a new neighborhood, just a few blocks south of Boundary Street (shortly to be renamed Florida Avenue), and property values there were on the rise. The extension of streetcar lines to the north of downtown and other improvements made the area ripe for development. It was at that time that electric-powered cars were introduced into the transit system. The stretch of S Street between 9th and 10th streets, paved only four years earlier, was roughly half filled when the Murrays moved in. Two of their new neighbors were William MacLeod, the longtime curator at the Corcoran Gallery of Art, and Alexander T. Hensey, the proprietor of the *Washington Herald*. The block included nine families who had made the 1888 Elite List and a private tennis club. The Murrays were the only African Americans on the block, not counting several live-in maids. Though the neighborhood around them would change, the Murray home at 934 S Street would remain in the family for the next seventy-six years.[15]

In the summer of 1890, the Murrays lost the youngest and oldest members of the family. In June, immediately after the move to the new house, thirteen-month-old Pinckney suddenly fell desperately ill. After experiencing convulsions for forty hours, he sank into a stupor. The doctor saw him just once, reporting, "This child was dying when I was called in." The diagnosis was infantile cholera, a highly infectious disorder of the alimentary canal prevalent in the summer months. It causes severe watery diarrhea that can lead to dehydration followed by shock and, in a matter of hours, death. Pinckney died on June 10. He was buried at Graceland Cemetery, an interracial burial ground in Northeast Washington.

Two months later, on August 8, George Murray died in Baltimore. He retained his physical strength until the last few days of his life. The "patriarchal colored man" had claimed to be 115. His son Daniel figured two years more, so 117 was the number in the *Evening Star* obituary and on the death certificate. The funeral was held at Bethel AME Church, where George Murray had served so long and faithfully. The church was filled to its full seating capacity as Bishop Alexander Wayland reviewed the life of the deceased. Among the mourners was William J. Hopper, a grandson of Murray's former owner. Eliza would last another seven years, living in the Forrest Street house with her daughter Catherine, who had moved back to the family home and continued to live there after her mother's death. Eliza died of a stroke at age ninety-three. Like her husband, she was eulogized at Bethel Church and buried at Laurel Cemetery, the black burial ground located on a hill just outside Baltimore's boundary.[16]

→ ←

In April 1891, a series of receptions for Diamond Back Club members and others in their circle was triggered by the visit of three out-of-town gentlemen who were staying with Robert Terrell. Terrell himself may have been in a partying mood, for it was at this time that his engagement to Mary Church of Memphis was announced. (She was the daughter of Robert R. Church, one of the richest black men in the South, and would marry Terrell in Memphis the coming October.) Between April 15 and April 28, no fewer than five stag card parties were staged. Perhaps the most interesting of them was the one James Bradford, the Diamond Back Club president, hosted on Saturday, April 18. Club member John H. Smyth, a former minister to Liberia, had been at the card party the night before but was absent this evening. Those who were present criticized the speech Smyth had given at the annual Washington Emancipation commemoration earlier in the day, wherein he made "an odious comparison between the blacks and the mixed blood Negroes in the United States." Smyth had been influenced by the president of Liberia College, Edward Blyden, who denigrated mixed-race people while promoting "purer" blacks. Though the men around the card tables condemned that—"The cry was union and not dissention"—in truth, many of them, certainly Murray, would not have objected to a sentiment extolling light skin over dark.

The combined guest lists for this series of gentlemen-only occasions read like a who's who of the black elite. Judging by their frequency of socializing together, with particular attention to those invited to his home, Murray's social circle at this time included John Mercer Langston, Pinckney Pinchback, Fred Barbadoes, John R. Francis, Robert Terrell, Christian Fleetwood, Wyatt Archer, James T. Bradford, William E. Matthews, John H. Smyth, Blanche Bruce, John R. Lynch, Frederick Douglass and his sons Lewis and Charles, Milton Holland, Charles Purvis, and the Harlans, father and son. If there was one sizable circle of black elites in Washington, it was a wheel divided into spokes, for there were many cliques within it. Paul Laurence Dunbar referred to "the war of the social cliques"; factions vied for social ascendancy, even as they overlapped and changed over time. Murray's clique, for example, shifted when Richard Greener left town and when O. S. B. Wall died; in addition, certain elites from other cities joined in during the period that they held government appointments in the capital. Those in Murray's social set were not his only personal friends in Washington; for example, he remained close to Spencer Murray even though they were associated with different cliques. Fred R. Moore, a confidential assistant to six consecutive secretaries of the Treasury, was a lifelong friend but was not active in the black elite; not all successful Washingtonians cared for the social whirl.[17]

In addition to social one-upmanship among elite circles, there was competition for federal and municipal positions, places on governing boards, even clients for lawyers. That led to jealousies, backbiting, and occasional intrigues, especially when spoken or unspoken racial quotas were involved. Daniel Murray instigated just such a spat in May 1891 when he slandered James M. Gregory and pressured him to step down from his position on the school board. Gregory was a well-respected Latin professor at Howard University, and he and Murray attended many of the same social events, most recently an April card party.

Murray's motivation was taken to be his own ambition for a coveted "colored slot" on the board. Gregory had served as a school board trustee since 1886, honorably so, as far as anyone knew, but now Murray claimed that he had borrowed funds from teachers he had appointed and suggested further that money had played into quid pro quo arrangements in Gregory's disposition of teaching positions in the public schools. Those charges caused an embarrassing sensation, well covered in the white as well as the black press. Murray was roundly criticized by both:

"[Daniel Murray] is at the bottom of this slander against Prof. Gregory," . . . "Caesar had just such friends as Mr. Daniel Murray is to Prof. Gregory." . . . "Prof. Gregory has been a victim of base treachery by ambitious candidates for the school board." . . . "Mr. Murray who is a presumed friend of Prof. Gregory is reported to have said that he advised him to tender his resignation before the charges could be investigated." . . . "The unmitigated baseness of those who inspired the charges is beyond expression . . . and only merits the pity of everyone who hitherto believed them to be capable of more lofty purposes and intentions than the employment of black-mailers." . . . "Gregory will not resign nor will he be removed to appease the appetite of ambitious candidates."

Gregory worried about his reputation being tarnished based on rumors alone. When, at his behest, the charges were investigated by the district commissioners, Murray was allowed to act like a lawyer, presenting "prosecution" witnesses and questioning "defense" witnesses. Gregory, sworn in at his own request, admitted having borrowed money but claimed a right to do so. He denied having provided school favors in return for financial considerations. In his harassment of Gregory, Murray apparently had his brother-in-law's career in mind in addition to his own desire for a school board post. Some of the newspapers reported that Bruce Evans was also behind the accusations but that Murray "kept his brother in law in the background." Questioning Gregory directly, Murray asked if it was true that he had offered to transfer the current principal of Mott School and give the position to Evans in exchange for Murray dropping the whole matter. Gregory replied that, aware that Evans was angry because he had not been appointed principal, he had made such a proposal but not with a view to his personal advantage, rather to avoid a school scandal.

The final call belonged to the commissioners, and they vindicated Gregory. Though they found "that in making loans from his personal friends among the teachers he acted indiscreetly," they declared him not guilty of any corrupt official action. When it was over, Gregory, satisfied that he had restored his reputation, voluntarily stepped down from the school board. Murray did not get his place, but the new trustee who did appointed Bruce Evans principal of Mott School.[18]

In November 1891, John Quincy Adams, the brother of Murray's German teacher, came to town. The brothers had founded the *Appeal*, a black newspaper promoting Republican politics, back in 1885. Cyrus Field Adams was in charge of the Chicago office, while J. Q. Adams managed the one in St. Paul. In the capital on work related to the paper, J. Q. Adams threw a Sunday eight-course dinner at the catering establishment of Gray and Brother for distinguished Washingtonians including Frederick Douglass, Blanche Bruce, Pinckney Pinchback, Charles Purvis, John R. Lynch, and Daniel Murray. The Adams brothers were part of a geographic network of black elites. There were clusters of upper-class African American families in Chicago, Cleveland, Memphis, Atlanta, Philadelphia, Boston, and New York. They lodged in one another's homes when traveling and expected to be entertained by their hosts. Richard Greener, for example, now living in New York, stayed with the Murrays during visits to Washington.

That Thanksgiving J. Q. Adams was the Murrays' guest, gathering with them around the holiday feast on November 26. Murray, Adams remarked afterward, "has an interesting family" and "His wife is an elegant entertainer and is ably assisted by her sister Miss Evans." Young Dan was now eleven, Henry nine, Nat seven, and Helene four. Anna's sister Mary gradually moved in with the Murrays; by the next year she gave 934 S Street as her address. Anna's brother Bruce, married with a child, continued to live with their mother, Henrietta. Like most in the black elite, the Murrays valued the home-centered life. Music was important to the family, the piano central. Education and good breeding were given the highest priority. Elite women were considered the moral centers of their homes. The men might rent a hall for a special occasion, but their wives and daughters tended to entertain in the home. Anna followed the tradition of hosting get-togethers for black elites visiting from out of town. One such reception was covered by the *New York Age*: "Mrs. Daniel Murray entertained a very pleasant tea party at her elegant residence. . . . The 'At-Home' was complimentary to Mr. and Mrs. Pinchback and daughter of New Orleans. Washington's inner circle was there and some very interesting stories were told. Mrs. Murray is a popular hostess."

J. Q. Adams described the Murray residence as "the most elegant in point of interior decorations of any in the city," replete with stained glass and rich frescoing and tiling. Often referred to as an example of the refinement and material prosperity of Washington's black upper class, the Murray home was even dubbed "one of the most handsome and commodious residences owned by a colored man in the country." One guest recalled that "Patrician taste was displayed everywhere" and "The rooms were arranged with such harmony and elegance that the most critical artist could not be offended."

An oak dining table and six leather-covered oak chairs sat in the dining room, a French clock gracing the fireplace mantel. Two cupboards, one walnut and one mahogany, held a set of French rosebud china, a dinner set of French china with scalloped edges, eighteen English crest china plates, crystal glasses with a Grecian border, colored champagne glasses, green hock glasses, and cut-glass tumblers, along with silver and fine linen embroidered tablecloths and napkins. The parlor furniture consisted of an overstuffed suite of five pieces, a walnut suite, two upholstered gold chairs, a Turkish chair and a Turkish rocker, other wooden rocking and straight chairs, a curio cabinet, and, of course, the piano. The first-floor library had a table and four bookcases. The bedrooms upstairs were furnished in walnut suites. There were lace curtains, paintings, and family photographs throughout.[19]

The holiday season of 1892–93 started well enough for the Murrays. On Christmas Day, Dannie and Henry sang in the boys' choir at St. Luke's. But before December was over, Helene contracted diphtheria, a highly contagious disease. As was the case with Pinckney, the infection took over quickly. Helene had laryngeal diphtheria, the form most likely to bring on serious complications such as extreme fever, severe cough, voice loss, and difficulty breathing. Death came on January 3, 1893, only four days after Helene first manifested symptoms. The next day she was laid to rest alongside her brother Pinckney at Graceland Cemetery. Helene's death at age five and a half would subdue the joys of future Christmastimes for Murray, as he later revealed to his old friend George Myers: "Eight years ago I lost my only daughter amid a scene of festivity which was the rule of my home during the holiday season. Since that time we have always been too sadly reminded of our loss to be anything else than quiet."

Having lost two children to infectious diseases, Murray joined the city's Sanitary League some weeks after Helene's death. Now forty-two, he displayed a new maturity and seriousness in general—there would be no more regular card parties.[20]

5

THE GOOD CITIZEN

A BABY BOY JOINED THE MURRAY HOUSEHOLD BEFORE THE year was out. Harold Baldwin Murray was born at Harpers Ferry on October 1, 1893. "The Ferry" had become the Murrays' regular vacation spot. Most years, Anna kept a cottage for the season and Daniel joined her and the children on weekends and during his annual leave. It was the place "where many of the society people recuperate," noted the *Washington Bee*, because "The visitor to Harper's Ferry is doubly paid, for he not only feels the thrilling impulses which come from a contemplation of the movement of the first martyr of a true and not spurious American freedom, but the natural beauty of the place appeals strongly to the most refined and exalted part of his being." If the site held meaning for all people of color, it was a truly sacred spot for Anna, as a descendant of two of John Brown's coconspirators. Anna was on the executive committee of the John Brown Memorial Association, which the year before had sponsored an event back in the city featuring Frederick Douglass sharing his reminiscences of Brown.

The Murrays and their friends spent the summer days out of doors, watching birds, picking wildflowers, fishing, hunting, bathing, rowing, picnicking, and generally reveling in the picturesque scenery. Playing croquet was a popular pastime. So was hiking. The higher one climbed, the more sublime the view of the two old rivers embracing. In the evenings they read books, played checkers and word games, and engaged in dramatic readings and musical performances.[1]

➢ ➣

THE WORKFORCE AT THE LIBRARY OF CONGRESS HAD YET TO significantly increase by 1893, but Murray's salary was raised to $1,400. The library's vast holdings were now dispersed among sixteen separate rooms and storage spaces in the Capitol. From the time ground was broken in 1887, Murray could witness the progress in the new building's erection each workday. Described as Italian Renaissance in style (but later more accurately recognized as Beaux Arts), it was a grand structure, covering nearly three acres of land. It was estimated when Congress passed the library bill that the new library's cost would be about $4 million; in the end $6.5 million were needed. The construction materials were granite, bronze, gold, mahogany, and fifteen varieties of marble. Following Spofford's vision, the design was a rectangle with a central dome covering an enormous octagonal reading room. Within the rectangle were four open courtyards. The main front faced the Capitol, rising four stories above grade. The granite exterior, roughly rusticated and vermiculated at the lowest level, grew finer and smoother with the height of the walls. The copper dome was plated with the purest gold, "polished so that it is as bright as a new wedding ring." The Torch of Learning, its flame also gilded, rose from the apex.[2]

➢ ➣

ON NOVEMBER 25, 1893, THE *EVENING STAR* PUBLISHED AN article by Daniel Murray entitled "District Taxation." It was written in response to the current assessment, which had been condemned as rife with errors and "alarmingly oppressive." Murray's suggestions for a new assessment and taxation law included a flexible rate of taxation and a sitting board of informed assistant assessors to replace the system of using temporary assessors who knew little about real estate values. Washington's Board of Trade, invested in this issue, took notice.

The Board of Trade had been formed in 1889. Its incorporators had visualized an organization of about a hundred representative businessmen, "having in view the better protection and promotion of their common welfare and the general interests of the city." The Board of Trade filled the void created by the lack of a locally elected city government. It addressed the civic concerns of Washingtonians in many areas such as urban development and planning, transportation, utilities, health and sanitation, crime, employment, and public parks, and it advocated municipal advances to the three district commissioners appointed by the President, and to the Senate and House committees charged with oversight of the District. In the years since its incorporation, the board had provided effective and forceful leadership and proved to be a potent lobby for the city's civic and economic interests.

Along with having control of the municipal government, Congress bore half the District's expenses. Early in 1894, efforts were made by certain congressmen to have the District bear 75 percent of or even the total financial burden. "So imminent was the matter that the Board of Trade was called to devise means of defense," divulged Murray, pointing out in his November *Evening Star* article that many people supposed that "Washington enjoys a favor through its relation to the general government" but that the costs of capital cities in Europe were defrayed to a greater extent than in the United States. The Board of Trade asked Murray to elaborate on that, and he obliged. On January 13, 1894, the *Evening Star* ran his article "Other Capitals," wherein he detailed the financial aid given by European governments to the cities that serve as their capitals and enhance the country's "prestige."

Two substantial and influential articles bearing Daniel Murray's byline, well researched and skillfully written, were published within an eight-week period. Clearly, he did not spend all his time at the Library of Congress fetching books.

Congress abandoned asking the District to assume more than half of its municipal expenses. Meanwhile, efforts to overhaul the city's system of taxation and assessment continued. On the morning of March 10, 1894, Daniel Murray was one of "a number of prominent business and real estate owners" who appeared before the commissioners at a public hearing on methods of assessing District property. He contributed substantively to the discussion, and his remarks were covered in that evening's newspaper, as were those of Brainard H. Warner, the president and one of the founders of the Board of Trade. Four days later, on the motion of Warner, Murray was elected to the Board of Trade. He drafted a new law of assessment and taxation that provided for a permanent board of assessors consisting of one chief and three assistants. Favorably received by the Board of Trade and the commissioners, a bill based on Murray's draft was sent to Congress, where it was pushed into law. "Here was one of the capitals of the world making its assessment and collecting the taxes under a law derived by a colored man," marveled one of Murray's colleagues at the Library of Congress. Murray later penned his own third-person characterization: "He was the first colored man in Washington elected to its Board of Trade. This honor was bestowed without the formality of an application, but because of a very signal service rendered by him to the city, in a matter then before Congress, the value of which Congress acknowledged. He is . . . an expert authority on methods of assessment and taxation and other matters of civic interest, the present system of assessment in this city having been largely devised by him."

B. H. Warner felt that "the organization should be made small enough to make membership creditable and desirable." He wanted a board "composed of men engaged in the transaction of business, who have become successful, practical, and possessed of sound common sense . . . men who understand that a broad liberal treatment is essential to the future development of the National Capital." He obviously saw these attributes in Daniel Murray. Originally from Pennsylvania, Warner was both a successful real estate developer and model of a man active in civic affairs. He was, for example, a Howard University trustee from 1892 to 1906, "perhaps the most influential member of the Board," according to university historian Rayford Logan. Warner and Murray were both members of the city's Sanitary League, and that may be where they first met.

As a real estate dealer and financier involved with many city enterprises, Warner was second only to Ainsworth Spofford among white mentors influencing Murray's work and business life. Murray claimed "an everlasting debt of gratitude" to Warner, who, he said, had been "instrumental in putting thousands of dollars in his pocket." At one time Warner "secured him property which was not open to him as a colored man and backed him up financially in the improvement of the piece." Murray was offered an astounding $25,000 for it afterward.

Contacts such as B. H. Warner helped Murray "amass a respectable fortune." According to the *Washington Bee*, "One of the best illustrations Washington possesses of a colored man accumulating wealth as represented in lands, stocks and bonds is Daniel Murray. Mr. Murray, in a quiet, unostentatious way, has gone ahead each year and added to his bank account and to his realty possessions. Not by sharp practices, but by legitimate deals and purchases." The *Indianapolis Freeman* reported Murray's worth in 1895 at $60,000, placing him among the ten richest African Americans in Washington, "whose names are accepted without question

on bonds and whose signatures convert a check into unchallenge-
able legal tender."[3]

The Board of Trade addressed issues through small working
committees that met monthly. Daniel Murray joined the library
committee, headed by Theodore Noyes, associate editor of the
Evening Star. The committee was charged with considering the
practicality of pushing for a public library. By the end of March
1894, the report submitted by the library committee, calling for
the establishment of a centrally located public library with extended evening and weekend hours for use by all classes of readers,
was adopted by the full board. In April the school board gave a
hearty endorsement to the project; its chairman named the seven
members of the library committee and described them as "some
of the best-known citizens of Washington." The commissioners
also promptly gave the plan their official endorsement. Librarian
of Congress Ainsworth Spofford offered his encouragement for a
public lending library, commenting, "It will raise the whole community to a higher plane of intelligence." He also predicted that
financing through Congress would be difficult and that wealthy
patrons might be more likely to underwrite the project.

Spofford was right. Nevertheless, the library committee's plan
was to seek congressional legislation creating a public library and
providing for its municipal maintenance with the cost to be borne
equally by nation and city, just as with the public schools. Congress
would also be asked to secure duplicates of books from various departmental libraries and a space in some public structure until permanent quarters in a new municipal building were available. At the
same time commitments from private individuals for donations of
books or funds to purchase them were sought. In December 1895,
the library bill was introduced in the Senate and House with Murray
a member of the sponsoring committee. Advocates in both chambers
were secured, but at the end of the session no action had been taken.
The campaign was diligently carried forward and met with partial

success in June 1896, when the library bill was passed by both chambers and signed by the President. The act stipulated that a lending library available to all city residents be established and maintained, but the bill was merely a creative measure with no reference to financing. In the next annual budget the commissioners requested $8,300 for maintenance of the library. It was stricken from the appropriations granted, and thus the library existed only on paper.

Finally, in an article headlined "A Long Hard Fight," the June 30, 1898, *Evening Star* announced that "The free public library of the District of Columbia is at last established on a firm foundation." Congress had approved an appropriation of $6,720, "which, though small, is yet sufficient to effect a beginning of the work." Small indeed: after staff salaries, there was all of $3,500 for rent, fuel, lighting, and every other expense of establishing a library. Then, at the beginning of the new year, an angel appeared in the form of the philanthropist Andrew Carnegie. At the Board of Trade annual reception on February 23, 1899, Daniel Murray was among the attendees who thrilled to the announcement that the public-spirited steel magnate was donating $250,000 to erect a public library building in the nation's capital.[4]

Over the same period in which Murray contributed to the establishment of a public library, he pushed for another long-standing interest: opportunities for industrial education in Washington's public school system. He published "Learning to Work: Argument for a Comprehensive Manual Training System" in the *Evening Star* of March 2, 1895. That was not his opening salvo; he had already lobbied for the issue before both the House and Senate District Appropriations Committees and gained prominence as "an active advocate of the new system." Senator Arthur Gorman reported that the Senate committee, of which he was chairman, was deeply impressed with Murray's argument: "He was broad and liberal in his view advocating the new system no less urgently as a great benefit to white boys as well as to colored."

"A boy who sees nothing in manual labor but brute force despises both the labor and the laborer," Murray wrote in the *Star* article, but manual training would "foster a higher appreciation of the value and dignity of intelligent labor and the worth and respectability of laboring men." Such education "fits boys not to become mechanics only, but men of intelligence and skill." Those studies, he concluded, "in which both head and hand are employed should be encouraged."

Philosophy aside, Murray had a particular motivation in advocating such training. As a contractor and builder, he hired all-black crews and was consistently looking to employ about fifty men. He "felt the need greatly of skilled mechanics and was obliged to refuse many profitable contracts through inability to secure the necessary workmen." According to a later feature on Murray in *The Colored American Magazine*, "No man in Washington ever did more to demonstrate the skill and capacity of colored mechanics than Mr. Murray."

The importance of manual training in school systems was widely recognized at this time. It was enthusiastically promoted by the school board and the school superintendents. In January 1895, the Board of Trade authorized a new standing committee on public schools. Murray was one of its five members. At the recommendation of the committee, the full Board of Trade endorsed the call for two manual training high schools, one for black pupils and one for white.

One of the new members of the school board in 1895 was Mary Church Terrell, the first black woman appointed a school trustee. Speaking to a reporter, she endorsed manual training not only for boys but for their female counterparts as well. Since the avenues of employment for young women of color were particularly limited, she hoped they would soon have the option in public school of "becoming first class milliners, dressmakers, scientific cooks and proficient artisans in whatever industry they may select." Hugh

Browne was the head of the department of physics at M Street High School (the contemporary incarnation, since 1891, of the Preparatory High School for Colored Youth), and was known for enlivening his "subject matter through emphasis upon its usefulness." In 1894, Murray had sought Browne's input on curricula for a manual training high school. In his reply, Browne embraced a philosophy of pragmatism in promoting manual training and its marketable value for the black man, given the "conditions in which he is compelled to earn his livelihood and unfold his possibilities." The added importance of industrial education for African Americans sounded practical coming from Terrell and Browne but racist when the white press suggested that industrial training should be black pupils' sole alternative. Such was the tone in an *Evening Star* article of April 22, 1896: "It is not saying too much to insist that a large percentage of those who graduate from the Colored High School are really no better off because of their experience in that institution, for they have learned only those things which cannot, except very vaguely and indirectly, be of any use to them along the lines of endeavor which must be theirs in life. Perhaps it might even be insisted that the time and energy devoted by many of those High School pupils to the acquisition of purely scholastic knowledge is simply wasted." Murray had made clear in his *Evening Star* article a year earlier that "the manual training school is not a mere training of mechanics," nor was it intended "to lower the intellectual standard or supplant the present curriculum" but rather to offer a "diversity of training."

With the backing of the commissioners as well as the school board and the Board of Trade, the request was made for a congressional appropriation of $250,000 for the construction of two manual training high schools. This request was renewed for several years running before Congress finally appropriated money for the white manual training school in 1898. It took another year for it to do the same for a black version.[5]

A year after Murray's admittance, Dr. Charles Purvis and James T. Bradford were elected to the Board of Trade. In another three years Robert Terrell, Bruce Evans, G. F. T. Cook, and Wyatt Archer were approved as well. Thus seven Washingtonians of color were members of the Board of Trade by 1898. Three of them—Bradford, Terrell, and Archer—were directors of the Capital Savings Bank, the first bank organized and operated by African Americans. By 1898, ten years after its establishment, the bank had "weathered, without a tremor, panics that buried more pretentious concerns beneath the waves."

Membership on the Board of Trade may have been considered an honor, but it entailed a lot of work, most of it none too glamorous, as the January 23, 1895, headline of a newspaper piece covering board activities—"The Sewer System"—conveyed. Board members grappled with many nitty-gritty issues from railway grade crossings to the cost of utilities to improved housing for the 70,000 people who lived in crowded, unsanitary dwellings along alleyways. Conducting studies, writing resolutions and bills, attending endless meetings: this was true civic service.

But there were perks as well. Each May, the Board of Trade sponsored an excursion for members and invited guests, most of whom were senators and congressmen. Murray's first such outing took place on May 17, 1894, two months after he joined the board. One of the guests boarding the chartered steamer at the 7th Street wharf that afternoon was his boss, Ainsworth Spofford. The company traveled leisurely down the Potomac River, then disembarked at Marshall Hall, an amusement park on the Maryland shore. Games and a shad bake were followed by speeches. So successful was the occasion that Marshall Hall became the traditional destination of the May excursion.

Most years, there were several hundred participants aboard the steamer. A band played on deck, while the men, released from the restraints of their working lives, indulged in card games, anecdote telling, and "an excellent punch." Arriving at Marshall Hall in midafternoon, they played baseball, bowled tenpins, and shot at clay pipes in the rifle gallery. Some watched the "famous operation" of planking and cooking the shad. The split fish were nailed to hardwood planks, which were propped upright inches from an outdoor fire. They were baked in that fashion, continuously basted with butter, until easily flaked with a fork. With as many as a hundred shad provided, it was quite a culinary feast. Its preparation and consumption were the highlights of each year's excursion. When it was time for the meal, banquet tables were set up in the dining room and open-air pavilion and, if the crowd called for it, on the green lawn as well. The shad fillets were accompanied by sauterne and claret. Some guests each year had not eaten shad before. All acknowledged its savory "toothsomeness."

Although billed as a time to get acquainted with legislators, the Marshall Hall outings were not merely pleasure trips. Once coffee and cigars were passed, speeches and toasts continued until twilight. "Distinguished Men Grow Eloquent over the Capital City" ran a headline covering the event one year, but not all the speeches were limited to praising "our fair city." Senators and congressmen were reminded that the Board of Trade existed "to voice the wishes of a city where the people had no vote" and were assured that the board "never asks for anything that is not needed."

Murray rarely missed the May excursion through the end of the decade, at least. The same went for the other annual Board of Trade occasion that assumed a social form: the reception at the Arlington each February. The most opulent hotel in town, the Arlington was located in the very fashionable Lafayette Square area, just a block from the White House. Like the excursions to Marshall Hall, these were all-male affairs, and though the men wore evening dress, the goal was much the same: an "opportunity for the exchange of ideas between men whose busy, everyday lives give them little time to meet each other socially," while working in a little business here, a little lobbying there.

Most of the guests invited to the receptions were national legislators or other high government officials, with the remainder "men distinguished in every active branch of business life" and "those representing the official and social circles of the city." Guests arrived at the Arlington about eight o'clock. Board of Trade members were identified by a red carnation in their lapels. They socialized with their guests in the spacious double parlors, decorated with cut flowers, potted plants, and trailing smilax vines draped about the chandeliers. After an hour of pleasant conversation on their feet, all were asked to be seated in the large parlor for the speeches to begin. Both board members and legislators offered remarks. Board officers impressed on the latter the growing needs of the city. The tone was friendly, with criticism communicated in a humorous vein. Next, the large folding doors connecting the parlors with the banquet hall were thrown open, and the company was served a buffet-style repast. The men returned to their chairs for a musical performance as cigar smoke floated overhead. Most years, it was midnight by the time the occasion broke up.

Murray's association with the Board of Trade brought him useful contacts and self-assurance as well as opportunities to contribute to the city's welfare. The annual receptions at the Arlington, mixing with senators, representatives, and businessmen, a red carnation pinned to his lapel identifying him as a member of the board, must have been especially gratifying.[6]

Even as he battled for the city's acquisition of a public library and manual training high schools, Murray applied himself to another cause: civil service reform. On May 8, 1894, at a "meeting of considerable consequence" at Willard's Hotel, Murray was among the "well-known business and professional men" who formed the Civil Service Reform Association of the District of Columbia. He was one of a committee of five appointed to draft a constitution. The document the committee issued set forth the objective of maintaining and extending the merit system of appointments, promotions, and removals of civil servants at the federal and municipal levels. The latter would be new in Washington, and the association circulated petitions to garner support for the merit rule in District offices.

A merit-based federal civil service had been created by law in 1883. The act had been intended to weaken the spoils system of granting appointments by substituting a measure of merit via competitive examination or other nonpartisan business method. Government jobs awarded through patronage politics went to those who had worked for a given party's election, in essence paying off political debts, often irrespective of competence. All agreed that top-level appointments and confidential positions such as personal secretaries should be controlled by the party in power. The civil service applied to departmental clerks and other jobs that ought to be dispensed independently of politics. It was through presidential action and congressional legislation that positions were added to— or subtracted from—the civil service.

The National Civil Service Reform League had been established for more than a decade before Washingtonians formed their local association. The national organization held an annual convention each December. Murray was elected a delegate to the 1894 meeting in Chicago, and to the 1896 meeting in Philadelphia. The year in between, Washington sponsored the event. Two days of talks resulted in a number of resolutions, including the following for the benefit of the locals: "We urge upon all seeking good government for our cities the paramount importance of securing the adoption therein of the merit system of appointment; and we respectfully urge upon Congress the extension of this system by law to the District of Columbia." The final round of presentations took place at the Cosmos Club the afternoon of December 13, 1895.

(The headquarters of the very exclusive Cosmos Club were located on Lafayette Square in the former Dolley Madison House, and meeting rooms were sometimes made available for other associations.) That evening a banquet at the Arlington was hosted by the members of the local association, Murray among them.

The progress of the District's Civil Service Reform Association was mixed. Protection from partisan dismissal was established, and the merit system was applied to more and more federal positions, but there would also be rollbacks in the years ahead. The association's advocacy for the extension of civil service to District offices continued without success into the next decade. Certainly there were foes of civil service reform. Many Washingtonians, both white and black, preferred to take their chances with the patronage system. The *Washington Bee* sniped at Murray, "Now that Daniel Murray had advocated democratic Civil Service for the Freedmen's Hospital, no doubt there would be a few vacancies in the Library of Congress if a similar method was adopted." Robert Terrell, like Murray, vigorously defended the civil service system as inseparable from good government, claiming that "by the civil service law more bright and capable young colored men had gotten into the public service without political influence than could ever have hoped to get in through the old spoils system."[7]

➤ ◄

ON JUNE 27, 1894, MISS MARY EVANS, ALMOST TWENTY-nine, married at the home of her sister and brother-in-law, where she had been living for at least two years. Mary had served since 1892 as "directress" of the physical education program for the colored school system. She took the position seriously and scientifically. In her classes, features of the Swedish Ling system of gymnastics were combined with those from the German Jahn system, the two influential models of the day. She authored a series of articles on "Health and Beauty from Exercise" for *Woman's Era*.

Published in Boston, it was the country's first journal produced by and for women of color. During her vacations, she visited schools in New England to learn how other institutions approached physical education. Perhaps it was during one of those trips that she met her future husband, the Boston lawyer Butler R. Wilson. He contributed editorials to *Woman's Era*, so they may have met through that association. Or perhaps they were introduced by Wilson's close friend and fellow Boston lawyer Archibald Grimké, brother of Mary's pastor at 15th Street Presbyterian Church.

Butler Wilson, four or five years older than Mary, was born in Georgia. After graduating from Atlanta University, he had headed north and earned a law degree at Boston University. He practiced briefly with Archibald Grimké and George L. Ruffin (the first black graduate of Harvard Law School) before establishing a solo practice, serving clients both black and white. Wilson, who had already taken on at least two race discrimination cases before he married Mary, was quickly becoming identified as a civil rights leader in Boston. He was a prominent member of that city's black elite, while his wife-to-be was "one of the leading girls of Washington."

Butler Wilson and Mary Evans were married by Reverend Francis Grimké. The S Street house was a perfect place for a home wedding; "its artistic interior . . . needed little decoration." *Woman's Era* covered the occasion, describing the June bride as "a picture in her white bengaline gown," and gushing, "The large number of guests present included almost all the representative people of Washington—the Bruces, Shadds, Purvises, Frasers, Cooks, etc., etc., etc." All the company—presumably including Mary's mother, Henrietta, and brother Bruce—wished the happy couple farewell as they hurried off for a honeymoon in New York and Newport.

Bruce had married a music teacher, Annie Brooks, four years earlier. Their daughter, Lillian, was now nearly four and their son, Joseph, two and a half. They resided with Henrietta in her house on 12th Street, Bruce's home since the age of seven. Bruce had received his first appointment in the public school system in 1885. Although he had continued his own education and earned an MD degree from Howard University Medical College in 1891, he had only practiced medicine briefly (but he did retain the "Dr." title). He was currently the principal of Mott School, where he had begun his own schooling.

The Murray sons' ages when Aunt Mary married in their parlor were: Dannie, fourteen; Henry, eleven; Nat, ten; and Harold, nine months. The first school for African American children in the Murrays' section of the city, Garnet School, was located at 10th and U streets. The fall before the wedding, Henry had been among the pupils injured there on an October morning when nearly all six hundred panicked boys and girls had rushed the exit in response to cries of "Fire!" It had turned out to be a false alarm, but nine children had been harmed in the crush. Henry's injuries had not been serious. Daniel Murray was a particularly warm and involved father at a time when many men left the day-to-day nurturing to their wives. He took "no little pleasure" in retelling the folktales he had heard as a boy to his own children, and they responded in kind. Murray found that his sons' "unwillingness to go to bed was overcome by the promise of a story . . . about Mr. Fox and Mr. Harry, or of Jack the Merchant's son." There were family outings; for instance, Harold later recalled that "since he was a tad of a lad he liked to go swimming in the Potomac River." But Daniel and Anna also made sure their sons learned what expectations accompanied a cultured, upper-class lifestyle. In February 1895, "Masters Daniel and Henry Murray" performed in two charity musicales, one to raise funds for St. Luke's and one for the Howard University Hill Relief Association.[8]

In the summer of 1895, Anna and the children had already spent two months at Harpers Ferry when Daniel joined them for his mid-August vacation. Even as they enjoyed their favorite outdoor activities, it must have been a wistful time. Come September, the two older boys would be leaving home to further their educations: Dannie at Oberlin College's Conservatory of Music, Henry at Cambridge Manual Training School for Boys.

Daniel Murray "is giving his offspring the best education possible," intoned the *Washington Bee*, "sparing no expense." Or effort. Murray undoubtedly researched manual training schools. The one he chose in Massachusetts for boys past eighth grade had been established in 1888 and, by the time Henry entered, "had gained an almost national reputation for its eminently practical, progressive, and unique features." The school stressed the difference between industrial education and manual training. The former amounted to instruction for a given trade. The latter taught one how to apply mind, eye, and hand together in order to understand the principles and systems underlying technical processes. The manual training school was incorporated into Cambridge's public school system. Nonresidents paid tuition ($150 per year) and were required to take an entrance examination. Henry received the highest score. His proud father made sure that this "signal success" was noted in the *Bee*.

Anna traveled to Massachusetts with her sons Dannie and Henry the first week of September 1895. Mother and brother settled Henry in his new situation and were perhaps still with him to celebrate his thirteenth birthday on September 14. Frederick H. Rindge was the founder and major patron of Cambridge Manual Training School. While Henry was a student there, the school's name was changed to Rindge Manual Training School to honor him. Its building was a distinguished structure of Romanesque style with hip roof and arched windows. When Henry entered, there were 172 boys (almost all white) spread over the four grades.

The boys wore square, squat white caps while busy at the bench, lathe, or forge. Woodworking, firefighting, blacksmithing, iron fitting, pattern making, and other technical courses were taught at the school. Mechanical drawing was integral to the curriculum. The pupils "always work from drawings, never from anything else . . . they understand, they interpret, and are able to put a drawing into three dimensions." All had an hour's class each day acquiring this "power of expression." The students took academic courses including languages, science, and mathematics at the nearby Cambridge English High School.

Though the manual training school accommodated a considerable number of tuition-paying, nonresident pupils, it was not a boarding school. Possibly Henry lived with his aunt Mary and uncle Butler; surely he at least visited them regularly. Only the Charles River came between the sister cities of Cambridge and Boston. The distance from Henry's school to the posh Rutland Square location of the Wilsons' spacious town house was less than three and a half miles. Henry could easily take a streetcar along the Harvard Bridge to cross the Charles River.

Anna and Dannie bid Henry good-bye and traveled on to Oberlin. As Henry had a local aunt and uncle for support while at school, so Dannie had his aunt Sarah and uncle Wilson in his mother's hometown of Oberlin. It is very likely that he lived with them, as they regularly boarded Oberlin students of color. Dannie was a violinist, embarking at age fifteen on a four-year course at Oberlin's Conservatory of Music. He had "exhibited a marked talent for music" early in life, according to his father. When all of three and a half, he had been described in the *Washington Bee* as "bright and promising." By eleven, he had begun studies at Washington's Bernays School of Music "at the solicitation of the master himself," the notable violinist Robert C. Bernays. Oberlin's Conservatory of Music would become world renowned and the oldest continuously operating conservatory in the country. Before Dannie's first academic year at Oberlin was over, Baltimore's *Afro-American* reported that Daniel E. Murray, sixteen, is "one of the finest of his age on the violin." By the end of 1897, he was, according to the *Cleveland Gazette*, "the best Afro-American violinist at the Oberlin conservatory and in this section of the country."[9]

→ ←

DR. ALEXANDER CRUMMELL RETIRED FROM ST. LUKE'S IN December 1894 after nearly a quarter of a century as pastor of his Washington Episcopal congregation and a full half century since his ordination. (He would remain in Washington, teaching at Howard University and organizing the American Negro Academy.) It was also in December 1894 that the remodeling of St. Luke's commenced. Daniel Murray, the chairman of the church's building committee, directed the work but declined the usual builder's fee. The remodeling was completed by the end of the following summer. The congregation had been gathering in the parish hall but on Sunday, September 8, 1895, returned to a church with numerous refinements to its interior.

Daniel Murray was elected vestryman at St. Luke's in April 1895 and the two Aprils that followed. But the 1897 term was his last. His activities with the church after that (other than remaining a congregant) involved St. Luke's Literary Guild. On December 10, 1896, he presented a talk on Napoleon. Six months later, the *Indianapolis Freeman* reported that "St. Luke's Episcopal Guild, the youngest member of Washington's triumvirate of high standard literary organization [the others being the Bethel Literary and Historical Association, and the Second Baptist Lyceum], has been addressed this season by some of the ablest men and women of the race." The list included Murray and several new associates who were making their mark in the nation's capital in the 1890s, such as Kelly Miller, a sociology professor at Howard; Lafayette M. Hershaw, a land examiner at the Department of the Interior and president of the Bethel Literary and Historical Association; and

Edward E. Cooper, the editor and publisher of the *Colored American* newspaper—all prominent among the city's black intelligentsia. The *Indianapolis Freeman* article referred to "the ablest men and women of the race." Among the women named was Anna Evans Murray.[10]

ACTIVIST COUPLE

Anna Murray's entry into public life can be dated to the mid-1890s. In April 1895, she appeared before the Board of Commissioners to urge that a black woman be appointed to the Board of Education. Although Anna promoted Helen Appo Cook, the wife of John F. Cook, surely she was satisfied when Mary Church Terrell won the spot. Both women were leaders in the District's Colored Woman's League. Anna was an active member of that organization as well.

The Colored Woman's League was formed in 1892 by a group of Washington female educators and community activists. When it was incorporated two years later, the officers included Helen Appo Cook, Mary Church Terrell, Charlotte Forten Grimké, Josephine Willson Bruce, Anna J. Cooper, and Mary J. Patterson. The specific object of league members, serving in the prevailing spirit of societal reform, was the education and uplift of African American women and children. Organization fostered concerted action. The Colored Woman's League was both the first black women's society of its kind in the country and the first with the goal of becoming national. Branches eventually formed in nearly every state. The president of both the local and national leagues was Helen Appo

Cook, who, Anna later declared, was "the mother of organizations among colored women in the country."

From July 14 to 16, 1896, the Washington league hosted the initial convention of the National League of Colored Women, held at the 15th Street Presbyterian Church, with delegates coming from as far away as Colorado. The *Evening Star* described it as "the most important gathering of colored women ever assembled on this continent." Anna (one of eighteen delegates from the District branch) served as head of the local committee responsible for visitor comfort. Although, at thirty-eight, she had two children at home, one still a toddler, she offered her residence for use as convention headquarters, and in its "cool spacious rooms were held the frequent meetings of the convention committees." Out-of-town delegates were even directed to 934 S Street for orientation and information upon arrival in the city. One new associate, struck by the figure Anna cut at the time, described her as "tall and distinguished looking, having a wealth of long silvery hair, although she appears not to have reached middle age." A number of the capital's attractions were recommended to the visitors, including tours of the magnificent, if incomplete, new Library of Congress.

Addresses, discussions, readings, and musical selections were part of each day's fare. The topics discussed ranged from education to home life and child rearing to consideration of various professions for women. Despite the intense heat, the church auditorium, decorated with flags and bunting, was nearly filled for every session. On Friday, July 17, the delegates were invited to make a pilgrimage to Harpers Ferry for a memorial service at John Brown's Fort, the engine house where Brown had made his last stand.

The next week, starting July 20, the meetings of the National Federation of Afro-American Women, organized at a conference in Boston a year earlier, took place in Washington at the 19th Street Baptist Church. One of the highlights was the participation of Harriet Tubman, "verging on toward ninety years of age." When the "venerable colored woman," who was "credited with having aided more escaped slaves to reach the Union lines by way of the 'underground railroad' than any other individual," was introduced, the audience, which included a good number of white ladies, "rose as one person and greeted her with the waving of handkerchiefs and the clapping of hands." Visibly affected by the tribute, gray-haired "Mother" Tubman, still "the possessor of a strong and musical voice," followed her remarks by singing "a genuine old plantation song."

The location and back-to-back timing of these two women's conventions was not a coincidence. Although the National Federation of Afro-American Women tended to be more politically minded than the National League of Colored Women, the missions of the two organizations were similar enough that a merger had been under consideration for some time. By midweek, the leaders of the two bodies, noting that "Our women are thoroughly alive to the great possibilities of a powerful body of Afro-American women in influencing public sentiment and legislation in favor of the race at large," decided to join forces under the name National Association of Colored Women. Mary Church Terrell was elected president of the consolidated organization. They adopted the slogan "Lifting as We Climb." The educated, cultured women of the association considered themselves, as Anna put it, "the leaven" whereby "our weaker sisters" would eventually rise.

The consolidation did not affect the identity of the Colored Woman's League of Washington, which continued to grow in membership and influence (by 1899, it was one of about two hundred clubs affiliated with the National Association of Colored Women). Anna's pet cause was advocating for kindergartens. Her years of teaching at Mott School had convinced her of the necessity for kindergartens, since many children lacked the influence of an educated home. "Where are you going to begin to mold character?" she mused, "Can you plant the seed in the harvest time and expect it to reap ripe, rich fruits? It must be sown in the spring time of life." When this process is not followed in the home, she reasoned, "we must take the best substitute we have—the kindergarten." This conviction grew during the National League of Colored Women convention.

Anna pledged herself to establishing kindergartens for black children, "that saving grace to the masses of our race," and persuaded the Colored Woman's League to promote the objective. "When I made this proposition to the executive board, the president thought it would be well-nigh impossible since the treasury of the league had been exhausted," she recalled, "By reason of my strong faith in the cause I had espoused, I simply asked permission to develop what I could." Anna, named chairwoman of the league's kindergarten committee, launched her efforts "without the first penny to begin with." After she succeeded in gaining the use of rooms in the University Park Mission near Howard, plus heat, electricity, and janitorial service, all free of charge, and scrounged tables, chairs, and other materials, the league pledged $40 for the project's support, and sympathetic individuals aided the cause as well. After just a few months of intense preparation, University Park Kindergarten, the first kindergarten for black children in Washington, opened in the autumn of 1896. Anna welcomed two classes of children, "a morning kindergarten for the poor and neglected children, and an afternoon kindergarten for those more fortunately conditioned," recounting, "From the poor children we requested, without demanding it, one penny a week; from the more fortunate ones, fifty cents a month." In addition to a safe and stimulating environment, the kindergarten provided meals, clean clothing, and medical attention as need required.

Three days before Christmas, the kindergarten committee of the Colored Woman's League sponsored a holiday dinner at the mission for the kindergartners. "Forty little children were filled and made happy with all the good things that belong to the Christmas time." Afterward, Anna Murray and Josephine Bruce each offered remarks, followed by a "mothers' meeting," the first in a series to be held over the coming year. These informal gatherings were developed to provide information—for working women in particular—on child care, health and hygiene, and home economy. At the occasion's close the little ones were given bags of nuts, candy, oranges, and raisins to take home, and their mothers basketsful of provisions.[1]

Anna also pursued her promotion of kindergartens through a second organization, the National Congress of Mothers, co-founded by Phoebe Hearst, an energetic patron of education and the arts, the widow of a former US senator from California, and the mother of the newspaper baron William Randolph Hearst. The newly formed organization, designed to facilitate the active partic-ipation of mothers in their children's education (and later evolving into the Parent-Teacher Association, or PTA), held its preliminary set of meetings in the nation's capital in February 1897. The first day's sessions, held at the Arlington Hotel on February 17, drew an enormous, standing-room-only crowd of two thousand people, male and female, black and white. Anna Murray, representing the Colored Woman's League, was one of a number of delegates char-acterized as "brainy colored women." She and other participants had set up a model nursery and playroom in the Arlington. Vis-ited by nearly everyone who entered the hotel, the room was fully equipped, including a baby used to demonstrate bathing and dress-ing "after the most approved methods." On the third and final day of the conference Anna was allotted two minutes to introduce her topic. From the inception of her work in early childhood educa-tion, she had been as interested in training kindergarten teachers as she was in establishing the classes themselves. Phoebe Hearst, already an enthusiastic proponent of kindergartens, learned from Anna of her efforts to establish kindergartens for black children in the District conducted by trained black teachers, and would prove a generous benefactor for both elements.

The philanthropist rented a house at K and 24th streets NW and there supported a free kindergarten for local youngsters from needy families of color. It was when Anna discovered that only white kindergarten teachers were available that she had conceived of the idea of starting a training school to prepare young African American women for the vocation. Phoebe Hearst, in her generous liberality, not only donated the first $1,000 to establish a Kindergarten Training School at the K Street location but also supplied books on early childhood education for the students and provided a kindergarten trainer of national reputation. Aspirants were asked to call on Anna Murray at her residence. Anna insisted that only those "of the necessary culture and education" and "conscious of the high purpose of kindergarten" be admitted to the class.

By June 1897, eighteen students had completed the program and were poised to receive their diplomas. "The event this evening will mark a new departure, being the first class of colored graduates in kindergarten science in this country," noted the *Evening Star*. "This work was undertaken by the Colored Woman's League, with Mrs. Daniel Murray in charge, and from a small beginning has now in successful operation five kindergartens, with more than one hundred children in attendance." The commencement exercises took place at the People's Congregational Church on June 7. Come 8 p.m., eighteen young ladies, all attired in white, "marched in to much applause and took their places on the stage," arranged in a large semicircle. It must have been a fulfilling moment for Anna, already seated on the stage. The exercises included three kindergarten plays performed by the graduates and an address delivered by the author, educator, and feminist Anna J. Cooper. The distribution of certificates of graduation to the class of '97 brought the evening to a close.

A few months earlier, on March 18, St. Luke's Literary Guild had hosted an evening of presentations on the many phases of women's work, both locally and nationally. It was a popular program with every seat in the parish hall taken. Mary Church Terrell spoke of the aims of the National Association of Colored Women. Anna Murray discussed not only kindergartens but day nurseries, advising working mothers to send their young children to nursery classes currently being established in the city instead of leaving them to their own devices. On a later date Anna described a day nursery supported by the Colored Woman's League: "We have a little house of four rooms right in the midst of an alley . . . where we take care of the children of the women who have to go out and work all day."

In the span of a year's time, Anna Murray, with the cooperation of the Colored Woman's League, managed to start several model private kindergartens for black children, develop a series of Mothers' Meetings, found and manage a training school for kindergarten teachers, and introduce day nurseries for strapped working mothers. In addition, within the same short period, she instructed a class of girls in domestic economy in her own home, teaching them "to sew and cook, to cut and fashion their own dresses, to read and write, and in every way possible to improve themselves." Besides being the chairwoman of the kindergarten committee, Anna served on two other Colored Woman's League committees, one with the goal of improving moral and social conditions in the alleys, the other charged with extending league work into new areas of concern.[2]

But this tireless clubwoman was just warming up. Anna was an indefatigable fund-raiser, and if it was necessary to borrow money, she voluntarily assumed the personal risk. She went among her friends and the churches in Washington garnering donations, many of them in the $1 to $5 range (Phoebe Hearst's gift an outstanding exception). Over two years, "she collected about $3,000 by her individual effort," her husband recalled, "and kept the system going until she was able to induce Congress to come to her aid." Anna felt that "The era of private philanthropy for free kindergarten instruction in the city of Washington had then come to an end and if the hopes of many of us were to be realized it would be necessary for Congress to make an appropriation." With the kindergarten classes and teacher-training program running smoothly, "I advised that we knock at the door of our municipality and ask that the kindergarten be made a part of our public school system." School superintendents judged that $12,000 would be a sufficient sum to "make a beginning in this most useful branch of education."

As "the mastermind of the project," Anna helped draft the first bill introduced to Congress promoting this advance, but the initial lobbying effort in February 1897 failed to generate congressional approval. The April issue of *Kindergarten News* observed, "All the educational people here are confident that Washington will have public kindergartens in the near future. An attempt was made to establish them this year, but our great and good Congress felt poor and the appropriation of $12,000 which was asked for scared them badly."

Anna described herself as "nothing daunted" and prepared for another run at congressional approval the next February. Now Daniel Murray worked his connections on her behalf. "My husband had been an employee at the Capitol," Anna recollected. "Through his efforts a hearing was secured for me before the Senate Appropriations Committee, of which Senator [William B.] Allison of Iowa was chairman." A committee of three from the Colored Woman's League was scheduled to attend the hearing on February 26, 1898. "When the morning arrived on which we were to make our plea before the Senate Appropriation Committee, both the other women deserted me, pleading engagements, and I was obliged to appear before the senators alone." As Anna, "with fear and trembling but strong in my cause," rose, Senator Allison cautioned, "be brief." She managed to make her request for funding for the kindergarten education of all District children succinctly. When she completed her remarks, Senator Allison said, "You have made a noble plea for your race."

Allison later said of Anna Murray, "She is an exceptionally bright and intelligent woman." He put his seal of approval on the kindergarten appropriation, but that was not the final hurdle. "There was the matter of having the conferees on the bill agree to this item," as Anna well remembered. Having already passed the House before the amendment was tacked on, the bill went to the conference committee for resolution. "Literally with my courage in my mind and my heart in my mouth, I went one evening after dinner, without an appointment, to the home of [Mahlon Pitney of the House Subcommittee on District Appropriations], a Representative in Congress from New Jersey and one of the most powerful of the House conferees. He permitted me to see him and, after I had stated my errand, agreed to give it his support." By late June, the District appropriation bill was finally ready for the President's signature.

Anna claimed she had called on "a heritage of courageous conviction" from her father in not allowing the many obstacles thrown in her path to dissuade her. And now, she exalted, "the $12,000 was ours—$8,000 to the white schools, $4,000 to the colored—this division being based upon our proportion of the population." Anna Murray was a true pioneer in early childhood education, her achievement marking the first time federal funds were allotted for kindergarten education. It was understood by Congress that this was the initial step in the incorporation of kindergartens into the public school system and that the amount appropriated would increase each year (as indeed it did). "Now the good news may be sounded!" wrote Anna in the September 1898 issue of *Kindergarten Magazine*. "I could shout with all the strength of my body in praise and thankfulness that this has been accomplished."[3]

Even with "the entire management, control and upbuilding" of the kindergarten enterprise "in her hands," Anna managed to make room for other concerns. One of them was the Sojourner Truth Home, which provided lodging for working colored women, in particular those "who are out at service during the day and who, from lack of means to provide for better accommodations, have been compelled heretofore to sleep in a room in an alley or other by-place." The home's name was "selected as a mark of respect to the memory of Sojourner Truth, a great evangelist among the people of the colored race" who had given herself the name Sojourner because she had "traveled from place to place, having no permanent home, but sojourning for a short time in each." On October 18, 1896, the same year the home opened, Anna presented a talk on "How to Be Useful," that is, self-supporting, industrious, and trained in household science.

Anna was also a booster of another "center of influence for good" in Washington: the National Association for the Relief of Destitute Colored Women and Children. This interracial organization had been founded in 1863 for the purpose of supporting "such aged or indigent colored women and children as may properly come under the charge of such Association; to provide for them a suitable home, board, clothing, and instruction, and to bring them under Christian influence." Over the years the association, which received a substantial annual appropriation from Congress, became increasingly dominated by African Americans in its membership and official positions. Anna was a member by 1894 at least. In 1899, more than a hundred boys and girls were being cared for at the home, along with about a dozen aged women. Anna served as treasurer that year. The roster of female officers and board managers represented the "highest type of cultured Negro womanhood," the peers of their charity-minded counterparts of "the more favored race."

Nor did Anna leave behind her passion for music while pursuing humanitarian work. For example, in the spring of 1897, she was one of a number of musically inclined Washingtonians of color interested in generating a new musical organization. Elected treasurer, Anna, together with the other officers, scheduled an open meeting for April 12. Two days before, the *Washington Bee* announced, "All lovers of music and all interested in the advancement of the people are cordially invited." Attendees discussed the establishment of a society for those given to a deeper understanding of the musical works of the best masters.[4]

→ ←

"THE COMING REPUBLICAN CONTEST FOR DELEGATES TO THE next National Republican Convention will be a hot one," the *Washington Bee* predicted in early September 1895. Grover Cleveland had pulled off a second presidential term following Benjamin Harrison's. Now District Republicans were anxious to again replace Democrat Cleveland with a man of their own party. The *Evening Star* reported that the Union Republican Club and the Republican members of the Board of Trade "have determined to take a conspicuous part in the selection of the two delegates" to the National Republican Convention, scheduled for June in St. Louis. Those parties sought a change in the present delegation from Washington and preferred a representative member of either the club or the board "to go as the white delegate and some prominent colored man to be his associate." The rumor around city hall and the District Building was that the particular men of "respectability and worth" they wanted to see paired were ex-commissioner Myron M. Parker and Daniel Murray, "the colored member of the board of trade." A pattern of such "racial combinations" had previously been established. As agreed upon, each male resident could vote for two candidates; "The one white man receiving the highest vote given to white candidates is to be declared elected; and the one Negro candidate receiving the highest vote among the colored aspirants is likewise elected."

The motivation of the Union Republican Club and the Board of Trade boosters was to promote men who would see eye to eye with them when it came time to "dispose of the federal patronage that will be given to the District," accusing those who had represented Washington at past national conventions of "neglect." The supporters of "the same 'gang' that has controlled affairs here for some time" predicted that when the election of delegates came in January, they "would be on top." The best bets from the old guard seemed to be the pair of Andrew Gleason and Perry H. Carson. Both had served as delegates at national conventions several times before. Andrew Gleason was an Irish-born contractor. "He is the friend of all classes," claimed a constituent, and though he "may not possess great power of oratory and the command of language as others, he has good common sense." Colonel Perry H. Carson, a garbage inspector with the United States Department of Health, was likewise a man who "never enjoyed educational advantages" but was held in esteem by the "common people."

Daniel Murray joined Carson in a crowded field of African American would-be delegates to the convention. Also running were Murray's fellow black elites, Dr. Charles Purvis and Milton M. Holland. As the New York Times Washington correspondent reported, "The intelligent colored people here are making what they are pleased to call 'an effort' to retire the Colonel, as they claim that he represents the worst element of the colored race in the District, and that the race has progressed beyond Col. Carson's ability to represent it." All the contenders seemed determined "to fight it out to the end."

Political meetings were held at black churches in every quadrant of the city, where the candidates could "put themselves on dress parade and tell the colored people of the District why they

want to represent them." All of the candidates stood for the restoration of District home rule "and pledged themselves to do all
in their power to secure it, if sent to the convention"—that is,
push it as a plank in the platform. A lot of heated discussion was
not necessarily pertinent to the issues. At a political gathering on
October 11, Perry Carson and Milton Holland "hurled charges of
race disloyalty at each other." Holland bounded to his feet when
Carson accused him of trying to pass for white and claimed that
he had advertised for a white servant for his family. Holland pronounced Carson "too ignorant to represent the colored people
here or anywhere." At a meeting a week later, Murray's remarks
followed those of Charles Purvis. "Mr. Murray declared that there
was a grave duty to be performed," reported the *Evening Star.* "He
stated that for many years the colored people had been sending
their representatives to national conventions, but that they accomplished nothing. He said a man with only ordinary characteristics
would be lost in a national convention. And he earnestly appealed
to his hearers to see to it that Mr. Parker and himself were sent as
their representatives." Carson was up next: "After hearing from all
those candidates, who think of themselves as intelligent gentlemen, I hardly think you want to hear from a man so illiterate as
they say I am. . . . They say they have always been interested in
the welfare of the race. That, perhaps, is true, but it has always
been for their own benefit." Carson was well known to all the inhabitants of the District, including those in the "mean, sordid"
localities where "kid gloves and white shirts have never been seen"
until this campaign. His speech was received with deafening applause.

When the voting on January 28, 1896, was over, not without "irregularities," Perry Carson and Andrew Gleason had been
elected delegates. It was generally an orderly election, but some,
including Murray, claimed there had been a good deal of repeat
voting. Yet there was no disputing that Gleason and Carson far

and away distanced all other candidates. The two "old war horses" would again represent the District.

The Republican National Convention was held in St. Louis on June 16–18, 1896. The front-runner, William McKinley—a former US congressman and governor of Ohio—handily won the nomination. "Speculation is rife as to what figure the Negro is to cut in the political arena before and after the election," noted the *Indianapolis Freeman*. Daniel Murray did more than speculate; he wrote a letter to McKinley's campaign manager, the industrialist Mark Hanna. Hanna, a longtime McKinley partisan, was a savvy, energetic GOP operative. Murray's introduction to him was undoubtedly provided by his close friend George A. Myers, an ally of McKinley and Hanna. He had served as a chief aide to Hanna at the nominating convention, working to secure the votes of black delegates. A top behind-the-scenes actor in Ohio Republican politics, or the "game," as he called it, Myers was the proprietor of Cleveland's Hollenden Hotel barbershop, one of the finest in the country (eventually boasting seventeen barbers and six manicurists) and a meeting place for Ohio politicos. Judging from Hanna's return letter to Murray, saved with his papers and stamped with the receive date of August 6, 1896, Murray had reminded Hanna that the black citizen was a prime factor in the political equation and proposed that he appoint a colored representative "to the Advisory Committee or to some other committee." Although Hanna thanked Murray for his advice, his response was thoroughly noncommittal, ending with the sentence "I will give your suggestion the attention to which it is entitled."

As it turned out, Hanna obviously realized its merit, as two weeks later he established the Afro-American Bureau, a branch of the Republican National Committee, with Ferdinand L. Barnett of Chicago and Richard T. Greener of New York in charge. F. L. Barnett was an attorney and editor, the husband of Ida Wells-Barnett, the better known of this activist couple. Greener told the

Chicago Tribune "that they would circulate a special line of literature prepared for the most part by colored men, arrange for meetings, and furnish speakers." They stumped for the ticket, used the
black press to get out the vote, and were successful in bringing disillusioned voters back into the Republican fold and more generally,
as Greener put it, "in reaching every available black vote."

Campaign clubs to promote the Republican ticket were organized. One of the most prominent in Washington was the "Henry
Cabot Lodge Sound Money Club." Henry Cabot Lodge was a senator from Massachusetts who, like McKinley, supported the gold
standard and high protective tariffs. The predominantly black membership "includes a number of Washington's leading lights, and important results are expected to accrue from its actions between now
and the 4th of March," the *Indianapolis Freeman* reported, adding,
"It is said to represent the Republican aristocracy of the District."
The president of the club was Robert Terrell. Among the "honorary
members" were Pinckney Pinchback, Charles R. Douglass, John R.
Lynch, James Bradford, Charles Purvis, and Daniel Murray.

Voting day was November 3, 1896. McKinley emerged the triumphant president-elect. George H. White from North Carolina
was elected to the House of Representatives, the twenty-second African American to serve in the House or Senate. Though McKinley
carried many Republican candidates on his coattails, White also
benefited from a three-way race that worked in his favor. Moreover,
his district was predominantly black, and the turnout among black
voters was greater than 85 percent. By the middle of the month,
Richard Greener was in Washington, staying with Daniel Murray.
It was a time for celebration. At a dinner in his honor on November 24, Greener responded to a toast to "Our next President," asserting that he "was convinced that Mr. McKinley would do more
for the colored man than any President we have ever had."[5]

In December 1896, Daniel Murray was elected president of the
Inaugural Welcome Club and Dr. John R. Francis vice president.

This club was responsible for sponsoring entertainments for out-of-town guests on occasions such as inaugurations and gave dances and assemblies throughout the season. According to Mary Church Terrell, though it was difficult to tell which social circle was ascendant at any one time, "there is one that comes more prominently before the public than the others," and that was the "charmed circle" within the Inaugural Welcome Club. Before the year was out, Murray held a meeting at his residence to make arrangements for the black inaugural ball. In mid-January, he secured the commodious Builders Exchange Hall for the venue. The main ball was scheduled for March 4, the same day as the inauguration ceremonies. Mark Hanna wanted to stage it in the new Library of Congress, but Ainsworth Spofford was not supportive ("Ruler over the Realm of Books Objects to Such Use of the Palatial Building" ran one newspaper headline), and it took place in the Pension Building.

"The colored citizens of the District are preparing for an inaugural welcome reception Friday evening, the 5th of March," noted the *Evening Star*. "Prominent colored citizens of the country who may wish to visit this city during the inaugural ceremonies are to be received and entertained upon that evening." There was no question that it was "to be a very select affair." The *Washington Bee*, which ran hot and cold when it came to lauding the city's black elite, pushed for exclusiveness: "There is every disposition to make the ball first-class. The committee should do one thing and that is to discriminate between what is and what is not. All names should be submitted to the executive committee. Some few years ago Tom, Dick and Harry, and his second female cousins and aunts were at the ball and no one knew how they secured admission." The *Indianapolis Freeman* predicted, "The ball will eclipse any social function ever attempted by the colored people of Washington."[6]

And so it did. As the same newspaper declared in its follow-up story, the inaugural welcome reception on March 5 "was the leading social function for the entertainment of visitors. Its conception amply illustrated the possibilities of the Afro-American society world at the nation's capital. The attendance marked the culture, beauty, refinement, and elegance of the race in the country at large, for nearly every state in the Union was represented, in the gay kaleidoscopic throng. The student of sociology, who made the Negro a specialty, missed a magnificent object lesson by their failure to be present." This was one time the black elite waived all notions of conservatism and understatement. As Baltimore's *Afro-American* described it, "Capital society really put on the dog":

> A canopy was stretched from the walk to the main entrance of the hall and a red plush carpet strip covered the walk to protect the entrained gowns of the women. Liveried coachmen delivered their charges into the care of uniformed footmen. And the women who entered the ballroom were as tastefully gowned, as refined in manner, as correct in their use of the English language, as graceful in their carriage as queens. Easily the belle of the ball was the beautiful Mrs. Daniel Murray. . . . She wore a white silver spangled mesh entrained gown, with a high staved neckline and long slightly puffed fitted sleeves. The eighteen-inch-waist-line basque came to a Y point and the long full skirt was entrained. Mrs. Murray led the grand march.

William Coalson, the only black man from Des Moines, Iowa, who attended the inauguration in Washington, went home with a report. He had not secured a ticket to the "swell colored ball" but had been permitted to enter and sit in the gallery, where he had watched seven hundred "high Washingtonians waltz." The *Freeman* piece concluded that "It was in every respect a gala night" and noted that Daniel Murray and his "tireless assistants have set a quick pace for future inaugural entertainment committees." A personal ad ran in the March 8 edition of the *Evening Star*: "Will

Lady who took through mistake sable fur cape from the inaugural Welcome Club's ball, Friday evening, the 5th, please return same to 2036 17th St. n.w., and receive hers?"

President McKinley was inundated with callers at the start of his administration. Yet when Daniel Murray and three other black leaders in Washington arrived at the White House on March 22, it was by the President's invitation. One can imagine the four men confidently bypassing those lined up without appointments. Just two weeks after the inauguration, the meeting was an honor and a very hopeful sign that McKinley would indeed do right by black Americans. The Bible upon which McKinley had sworn to protect and defend the Constitution at the inauguration ceremony had been a gift from the bishops of the AME Church. The newly minted President had kissed it to seal his oath. In the address that had followed, he had declared that "Lynchings must not be tolerated in a great and civilized country like the United States; courts, not mobs, must execute the penalties of the law." The conference Murray and his associates had with President McKinley that March afternoon was on "District matters." Without a doubt, it would have included not only discussion of home rule but more patronage for African American citizens. Whatever Murray's beliefs about civil service reform, they did not exclude his interest in seeing African Americans appointed to office. The *Indianapolis Freeman* reported that Washington politicos claimed that "new leadership means a new virility for Republicanism for all it is worth" and observed, "The District of Columbia is fertile in stellar lights, and both young and old warriors will engage in the battle royal." The article went on to state that Daniel Murray and other prominent men of color named "will all have a finger in the pie."[7]

→ ←

FOR AINSWORTH SPOFFORD AND HIS STAFF THE YEARS IN which the new library was under construction were "simply a period of marking time, as the situation continued to deteriorate." At 3:30 in the afternoon of December 3, 1895, "lusty cries for help rang out in the attic . . . and echoed through the courts and corridors." When Daniel Murray and fellow assistant librarian Hugh Morrison rushed to the area in the attic "from where the cries seemed to come, they could see nothing but a mighty mass of newspaper files which had toppled and entombed J. H. Marcellus," a bookbinder, whose work had taken him to a narrow attic passage lined high with "monster files of newspapers." It turned out that Marcellus had become momentarily unsteady and, reaching for support, had disturbed the poise of one of the stacks, which had toppled and pinned him down. "From the weight of the papers, probably a ton, which had fallen, it seemed to the rescuers that Marcellus must have been crushed," and indeed, except for the speedy aid rendered by Murray and Morrison, the bookbinder might have suffocated but instead was rescued unharmed.

Among those detailed to the book service, Murray worked closely with John G. Morrison and Hugh Morrison. Though sometimes referred to as "the Morrison brothers," the two were not related. John was a Washingtonian and had worked at the library since 1883; Hugh, from Baltimore, had arrived in 1890. The daily duties of all three men were the same: locating and supplying books and information to government officials and general readers, and replacing books on shelves. Their normal work hours, from nine in the morning until four in the afternoon, were stretched when Congress was in session. Murray had the additional responsibility of bringing in the mail from the post office each morning. "He is what we call confidential mail clerk," explained Spofford, "and has the locked bag containing all the letters—copyright letters and registered mail, etc." Another assistant librarian, David

Hutcheson, born in Scotland in 1844, thus fifty-two in 1896, had joined the staff in 1874 and was eventually considered head of the library service, which to Spofford meant, "He is my representative to supply books and information, and to answer all inquiries that are needful to be answered."

No matter how the library business grew, Spofford remained involved "in the countless minutiae of insistent, direct, undelegated labor." His organizational flowchart was nearly flat. Despite nominal designations such as Hutcheson's or the head of copyright or the law library, he maintained, "I generally direct and apportion all the Library business," adding, "I am accustomed to call upon any competent person to do any work I see fit in the Library." He exercised loyalty toward his employees: "If an assistant is faithful, accurate, expeditious, and industrious, I think it is exceedingly well to keep him in service." When it came to salary increases, he believed that the principal determining factors were "length of service and diversified ability or expertness in work, of which I must be the judge, of course."

But big changes were afoot. By 1896, there was a jump to forty-two assistants under Spofford. Most of the new hires were due to the rise in copyright business. There were now twenty-six staff members assigned to that area; eleven, including Murray, in library service. That was just the beginning. All, including Spofford, understood that the new library would require not only an additional leap in personnel but a true organizational structure. In his annual librarian's report dated May 28, 1896, Spofford wrote, "The reorganization of the library force and the necessary provision for the administration of the Library in the new building, now nearly completed, has been fully set forth in the special report of the undersigned, laid before Congress at the beginning of the present session, in December, 1895, and heretofore printed." As eventually adopted, the new scheme called for the formation of various administrative units under the Librarian of Congress and a chief assistant librarian. The divisions consisted of a reading room, an art gallery, a hall of map and charts, a periodicals department, a manuscript department, a music department, a catalogue department, a copyright department, and the law library, each headed by a chief with direct charge of his operation.

The reorganization of the library was approved by Congress on February 19, 1897, to become effective the following July 1. For the fiscal year ending June 30, 1898, Congress provided for an increase in the library's personnel from 43 to 187! Of that number, 108 would be library staff proper and the rest custodial and maintenance employees under the separate authority of a building superintendent. The new library was completed by March 1, 1897, ten years after it was begun, but because Congress unexpectedly scheduled an extra session, the books could not be moved to the new building until late July.

On June 30, 1897, President McKinley nominated John Russell Young, a journalist and former diplomat born in Ireland, as the new Librarian of Congress. He was confirmed by the Senate the same day. Young took the oath of office as the seventh Librarian of Congress on the morning of July 1. Although a fellow journalist described him as "almost a born literateur," to the disappointment of many, he was not a professional librarian. According to the *Library Journal*, "Mr. Young, so far as is known, has had no experience in, or general acquaintance with library work." Indeed, it was remarked that his chief qualification seemed to "lie in political preferment." But he was a skillful administrator. His first act was the appointment of Ainsworth Spofford as chief assistant librarian. Exactly when Spofford had arrived at the realization that he would be passing on the torch, and whether it came slowly or at once and under what outside influences, is unknown. Young noted McKinley's intention to nominate him in his diary two months before it was announced. Whatever the full background, the transition was handled gracefully by all parties. Spofford's letter to President

McKinley, dated June 28, 1897, informing him that he "preferred not to be a candidate" as future Librarian of Congress was published in the July 2 edition of the *Evening Star*. As Library of Congress historian David Mearns pointed out:

> For Mr. Spofford, the change meant release from intolerable burdens. He was a bookman, not a bureaucrat, and no one was more sure of it than he. Indeed, it is just possible that the plan for reorganization of the Library had provided the post of Chief Assistant Librarian in order that he might have a place of dignity and prestige where his great genius (and it was very great) might exercise its full powers. He was not at his best as an administrator. . . . He took the "stepping down" with the grace that was his nature. . . . There was no pomposity about him; he was no servant of his own power, no slave of his ambitions.[8]

Young, who was officially charged with the supervision of the move from the Capitol and implementation of the new organization had, by mid-July, set up his office in the otherwise empty new edifice. Over in the Capitol, Spofford "conducted the day-to-day services of the Library, trained the rapidly increasing staff in the requirements of their positions, and consulted with his superior by mail." Qualified staff members were assigned charge of manuscripts, periodicals, maps and charts, cataloguing, and other new divisions. "The persons now acting under Mr. Spofford's direction as the practical heads of these departments will be examined by Mr. Young personally," reported the *Washington Post* on July 12, 1897. The article went on to state that although there was no desire to necessarily "disturb any one now in the Library," some changes were expected and "new blood will be infused where requisite for the good of the public service and the improvement of the Library force." Promotions, particularly those made in-house, began to be

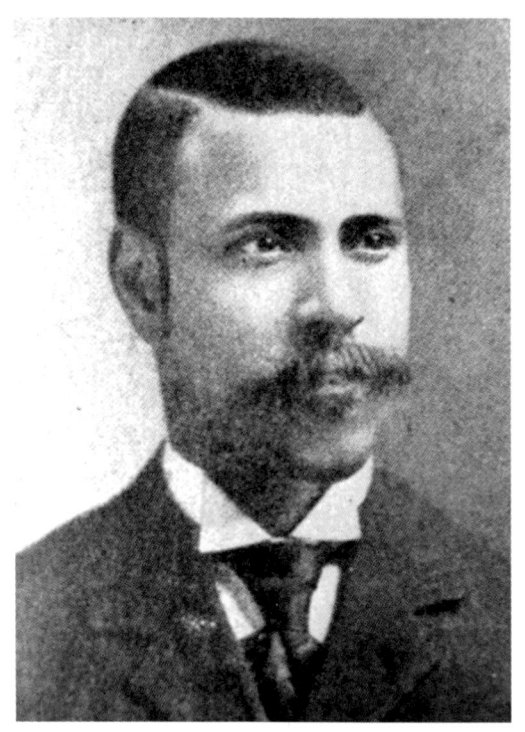

1. LEFT: Daniel Murray photographed in 1896 at the prime of life.
2. BELOW: Diagram of the main floor of the US Capitol. The Library of Congress was housed in the Capitol until 1897. Daniel Murray was offered a job in the library while working as a waiter in the Senate Restaurant.

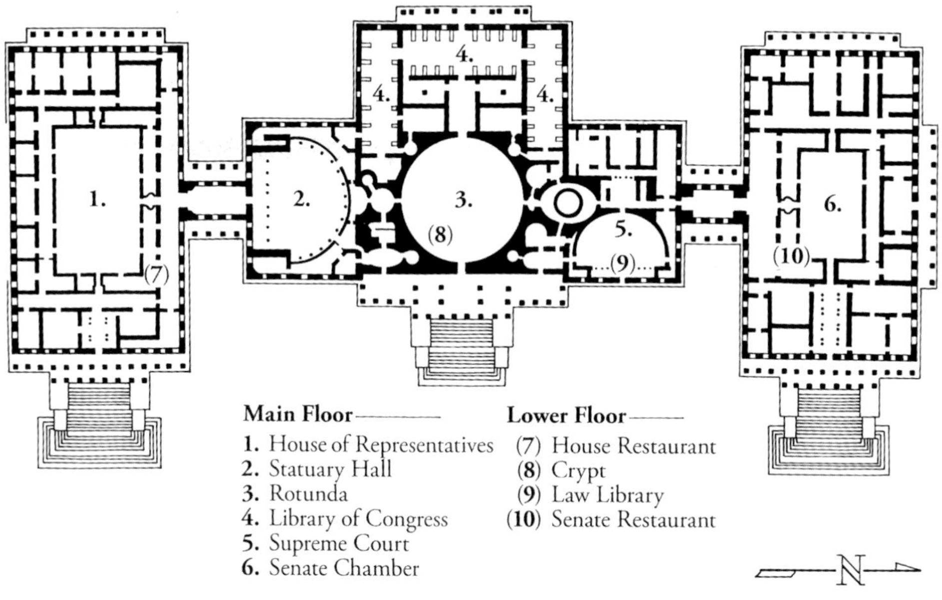

1.
2.
3.
4.
4.
4.
5.
6.
(7)
(8)
(9)
(10)
Main Floor
1. House of Representatives
2. Statuary Hall
3. Rotunda
4. Library of Congress
5. Supreme Court
6. Senate Chamber
Lower Floor
(7) House Restaurant
(8) Crypt
(9) Law Library
(10) Senate Restaurant
N

3. ABOVE: Library of Congress interior, circa 1866. Murray began working at the library on January 1, 1871.

4. LEFT: Ainsworth Spofford as he appeared at the time he hired Murray. Appointed by Abraham Lincoln, Spofford served as Librarian of Congress from 1865 to 1897.

5. ABOVE: The Oberlin Rescuers. In 1859, Anna Evans's father, Henry Evans *(seated, farthest right)*, and uncle Wilson Evans *(standing, fifth from right)* had been two of the Oberlinians who had been jailed in a famous fugitive slave case.

6–8. BELOW: Lewis Sheridan Leary *(left)* and John A. Copeland Jr. *(middle)*. Other abolitionists in Anna's family included her uncle Sheridan Leary and cousin John Copeland, two of John Brown's Raiders at Harpers Ferry. John Mercer Langston *(right)* in 1849. A lawyer and leading citizen of Oberlin, Langston moved to Washington, DC, after the Civil War, and later served in the US Congress.

9. ABOVE LEFT: Young Anna Evans. Anna manifested a strong genetic tendency in the Evans family of premature white hair.

10. ABOVE RIGHT: Bruce Evans as a young man. The youngest of Anna's siblings, he and his sister were always close. Beginning in 1910, their families lived just a few blocks from each other.

11. BELOW: 15th Street Presbyterian Church, where the Evans family worshipped. Anna married Daniel Murray here but afterward attended St. Luke's Protestant Episcopal Church, where her husband was a founding member.

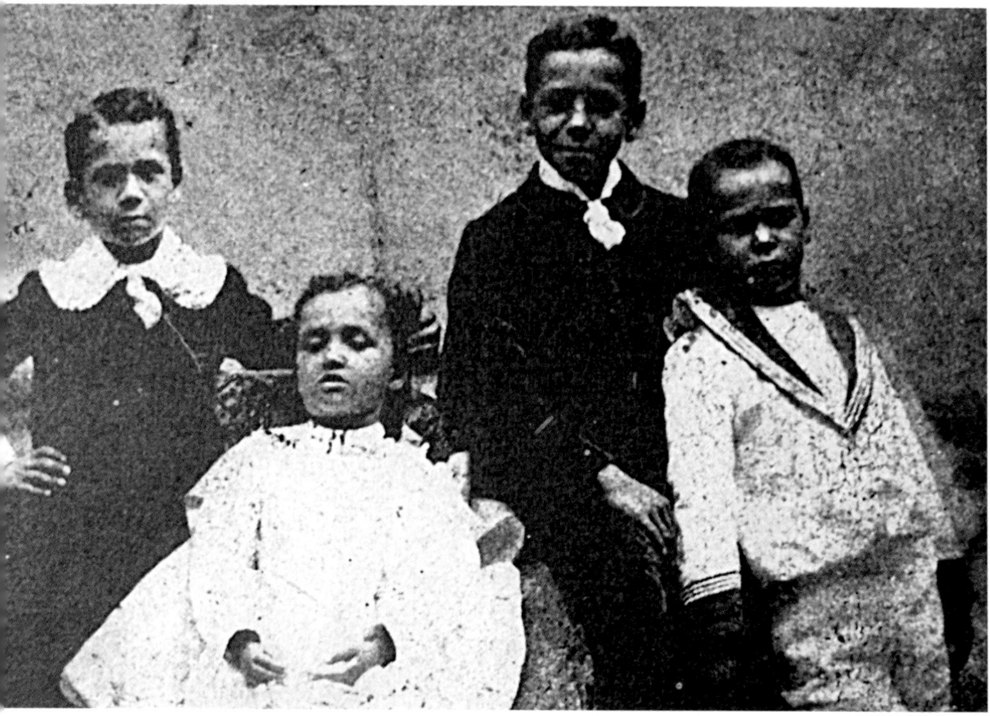

12. ABOVE: Murray children *(left to right)*: George Henry (known as Henry), Helene Ethel, Daniel Evans, and Nathaniel Allison. There were seven siblings in all. Pinckney died before this photograph was taken, while Harold and Paul were yet to be born.

13. LEFT: Helene, the Murrays' only daughter, died from diphtheria in 1893 at the age of five and a half, after an illness lasting only four days.

14. LEFT: The Library of Congress, showing an abundance of books overflowing the shelves.

15. BELOW: This illustration, which appeared in *Harper's Weekly* in February 1897, depicts the library in its ever-increasing congested state. In midstride, on the right, is Ainsworth Spofford, and to the left, holding a lamp, is David Hutcheson, who would be appointed the reading room superintendent when the staff was expanded and reorganized in the new dedicated library building.

16. ABOVE: Newly completed Library of Congress. The Beaux Arts building remains one of Washington's foremost architectural gems. (Today the Library of Congress is made up of several buildings, with the original known as the Jefferson Building.)

17. BELOW: Diagram of the main floor of the Library of Congress. The design was a rectangle with open courtyards and a central dome covering an enormous octagonal reading room. An underground tunnel with a mechanical trolley for the transport of books ran between the library and the Capitol.

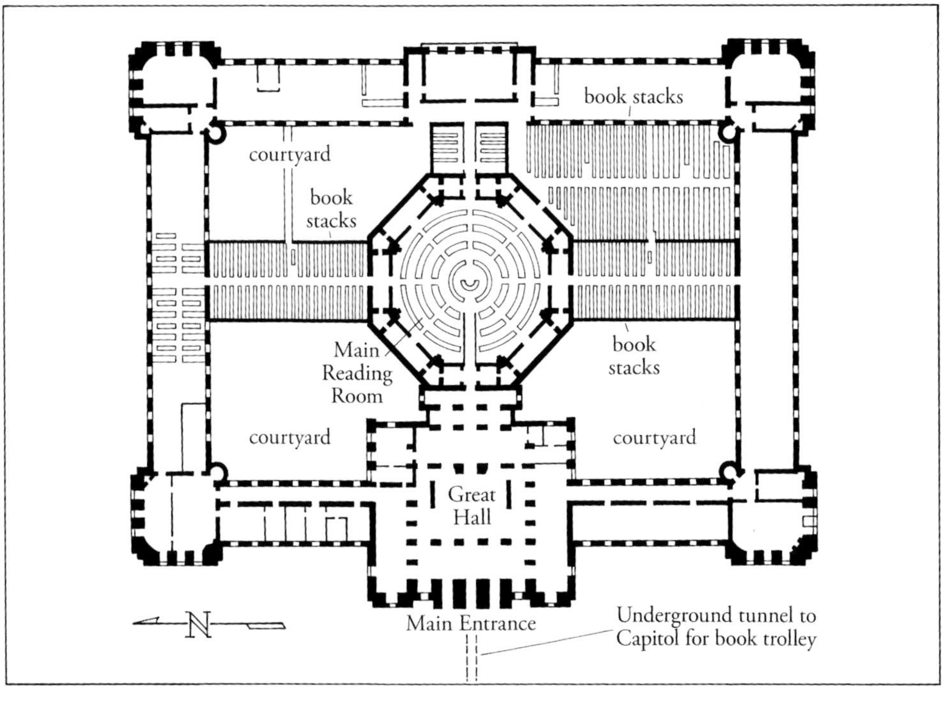

book stacks

courtyard

book stacks

Main Reading Room

book stacks

courtyard

courtyard

Great Hall

N

Main Entrance

Underground tunnel to Capitol for book trolley

18. Old library, now empty, 1897. Approximately eight hundred tons of books, pamphlets, periodicals, maps, manuscripts, prints, musical scores, and other collections, including seventy tons of copyright deposits, were transported across the street to the new building, a process that took months.

19. The elaborate Main Reading Room. Mahogany desks, accommodating as many as two hundred fifty readers, were positioned in concentric rows facing a circular station in the room's center. Murray worked in a few different departments but spent most of his time assigned to the reading room. During his fifty-two years at the Library of Congress, the staff grew from twelve to more than five hundred.

PRELIMINARY LIST

of

BOOKS AND PAMPHLETS BY NEGRO AUTHORS

for

PARIS EXPOSITION and LIBRARY of CONGRESS.

Compiled by

DANIEL MURRAY, LIBRARY OF CONGRESS,

WASHINGTON, D. C.

For the AMERICAN NEGRO EXHIBIT,
Paris Exposition of 1900,
Thos. J. Calloway, Special Agent.

20. TOP LEFT: Cover of Daniel Murray's *Preliminary List of Books and Pamphlets by Negro Authors.* The number of titles within was 270. Eventually Murray compiled a list of 7,500.

21. BOTTOM LEFT: The American Negro Exhibit at the Paris Exposition of 1900. Murray shipped sixteen glass-encased sheets bearing 980 bibliographic entries attached by hinges to stationary posts, along with 214 books, more than 160 pamphlets, and 2 bound volumes of newspapers across the Atlantic.

22. RIGHT: W. E. B. DuBois at the Paris Exposition. DuBois described Murray's literary display as "the most unique and striking" part of the American Negro Exhibit.

23. LEFT: Anna Evans Murray at age thirty-nine. She was described at this time as "tall and distinguished looking, having a wealth of long silvery hair, although she appears not to have reached middle age."

24. BELOW: Murray home at 934 S Street. Built by Daniel Murray in 1890, this four-story town house in northwest Washington would be home to Murray family members until 1965.

Three Harpers Ferry scenes. 25. TOP: Postcard view from 1908 of the Potomac and Shenandoah Rivers meeting at Harpers Ferry. 26. MIDDLE: Storer College's Lincoln Hall. During the summers, this college residence hall was made available to vacationing African American families. The Murrays first stayed here in 1883 but would later rent a cottage of their own each summer. Note John Brown's Fort to the left. 27. BOTTOM: The National Association of Colored Women at Harpers Ferry in 1896. Participants took a break from their conference in Washington to visit John Brown's Fort. The fort where Brown's band had made their last stand was transported to several locations before the National Park Service acquired Harpers Ferry, and in 1968 moved the structure close to its original site.

28. TOP LEFT: Bruce Evans in 1896, at age twenty-nine.
29. TOP RIGHT: His wife, Annie Brooks Evans, photographed by notable African American photographer Addison Scurlock.
30. LEFT: Their daughter, Lillian, as a fashionable toddler. Early in life, Lillian displayed remarkable musical talent. She later gained fame as an opera singer.

31. TOP: Anna's sister, Mary Evans Wilson. She married Butler Wilson, and their wedding was held in the Murrays' parlor. The Wilsons became members of Boston's black elite and leaders in the NAACP.

32. BOTTOM: Henrietta Leary Evans, mother of Anna, Bruce, and Mary Evans, photographed by Addison Scurlock. She was a speaker at the 1906 meeting of the Niagara Movement at Harpers Ferry.

33. LEFT: Daniel and Anna Murray's eldest child, Daniel Evans Murray, photographed by Addison Scurlock. Called Dannie by the family, he became a professional violinist.
34. BOTTOM: A member of the New York City music scene, Dannie formed and managed the Port-Au Peck Quartette, which included future famous bandleader James Reese Europe on piano.

DANL. MURRAY   JAS. R. EUROPE
TOM . BETHEL   ARTHUR PAYNE

THE. PORT-AU PECK
QUARTETTE

DANL. MURRAY, MGR.
148 W. 52ND ST.   N. Y. CITY
TEL, 8989 COLUMBUS

35. TOP LEFT: George Henry Murray attended Harvard University for two years and was later awarded a law degree at Howard University.

36. TOP RIGHT: Harold Baldwin Murray graduated from Cornell University in 1916, having majored in mechanical engineering.

37. LEFT: Daniel and Anna Murray's youngest son, Paul Evans Murray, earned a law degree from Howard University.

38. RIGHT: Nathaniel Allison Murray received a degree in agriculture from Cornell University in 1911. He, along with six other Cornellians, founded the country's first black college fraternity, Alpha Phi Alpha.

39. BELOW: Alpha Phi Alpha 1931 convention with Nat Murray (*front row, third from right*) seated next to W. E. B. DuBois (*fourth from right*).

publicly announced by mid-July, with David Hutcheson formally named superintendent of the reading room.

On July 28, Daniel Murray was promoted to chief of periodicals, his salary having already been raised to $1,500, effective the first of July. Though the advancement undoubtedly came through the good offices of Spofford, it carried Young's stamp of approval. The *Washington Bee* sang, "Librarian Young Wednesday last after a full canvass of the men in the Library of Congress, tendered to Mr. Daniel Murray the position of chief of the periodical department in the New Library building." The organizational plan called for a superintendent of the periodicals department earning $1,500 annually, with three attendants and collators under him. The newspapers, magazines, journals, and other serials preserved by the library covered a broad range. "This vast mass of periodicals, bound and unbound, comprises a department of the Library of immense and constantly increasing value," Spofford opined, "They afford the completest mirror of the times to be derived from any single source." No other area of the library was so widely used.

The mammoth movement of material across 1st Street, from the old library to the new, finally commenced on July 31. Staff and hired men worked in concert. Books, color-labeled for their final destination, were lifted into cases placed on handbarrows. Two workers hefted each handbarrow by the flanking handles. Wooden chutes were employed where descents were faced, as from the library galleries or down the long flight of stairs outside the Capitol. A witness at the base of the Capitol steps recalled seeing bookcases flying down the chute and men catching them at the bottom and hoisting them onto wagons. Horses drew the wagonloads across the road, where many hands dispersed the books to their new resting places. The repetitive, arduous process, which transpired during the dog days of summer, continued week after week. Approximately eight hundred tons of books, pamphlets, periodicals, maps, manuscripts, prints, musical pieces, and other collections, including seventy tons of copyright deposits, were transported. In the end, not a book was lost. Bernard Green, the new library's building superintendent, witnessed a deeply moving portrait of the now former Librarian of Congress, the seventy-two-year-old man who had been the life and soul of the unique institution for over three decades. Green spied Spofford seated at rest in the old library, the shelves now empty, the floors swept clean. Against the library rule he had devised and enforced, he had his hat on.[9]

The new Library of Congress was designed not only to hold the nation's ever-increasing supply of books but to awe all who took in this astonishing architectural masterpiece, to refine and elevate the public taste. An elaborate fountain featuring Neptune and his court in bronze provided a refreshing welcome to the visitor upon reaching the front of the edifice. Flights of wide granite stairs led to three pairs of sculpted bronze doors. The massive entrance doors communicated directly with the great hall of the main floor. The interior was overwhelming in its size and grandeur. The various administrative units were dispersed over three stories, starting with the ground floor. The spaces on the main or library floor included, in addition to the great hall, the main reading room, the periodicals room, and the librarian's office. The second story was also known as the museum floor because of the exhibitions displayed there. On the attic level were a kitchen and restaurant.

The central reading room or rotunda was 100 feet in diameter, covered by the glorious dome, a lofty 125 feet above. Here, the "two great ends of architecture, use and beauty," were realized in a design at once "harmonious and imposing." How Daniel Murray, perhaps a bit puffed by his new promotion, must have relished striding across the enormous space, decorated with statuary, grand arches, stained glass, and gilded rosettes. Adjoining the rotunda and extending north, south, and east were the book stacks, accessed from alcoves near the room's perimeter. The iron network of stacks began on the basement floor and rose nine tiers high.

Altogether there were forty-four miles of shelving, capable of accommodating two million volumes, more than double the number
the library had amassed by the time of the move.

Mahogany desks, able to accommodate as many as 250 readers,
were positioned in concentric rows facing a circular station in the
middle of the room. This was the hub for book request and delivery. An ingenious and efficient mechanical system allowed as little
as three to five minutes to elapse from the time a book was ordered
until it was in the patron's hand. The process began when a ticket
for a desired volume was filled out. The attendant then whipped
the slip to the appropriate stack and tier by way of pneumatic tube.
The requisite book, collected by the attendant in that story, was
delivered to the reading room station via a book carrier operated
by an electrically powered revolving chain system. Amazingly,
the extensive system of pneumatic tubes and cable book trolleys
extended to the Capitol itself. Not only did pneumatic tubes run
underground from the library to the Capitol, but a sizable tunnel
(six feet high and five feet wide) a quarter of a mile long had been
dug that enabled books requested by senators or congressmen to be
dispatched by "electric railroad" directly to a small receiving room
just to the rear of the Capitol's Statuary Hall. Even that journey—
from order to delivery—regularly took less than fifteen minutes.

With her husband's annual leave suspended for the summer
of 1897 (as it was for all library employees over that busy time),
Anna Murray spent much of the season traveling. She, along with
Henry, Nat, and Harold, went to Oberlin for a visit with Dannie and the extended family. Leaving all but Harold, not yet four,
behind, Anna next sojourned to Chicago. There she spent part of
her time with Dr. and Mrs. Charles E. Bentley. Dentist Charles
Bentley was the "best known high-achieving black in Chicago."
Earlier that summer he had married Anna's friend Florence Lewis,
a journalist and clubwoman from Philadelphia. The Bentleys and
Murrays would grow close and remain so for decades. Reuniting

with Henry and Nat, Anna and her three younger boys traveled on to Boston. Surely, she proudly shared the news of her husband's advancement at the library with the folks in Oberlin and Boston as well as friends in Chicago.

In addition to the *Washington Bee*, notice of Daniel Murray's promotion to chief of the periodicals division was carried in the *Cleveland Gazette* and *Indianapolis Freeman*. How especially gratifying it must have been for Murray to discover that the August 22, 1897, *Washington Times* article on "Successful Colored Men" included a biographical sketch of him, alongside his pen-and-ink likeness. "Among the colored self-made men Mr. Daniel A. Murray stands conspicuous," the piece ran. "His position at the Library has given him great prominence, and it is safe to state that he is known to almost every colored man of note in the country, and to most of the statesmen."

So far, 1897 had been a very good year for Daniel Murray, now forty-six. At the Board of Trade reception in February, banks of palms overflowing the corners and clematis and evergreens covering the walls and ceiling transformed the Arlington parlor into a "green bower," as described by the *Evening Star*: "In this green bower there assembled the leading men of the nation and of the capital city. Men famed in the halls of legislation, distinguished jurors, bankers, leaders in commercial enterprises of all kinds, moved about in this green bower, chatting pleasantly on all subjects." He was one of those men. The new President of the United States—whom he had helped to elect and believed in—had sought his advice. And now he could savor his promotion to superintendent of one of the Library of Congress divisions, with a nice rise in salary. His high standing among the citizens of Washington seemed solid. Daniel Murray, it was said, "enjoys the distinction of being one man of color on whom the 'color line' is very seldom drawn."[10]

7

BACKSLIDING

B UT THE COLOR LINE *WAS* DRAWN ON DANIEL MURRAY. AF-
ter less than two months at the helm of his own division, he
was demoted as John Young implemented personnel changes that
reassigned him to his former position. Murray's humiliation was
exacerbated by a substantial decrease in salary. It was dropped not
back to $1,400, which is what he had been earning at least since
1893, but down to $1,200. According to Edwin Lee, a white co-
worker who wrote a 6,000-word biographical essay on Murray published in *The Colored American Magazine* in 1902, the change had
been deemed necessary because of "the friction incident to caste,"
adding that "Mr. Spofford was unable to hold him in the place."

Murray, embarrassed, worried that his standing in the community would be affected. He said as much in a letter to Young's confidential assistant, Thomas Alvord, dated September 3, 1897. It was
accompanied by a clipping from the *Washington Times*: the recent
article on "Successful Colored Men," lauding Murray's achievements and prominence. "It will explain," Murray wrote, "how difficult it is for me to accept a lower place in the Library." Murray
made reference to a conversation he'd had with Young, presumably the one in which the Librarian had revealed his decision to

bring in a new man as head of the periodicals department. Murray informed Alford that Young had invited him to "suggest a solution" as to his own disposition. He now proposed that he take the position of superintendent of the congressional reference library at the Capitol (where, for the ready convenience of congressmen and senators, a station with a collection of reference books and catalogues, monitored by library staff, was planned) and that the employee slated for that position, James Q. Howard, be made chief of manuscripts. Murray went on to add a political spin: "This would give the colored people a small division which it was thought had been done when I was temporarily made head of the Periodical branch. The 1,500,000 Colored Republicans who supported Major McKinley I am sure would appreciate the recognition and it would be good politics to do it." That statement echoed the one the *Washington Bee* made in announcing Murray's promotion, stating that it was "very gratifying to the friends of the administration and justifies the belief that the colored man will receive full recognition at the hands of President McKinley. Librarian Young has thus justified by his action in this case that the color of the man will prove no bar to advancement if the subject is worthy."

Although Young himself was a political appointee, he expressed determination to base his hiring on aptitude, not patronage or partisan politics. And though he claimed to be sensitive to those already in service as well as to a diversity of gender, color, and geography, he made it clear that such considerations were secondary to fitness. The announcement that the job of periodicals supervisor had been awarded to Allan B. Slauson from Oregon, a newspaperman educated at Cornell University, ran in the *Evening Star* on September 1. A few days earlier, the same paper had noted that "Mr. Young is determined to recognize the Pacific Northwest in his appointments, and will see that no part of the country is neglected."[1]

Young reported that there were only five men from the old staff who had not been given places in the new library, three because of superannuation and two "in the interest of the library." One of the latter was William H. H. Hart, a black staff member hired by Spofford in 1893. "W.H.H. Hart, professor in criminal law at the Howard University law school, has been dismissed from the Library of Congress," disclosed the *Washington Bee*. "This is somewhat a surprise, as Mr. Hart was one of the most efficient men in the Library." Striking a cautiously optimistic note, the *Bee* concluded, "The new librarian has received no instructions to retain negroes or to appoint them. Nothing should disappoint office seekers at this time." The *Evening Star* seemed to agree, predicting it "likely that [colored persons] will be given places by Mr. Young." Of course many applicants, regardless of race, were unsuccessful in obtaining positions. John W. Cromwell was one of the candidates of color turned away, despite John E. Bruce's recommendation that his fellow journalist Cromwell was "in every way qualified" to fill the job of assistant librarian. As it turned out, Young hired three African Americans, as best as can be determined. In 1895, there were six black employees, or 16 percent of total staff. With Hart dropped and only three new men hired, that percentage, based on a staff increase to 108, fell to 7.4 percent. (The discrepancy would grow more pronounced in future decades. By 1921, when approximately 625 people were employed by the library, only 35, or 5.6 percent, were African American.)

One of the three new employees of color was Paul Laurence Dunbar. He was recommended by Robert G. Ingersoll, a progressive with cultural and political influence, who wrote a letter on his behalf that included the pronouncement "He has written verses worthy of the greatest American poet." The *Evening Star* noted Dunbar's hire, referring to him as "the celebrated negro poet." Dunbar's post was deck attendant, retrieving and reshelving books. Josephine Bruce visited him on the job: "Climbing four short flights of stairs in the north stack of the library, I found my poet, seated humbly at a desk." Queried by Dunbar's first biographer, Murray recalled that initially Dunbar "was made an assistant to me that he might learn library methods and have, at the same time, one who would take an interest in his advancement."

As for Murray himself, his suggestion for shifting supervisors went unheeded. Murray's idea that James Q. Howard be made chief of manuscripts was an apt one. The author of histories of Lincoln and Hayes, he was, as Murray pointed out, "specially fitted for such a place." The problem with Murray's overseeing the congressional reference library at the Capitol was the same one as his supervising the periodicals department: attendants were assigned to the chiefs of both these administrative units. Herein was the fear of "friction incident to caste." Requiring white employees to report to a black superintendent was apparently deemed inadvisable. It was one thing for Dunbar to be under Murray's oversight, but a staff of white underlings was quite another. After all, the exterior ornamentation of the library itself made clear the supposed inferiority of people of African descent. At the keystones of thirty-three arches sat sculpted heads representing the races of the world: "Over the main entrance are the types of the highest order of men, such as the Greek, the Latin and the Saxon, while at the back of the building you find the lowest types, such as you find in Africa and in the South Sea Islands." Murray was duly assigned to the catalogue department, where he would be one of sixteen assistants under that division's supervisor.[2]

The new Library of Congress officially opened to the public on Monday morning, November 1, 1897. All was in readiness. Librarian Young and Building Supervisor Green had made sure of that, together reviewing every element of the operation from cellar to attic the day before. The fair skies and autumnal temperatures of Sunday had transitioned to inclement weather overnight. It was "raining volumes" at 9 a.m. when the library doors gave way to "an enthusiasm that rain could not repress." By afternoon, there were five hundred people in the building at any one time. Although the library—the finest architectural treasure in the nation's capital—had been accessible for touring for many weeks, this was the first day that the reading room was open to the public, and even then only for those actively engaged in study and willing to dispense with conversation. Those requesting books were highly impressed with their delivery via the "newfangled" apparatus of pneumatic tubes and electric book carriers. Supervisor of Periodicals Allan Slauson, having "worked his force so well," had ensured that all was in shape for patrons seeking newspapers, journals, and magazines. For Slauson and most of the staff, there may have been a feeling of fresh beginning, but for Daniel Murray the rainy day likely matched his sense of letdown. Working in one of the catalogue department offices, he was perhaps just as glad to be apart from the crowd enjoying the bustle of opening day.

By the spring of 1898, Murray was reassigned to the Smithsonian Collection, the 100,000 scientific works on deposit at the library. "The long sets of well-bound books representing the most authentic scientific literature of the world" were arranged in a dedicated library room. Murray reported to Cyrus Adler, the librarian of the Smithsonian Institution (Adler was employed by that entity as well as the Library of Congress). He may well have appreciated working under a renowned scholar like Adler, but he chafed at his $1,200 salary, lower than that of other employees with similar duties. Not easily cowed, on August 23, 1898, he wrote a letter of protest to John Young:

> I venture to call your attention to the promise made long ago to urge Congress to restore my salary to $1500 again, the amount received when I was summarily reduced. I rehearsed to you yesterday the conversation had with Sen. Allison and his interest in seeing me treated with the consideration to which I believe I am fairly entitled. I would suggest that in

your estimate for salaries, one of the $1200 in the reading room be changed to $1500 making three at $1500 instead of two as at present. In the old Library there were three at the desk at $1400—the two Morrisons and myself. Their salaries were not reduced, but mine was. The service I perform in connection with the scientific branch, i.e. the Smithsonian deposit, justifies the restoration of salary.

Submitted "Very respectfully," Murray's effort came to naught. The compensation inequity was ignored.

Despite that injustice, Murray gamely carried on. The new reading room for the blind, where those with "clouded vision" found "raised-letter volumes on different subjects," was Librarian Young's innovation and special interest. Readings were presented each afternoon. One of the participants was poet Dunbar, who read his poems with "a musical voice." Murray suggested that a concert for the blind be staged for November 1, 1898, when his eldest son would be in town. "Those who participated in the program were colored . . . a large majority of the visitors were white people." The program featured several violin solos by Daniel Evans Murray, accompanied on the piano by his mother. Young was "gratified over the success" of these offerings, popular with patrons both with and without sight.

In recommending Dunbar, Robert Ingersoll had averred, "He is crazy to . . . be in the company of books." True as that was, the position did not work out for Dunbar, and he resigned at the end of 1898. The long hours left little time for his own literary work. Moreover, the dust and moldiness of books in hot, closed spaces affected his already strained health. His wife, Alice, later wrote of this and its connection to Dunbar's poem "Sympathy," which opens "I know what the caged bird feels, alas!" and closes with the more familiar line "I know why the caged bird sings!" According to Alice Dunbar, "The iron grating of the book stacks in the Library of Congress suggested to him the bars of a bird's cage. . . . The torrid sun poured its rays down in the courtyard of the library and heated the iron grilling of the book stacks until they were like prison bars in more sense than one. The dry dust of the dry books . . . rasped sharply in his hot throat, and he understood how the bird felt when it beat its wings against its cage."

Daniel Murray kept his job at the Library of Congress until his retirement, but his advancement was stalled. His salary never rose for the twenty-five-year remainder of his tenure. John and Hugh Morrison, by comparison, would receive raises and enhanced titles. Murray was reassigned to the general reading room service before 1899 was over. In that same year it was decided to reduce the term "assistant librarian" to "assistant," though Murray continued to use the two-word descriptor.[3]

→ ←

MURRAY'S DISHEARTENING PERSONAL REVERSAL WAS JUST ONE manifestation of newly emerging color prejudice in the nation's capital over the 1890s, which proved to be a period of deteriorating status and bleak reckoning for black elites.

When federal troops enforcing Reconstruction-policy compliance withdrew from the South in adherence to the 1877 Wormley Agreement, rollbacks for that section's blacks came swiftly. In the name of reconciliation with the former Confederate states, the national government not only revoked its commitment to black advancement but delivered its new citizens into the hands of white supremacists, who lost no time in renewing their oppression. Local and state governments restricted the political, economic, and social status of African Americans by legalizing segregation and discrimination. Such racist statutes, constituting an uglier, more pervasive form of racism than had existed before the Civil War, became known collectively as "Jim Crow" laws. The name was derived from black figures mockingly caricatured by minstrel-circuit performers in blackface.

If those laws stunningly ignored the validity of the Thirteenth, Fourteenth, and Fifteenth Amendments to the US Constitution, southern white supremacists did not stop there. They also employed extralegal techniques of intimidation and violence to keep black people "in their place." Government at every level failed to protect African American citizens against lawlessness as extreme as murder. The lynching of blacks increased steadily through the 1880s and 1890s. The United States might tout its being, first and foremost, a nation of laws, but not even murder-by-mob led the federal government to abandon its policy of noninterference in southern affairs. It not only declined to intervene in Jim Crow injustice, it actively facilitated retrogression with the Supreme Court decision of 1883 that gutted the Civil Rights Act of 1875, which had ensured public accommodation regardless of race. Lawsuits from a number of plaintiffs denied service at public facilities due to color were considered together. The high court claimed that the Fourteenth Amendment applied to state violations of equal protection only, not to race discrimination by individuals, including in that descriptor restaurant, hotel, theater, and transit owners.

Devastating reversals for southern blacks may have come rapidly, but for Washington's people of color change was delayed and a staggered process at that. According to the *Colored American*, "There were few tangible evidences in Washington of race prejudice" as late as 1887. Racism had never gone away altogether of course, but incidents during the period of advancement had tended to be called out as anomalies or dismissed as vestiges. In response to one instance in a restaurant, the *People's Advocate* fumed, "This is as much against the spirit of our institutions as distinctions on the color line in the theatres, hotels, steamboat or railroad, and only in such states as Georgia or Kentucky is this discrimination now practiced." When a government clerk, Theophilus Minton, the scion of a top black elite family, was refused a glass of milk at a public house, the *Weekly Louisianan* remarked, "Prejudice against color still expresses itself at the National Capital," the modifier "still" seeming to imply that such cases represented the last traces of exclusion. Instead, prejudice in the District would grow and incidents in which even upper-class African Americans were subject to segregation and discrimination would proliferate over the 1890s.

Such an incident, one with spreading repercussions, occurred on the afternoon of February 10, 1890, when ex–minister to San Domingo H. C. C. Astwood was invited by a white associate to share a meal at the Riggs House. The two men took seats in the hotel dining room to discuss a business proposition. Shortly thereafter, Congressman Thomas W. Grimes of Georgia entered the room. "As soon, however, as he saw Mr. Astwood he arose, and, going to the office, paid his bill, declaring that he would not stay at a hotel which received negroes as guests." Astwood was taken by surprise. "I have frequently stopped at the Riggs for a considerable length of time and had no idea any unpleasantness could possibly arrive now on a question of color," he told the *Evening Star.* He added that at the Riggs House, as well as at the Ebbitt House, which he also frequently patronized, not "the slightest objection" had ever been raised. Indeed, as one commentator noted, "Well-known negroes have been accommodated in the hotels of Washington without causing a stampede of white guests" for twenty years before this ruckus. Yet when reporters queried local hoteliers after the incident, most squirmed and revealed a reluctance to serve guests of color. "Nobody wishes to offend them," the clerk at the Arlington responded, "but as a matter of protection of our business, we cannot receive them." Astwood published an open letter of protest directed to Grimes in the *Washington Bee* of February 15, accusing the congressman and "others of your section" (one of whom characterized the matter as "a white gentleman eating batter cake with a nigger!") of "forcing the hotel keepers of Washington to submit to a barbarous discrimination."

Black elites were shocked and humiliated by such latent discrimination coming to the fore. Charles Douglass, son of the great abolitionist, certainly was when he and his wife were turned away from the restaurant of Maryland's "queen resort of the Chesapeake" that summer. The Bay Ridge Resort boasted of its "first-class hotel and restaurant," and Douglass had been served there in the past, but now his black elite status was not enough to surmount the new color bar.[4]

Back in the capital, "It seems colorphobia has taken a strong hold," the *Washington Bee* observed. Partition by color along the Potomac River bathing beach came next. In May 1891, the *Evening Star* reported that dressing rooms and a wharf would be provided for white people at one end of the beach and the same set of facilities for black people at the other end, and "in order that decorum and good feeling may be maintained it will be insisted upon by the policemen in charge that each color shall keep to themselves." To complaints about such segregation, the superintendent for the project replied, "It is my aim to make the beach a popular bathing place, and everybody knows that can never be if the two races are forced to mingle." A supporter of race separation offered this strange logic: "The white boy is not indignant that he has to bathe alone, for which reason I cannot see why his colored friend should be." Black residents could easily "see why." A letter to the editor of the *Evening Star* from an African American pastor articulated their alarm: "If the beach is to be a public place why not open it alike to all respectable persons? Why should there be a separate 'Jim Crow' pool? . . . It is bad enough when private individuals discriminate against us, but it will be far worse when the best government under the sun assumes such an attitude against its citizens."

In 1894, Robert and Mary Church Terrell ran up against housing bias when they attempted to buy a home in a white

upper-middle-class development called LeDroit Park. Located
to the south of Howard University in what were then the suburbs of Northwest Washington, the architect-designed homes
were elegant and expensive. "It was easy to find houses where
self-respecting people of any color would not care to live," Mary
Church Terrell recalled, but just getting realtors to show the couple available properties in LeDroit Park proved knotty. When they
made a bid on a house, the owner refused to sell to them. A sympathetic white acquaintance intervened by buying the house and immediately reselling it to them. "It is not because colored people are
so obsessed with the desire to live among white people that they
try to buy property in a white neighborhood," Mary Church Terrell explained. "They do so because the houses there are modern,
as a rule, and are better in every way than are those which have
been discarded and turned over to their own group."

A situation involving racial ostracism that played out in 1895
affected the Daniel Murray family personally. Congress had decreed that due to health concerns, Graceland Cemetery, where the
remains of one-year-old Pinckney Murray and five-year-old Helene Murray had rested since 1890 and 1893, respectively, would
no longer allow interments and the bodies buried there would be
removed. The officials of the Graceland Cemetery Association
purchased land in Southeast Washington—to be known as Wood-
land Cemetery—to which bodies that were not claimed by relatives
for reburial elsewhere could be transferred. Graceland had been
incorporated in 1870 when a group of progressive white Washingtonians had bought thirty acres of land for an interracial cemetery.
Besides the Murrays, black elites who had purchased lots there included the Douglass, Wall, Grimké, Purvis, and Cromwell families. At variance with the parklike setting of Graceland, Woodlawn
was characterized as "nothing more than a potter's field," and too
distant from the city's center besides. Given that most cemeteries
in Washington now refused to accept black dead, for those like

Murray who found this new burial site unsuitable, this presented a dilemma.

Murray attended the gathering of disgruntled Graceland lot owners "protesting against the further removals of bodies" held at Metropolitan AME Church on July 23, 1895. "The Protective Association of Lot and Site Owners in Graceland Cemetery" completed its organization that evening, with Murray chosen as secretary and treasurer. At a meeting six weeks later, Murray reported that efforts were being made to locate a worthy burial place where "colored people . . . could deposit their deceased relatives." In the meantime lot owners had obtained an injunction restraining "disturbance of their dead." The injunction, however, was temporary. Counsel for plaintiffs Harrison Davis, Daniel Murray, John W. Cromwell, Wyatt Archer, Lewis Douglass, and seven other lot owners in equity case 16730 presented evidence from various angles in support of the injunction. Exhibit A was Murray's own deed identifying him as a lot owner "entitled to perpetual use." The lawyers for the Graceland Cemetery Association countered with their mix of arguments. On October 12, 1895, the chief justice of the District of Columbia Supreme Court ruled against the complainants, and the restraining order was dissolved.

Efforts to locate a more desirable burial ground willing to receive the bodies of African Americans for reinterment were fruitless, though appeal was made to more than thirty cemeteries. Woodlawn was the only option. The Murrays eventually relented, and the graves of their lost children were opened and their remains transferred to Woodlawn. The gruesome removal of Helene's body was especially painful. Because she had died of diphtheria, it was required that her body be "thoroughly wetted before removal from the grave with a solution of chloride of lime of the strength of one pound to each two gallons of water."[5]

As the 1890s continued, so did the trend toward increased exclusion. Acknowledging that black Washingtonians had lost ground was a slow and reluctant process. "Indignities had been heaped upon the colored people for years, but they had not awakened to the fact until . . . recently," observed the *Washington Post*. When, on October 30, 1892, T. Thomas Fortune, the editor of the *New York Age*, presented an address titled "Can the Afro-American race hold its place in American civilization?" at Second Baptist Church, the *Post* covered it. While recognizing that "further South it was worse," Fortune maintained that "There was more prejudice in Washington, under the dome of the Capitol, which was the bulwark of the Constitution, than the mind could measure." He pointed out that when he left the church that evening, if not for the hospitality of a local friend, "he would not know where to apply for food or lodging . . . without the possibility of meeting an insult."

Other activists spoke out as well. At the convention of the National Equal Rights Association held in Washington in May 1894, the committee on discrimination in the nation's capital issued a long list of grievances. The document stated that "Within the shadow of the dome of the Capitol no man can be convicted of murder if the victim be a negro and the criminal a white man, while the courts are swift and merciless in the punishment of colored persons." When, in July 1896, the Washington conference of the National Confederation of Afro-American Women was about to begin, an *Evening Star* reporter interviewed one of its spokeswomen. The unnamed clubwoman decried, "It cannot be denied that sentiment against the negro and his rights is growing rapidly. As the black man acquires money and education new barriers are raised against him; sometimes old obstacles . . . are being rebuilt."

But some leaders had a hard time admitting that the trend was real. A Treasury Department clerk and community activist, Andrew Hilyer, addressed the Bethel Literary and Historical Association on the subject of race prejudice in March 1892. "The anti-color feeling appears to be growing stronger, but this is not actually so," he claimed, even as he acknowledged that "invidious distinctions are made on account of color in public licensed hotels, dining halls, places of amusement" and "barriers are set up against us in the avenues of remunerative employment." Yet, he insisted, "The feeling is not getting stronger. We are getting nearer to the point of greatest resistance," and "short revivals of anti-color feeling" are to be expected in the course of breaking down that resistance.

John Mercer Langston, who had given his all to foster the rise of prospects for black Americans, was especially loath to concede to a backslide, even by 1897, when his young law partner, Thomas L. Jones, lost his suit against a Washington restaurant owner for denial of service, a violation of the local civil rights law of 1873. At the trial, "The defense challenged the two colored members of the jury panel, and white men took their places." After only forty minutes' deliberation, the jury found the defendant not guilty. It was at an assembly at Metropolitan AME Church, called to discuss the repercussions of this court defeat, that Langston offered his painfully poignant musings: "I have seen many changes in the advancement of the colored people in this country. Sometimes we seem to have reverses; our cause seems to go backward. Then we bestir ourselves more vigorously and undertake to educate public sentiment in our favor, and again we begin to move forward, better perhaps than ever before. . . . When Frederick Douglass was alive, how bright everything looked for us. Then we felt that the time would soon arrive when the rights of the negro would be universally respected, and that the white man would not in any quarter be considered superior to the negro."

Why did it take well over a decade from the date of the Wormley Agreement for black Washingtonians to experience the effects of the government's retreat from Reconstruction-era commitments? The time it took for African Americans in Congress, all representing southern states, to be replaced by white counterparts was one factor. Those new legislators, with their white supremacist

orientation, wielded political clout, not just with national legislation but, given that Congress controlled the District, locally as
well. They also, as was apparent in the Astwood incident, affected
the tone of everyday life for the city's blacks, importing their brand
of open, rabid racism.

When, in 1883, the US Supreme Court severely limited the interpretation of the national civil rights bill, wholesale panic among
District blacks was tempered by knowing that local antidiscrimination laws remained in effect. But it was now obvious from the
Jones case that those laws could not be relied on. Indeed, they were
silently dropped from future printings of DC's cumulative laws.

In 1896, another major blow came from the Supreme Court
with the *Plessy v. Ferguson* decision. Louisiana had passed a
separate-car act in 1890 that required railroads operating in the
state to segregate passengers on the basis of race, providing equal
but separate accommodations. Though the 1883 Supreme Court
decision had allowed discrimination by private businesses, it af-
firmed the Fourteenth Amendment's applicability to state violations of equal protection. Now the legality of segregation on public
facilities imposed by the state could be challenged, and opponents
decided to do just that. Homer Plessy, a Creole from New Orleans, was chosen as the test plaintiff. After purchasing a first-class
ticket, Plessy refused to sit in a Jim Crow car and was duly arrested
and charged. When the suit he brought reached the US Supreme
Court, it ruled that since the Louisiana law called for equal accommodations, even if separate, the equal protection clause had not
been violated. Again, the intent of the Constitution's Fourteenth
Amendment was undercut by the nation's highest court. The federal government could no longer be trusted as the African American's protector. Meanwhile, most white citizens in the nation who
had formerly supported the black man's rights grew quiet in his
cause. When the unidentified clubwoman voiced her concerns over

growing race bias to the *Evening Star* reporter in July 1896, she noted, "It is only to a few enlightened minds that the cause of the negro has any interest at all."

Given the repercussions of the *Plessy* case, the process of change for black citizens outside the South picked up steam. So did the attention of black elites: they traveled the country by train, so separate-car laws passed in southern states impacted them directly. Soon enough, well-to-do African Americans boarding a train in Washington would be forced to move to a Jim Crow car upon crossing into Virginia, no matter that they held first-class tickets. Those facilities, often the noisy coach nearest the engine and sometimes doubling as the baggage or smoking car, were notoriously inferior. The "equal" modifier in the "separate but equal" policy established by the *Plessy* decision was manifestly a ruse. Such humiliation was difficult to circumvent. Once at their destination elites commonly stayed in one another's homes to avoid possible discrimination at hotels, but traveling by train was the only option before automobiles were common.

Recognizing that they were not to be considered exceptions to the new rules was a bitter pill for Washington's black elites to swallow. They were used to a flexible color line that allowed for class and recoiled to see it tightened. Again and again, they attempted to keep the focus not on color but on "respectability." As the *Washington Bee* explained, "There are some colored people, as well as white, that ought not to be served in any respectable saloon, and why? Because of their very bad manners and their unkempt appearance." But as the 1890s drew to a close, the new order could no longer be denied. Andrew Hilyer himself articulated the fresh return of the old complaint: "White people have quite unanimously agreed to class all Afro-Americans together. No matter how light colored they may be or how intelligent, cultured, or wealthy, they have determined that all shall be subject to the same proscriptions and discriminations."[6]

A determination to block the backward slide was imperative. Who would lead the call? Frederick Douglass had passed away in 1895. John Mercer Langston had died shortly after the defeat in the Jones civil rights case. Buried at Woodlawn cemetery, he had been followed there by Blanche Bruce a few months later. The seasoned race men Pinckney Pinchback and John R. Lynch were still active. George H. White was currently serving in Congress. Daniel and Anna Murray were among the Washington community leaders who would pick up their game and expand their stage, while new activists emerged on both the local and national scene. All were ready to act but were not necessarily in concert on how best to reverse the eroding status of African American citizens.

Among a diversity of approaches, most race leaders sanctioned one avenue to power: increased economic solidarity and self-sufficiency. If white people were "determined to make them rise or fall together," black people would be obliged to develop, through mutual support, control of the economic factors that would ensure their collective livelihood and well-being. They would need to enter into every channel of business and build their own banks, factories, and stores.

Difficulties for blacks in establishing successful new enterprises in the past had included securing capital and contending with a lack of patronage, even among those of their own color. In May 1890, for example, Howard University's alumni association was called out by the *Washington Bee* when a white caterer was hired for a special event instead of a colored counterpart and low bidder, Emanuel E. Murray (no relation to the Daniel Murray family).

Then there was the sticky complication of race discrimination evidenced in black-owned businesses. Back in 1887, an African American justice of the peace, E. M. Hewlett, had claimed in a newspaper editorial that "There is not a hotel or restaurant in this city, kept by a colored man, where . . . every respectable and well-behaved person could not be served," but that was no longer the case come the 1890s. Discrimination imposed by black businessmen increased over that decade as proprietors of barbershops, restaurants, and other facilities, ostensibly open to the public, drew the color line. Caterer Emanuel E. Murray's establishment included dining and ice cream parlors, and in 1891 he himself was accused of "discriminating against his own race." Murray claimed he lost money admitting black customers because of the resultant loss of white ones. The *Bee* expressed understanding: "In view of the relentless warfare now being waged against Murray would it not be well to remember that the white people of this country set the standards for us in the matter of race discrimination? . . . As long as a considerable number of white people in this city demand a separate dining room there will be colored men who will supply that demand." A commentator on the scene likewise observed, "This latent spirit of discrimination would be found to exist in a proprietor no matter what his color, provided the great mass of his customers were white."

In 1896, the restaurateur S. G. Thompson "opened a first-class dining parlor" and tried to do the right thing by accommodating "respectable people of all classes and nationalities." However, Thompson rented his space and his white landlord informed him that "he didn't want negroes served in his dining room; in fact his place was too good for colored people." Thompson was highly insulted, but when he insisted that "he would serve any respectable person for his money," his landlord threatened to eject him.

Notwithstanding such conflicts and complications and despite the risks and challenges, new efforts were made to encourage businesspeople to establish commercial entities that hired black employees and relied on black customers, and African Americans at large to support those enterprises. Cooperating out of race coherence and loyalty, both proprietors and patrons would attain economic independence. *Why give your money to white businesses that will not hire you and, when they serve you at all, do so only in degrading or limited ways?* If alternatives were provided, black people could not only circumvent stigmatization at white-run concerns but gain new opportunities for jobs and shopping venues and keep their money in their home communities.

8

CONFRONTING LOST GROUND

PARALLEL INSTITUTIONS COULD BE DEVELOPED IN COM-
merce and other aspects of black life, but there was no possibility of constructing an alternate political system. Race leaders
coalesced in the goal of full citizenship as granted in the Constitution's Reconstruction amendments. Two torchbearers who
moved in the same circles as black intellectuals and activists in the
nation's capital, Professors Booker T. Washington and W. E. B.
DuBois, gained national prominence in the 1890s promoting different pathways to reach that goal. Washington was the founder
and principal of Tuskegee Institute in Alabama. Known for his
ideology of accommodation to white privilege, he was willing to
embargo the push for political equality while the black man advanced his economic security. As a means to that end he promoted
mechanical training like that offered at Tuskegee. DuBois, twelve
years younger than Washington and the first African American to
earn a Harvard PhD, was, by the late 1890s, teaching at Atlanta
University. He did not disagree with Washington on the value of
economic advancement or industrial education, but he thoroughly
rejected his gradualism when it came to demanding full rights. He
viewed the vote as the primary badge of citizenship, agreeing with

Senator Charles Sumner, who had asserted long before that there "was no substantial protection for the freedman except in the franchise." He also resented Washington's conservative philosophy of accommodation; he favored a protest ideology.

Stances among leaders varied on a host of other race matters as well. Andrew Hilyer thought that prejudice "increases as the two races come in contact and measure arms with each other"; while Mary Church Terrell believed the opposite. Intermarriage with whites, black emigration, and race separatism were other issues on which opinions diverged. On the other hand, in many cases there was no conflict in pursuing multiple advancement strategies together, even as their emphasis and priority were debated. Industrial training and liberal education were not mutually exclusive options, for example; nor were self-help and government concessions.

All activists recognized the power of organization. Diversity of viewpoint was one thing; fractiousness due to ego or personal animosities that got in the way of unified action was another. Taming the captiousness of leading personalities and untangling a web of perspectives in order to establish a progressive movement would be a challenge. T. Thomas Fortune lamented, "Whenever you get half a dozen Afro-Americans together to accomplish anything you have the elements of a big row. Each man wants to boss the job himself. Until we learn how to stand shoulder to shoulder . . . we can accomplish nothing."[1]

➤ ◄

ON DECEMBER 29, 1898, THE FIRST TRULY NATIONWIDE CIVIL rights organization in the United States, the National Afro-American Council (NAAC), convened in Washington, DC. Fortune, prompted by AME Zion Bishop Alexander Walters, had put his money where his mouth was. He had tried before to form an organization bent on ameliorating race relations, but his Afro-American League had failed to generate momentum and had collapsed. The NAAC was conceived on September 15, 1898, in Rochester, New York, by a small group of activists who decided "not to reorganize the old league, but to form a new one." The two leaders, Fortune and Walters, both born slaves in the South, now lived in New York and New Jersey, respectively, and presented a contrast in type. Fortune, called Tim by his friends, was an often acerbic journalist; he tended to be erratic, excitable, and rash and was the more radical of the two. Walters, the charismatic clergyman, was even-tempered and a skilled organizer. The council was designed to succeed as a national organization where the league and other efforts had failed. Learning from past mistakes, it aimed to form local branch chapters, rally the support of the "Negro masses," act continuously between meetings, establish firm financial footing, seek press coverage, and attack southern discrimination directly.

On November 1, Alexander Walters, the NAAC president (Fortune having declined the office), called for a conference in Washington in late December to complete the council's organization and formulate a plan of action. The council was inaugurated against a backdrop of increasing denial of African American political participation and a growing rate of lynchings in the South. The impulse to organize had been galvanized by an atrocity that had occurred in February in Lake City, South Carolina, where Postmaster Frazier Baker had been harassed for months because white citizens resented the appointment of a black man to supervise the post office. In the predawn hours of February 22, a lynch mob set fire to the post office that doubled as the Baker home and shot at the family as they attempted to flee the burning building, killing the postmaster and his two-year-old daughter, Julia. Walters warned in response that it was "absolutely necessary that we organize for self-protection." Between the NAAC's creation in September and the conference scheduled for the end of the year, another ghastly outrage occurred. Beginning on November 10, a white mob of at least a thousand armed insurgents in Wilmington, North Carolina's largest city, overthrew the legally elected interracial local government by force, violently attacked black citizens at large, and chased hundreds out of town.

Even before the Wilmington race riot further aroused activists, a District NAAC chapter was formed, with Edward E. Cooper, the editor of the *Colored American*, as its president. Local Council No. 1 handled the arrangements for the December conference. Daniel Murray served on the invitations committee. The Rochester meeting had not been largely attended; the notice given had been short, and many potential attendees had found the location too far north. This time there was ample notice, and the event was in a more central location. "Afro-American men and women from all parts of the United States who are interested in the future welfare of their race" were invited to converge on the nation's capital on December 29. Murray and the other members of the invitations committee must be credited with the broad spectrum of participants—journalists, educators, lawyers, politicians, government officials, clergy, and community activists—who came from far and wide. The head of the program committee, lawyer and sociologist Jesse Lawson, held a meeting at his home on December 19 at which the chairmen of the local arrangements committees finalized plans.

The first annual meeting of the NAAC, presided over by Bishop Walters, was designed to "eclipse any previous assemblies for racial organization." The program listed day and evening sessions for Thursday, December 29, and Friday, December 30. Meeting at Metropolitan Baptist Church (not to be confused with Metropolitan AME Church), "an audience of over a thousand colored people crowded the main floor and galleries" for many of the sessions. Among the "race's 'stars' " on the program were Paul Laurence Dunbar ("The Negro in the Department of Letters"), Ida Wells-Barnett ("Mob Violence and Anarchy"), Kelly Miller ("Higher

Education"), E. E. Cooper ("Influence of the Press"), T. Thomas Fortune ("Our Economic Status"), Pinckney Pinchback ("The Negro in the Nation's Wars"), and Booker T. Washington ("Industrial Education"). The last address was scheduled for Friday, with Murray among those set to respond, but Washington sent regrets at the last minute.

Alexander Walters was reelected president and Ida Wells-Barnett secretary. The newly constituted executive committee was composed of two representatives from each of thirty-nine states (of forty-five total) plus the District of Columbia. Daniel Murray and E. E. Cooper represented the District. Other members of the executive committee who were close Murray associates included T. Thomas Fortune, Cyrus Field Adams, Pinckney Pinchback, John R. Lynch, Jesse Lawson, and George H. White; all were current Washington residents or regular visitors but represented the states from which they hailed. The executive committee in turn appointed a fifteen-member steering committee, "the real working force of the organization," to "assume charge of the work until the next National conference." This group was further narrowed to a three-member subcommittee: George H. White, Daniel Murray, and Cyrus Field Adams were allotted the power to act for the executive committee "in all matters of legislation."

The Address to the Nation, adopted by the NAAC on December 30, described eight areas of concern. The first five named growing problems concentrated in the South: attempts to eliminate the black man from politics via new state constitutions intended to disenfranchise him, lynchings and other violent forms of lawlessness, degrading separate-car laws, the horrors of convict camps and other prisoner abuses in penal institutions, and the inadequacy of schooling for black children. Each was accompanied by suggestions for redress. The remaining three items were recommendations for black Americans. The NAAC promoted both industrial and higher education, encouraged business enterprises of all sorts, and supported migration from the South to states where law was respected but not immigration to foreign countries ("We shall remain here and fight out our destiny in the land of our fathers"). The address was submitted to President McKinley the next day. The audience that Alexander Walters and twenty-some members of the executive committee, including Murray, had with the President was initially assessed "quite satisfactory." Disappointment followed, however, when the delegation "could get no public statement" on their cause issued by McKinley.[2]

"A banquet in honor of Congressman George H. White is being arranged, and the function promises to be . . . a social reunion of 'giants,' " the *Colored American* announced two weeks before the event. "It will be designed as a message to the country, testifying to the race's appreciation of Mr. White's masterly services, and pledging the support of a solid constituency in the struggles that are to come." White, the sole remaining black congressman, had been narrowly reelected in November. On the evening of January 3, 1899, "Negroes of national repute gathered around the banquet board" at the Delmo-Koonce banquet hall on the ground floor of Odd Fellows Hall, decorated with "banks of roses and the American colors." The tables were "embellished with pyramids of fruit," and the elaborate menu consisted of eight courses. "The dinner was a race affair, from top to bottom," observed the *Colored American*. "It was in honor of a colored leader, attended wholly by colored guests, served by a colored caterer in a building owned by the colored Old Fellows and managed and paid for by colored citizens." More than sixty gentlemen attended the fete. When Representative White rose to speak, they "stood, cheered and waved their handkerchiefs." The banquet "was a glorious success, and a fitting climax to the practical work of the National Afro-American Council of the previous week." Daniel Murray, one of the subscribers, served on the committee of arrangements, and responded at the dinner to the toast, "The President of the United States."

Then Murray got to work. On January 25, he contributed an article on the purpose of the NAAC to the *Evening Star*. His communication, he claimed at the outset, referring to various rumors about the organization, "was an authoritative statement." He reviewed some of the issues in the NAAC's Address to the Nation. In summary, the council's goal was "to secure all the benefits of compact organization . . . to get for the negro in this country a fair and honest hearing for his cause [and] appeal to the Christian hearts and consciences of the American people to aid him in securing justice." He anticipated the time "when the blindness of prejudice is cured." Meanwhile, "A man who would manifest his prejudice by introducing a bill curtailing or in any manner restricting the rights and privileges of the colored race would be a marked man." Murray looked to the present administration to "remove obnoxious restrictions upon travel and suffrage." In expanding on railroad segregation and the wish "to prevent any person's prejudice being satisfied at the expense of the entire community," he did not refrain from playing the class card. Echoing the stated stance of the NAAC, he backed a system whereby patrons would pay "according to their means and intelligence, those who like exclusiveness paying first-class fare, others second or third. Nine-tenths of the colored people would take third-class because of its cheapness." He underscored the NAAC's lack of party orientation ("If the colored voters' attitude were uncertain . . . the republicans would be obliged to win his vote and not be able to count it as assured") and the importance of forming branch councils. He also noted that "women are eligible for membership and are expected to be powerful agencies for the work" (in the coming months a female would be added to each state's representation on the executive committee).

Murray was a prime player on Washington's branch council,

too. He presided over a meeting of Local Council No. 1 four days
after his *Evening Star* article appeared. Jesse Lawson, referring in
his opening comments to the NAAC marking the beginning of a
new era for black Americans, now "united in their demand for fair
play, and for equal rights and equal protection . . . under the ae-
gis of the law," delivered a speech that struck so many memorable
notes that the assembly voted to adopt it as a public address. "We
are ten million souls and all native-born," Lawson intoned. "We
are Americans in every fibre of our being, and we have the aspirations common to the citizens of this Republic." Two of the issues
discussed at the meeting were the need for more participation in
the District government and the lack of any representation on the
US Congress's Industrial Commission.

Murray addressed both those matters in his subsequent report
to the national organization. The NAAC had created various departmental bureaus, with Murray appointed director of the legal
and legislative bureau (other bureaus included literary, emigration,
and business). In March 1899, he submitted his first bureau report
(known from drafts in his papers). The bureau's letterhead gave the
address of the "Office of Director" as 934 S Street, Murray's own
home. George H. White was the bureau's general counsel, and
Murray recruited sixteen other men (including his brother-in-law,
Bostonian Butler R. Wilson) as assistant counselors. Murray's report elaborated on three current issues.

One was the local concern over the near exclusion from representation in the DC government, despite the fact that Washingtonians of color constituted a third of the population (one
major exception was Henry P. Cheatham, appointed the District's
recorder of deeds by McKinley). In his *Star* article, Murray had
advised African Americans to "look more carefully after those
exercising the power of appointment," adding, "If we are fairly
treated we will be given recognition in offices in accordance with
our deserts, and we will not have to beg for it." The local council

had called for suffrage to be restored to Washington residents and more black candidates to be appointed to District offices, in particular a judge on the municipal court bench, an assistant district attorney, and at least one representative on the Board of Assessors. In his bureau report Murray singled out the last, noting "The Republican Commissioners in the District of Columbia, appointed by a Republican President, used the power placed in their hand to deny to the 90,000 colored citizens of Washington a representative on the Board of Assessors . . . the first time in thirty years that such a condition has [occurred] under a Republican administration." As an ambitious District resident, Murray could always be counted on to warm up to this subject.

The other two issues were wider in scope. In June 1898, Congress had created a nonpartisan, nineteen-member Industrial Commission. "Notwithstanding the united and persistent effort made," noted Murray in his report, the commission had failed to include a single black member. Agreeing with the local council's insistence that "fully 95 per cent of our race belongs to the industrial forces in America and the labor problem cannot be solved without considering us as a factor," the report continued, "To cure this serious omission, your Director prepared the following bill." Murray inserted in full a bill outlining provisions for a "Freedmen's Inquiry Commission," creating a five-member commission "to make a comprehensive investigation of the condition of the people of the Negro race in the United States, their relation to the labor problem, their industrial status, their educational progress, and the best means of promoting harmony between the races." After having the proposed bill reviewed by several congressmen, Murray saw that "a copy was laid before the President of the United States." Murray requested the full council's approval.

The next issue was connected to the NAAC's goal of lobbying Congress to uphold the Reconstruction amendments. One way of addressing this, and the one the council had recommended in its Address to the Nation, was to secure, in Murray's words, "a law reducing the representation in the Congress and electoral college of such states as have bogus constitutions sought to deprive American citizens of constitutional rights and at the same time enjoying representation based upon their enumeration." Where the right to vote was denied or abridged, a corresponding reduction in representation was mandatory under section 2 of the Fourteenth Amendment. "In the Southern States, where from 40 to 60 percent of the population is disfranchised by state law, the change would be radical," estimated the *New York Evening Post*, "South Carolina, for instance, would come up to Congress with three Representatives instead of seven, as at present." The timing for pushing diminution seemed propitious. The twelfth census would be conducted in 1900, and fresh data quantifying the discrepancy could be gathered. After consultation with George White, Murray communicated, by letter and in person, with the congressional chairman of the census committee and the director of the census. He requested an amendment to the census bill that would require tabulation of the number of persons currently qualified to vote in each state along with the total number of male citizens over the age of twenty-one. After initiating his efforts, he realized that he had a like-minded ally in Congressman Edgar Crumpacker from Indiana, a member of the census committee. On February 4, Crumpacker "introduced a bill embodying the essential features of the Bureau's amendment." Like Murray, Crumpacker saw expanded census data collection as "the first step in the movement to reduce the representation of the states which have disfranchised a large portion of their former voters." Not all race leaders approved of the strategy since it acquiesced to the loss of voting rights rather than demanded that they be restored. But reduction would "break up the menace of the solid South," and Murray recommended that the council endorse the Crumpacker bill.

In addition to contesting injustice through national legislation, the NAAC was determined to directly "test the constitutionality of laws which are made for the express purpose of oppressing" African Americans. Though not mentioned in Murray's report, a fourth issue the bureau was working on was the exploration of a basis for a constitutional test case challenging disenfranchisement of black voters in the South. Murray likely mentioned this in a letter to Alexander Walters that preceded his March report, since February 25, 1899, is the date of a reply from Walters, reading, "I endorse most heartily every word of your letter, especially your plan to secure a good case." Starting with Mississippi in 1890, southern states had contrived new constitutions aimed at disenfranching African American voters. The relevant section of the Louisiana Constitution of 1898, establishing literacy and property requirements, was accompanied by a clause that read, "Literacy and property tests for registering to vote will not be given to any individuals whose fathers or grandfathers were legally entitled to vote on January 1, 1867." Since no black man in the state had been entitled to vote by that date, blacks were largely excluded from this so-called grandfather clause. Contending that "Suffrage is a federal guarantee, and not a privilege to be conferred or withheld by the state," challenging the grandfather clause was one way to force the nation to uphold the Fourteenth and Fifteenth Amendments.

Daniel Murray would pursue those four issues for years to come. Why was Murray chosen as director of the NAAC's legal and legislative bureau? Though he was not a lawyer, Walters had found him the man "best suited" to take charge. Murray was an active community participant in the seat of the federal government and knew many lawmakers personally but, in keeping with the NAAC's nonpartisan status, was not a politician. He also had, as he wrote his friend George Myers, "considerable experience in drawing bills for legislative purposes" and access to research at the Library of Congress. There, when he had been detailed to the Law Library early in his tenure, Murray had become "well grounded in the principles of the law." Moreover, according to his coworker Edwin Lee, Murray had an "amazing talent joined to a constancy of mind, self-possession and untiring energy that insures success, if possible, in spite of every obstacle." In addition to his work ethic, he was especially motivated by desiring, as he wrote to the journalist and race leader John E. Bruce, to do something of "lasting benefit to my race."

Alexander Walters came to Washington to conduct a meeting of the national steering committee and officers of the DC branch council on April 7, 1899. "The Bishop expressed himself as fully satisfied with what has been accomplished, and confesses that results even at this early date have far exceeded his most sanguine expectations," reported the *Colored American*. While Walters and Fortune were in town, articles incorporating the National Afro-American Council were placed on record. In addition to those two men, Murray was one of the other twelve incorporators.[3]

→ ←

ANNA MURRAY WAS NOT ABOUT TO BE LEFT OUT OF WORKING for the race. She served on the Associate Committee of Ladies at the NAAC conference in December 1898, despite the arrival of a new baby boy four months earlier. Forty-year-old Anna had given birth to Paul Evans Murray at home on August 28. Like her husband, Anna was very active in the new year and not put off by the record-breaking "Great Blizzard" of February 1899. "There are no local precedents for this storm which has Washington in its grip," the *Evening Star* reported on February 13, "After a week of snowing and low temperatures the city is visited by a blizzard which has brought high winds and, thus far, about sixteen inches of snow in addition." The capital was again hosting the National Congress of Mothers convention, which was scheduled to begin on February 14, but given "the paralysis of almost all the street car lines, the general blockage of the streets and the crippled condition of the telephone service," it was postponed for two days. Among the delegates who "braved the terrors of snow-blocked streets" were Helen Cook and Anna Murray from the Colored Woman's League and Mary Church Terrell, representing the National Association of Colored Women. All three spoke on the last day of the conference, February 18. CWL president Helen Cook discussed the accomplishments of the league, including the updated number of kindergartens supported by the public school system (sixteen: ten white, six colored), the training school for kindergarten teachers, and the day nurseries for the children of working mothers. The chairman of the league's kindergarten committee, who "bore a conspicuous part" in the successes Cook detailed, spoke next. Anna Murray, according to *Kindergarten Magazine*, gave one of the "most stirring addresses" of the conference, stressing the importance of kindergartens. "The seed time must be taken for character sowing," she insisted, "not the harvest time." Terrell, too, addressed early childhood intervention; in reference to "the prejudice and discrimination against the colored race," she "urged the mothers to teach their children to recognize no distinction except that which is based on merit."

Like the missions of the CWL and NACW in general, Anna's activities became more overtly political. Educated black clubwomen were increasingly aware that their reform efforts involved political struggle. Anna would now confront race issues by name and identify her cause as one of them. She would write articles for newspapers and magazines and embrace the role of "race speaker," traveling to conferences and meetings in states across the country to deliver her message: proper home training and early childhood education were keys to race progress. She agreed with Mary Church Terrell's assertion that "The real solution of the race problem lies in the children, both so far as we who are oppressed and those who oppress us are concerned."

Terrell minced no words in articulating the challenge for

elite clubwomen. To live up to the NACW motto, "Lifting as We Climb," meant "coming into closer touch with the masses of our women, by whom, whether we will or not, the world will always judge the womanhood of the race. Even though we wish to shun them, and hold ourselves entirely aloof from them, we cannot escape the consequences of their acts. So, that, if the call of duty were disregarded altogether, policy and self-preservation would demand that we go down among the lowly . . . to whom we are bound by the ties of race and sex, and put forth every effort to uplift and reclaim them."

Despite Terrell's bare mention of the "call of duty," sympathetic and sincere concern for their less fortunate sisters did motivate elite clubwomen (though few literally went "down among the lowly"), but their sense of noblesse oblige was now balanced by recognition that their own advancement was tied to the progress of blacks at large. Among "efforts put forth for the elevation of women of the race," Anna maintained that instilling values and character in early childhood was the "one safe, sure guide . . . to remove the cause of the many accusations that have been made against us as a race." Believing that "it is the women of the South who stand in the greatest need of our help," she determined, "now that my work is firmly secured in Washington," to turn "my strongest energy toward planting it in the Southland."

A National Congress of Mothers convention was scheduled for the latter part of May 1900 in Des Moines, Iowa. A Kansas City black newspaper announced that Anna E. Murray, a "colored women of national prominence," would take the platform and disclosed that "Mrs. Murray's photograph shows a very beautiful woman with snow white hair that makes her face appear young," adding that it revealed "not the faintest trace . . . of her colored ancestry." A thousand people attended the congress, which started May 21. Domiciled during her time in Iowa at the home of "one of

Des Moines wealthiest and most prominent citizens," Anna "was delightfully entertained by the colored women of Des Moines" over the days of the convention.

The *Iowa State Bystander*, a voice for that state's black residents, devoted a major article to Anna's speech under the headline "An Elegant Address Before the Congress," claiming it was "the feature which at yesterday forenoon's session attracted widest attention." Her topic, as listed in the program, was colored women's clubs, but as the *Bystander* piece noted, "This theme served rather as a starting point from which, without entirely dissociating her argument from the subject, she entered on a discussion of the race problem generally." Speaking "without notes, easily, slowly and most impressively" and "with the deep conviction that her message was an important one," Anna said she was dedicated to "the work of home-building among the colored people," who, under slavery, "were the victims of a ruthless violation of family sanctity." Since "the children of the race are the fathers and mothers to be, the citizens to be," kindergarten teachers must be trained and sent "throughout the length and breadth of the southland." Unschooled people of color must be lifted up, "and this can only be done by beginning with the child." That, she concluded earnestly, "is the solution to the race question."

Anna "was applauded frequently, and her address plainly touched a sympathetic chord in the hearts of the audience." At the close of the session both white and black women pressed forward to the platform to meet her. Anna was "overwhelmed with hearty congratulations." Weeks after the event, "many complimentary echoes" were still being heard. Anna's participation in the convention was covered not only in the Iowa newspapers but also in those of Indiana, Kansas, Ohio, Minnesota, Nebraska, and of course Washington. Anna Murray, according to the *Colored American*, "made one of the most forceful speeches of the convention, which for eloquence, logic, sound judgement and pathos will stand as one of the most important utterances which has fallen from the lips of any race speaker in recent years."[4]

The same newspaper remarked that "a commendable feature" of the National Congress of Mothers was its "freedom from race prejudice." Just two weeks after Anna's speech at the congress, a color-line incident marred the convention in Milwaukee of another national women's organization, the General Federation of Women's Clubs. Anna's "happy experience and royal welcome at the Des Moines Mothers' Congress" was "in glowing contrast to the Milwaukee Federation fiasco." Josephine St. Pierre Ruffin, one of the four thousand clubwomen who converged on Milwaukee the first week of June 1900, was the central figure in the controversy. Ruffin had founded the New Era Club in 1873 (first called the Woman's Era Club, in 1896 it became part of the NACW). "An intelligent and highly educated woman," Ruffin, approaching sixty, was "attractive in appearance, being very light in color, and having a soft pompadour of gray hair." Ruffin, the widow of George Ruffin, the first African American municipal judge, and those in her Boston circle, which included Anna's sister Mary and her husband, Butler Wilson, were accustomed to interacting with white Bostonians, even socially.

The New Era Club belonged to the General Federation of Women's Clubs, and Ruffin had the certificate of membership to prove it. On her arrival she was issued a badge after showing her credentials, but minutes later, upon "the discovery that Mrs. Ruffin was a negress," it was demanded that she return it. As the representative of a predominantly black club, she was refused a seat at the convention. Most of the enmity came from the southern contingent, which wanted to amend the federation's constitution by inserting the word "white" before "clubs." Many members from other sections disapproved of Ruffin's ejection but thought it "wise to take no action in the matter, owing to the bitterness of the feeling of the southern states," and were not willing "to do anything that threatens disruption of the Federation." Ruffin resisted her exclusion, initially refusing to surrender her badge, but eventually left to fight another day. "It is the high-caste negroes who bring about all the ill feeling," the federation president, Rebecca D. Lowe of Georgia, pointed out. "The ordinary colored woman understands her position thoroughly."

Anna was one of "a number of educators of national prominence" invited to present papers on various aspects of "the status of the race" at the fourth annual Hampton Negro Conference, which commenced on July 18, 1900. Hampton Normal and Agricultural Institute, an industrial and teacher-training school in Hampton, Virginia, founded "for the education of Negro young men and women" three decades earlier, sponsored the event. Conferees were "handsomely entertained during their stay" with a reception as well as diversions such as boating, sailing, fishing, and bathing. Anna was scheduled to give a presentation on "The Kindergarten," but again her remarks took a political turn, and when the conference proceedings were published in Hampton's journal, the *Southern Workman*, in September 1900, her address appeared with the title "A New Key to the Situation." That key was "education of the right kind and at the right time," namely early childhood. That, Anna asserted, would be "the sure solution of America's gravest problem—the race problem." Wishing to widen the scope and influence of the kindergarten and with particular interest in "the children of the Southland," she advocated training kindergarten teachers for that section. She had already "supplied a call for two teachers in the South," and now proposed that competent young women be recruited from black institutions such as Tuskegee and Hampton for training in Washington, the school there to serve as a supply station for kindergarten teachers. "I have a bill prepared which I shall at the proper time present to Congress," she announced; it called for the appropriation of "$1,000,000 to each of the Southern States—for the establishment of kindergartens, equally among black and white children—$1,000,000 to be reserved for the support of the training school in Washington." Anna's request for congressional funding was a tall order. Meanwhile, private donations, including additional generous gifts from Phoebe Hearst, continued to support the training school. (In 1901, it would be incorporated as the National Kindergarten Training School, with Phoebe Hearst as president and Anna Murray as secretary.)

Among African Americans active on the lecture circuit, Anna, noted for the excellence of her diction and delivery, was considered one of "the best women orators of the present day." She gave many talks in Washington and was a regular participant in the Bethel Literary and Historical Association. In October 1900, she was on the road again. The *Colored American* announced, "Mrs. Anna J. Murray, whose scholarly and magnetic addresses on kindergarten work have attracted much attention at the hands of the press and leading men and women of both races, will shortly make a tour of the middle West in the interest of her noble cause."

Anna revisited Des Moines by special request. Her earlier trip there had inspired results. The president of the local Mothers' Club had used the impact of Anna's visit as a recruiting tool, while another group of women had formed the Anna Murray Aid Society. Anna delivered remarks before the white Woman's Christian Temperance Union in Des Moines and also in Chicago, the city she proceeded to next. She was invited to speak to the Chicago Women's Club and the Women's Club of Evanston, "the two swell clubs of the state." Her ten-day stay in Illinois was "almost wholly among the white people, since they have arranged each day's program." She received invitations from the Chicago Institute and the Armour Institute of Technology, two of the most prestigious and liberal educational institutions in the city. The Chicago Institute was a new private experimental school for kindergarten through

the academic grades, as well as for the training of teachers (it became the University of Chicago School of Education the year after
Anna's visit). The Armour Institute, where Anna was a guest at a
dinner and evening reception, emphasized practical education and
included a department of kindergartens.

Daniel Murray was supportive and proud of his wife's acknowledged place as a pioneer of early childhood education. "Mrs. Murray numbers among her friends Mrs. Phoebe Hearst, a very rich
woman who . . . has now arranged with Mrs. Murray to give to the
colored girls the same training [as white ones]," he informed his
friend George Myers, "This will strengthen the whole scheme by
equipping a sufficient corps of teachers who can go South and extend the system to the teeming millions of that benighted land."
Elsewhere, he boasted of Anna's "phenomenal success" as promoter of the kindergarten: "She has been most active and zealous
in bringing its benefits as a factor to solve the race problem to the
notice of the colored people of the United States," adding, with
a touch of hyperbole, that his wife had become "widely known
among educators throughout the world."[5]

9

NATIONAL AFRO-AMERICAN
COUNCIL

B Y THE CLOSE OF 1898, MANY RACE LEADERS WERE BECOM-
ing disenchanted with the McKinley administration. The
President was not stepping up to the plate on issues of importance
to African Americans. He had undertaken no action to combat
lynchings and had been "silent on the outrages" that had occurred
in the Carolinas and elsewhere. His annual message to Congress
on December 5, 1898, contained no words of encouragement for
black Americans. He was focused on reconciliation with the South.
"It will be my constant aim to do nothing, and permit nothing to
be done, that will arrest or disturb this growing sentiment of unity
and cooperation," he pledged, "but I shall do everything possible
to promote and increase it." The diminution of sectional animos-
ity that the President sought came at the price of African American equality. During the NAAC's December 1898 Washington
conference, several participants were quoted in the newspapers as
expressing their disappointment in McKinley. Executive committee member H. C. C. Astwood, ex-minister to San Domingo and
the injured party in the earlier Riggs House incident, claimed that
"they were all angry because the President failed to say anything
relative to the race troubles in his message," adding, "If he did not

say something shortly he would be derelict in his duty." The council president himself, Alexander Walters, lamented, "The President of the United States, whose duty it is to see that the citizens are protected, has abandoned us to our fate." The day the NAAC conference commenced, a black delegation from Pennsylvania called on McKinley "to protest against lynching and race riots in the South" and "to urge . . . the enactment of legislation looking to the prevention of such crimes." McKinley, in a typical response when face-to-face with disgruntled black citizens, breezily "assured his visitors that none of them regretted the troubles more than he, and that the entire machinery of the Government had been put in motion to run down the perpetrators of the most recent outrages."

In an article in the *Evening Star* of January 25, 1899, Daniel Murray refused to criticize the President in the name of the NAAC, an organization that—despite "the utterances of some of its members"—did not "arise from hostility to the present administration." He reminded his readers that McKinley had two more years in office and one ought not to "render a verdict on the administration before all the evidence is in." That might have been his public statement, but in fact he, too, was frustrated with the President. His attitude toward McKinley was mixed in with his own ambition. Murray had attempted, without success, to secure an assistant assessor appointment in 1894. Four years later he tried again. As a "student of public economy who has given full consideration on the subject," he penned a letter to the editor of the *Evening Star* to counter the view that large business properties in the city were being underassessed. Published on January 17, 1898, his letter argued that those who would heavily tax such enterprises neglected to consider the jobs and other benefits that came with investment of capital. Having shown off his expertise in the field, he presented himself as a candidate for assistant assessor two months later.

The four-year terms of the current assistant assessors (a position that paid $3,000 per year) were set to expire in August, though they could be renewed. "Daniel Murray, a well-known colored man, is reported to be strongly backed for a place on the board, and it is claimed that he is the originator of the bill providing for the board of permanent assessors," reported the *Evening Star*, "It is also claimed by his friends that he was promised the place four years ago." Murray's friends and associates were indeed "making strenuous efforts to have him appointed." A delegation of black men called on the district commissioners on the morning of July 27 and presented petitions endorsing Murray for assistant assessor: "Mr. Murray would be very pleasing to the colored people of the District, as he is a man who enjoys not only their respect and confidence, but also that of the white population." As it turned out, neither Murray nor any of his African American competitors got the job; rather, the incumbents were reappointed.

Murray was still chafing over this months later when he submitted his first NAAC bureau report and referenced the issue of exclusion from District affairs. Employing almost the same language, he complained to George Myers in June 1899: "We are struggling in Washington to secure some representation in the District government. . . . I would like you to write the President and ask him to insist that the Commissioners who are his appointees give us a seat on the Board of Assessment and Taxation. This is the first Republican administration for thirty years that we did not have representation in the Assessment Board. Sen. Hanna told me we were to have it." Murray elaborated on the discontent engendered by lack of sufficient representation in the city government in letters to his Ohio friend throughout the summer, claiming that Washingtonians of color considered the slight "evidence of unfriendliness and indifference on the part of the administration towards its faithful friends in the late election." He continued, "The feeling here is very bitter and the people say they will do all in their power to induce their friends in the states of Ohio, Maryland and

Kentucky to remain away from the polls, or make terms with the Democrats. . . . I would not be surprised to see the Afro-American Council pass a resolution of condemnation if the action of the Commissioners is not amended."

Murray expressed confidence that a letter from Myers "would have great influence," and "one word" from the President in turn would "secure the desired end." With Ohioans McKinley and Mark Hanna, now a US senator, in power in Washington, Myers's influence extended to the White House and Capitol. If Myers was, as the *New York Times* described him, one of the "close personal as well as political friends of the President," he was closer yet to fellow Clevelander Hanna, whom he referred to affectionately as "Uncle Mark." Myers repeatedly declined their offers of appointed national office in return for his yeoman's service to the GOP, preferring his role as behind-the-scenes politico. He advised McKinley in his appointments of African Americans to federal posts, and he now lent his support to Murray's cause for increased patronage at the District level and urged his connections to do the same. Myers wrote to Murray in August 1899 that with so many people bringing the matter to the President's attention, it "gives him no excuse for taking any middle ground." Excuse or no, whether McKinley would intervene in District affairs on behalf of Washingtonians of color remained to be seen.[1]

Murray and his colleagues' incipient ire with the McKinley administration was initially raised because of limited use of black troops and appointment of black officers in the Spanish-American War. On April 25, 1898, barely a year after McKinley became commander in chief, the United States declared war on Spain, provoked by the sinking, due to a massive explosion (the cause of which was never determined), of the battleship USS *Maine* in Havana harbor two months earlier. The battleship had purportedly been sent to the port because the United States objected to the repressive measures Spain was taking to suppress Cuba's rebellion against its rule. But once in, the United States fought for domination in place of Spain in two theaters of action, Cuba and the Philippines. In the latter place, Admiral George Dewey scored an early decisive victory on May 1, when he decimated the Spanish fleet in Manila harbor.

Even before war was officially declared, George H. White, speaking in the House of Representatives, pledged, "The black phalanx is ready to be mustered in." There were four segregated regiments in the standing army, and they were dispatched to Cuba with white officers in command, lieutenant being the highest rank allotted to black men. Tens of thousands of volunteers needed to be organized to add to the regular army, but only reluctantly and sparingly were black regiments formed, in some cases only when necessary to reach state volunteer quotas. Just a few of those segregated units were led by African American officers. Black men wanted to serve for the same reasons as they had in the Civil War: to prove their loyalty to the flag and, as Murray put it, "demonstrate the capacity of the race," both in the hope of influencing the status of black citizens at conflict's end.

The *Colored American* was blunt and succinct: "We want colored troops with colored officers." In June 1898, "it was decided that three of the most influential colored men then in Washington should call on the President." Daniel Murray, George H. White, and John R. Lynch, with Murray as spokesman, met with McKinley and put forth the same suggestion that Murray had outlined three weeks earlier in an *Evening Star* article. Headlined "Leaders Feel They Have Been Discriminated Against," it urged that the District of Columbia, Maryland, and West Virginia be allowed to furnish a complete regiment of black troops. "There are now in this city an efficient organization of four companies, drilled and equipped, ready to enlist at the word," Murray averred. "Assurances are at hand from similar organizations in adjoining states ready to merge their numbers in the regiment." He recommended that

Medal of Honor recipient Major Christian Fleetwood be bestowed the rank of colonel and lead the regiment. Murray concluded, "It could be arranged to make this one of the regiments composed of immunes, since colored men generally are proof against such climatic conditions as exist in Cuba or the Philippines."

There would be no tristate regiment commanded by Fleetwood as Murray proposed, but McKinley, who had called for regiments of so-called immunes, decreed on May 26 that some of the ten new specialty regiments would be composed of "persons of color." These were the regiments Murray referred to. The moniker "immune" was applied to soldiers recruited from southern states and among black men generally, who, due to their experience (or that of their ancestors) living in hot climates, were supposed (incorrectly) to be resistant to tropical diseases such as yellow fever, which had already taken many American lives.

Four segregated immune regiments, designated 7th through 10th, were formed. Though their lieutenants were black, the company captains, as well as the field and staff officers, were white. As with the regular army, the War Department refused to commission black officers above the rank of lieutenant. The 8th Immunes included two companies of Washington men. The second of them, Company G, was mustered into service on July 11, 1898. Selected from the two hundred who had volunteered, eighty-two men left the capital that evening to join their regiment at Fort Thomas in Kentucky. (Native Washingtonian Benjamin O. Davis, Jr., was a lieutenant in Company G and was destined to become the nation's first African American general in 1940.)

The bloody battle of San Juan Hill, which made Theodore Roosevelt famous, took place on July 1, 1898. Three of the four black regiments in the regular army, nicknamed "Buffalo Soldiers," participated in the taking of the hill. As it happened, the victory marked the war's final turning point, and only one of the ten immune regiments ever got as far as Cuba's shores. The war ended with the signing of the Treaty of Paris on December 10, 1898, transferring control of Cuba and the Philippines from Spain to the United States. The 8th Immunes were mustered out the following March. Noted the *Evening Star,* "Two companies of the regiment are composed of Washington boys . . . and the colored citizens propose to give them an ovation when they reach the city." Daniel Murray hosted a meeting at his home on March 7 to complete the reception arrangements. The next evening, the companies, accompanied by the regiment's forty-piece band, were met at the 6th Street station and paraded down Pennsylvania Avenue, escorted by twenty-four of the city's mounted police, to their reception at the Center Market Armory.

But the Treaty of Paris did not spell the end of action in the Philippines. On February 2, 1899, hostilities broke out between the United States and Filipinos resisting the takeover. They were the same insurgents who had fought Spanish rule earlier, now equally inclined to turn their guns toward the new occupiers. By this time, many African Americans were expressing concern about the nation's imperialism and race-based subservient treatment of Cubans and Filipinos. Nevertheless, when the War Department announced that although military reinforcements were needed, the authorization of additional black troops would not be considered, it was to the dismay of many black citizens. The *Colored American* weighed the options: "Stripped of patriotic considerations, our racial sympathies would naturally be with the Filipinos. They are fighting manfully for what they conceive to be their best interests. But we cannot, for the sake of sentiment, turn our backs upon our own country, to give aid and comfort to any people in arms against it."

By the summer of 1899, Murray could no longer hide his disillusionment with McKinley. Just six months after publicly giving the President the benefit of the doubt, he published a "Bill of Grievances" in the July 15 *Colored American.* He covered three issues: slights in the military, lack of representation on the National Industrial Commission, and denial of suffrage and other participation in District governance. He also harped yet again at an ongoing point of contention: the assumption that black men would support the Republicans without question or concessions. The day before the article came out, he poignantly confided to George Myers that his disappointment in the President was intense since "I was never more enthusiastic for the election of any man than for Mr. McKinley."

Less than two weeks later, Murray received the opportunity to voice his grievances directly to the President. On the Sunday afternoon of July 23, Murray "handsomely entertained Col. John R. Marshall of Chicago at his elegant home," where "quite a number of distinguished gentlemen called to pay their respects to the gallant commander of the Eighth Illinois Volunteer Regiment." Marshall, the first African American colonel in the US Army (commissioned in June 1898), had conferred with President McKinley the day before.

Murray later recollected the story. Colonel Marshall had come to Washington after the War Department had decided that "no more Negro Regiments were to be organized, [and] a wave of discontent among the colored people swept over the country, coupled as it was with the dissatisfaction on the Industrial Matter [and] the Lynching cases." Calling on the President, Marshall had "urged him to reverse the decision" of the War Department. McKinley had remarked, perhaps disingenuously, "that his advice led him to believe that the colored people were well satisfied with what he had done for them and were not anxious about further service in the army." Marshall responded, "You have been misinformed Mr. President and I would suggest that you send for some thoroughly reliable colored man who will honestly tell you the truth." Marshall suggested Murray, whom the President knew, who would be frank, "without any fear that the same might affect his personal fortunes." That, Murray recalled, "occurred on Saturday and on Tuesday I was summoned to the Executive Mansion, and remained two hours and a half in consultation." That was the conference length Murray gave looking back; at the time, he said the interview had lasted for "nearly an hour."

Either way, it was a substantial conversation. Murray discussed with the President the same three matters he had reviewed in the *Colored American* article. He was asked to put it all down in writing, which he did the next day. George B. Cortelyou, acting secretary for the President, acknowledged Murray's summary with a lukewarm tone in his letter of August 11, 1899: "After the very full interview accorded you . . . it is hardly necessary to add anything to what was then discussed. . . . From the liberal purpose repeatedly evidenced by the Administration, I feel sure you will be able properly and fairly to advise any who may make inquiry of you on the lines concerning which you write."

Despite Cortelyou's noncommittal response, Murray felt good about the conference, especially once McKinley authorized the formation of two new segregated regiments in September. Designated the 48th and 49th Volunteer Infantry Regiments, though their field-grade officers were white, all company-grade officers, including some with the rank of captain, were African American. They fought to their honor in the conflict officially named the Philippine Insurrection (ten times more US troops died suppressing Filipino resistance than had died defeating Spain). Murray later claimed that it had been at his conference with McKinley that "it was decided to reverse the War Department and organize the 48th and 49th regiments as colored troops, and give to each company a colored captain, a gain of one rank above what had been previously accorded." He bragged to Myers, "I feel I am entitled to a large share of the credit." Myers wrote back that he deserved a share of the credit. Surely Colonel John R. Marshall and others who had coaxed the President into his decision felt the same way.

Another matter came up at Murray's White House meeting with McKinley that he shared with Myers: "The President told me that had he known all the circumstances surrounding my candidacy for Asst. Assessor and that I was the author of the law, he would have seen to it that I was appointed." There was a fresh opportunity to name Murray or another African American come that November, when a vacancy was created by an assistant assessor's resignation due to illness. The opening was filled with a white man.[2]

In the summer of 1899, the industrious Murray was not only working his library job and managing the NAAC bureau; he was— while still not giving up on a District appointment—also writing a book, according to the *Colored American*. The NAAC annual meeting was scheduled for August 17–19 in Chicago, and, despite this overload, Murray was planning to attend at least as late as August 11, when he wrote to George Myers that he would present his bill creating a Freedmen's Inquiry Commission "along with my report to the Council in Chicago on the 18th inst." He added that the bill would also be submitted for endorsement at the National Association of Colored Women's convention, scheduled in Chicago just ahead of the NAAC meeting. Anna Murray planned to attend the convention but was kept home by the "illness of her infant." The health of twelve-month-old Paul may have played into her husband's belated decision not to travel to Chicago either. Although listed on the program, "Mr. Daniel Murray seems to have kept to his books," observed one newspaper account.

Murray's legislative bureau report was read by another delegate. Council president Alexander Walters relayed Murray's request "that the bills that have been prepared by his department to be presented to Congress be endorsed by the National Council." One of those was "a petition to Congress to authorize the President to appoint a Freedman's Inquiry commission," which the council's final resolutions duly comprised.

"A petition to Congress for the suppression of mob violence" was another. "The country is drifting into anarchy," the council warned in its subsequent Address to the Nation. "Day by day the lawless and barbarous spirit of the mob becomes more defiant." The lynching of Georgian Sam Hose in April was so ghastly it received nationwide coverage. Hose had killed a white man who had pulled a gun on him and had subsequently been lynched by a mob, which slowly drew out the process by grisly torture. In the face of rising mob violence, the NAAC called for a day of fast and prayer on June 2 and asked ministers to address the issue from their pulpits the following Sunday. Just a week before the conference, across the Potomac River from the nation's capital in Alexandria, Virginia, a lynch posse forced a black man from a local jail and hung him on a city lamppost. Though authorities were on the scene, not a single participant was arrested. Regarding a legal remedy, Murray's report claimed that federal law "could be cured by amendment which he had prepared and would later lay before Congress," whereby "adequate punishment is provided and its infliction not left to local authorities." Edward E. Brown, a Boston lawyer, championed that approach on the conference floor, seconding the need to make lynching a federal crime that imposed severe penalties on those who would circumvent the legal system. The NAAC resolutions determined "that Congress be asked to so amend the revised statutes of the U.S. as to place beyond quibbles the authority of the general government to act at once in the case of lynchings."

The legal and legislative bureau was charged with drafting an anti-lynching bill for Representative George White to introduce in Congress. Murray was reelected chair of the bureau, despite being "conspicuous by [his] absence." Ida Wells-Barnett was elected chair of the new anti-lynching bureau. "The work of that bureau is the same as that which I have individually conducted for the past seven years," explained the relentless activist, "agitating, investigating, and publishing facts and figures in the lynching evil."

W. E. B. DuBois was elected the new head of the business bureau, the delegates having been impressed by the "the scholarly and brainy Professor's" presentation on "Business Enterprises of the Race and How to Foster Them." In other proceedings, the delegates resolved to end race-exclusive suffrage in the South, affirming the legislative bureau's intention to challenge Louisiana's grandfather clause.

On September 7, Alexander Walters traveled to Washington and held a special meeting with a subset of the NAAC's executive committee at Daniel Murray's house, where "considerable business left unfinished by the Chicago convention was disposed of." An NAAC delegation met with President McKinley on October 3 and presented the address adopted at the Chicago conference. "The constitution of the United States is to the Afro-American the bedrock upon which is founded all true civilization, and he wants it enforced in its entirety," the address read. "So long as the rights of the humblest citizen are trampled on with impunity civilization falls of its purpose and the ends of government are subverted."

On the evening of October 12, 1899, Local Council No. 1 held a public meeting at the Conservatory of Music, the audience filling the main hall. The current president, Pinckney Pinchback, presided. Jesse Lawson, a delegate to the Chicago convention, reviewed the convention's proceedings. Daniel Murray, reporting on the progress of the legal and legislative bureau, said he was working to pass three bills. One was the measure authorizing a Freedmen's Inquiry Commission. Another was the Crumpacker bill, sanctioning a reduction in representatives in accord with permissible voters; it had been set aside in the last congressional session, and Representative Crumpacker intended to resubmit it in the next Congress. The third bill Murray discussed was an amendment to the Revised Statutes of the United States that would compel federal officers to protect persons charged with crimes from lynch mobs and, as necessary, prosecute offenders in federal courts. This was the strategy behind the anti-lynching bill that George H. White announced he would be introducing in Congress.

White declared at the public meeting that McKinley and members of his cabinet promised to support the anti-lynching bill. In subsequent weeks the attorney general, John W. Griggs, presumably with the President's approval, did lend assistance. White, Murray, and Edward E. Brown, one of the legislative bureau's assistant counselors and a new member of the NAAC executive committee, conferred with Griggs and other authorities on several occasions to shape the proposed measure. The *Colored American* predicted that the bill "to prevent lynching and to permit the cooperation of federal officials in enforcing the laws when the state is unwilling . . . promises to be one of the most significant issues to be argued in the coming Congress."[3]

An important ongoing NAAC objective was the support of local council issues and efforts. The Washington chapter sponsored "Afro-American Council Day" at the Second Baptist Church Lyceum on November 26, 1899. The talks presented to the overflow crowd included one by Murray outlining the practical movements the NAAC had under way. Many participants enrolled in the civil rights organization afterward, the show of interest undoubtedly spurred by a recent case of segregation at the Grand Theater, whose new management was accused of "importing Georgia methods into the Nation's Capital." Barely a week before, an M Street High School physics instructor, in the company of his family, had resisted being booted out of the Grand's orchestra seats. He had been taken into custody and charged with disorderly conduct. "This outrageous discrimination," observed the *Colored American*, "has stirred up the colored citizens of Washington more deeply than has been the case with any similar demonstration of race prejudice in recent years." The NAAC took up the cause. At a meeting at Murray's house on November 30, the sub-executive committee, fearing that the ostracism was "likely to be far reaching in its consequences unless speedily rebuked," adopted a resolution as the voice of the council. "The Grand Opera House of this city has refused admission to the desirable seats of that theater to respectable and orderly colored people in open violation of the laws," it read. "The National Afro-American Council hereby tenders its moral and financial support . . . and it is advised that criminal and civil proceedings be . . . instituted at once." Murray wrote an article for the December 9 *Colored American* supporting the suits filed by two complainants, "ejected from the Grand because of color," against the theater managers for violating the District civil rights act. In the end the suits brought no redress, rather only added finesse by the Grand's management to keep its orchestra seats all-white and regular snipes from the black press at the "Jim Crow theater."

The regular, semiannual meeting of NAAC officers and executive committee members took place at the Conservatory of Music on Thursday and Friday, December 28 and 29, 1899. Called to order by Alexander Walters, most of the sessions centered on the work of the legal and legislative bureau. Crumpacker's bill, White's anti-lynching bill, issues to be laid before the National Industrial Commission, and the test case challenging the constitutionality of Louisiana's election law were all discussed. On the latter topic, Frederick McGhee, an attorney from St. Paul who, like Edward E. Brown, was one of the legislative bureau's assistant counselors and a member of the executive committee, "made a decided impression as a speaker and thinker." Efforts had been under way for months to raise money to meet the expenses of the lawsuit. In other business, a new sub-executive committee, charged with acting for the council between national conventions in matters of legislation, was formed. Chaired by Jesse Lawson, the nine-man working group included Murray, White, and Brown. The council met in private session throughout the two-day conference but hosted a public meeting on Friday evening at which Bishop Walters "described the grand results achieved by the conference and declared that the Council was here to stay."

On Saturday afternoon, December 30, George White hosted a dinner at "Gray's famous hostelry" for a "select party" of twelve gentlemen. Just the meat dishes featured on the elaborate menu included chicken gumbo, broiled lake trout, lamb chops, roast rib of beef, roast ham, and tongue. The wine served was North Carolina scuppernong, a homegrown specialty from White's native state. The meal was finished off with café noir and cigars, followed by "Eloquence." George White, Daniel Murray, Tim Fortune, Alexander Walters, Edward Brown, Frederick McGhee, Pinckney Pinchback, Edward Cooper, and John Bruce were among those who enthusiastically contributed to the "running conversation on the work of the Council and the best means of enlarging its scope." Bruce concluded, "The little dinner of Congressman White's . . . will be remembered for a long time by all who were privileged to enjoy his hospitality, his rare old scuppernong and his fragrant Perfectos."

Murray may well have rushed off, leaving the others still smoking cigars at 4 p.m., because he was in charge of an event that evening, the National Afro-American Council/American Negro Academy joint reception at Odd Fellows Hall. The American Negro Academy, a scholarship-promoting organization of black intelligentsia, staged their annual meeting in Washington on December 27–28. W. E. B. DuBois was one of those who did double duty. The public reception was "designed to show Washington's hospitality toward its holiday visitors and organization delegates." According to the *Colored American*, "Mr. Daniel Murray was an energetic chairman on arrangements, and raised Washington's stock several points higher in the society market."

The agenda for the coming year mapped out, the council's prime players got busy. On January 20, 1900, Representative

George White introduced the first federal anti-lynching measure, "A Bill for the Protection of All Citizens of the United States
Against Mob Violence, and the Penalty for Breaking Such Laws."
Not until February 23 was White given the opportunity to enter
its text into the *Congressional Record* and present his colleagues with
an impassioned plea for an end to the barbarism of lynching. The
bill, H.R. 6963, was referred to the Judiciary Committee.

To present issues bearing on the social and economic status of
African Americans to the National Industrial Committee, a committee with George White as chairman and Murray as one of its
four other members was appointed. In early February, the NAAC
committee testified at length before the commission. "With the
hope of inspiring remedial legislation," committee members described the oppressive conditions that confronted the black
workingman, including discrimination by trade unions and organized labor generally, as well as the convict lease system and unfair
tenant/landowner arrangements such as peonage.

On March 3, 1900, a meeting to discuss a court challenge to
the suffrage clause in Louisiana's state constitution was conducted
in Washington. Participants in this "important conference of representative negroes" included T. Thomas Fortune, George H.
White, Jesse Lawson, E. E. Cooper, Daniel Murray, and Booker T.
Washington. They endorsed the action of the NAAC to test the
constitutionality of Louisiana's grandfather clause, all the way to
the Supreme Court if necessary. The case was the first time that
discrimination in state election laws would be tested in the courts
by a civil rights organization.

An identical article covering the Saturday meeting, presumably
submitted by NAAC press representatives ready to serve notice of
the council's intention, ran in the *New York Times* and many other
papers throughout the country. The article pointedly noted that
"The conference was not held under the auspices of the NAAC"
and made no mention of Booker T. Washington's presence. Wash-

ington's participation is confirmed by a letter to his secretary, describing "the conference which I held in Washington last Sunday," misidentifying the day of the week. This was in keeping with the way Washington preferred to operate—covertly—in order to protect his reputation as an accommodationist with white power brokers. Though Washington preached to the black population, "I see no good for you in politics, but I see plenty of harm. . . . Live on friendly terms with the Southern white people," behind the scenes he disregarded his own advice. In the instance of the Louisiana test case, Washington was quietly supportive and made monetary donations to help finance the suit.

Daniel Murray remained desirous of a District appointment. "If the president should tender to me a place on the Board of Education when [re]organized I should highly appreciate his consideration," he wrote George Myers in early May 1900. "There are to be seven members of the board and it's generally conceded that two of the seven will be colored men. I would like to be one of that number." Let his competitors canvass personally, Murray declared, "I will not enter into a scramble for the place." What he meant was that he would not make an obvious play for the position. Though the appointments were in the hands of the district commissioners, he asked Myers to write President McKinley on his behalf. John E. Bruce penned a lengthy and laudatory article on Murray for the April 28 *Colored American*, promoting his friend for the board. On May 26, Murray informed Myers that his appointment was very probable. But by the last week in June he had become a bit frantic. Having encountered the President and "embraced the opportunity to talk of the Board of Education," he wanted Myers to follow up with a wire, asking the President to "insist" that the commissioners select him for the board. Believing that McKinley favored him, Murray told Myers that if the President followed through ("all depends on his backbone") and "assumes the credit" for appointing a black man to District office, "it will offset the lynching matter and furnish a strong argument for his [reelection] campaign in every section of the country." This was an outrageous sentiment, even if in a confidential letter, and one hopes that on reflection Murray would see it as a rash, self-serving comment not worthy of him. As it happened, he had no better luck being appointed school board trustee than he'd had trying for the assessor job.[4]

The Republican National Convention was scheduled for June 19–21, 1900, in Philadelphia, and Murray again took a run at becoming District delegate. According to the *Colored American*, "A boom of no mean dimensions has sprung up in favor of Daniel Murray and it is understood that he will have the backing of the Board of Trade, of which he is a member, and the business and real estate interests generally." The election of party delegates was the one instance when Washingtonians, both black and white, could vote, and the paper claimed that "The conviction is stealing over the rank and file of the Negro voters of the District that Mr. Daniel Murray is excellent delegate timber," elaborating, "Mr. Murray is active. He is public-spirited. He is always helping somebody. He never shirks a duty. He is above petty methods. His political honor is unpurchaseable. Mr. Murray is the right kind of a man to represent our people." He lost.

Murray was, however, part of the committee the NAAC—claiming to represent more than 200,000 black voters residing principally in fourteen states—dispatched to the Republican National Convention to "take a strong stand against mob violence" and the suffrage laws of southern states, which "in effect nullify the Fourteenth and Fifteenth Amendments of the Constitution." George Myers was elected alternate Ohio delegate, and he and his wife, whom the Murrays had never met, visited Washington ahead of the convention. Two weeks before, a biographical sketch of Myers authored by Murray had come out in the *Colored American*.

John P. Green, formerly an Ohio state legislator, who, with the influence of Myers, had been appointed US postage stamp agent in 1897, threw a party for black elites on Friday evening, June 15, which began at eight o'clock and continued until midnight. "One of the most unique social functions that has taken place in Washington for a long time was the reception given by Hon. John P. Green and wife at his capacious residence . . . in honor of Mr. and Mrs. George A. Myers of Cleveland, Ohio," gushed the *Colored American*. "The parlors were beautifully decorated with flowers and exotics of all kinds, while the first floor was given over to those who had charge of the culinary art." Anna and Daniel Murray attended this gathering of "Washington's best society," as did Alice and Paul Laurence Dunbar, Bettie and John R. Francis, Mary and Robert Terrell, and many other elites.

The Republican National Convention began on June 19 at Philadelphia's Exposition Auditorium. William McKinley was unanimously nominated for a second term, and New York governor Theodore Roosevelt was selected as his running mate. The convention declined to include planks denouncing lynching or endorsing representational reduction in the platform. (McKinley would be easily reelected the following November, again running against William Jennings Bryan. Most African Americans permitted to vote saw McKinley as the lesser of two evils, despite knowing that the Republican Party, as T. Thomas Fortune put it, "promises us before election all we deserve, and gives us afterwards what it thinks we ought to have.") On the social side, Murray thoroughly enjoyed himself in Philadelphia with George and Maude Myers and long recalled the time the three of them went in search of an egg phosphate and were amused by the clerk's reluctance to admit that he was not familiar with the drink. Back in Washington, Murray found the July weather so warm that he had "little inclination to move after reaching home" via streetcar from his workday at the Library of Congress.

On July 28, the Sub-Executive Committee in Charge of Work formally issued the call to all NAAC members to meet in national convention, in the state senate chamber in Indianapolis, Indiana, on Tuesday, August 28, 1900. The place and date of the annual meeting had actually been set a year in advance. The *Indianapolis Freeman* named Daniel Murray among "the prominent leaders and speakers of the council who will be here." There were three to four hundred people in attendance when the conference commenced, a much better turnout than the year before, but no Daniel Murray. Back in July, Murray had said he expected his normal energy to return "just as soon as the weather is a little less charged with calorie." Perhaps he had not recovered his vigor by the hotter month of August. Whatever the reason, he was, for the second consecutive year, a no-show at the national convention.

Murray's legislative bureau report was scheduled for August 29. His paper, read by one of the DC delegates, "provoked quite a discussion," taking up most of that Wednesday morning. In proposing remedies for lynching and separate-car laws, Murray blasted the South. He referred to the white man's "hatred of the Negro in the South" and recommended that "the race, in states that have discriminating laws, refuse to ride on railroads or engage in any form of diversion in which they are subjects of discrimination." When the reading concluded, "a score of delegates were on their feet, clamoring for recognition." Though most approved of Murray's boycott plan, Georgian Richard R. Wright, Sr., and other southern delegates, who had to negotiate their home terrain through strategic accommodation to Jim Crow realities, denounced Murray's statements and resented his attacking their section "so vigorously at long range." Meanwhile, Frederick McGhee, having presented an enthusiastic welcome address, contributed actively to the proceedings throughout the four-day conference. According to John E. Bruce, the St. Paul lawyer had a winning personality: "Mr. McGhee is an inimitable wit, and bears a striking resemblance to Hamlet. His eloquence is fervid and his manner engaging as a speaker." Before the convention was over, McGhee was elected the new director of the legislative bureau.[5]

→ ←

THE SEVEN MURRAY FAMILY MEMBERS GATHERED AT THEIR S Street home to celebrate the Christmas holiday together in December 1900. Paul, a two-year-old toddler; Harold, seven, a student at Garnet School; and Nat, sixteen, an M Street High School junior, were joined by their older brothers, Henry, eighteen, and Dannie, twenty. Henry was a freshman at Harvard University, a mechanical engineering student in the Lawrence Scientific School, enjoying his Christmas break. Dannie, after completing his studies at Oberlin, where he'd won the position of lead and solo violinist of the conservatory orchestra, had moved to New York City. There he had studied under famed German violinist Henry Schradieck and become a member of his society orchestra. Dannie was a versatile musician. He had "the power of throwing all of his own soul and feeling into his instrument," whatever the genre. A composer of popular songs, he also rearranged old plantation melodies and folk songs for violin and orchestra. He was cocomposer of a "coon song" titled "I'm Happy When I'm by My Baby's Side." It had "reached its fourth edition, and is said to be extremely popular in the New York vaudeville theaters," reported the November 25, 1899, *Colored American*, "Young Mr. Murray received quite a handsome sum for the song." Dannie boarded in the borough of Brooklyn with his father's close friend Fred R. Moore (now a "solid business man of Gotham"), who himself visited with the Murrays in the early part of December. Cyrus Adams's two-week stay overlapped with Moore's. On more than one occasion, Murray invited John Green over to share oysters with his out-of-town houseguests. At the end of the month, the Murrays received a visit from Charles and Florence Bentley of Chicago.

Through December, Murray traded information with George Myers on their wives' health. To the news that Maude Myers was ill, he responded, "I know somewhat of the pains experienced from the trouble mentioned, since I have known Mrs. Murray to suffer intensely for days. Usually she found relief in the application of turpentine strips, that is, hot cloths wrung out [in] turpentine water." The nature of Anna's ailment is unknown. Turpentine was used medicinally primarily as a topical treatment for rheumatic disorders and muscle pain. Playing hostess to a houseful of company, not to mention her activity as kindergarten advocate (she had returned from her speaking tour in the Midwest only on November 4), it is hard to imagine Anna, at forty-three, not up to any challenge. Maude Myers's illness, on the other hand, resulted in hospitalization. With wishes for her recovery and in light of the Christmas season, Murray sent her a jar of brandy peaches, "put up by Mrs. Murray for me because I like them."

A fascinating development involving Anna's extended family had transpired the year before. On July 29, 1899, a Washingtonian, Thomas Featherstonhaugh, had unearthed the remains of Lewis Sheridan Leary and seven other of John Brown's foot soldiers killed in the Harpers Ferry raid four decades earlier. For years, Featherstonhaugh, a recognized authority on Brown and his band, had periodically searched for the graves of the raiders, who had been hastily buried somewhere along the bank of the Shenandoah River. With the help of now-elderly locals who had been involved in the burials, he finally discovered them near the water's edge of the south bank, about a half mile upriver from the town. Some digging revealed two pine store boxes sitting in shallow trenches. Inside, what little remained of the eight bodies was enveloped in the woolen remnants of the blanket shawls that they had worn the night of the attack. Featherstonhaugh wanted to see the bones properly reinterred next to the body of their leader on the Brown family farm in North Elba, New York. The remains were dispatched to that site in the northern Adirondacks. All that was accomplished in stealth to avoid interference of any kind. Anna's mother, Henrietta Leary Evans, may well have been aware all along of Featherstonhaugh's goal, as he had previously interviewed her to learn what he could about her brother Sheridan. It would be fitting if she did have a heads-up on this posthumous movement, given that she told Featherstonhaugh she had learned of her brother's participation in the Harpers Ferry raid only when his name had been listed in the newspapers among the dead insurrectionists.

The single coffin holding the bones of the eight comrades, draped in an American flag, was lowered into the ground next to John Brown's body on August 30, 1899. Three thousand people were present to see the men honored as heroes in a dignified but emotional ceremony. President McKinley, though in nearby Lake Champlain (where he had gone to vacation immediately after his July conference with Daniel Murray), declined to attend what, for many, was a controversial proceeding.

There is another chapter to this story. Mary Leary Langston, still living in Lawrence, Kansas, had been widowed for a second time when Charles Langston had died. In 1902, her grandson, Langston Hughes, destined for literary fame, was born. She raised him, due to difficulties in her daughter Caroline's marriage. As her grandson grew up, she sat in her rocker with him on her lap and told "long, beautiful stories about people who wanted to make the Negroes free." She said that the bullet-ridden blanket shawl she had wrapped him in as a baby was the one her first husband, Sheridan Leary, had worn the night of the Harpers Ferry attack. Langston Hughes inherited that family heirloom. He treasured it, along with the tales his grandmother had shared with him, and in 1943 donated it to the Ohio Historical Society. Hughes relayed the family tradition as he understood it: the blanket shawl had originally belonged to Sheridan Leary's grandfather, and "some good person" had sent the muddy woolen cloth to his grandmother

Mary shortly after the 1859 raid. Such a provenance is doubtful, to say the least. All the raiders wore the same shawl blankets that Brown distributed. It is improbable that a sympathetic soul, who might have retrieved Leary's blanket and sent it to his widow, was on the scene. One of those who participated in the reburial event forty years later was Richard Hinton, a comrade of John Brown in the struggle to secure a free-soil Kansas. He traced Mary Leary Langston's whereabouts to Lawrence. She had written in early August to the minister who would be presiding over the religious exercises at the reinterment ceremony, revealing her keen interest in the proceedings. During Hinton's monthlong visit to Kansas in early 1900, he very likely delivered the blanket to her. It can only be said that it was one of the blanket shawls found with what was left of the bodies, given that just a single set of remains could be individually identified.[6]

→ ←

HIS RACE ACTIVISM NOTWITHSTANDING, MURRAY STILL played a good game when it came to assimilation into the white-dominated culture. He belonged to the National Geographic Society, then a prestigious club whose members were elected. On October 26, 1897, he and Anna attended the reception for the arctic explorer Dr. Fridtjof Nansen, "one of the most notable social events in the history of the society." The reception drew an enormous crowd, replete with a number of cabinet secretaries, but the Murrays were nearly the only African Americans on the long reception line whose hands Dr. Nansen shook. Murray continued his service on the Board of Trade and was present at the February 1899 annual reception celebrating "the city's great future." He was a proud selectee for Admiral Dewey's escort to the nation's capital in October 1899 and the following year joined the integrated committee responsible for arranging financing for the District of Columbia centennial commemoration. On January 20, 1901, he and

Anna hosted "quite a company of our white friends of prominence in the city" for an at-home entertainment featuring their son Dan on the violin. The audience of about thirty included Republican Party leaders and their spouses.

Murray continued to cultivate influential white contacts, endorsing Andrew Hilyer's advice to "keep ourselves in touch with them. Show appreciation of their friendship." For example, at an afternoon ceremony in a Senate room at the Capitol on March 2, 1901, Murray presented an engraved ebony-and-gold-mounted walking stick to Senator William E. Chandler of New Hampshire "on the part of the colored press and people." In his short speech that followed, Murray thanked the senator for his steadfast defense of black rights inherent in the US Constitution. Murray's relationship with Senator William B. Allison of Iowa grew into friendship, close enough to exchange family news and birthday wishes anyway. Murray had regular opportunities to cultivate other lawmakers, thanks to his position at the Library of Congress, especially once he was assigned to its Capitol Station in late 1901. Murray disclosed to George Myers that the duty was demanding "but brings me more in touch with the Members and Senators. The most pleasing part is that a request was made to the Librarian to detail me [there]."

If the matrices of associations with whites came with contradictory pressures, contradictory pressures certainly led black elites both toward and away from the African American majority population. They were, in some respects, compelled to do more by way of solidarity with all people of color, especially if those in power were not making distinctions, which increasingly became the case. But that did not sway them from adhering to their own social biases. It is an irony that although the elites understood that their advancement was inextricably tied to the progress of black Americans as a whole, more and more as the "one-drop of African blood rule" gained ground, they nevertheless kept their own caste and color barriers intact. Holding themselves, as Mary Church Terrell admitted, "aloof from the less fortunate of their people" and wary of discrimination by whites of their own class at public facilities and diversions, they developed a deeper social insularity, "preferring to enjoy themselves in amusements of their own making." A prime example of this was the exclusive Highland Beach enclave, developed by Charles Douglass after his humiliating rejection at a resort in the same Chesapeake Bay area. As the *Washington Bee* noted in August 1895, it was "the first and only seaside resort owned and controlled by a colored man in America." Douglass sold lots to other upper-class blacks, who reveled in the relaxation that their private summer community afforded. The select set was regularly accused of applying its own version of the color line, the "brown paper bag test." The phrase was a metaphor for the selective advantage that African Americans whose skin tint was lighter than the standard brown paper bag enjoyed.

When Josephine Bruce was asked, in 1890, how upper-class black Washingtonians used their leisure time, she responded, "Pretty much as other people do, I imagine. We are card players and have our whist and euchre clubs. Some of our gentlemen are excellent chess-players and get much entertainment from the game. We are theatergoers, too, and are much given to dancing, to dinner parties and to receptions. We receive and return calls, read, drive, dress and, in fact, live just about as ladies do everywhere, who have education and means for social enjoyment." The cavalier, myopic attitude inherent in this comment modified a bit with time. Although the elite continued to indulge in purely social occasions, for the Murrays and many in their circle, including Josephine Bruce, the quantity of such outings eased. When Daniel and Anna took time from their political and civic activities and family life these days, they were most likely to take in a lecture or musical performance. The parties they did attend tended to be ones like that hosted by Kelly Miller and his wife on September 25, 1899. A benefit for the Colored Woman's League's day nurseries, the elite gathered on Miller's "velvety lawn" for a garden party. The Howard professor, "attired in a serge coat and duck trousers, looked the part of the 'landed proprietor.' " Netting a handsome sum for day nurseries while "the people can be seen that one most heartily enjoys seeing" conspired to make the affair "a brilliant success."[7]

The festivities surrounding the second inauguration of William McKinley on March 4, 1901, constituted a major exception to the Murrays' scaled-back socializing. As president of the Inaugural Welcome Club, Murray held the first of several organizational meetings at his house on December 5 to plan the all-black inaugural ball scheduled for the evening of March 5. He expressed confidence "that the proposed entertainment will be even more brilliant than that of 1897."

Murray wanted to be placed on the executive committee that organized the inauguration itself, and in early December George Myers sent a letter to Senator Mark Hanna recommending his friend. Murray was not assigned to the executive committee, but he was "perfectly satisfied" with the prize he was offered because of Myers's intervention, namely, chairman of the committee on public comfort no. 2, charged with "looking after all the colored organizations and visitors coming to the inaugural ceremonies." So tickled was Murray that he had "distinctive letterhead" prepared for his committee. His appointment not only came with a clerk and a messenger but "gives me some patronage." The patronage he referred to was the power to name more than thirty-five local associates to serve on the committee under him, plus delegates in large cities from which residents would be traveling to Washington. As he explained to George Myers, in asking him to assume that role in Cleveland, that would "avoid the embarrassment hitherto encountered by the inability of the Committee to learn . . . the racial identity of the numerous applicants for quarters."

Meanwhile, competition for throwing the inaugural ball

emerged from the Cosmos Club, a black elite club based on the white association of the same name, formed a year earlier. Pinckney Pinchback was a vice president of the Inaugural Welcome Club but deserted his longtime friend to help lead the Cosmos Club event. Murray energetically accepted the challenge of outdoing the competing ball. He expected that his role as chairman of the committee on public comfort no. 2 increased his chances of "getting a good hall for *our* Inaugural Ball." On February 23, he described for George Myers the "tremendous fight" that had ensued: "The other fellows led by John F. Cook, Pinchback, Whitefield McKinlay and Terrell paid $200 for the Hall of the Builder's Exchange which had been promised to us for $100. They then set out to malign and misrepresent us. . . . Their aim was by closing every Hall to us, to prevent our having any ball except under their management." He then revealed the happy turn of events: "The splendid Armory of the Washington Light Infantry with its six hundred electric lights and corresponding features was granted me as chairman of the committee on public comfort. . . . Washington in its Social Circles is rent asunder and we are on top. We have the finest hall in the city and it's the talk of the town."

Following the big night on Tuesday, March 5, the St. Paul *Appeal* judiciously reported that the Inaugural Welcome Club had given a grand ball that "was a very swell affair" and the Cosmos Club had given a grand ball that "was a very swell affair." Paul Laurence Dunbar elaborated, "Both were tremendous successes, though the visitors, who, like the dying man had friends in both places, had to even up matters by going first to one and then the other, so that during the whole of that snowy March night there was a good-natured shifting of guests from one ballroom to the other. Sometimes the young man who happened to be on the reception committee at one place and the floor committee at the other got somewhat puzzled as to the boutonniere which was his insignia of office, and too often hapless ones found themselves standing in the midst of one association with the flower of the other like a badge upon his lapel. Each faction had tried the other's mettle, and the whole incident closed amicably." Murray's take was a shade different. He agreed with the Cleveland *Plain Dealer*'s assessment that the Inaugural Welcome Club "had a larger and better hall, better music, better supper, and a larger and more representative crowd." Six hundred persons had attended the affair, with its sixteen-piece orchestra, "sea of glass" dance floor, ten cases of champagne, and twelve gallons of Roman punch. Murray boasted, "The Ball was an unqualified success in every way, the efforts of the Cosmos people to down the man from Maryland not meeting with any success."[8]

➜ ←

PARTY OVER, IT WAS BACK TO THE STRUGGLE AT HAND. THE Crumpacker reduction bill, after repeated attempts to gain ground, was tabled from further consideration by vote of the House of Representatives in January 1901. The effort to gain authorization for a Freedmen's Inquiry Commission was in limbo. Adequate financing was a barrier in proceeding with the court challenge to Louisiana's grandfather clause. George H. White's last day in the US Congress was March 3, 1901. Discriminatory election laws voted in by the North Carolina legislature had rendered his election to a third term an impossibility. His anti-lynching bill, trapped in committee, died there. McKinley had not supported the measure as White said he had promised to do.

George White's parting speech to the now all-white Congress was poignant: "This, Mr. Chairman, is perhaps the negroes' temporary farewell to the American Congress, but let me say, Phoenix-like he will rise up some day and come again. These parting words are in behalf of an outraged, heart-broken, bruised, and bleeding, but God-fearing people, faithful, industrious, loyal people—rising people, full of potential force."[9]

10

BLACK HISTORY PIONEER

IN JANUARY 1900, DANIEL MURRAY RECEIVED A SPECIAL AS-
signment at work. Librarian John Young had unexpectedly
died a year before. The new Librarian of Congress was Herbert
Putnam, the first professional librarian appointed to the position.
Putnam approved a request from the organizers of the American Negro Exhibit, planned for the upcoming Paris Exposition,
that the library furnish a bibliography of works authored by black
Americans and collect some of the books and pamphlets listed
therein. Murray was put to the task.

Participation in the Exposition Universelle was something the
National Afro-American Council had long had in its sights. Indeed, it had been one of the objectives set at the formation of the
council at Rochester in September 1898. That was just six weeks
after Ferdinand W. Peck, a civic-minded businessman from Chicago, had been appointed commissioner general for the United
States at the world's fair that would open in the heart of Paris in
April 1900. Twelve commissioners were to be appointed under
Peck. The Washington branch of the NAAC had called for inclusion in that group at the meeting Murray had presided over in
January 1899. Although that had not transpired, black leaders had

continued to press for some avenue of representation. According to Murray, Peck had "stoutly resisted" the idea of giving up any of the nation's limited space to African Americans. Murray had appealed directly to President McKinley during their July 1899 conference and claimed that "Mr. Dawes [Comptroller of the Currency Charles G. Dawes] later said the President had at my instance overruled Comm. Gen'l. Peck." But other prolocutors, including Booker T. Washington, applied pressure as well. It was Thomas J. Calloway who engineered the final push.

Calloway, a graduate of Fisk University formerly employed by the US War Department and Tuskegee Institute, resided in Washington. On October 4, 1899, he sent a letter to more than one hundred race activists, seeking their backing for promotion of a separate African American exhibit at the fair. "We owe it to ourselves to go before the world as Negroes," he wrote. "The Europeans think us a mass of rapists, ready to attack every white woman exposed, and a drug in civilized society. This information has come to them through the horrible libels that have gone abroad. . . . How shall we answer these slanders?" One way, he continued, would be a "well selected and prepared exhibit representing the Negro's development" at the Paris Exhibition that "thousands upon thousands" would view: "Not only will foreigners be impressed, but hundreds of white Americans will be [too]." He asked for the views of his correspondents and was pleased when "nearly all replied, and the responses were practically unanimous" in their support.

President McKinley was moved by the prompting of these distinguished individuals. On November 2, he met with General Commissioner Peck, and it was decided that the United States would sponsor an American Negro exhibit and that Thomas Calloway would be the special agent in charge. Calloway officially received the job on November 15. Congress appropriated $15,000 for the exhibit. With the exposition opening on April 15, he had no time to waste.

The exhibit would highlight African American progress since Emancipation by reviewing "the history of the American Negro, his present condition, his education, and his literature." On December 18, Calloway met with Librarian Putnam to discuss a "Negro book exhibit" and followed up with a written request the next day. In his return letter, dated January 5, Putnam assured Calloway that the library service superintendent, David Hutcheson, would give such assistance "as may be practicable" and is "apt to assign the work to Mr. Daniel Murray," adding, "We cannot specifically detail him for any given period for work so special, but will assign to it such portion of his time as is not required by routine duties."[1]

Murray took on the special assignment with zeal, never limiting himself to working on it when on the clock at the library. He "labored late at night and with great expense of time," recalled Calloway. "It is not often we find men who without compensation will devote themselves so earnestly for the benefit of the race."

In short order Murray produced a preliminary list of 270 books and pamphlets authored by African Americans, along with some of the works themselves to be displayed in Paris. He boasted that his list "was compiled in less than two weeks, mainly from memory." Not quite. In a fuller telling, he reported to Hutcheson that upon getting the assignment, "I immediately set about formulating a plan which offered a reasonable prospect of securing a creditable result. . . . To facilitate the quest, with the aid of the Assistants in the Library . . . and inquiry among colored men habitually active in ferreting out such information, I was able to publish on the date above given [January 24], 'a Preliminary List' containing 270 titles." He explained further that he had started with a base of 153 books and pamphlets compiled five years earlier by the Bureau of Education and added 117 titles.

The *Washington Post* carried an advance notice on January 22. The Negro literary exhibit for the Paris Exposition has "been put in operation under the charge of Mr. Daniel Murray, long known to every frequenter of the Congressional Library," it reported. "Mr. Murray is given authority to select from works by colored authors which are within the Library collection, and to secure by one means or another copies of works scattered throughout the country which are not so included. . . . Not all the books secured will be sent to the exposition. Only works of real literary merit will be forwarded." The article went on, in complimentary fashion, to describe the books of several authors.

Murray's preliminary list of 270 titles was just a starting point. The date on the *Post* article was also the date on the circular he prepared "to acquaint the public with the purpose of this Library to compile a bibliography of all books and pamphlets which colored authors had at any time published." The circular was in the form of an open letter requesting help (titles, books themselves, any relevant intelligence) in identifying books or pamphlets written by black Americans. Sent out with the circulars, along with the preliminary list, was a prepaid return envelope addressed to Murray. The circular promised that at the close of the exposition "the whole collection will be installed in the magnificent Library of Congress to be on exhibition and for consultation for all time."

Murray started by forwarding the circulars to 180 schools for African American youths. Eventually he sent a thousand circulars to institutions and individuals. Published in many newspapers as well, the circular lent "wide publicity to the quest for books and pamphlets" and, Murray found, "had the effect of calling public attention to a previously neglected field of literary endeavor." Even to many of the country's librarians, "the 270 titles of books and pamphlets were a revelation."

Murray's quest was not straightforward. "You will I am sure appreciate the immense labor necessary to develop and render approximately complete a work of this kind," he wrote to supervisor Hutcheson. "How separate the books or pamphlets by Negro authors from the general mass," he posited, "since who is gifted with that prescience necessary to divine the nationality of an author by a simple glance at his works." Murray chased down contenders based on "the imperfect recollection of individuals." Many books included a portrait of the author, but "when this distinguishing mark was omitted, evidence had to be gathered externally, and when this was not forthcoming, the effort was abandoned." Murray's list, therefore, grow as it might, would always fall short of crediting additional titles to which "the Negro race is justly entitled." Even with those difficulties, he asserted, "I did not give up the effort, since I appreciated the fact that such an opportunity might not come again in a lifetime."[2]

In mid-February, General Commissioner Peck wrote to Librarian Putnam and requested that Murray accompany the collection to Paris. He offered to pay Murray's travel expenses if the library would "continue his salary while abroad in charge of the Library's collection of books." Putnam asked chief assistant librarian Ainsworth Spofford for his input on the matter. It came back lukewarm. Most of it consisted of concerns about sending the books, some of them irreplaceable, overseas. "In regard to . . . detailing Mr. Daniel Murray to take charge of the exhibit, with a continuance of his salary in the employ of the Library, I have to say that such permission is wholly without precedent in the past service of this library."

Thus was Murray's opportunity to see Paris dashed. On March 6, 1900, Murray accompanied Thomas Calloway and his family from Washington to New York, where the Calloways boarded an ocean steamer for Paris the next day. Under that March 7 date, Murray penned a note to David Hutcheson, alerting his supervisor to a last-minute change: "Referring to our conversation yesterday my plans are now changed since Mr. Putnam thinks and I agree fully that a more effective display can be made at Paris by adopting another plan. . . . Mr. Putnam suggests that I defer the extended trip until I had the new arrangement well in shape. . . . I shall return Monday." It would seem that Murray had intended to hand over his part of the exhibit as he saw Calloway off and then conduct further bibliographical research in New York but instead returned to the library to reconfigure the display.

By the last day in March, Murray had 980 titles in hand. The enhanced method of displaying his bibliography consisted of engrossing the catalogue entries on sixteen large sheets (18 by 24 inches) and then encasing them in frames under glass that were attached by hinges to stationary posts. The entries were arranged under subject headings such as education, sciences and arts, religion, and fiction. Over the month's time that the display of the 980 entries was under preparation Murray "pushed night and day" to accumulate more titles. By the time it was ready in early May, he had "succeeded in securing identification to twelve hundred books and pamphlets," as he bragged to George Myers, commenting, "Marvelous isn't it?"

On May 14, 1900, the sixteen glass-encased sheets bearing 980 catalogue entries along with 214 books, more than 160 pamphlets, and two bound volumes of newspapers were shipped across the Atlantic. Thomas Calloway, in Paris with W. E. B. DuBois, oversaw the collection and display of the exhibit materials. The American Negro Exhibit was housed in the Hall of Social Economy, located in the center of the fair on the bank of the Seine. Dense but artfully arranged, the exhibit took up about a fourth of the space assigned to the United States in that building. On display were models, portraits, graphics, photographs, books, and various paper materials. The latter included some 360 patents issued to African Americans.

Calloway was a colleague of both Booker T. Washington and DuBois, and there were features in the exhibit reflective of the positions and priorities of both standard-bearers. Washington contributed a series of photographs from Tuskegee portraying groups of African Americans working as agricultural laborers and industrial producers. DuBois's submissions aimed at breaking down that very stereotype. He prepared colorful statistical charts showing various aspects of progress, one set illustrating conditions in the country at large, the other focused on Georgia. He also contributed a series of photographs that celebrated black self-assertion. He described the exhibit as depicting an "honest, straightforward" picture of African Americans "without apology or gloss, and above all made by themselves." Calloway thought "the most credible showing in the exhibit is by Negro authors collected by Mr. Daniel Murray," and DuBois concurred, describing it as "the most unique and striking" part of the exhibit.

Fifty million visitors attended the fair. The American Negro Exhibit was a sound success. The exhibition commission's official press representative lauded it as "intelligent and valuable," expounding, "Marvelous as has been the progress of the United States in other ways, none have equaled the facts of the progress of the American Negro." The exhibit won fifteen medals, including a grand prix overall. DuBois regretted that the awards were made before all of the features, including the literary display, were installed, with the result that some of the strongest elements never had a chance to be considered by the judges.[3]

Throughout the tenure of the exhibit, article after article appeared in newspapers across the country on Daniel Murray and his project. "It is perhaps not an exaggeration to say that no one would have believed that the colored race in this country was so prolific in the production of literature," the *New York Times* pronounced. Even the leading literary paper in England, the *Academy*, took note and, like most of the other periodicals, expressed astonishment and praise.

The journalist Richard Henry Stoddard, in his *New York Mail and Express* piece, on the other hand, dismissed Murray's bibliography, scornfully declaring that "there is no such thing as Negro literature" and that "the Negro has furnished inspiration rather than found it." Murray published a clever response to Stoddard, the compiler of the *Cyclopedia of American Literature*, that ran in several Washington newspapers. "What feelings of wonder must arise when I tell you I have now completed and identified fully eleven hundred titles of books and pamphlets by Negro authors, many of them exhibiting excellence in a literary sense," he wrote. "If another edition of your excellent work is contemplated, this information must be of the greatest benefit, since a 'Cyclopedia of American Literature' that omitted to notice so large a number of American books . . . cannot justly lay claim to completion."

A more substantial critique, carried by the *Washington Bee*, was filed by editor and literary critic Frank H. Severance, who, unlike Stoddard, treated the authors in Murray's bibliography seriously. "We might as well be entirely frank in the appraisal," he began, "Much of it is rubbish, none of it is very great." No Shakespeare, no Homer. Yet he judged the collection to be of value as a history of blacks in America written by blacks, singling out DuBois's *The Suppression of the African Slave-Trade to the United States of America* as "of sterling worth." Poetry was "the field in which the negro has made his most distinct mark," he intoned, with Paul Laurence Dunbar first in rank. He found the collection rich in memoirs and "what may be called literary curios," naming memoirists Paul Jennings and Elizabeth Keckley, among others.

The memoirs of ex-slaves Paul Jennings and Elizabeth Keckley were singled out as "curious" in many articles. Jennings had been James Madison's manservant. His *A Colored Man's Reminiscences of James Madison*, published in 1865, has been decreed by the White House Historical Association to be the first memoir of life in the executive mansion. Not more than 150 copies of Jennings's slim book were printed, and Murray may well have saved it from utter obscurity.* Elizabeth Keckley was seamstress and companion to Mary Lincoln. Her memoir, *Behind the Scenes, or, Thirty Years a Slave, and Four Years in the White House*, was published in 1868. It was Keckley herself, old and infirm, who presented a rare copy of her book to Murray, seven years before she died in Washington's Home for Destitute Colored Women and Children. Her memoir had been suppressed after the initial hoopla its publication had caused. The revelation that a black woman had been Mary Lincoln's closest confidante outraged many and embarrassed the former First Lady and her son.

Other ex-slave memoirs now considered extraordinarily significant resources that Murray included in his preliminary bibliography (and that had been absent in the earlier Bureau of Education list) were Solomon Northup's *Twelve Years a Slave* (1853) and Linda Brent's *Incidents in the Life of a Slave Girl* (1861). Murray was well aware of the facts rediscovered by historian Jean Fagan Yellin in the 1970s, namely, that Linda Brent was the pseudonym of Harriet Jacobs and that Jacob's narrative was an authentic, not fictional, account. Jacobs died in Washington in 1897. Cornelia Grinnell Willis, who had purchased Jacob's freedom circa 1852, sent Murray a copy of Jacob's memoir with an accompanying letter.

Murray's bibliography contained many entries that are today considered historical or literary classics or both. On the other hand, his emphasis on ever lengthening his list resulted in the

---

* It was in researching my biography of Paul Jennings (*A Slave in the White House: Paul Jennings and the Madisons*, 2012) that I became aware of the work of Daniel Murray. Besides including Jennings's memoir in his preliminary list, Murray composed a sketch of Jennings (who died in Washington in 1874) after interviewing his son Franklin, and his interview notes supplied me with several key biographical revelations. Murray presented bound copies of his typewritten manuscript, titled "Paul Jennings and his Times, President Madison's Biographer and Valet," to the American Antiquarian Society and President Theodore Roosevelt. The latter copy was transferred from the White House to the Manuscript Division of the Library of Congress in 1913.

inclusion of many titles of dubious literary worth. He wrote to George Myers in May 1900, "Have you not some printed pamphlet bearing your name that I can have so as to include your name in the Bibliography. If it's a campaign pamphlet and issued in your name, that will give me something." When the *Report of the Librarian of Congress* for the fiscal year ending June 30, 1900, was prepared, it included a paragraph on Murray's project, noting that his bibliography "already comprises over 1,400 titles." The next year's report included Murray's *Preliminary List of Books and Pamphlets by Negro Authors* in its compilation of publications. Murray must have felt gratified to see that in print.[4]

His role in the Paris Exposition complete, Murray continued "in my leisure hours at night, and sometimes in the morning and at noon" to "prosecute the search." His absorption in his project—a "task of herculean proportions" as he described it—undoubtedly accounts for his paying less attention to NAAC political issues and his absence at the August 1900 convention. No longer satisfied with bibliography and book collecting alone, before April 1900 was over, he was seeking data for biographical sketches of notable African American authors. On May 5, the *Colored American* revealed that Daniel Murray had "decided to attempt a more ambitious line of investigation." He was writing a book, "desirous," as he told George Myers, "of giving to the world a history of Negro literature."

Murray's inclination to take a pioneering role in what later would be referred to as the black history movement can be traced back to 1894. Prompted by a letter from Frederick G. Barbadoes in October of that year, seeking interest in the preservation of the "history of the Colored People of African descent in the United States," Frederick Douglass, Alexander Crummell, Francis Grimké, John Cromwell, Eugene Johnson, and Daniel Murray joined forces in support of the notion. "The pressing necessity for such a history at this time, when we are being so unfairly criticized by published statements, so inhumanely treated by mob law; our constitutional rights violated by State enactments; by congressional and executive indifference to our condition, is apparent to all," read the circular issued under the signatures of those five race men. Gathering the facts on black Americans' past and present "will fill the existing blank in the true history of our country and prevent further misstatements as to our title of citizenship."

Murray's active interest in African American literature had begun years before the Paris Exposition, when he read Henri Grégoire's *An Enquiry Concerning the Intellectual and Moral Faculties, and Literature of Negroes*. Published in English in 1810, Grégoire's work undermined conceptions of black inferiority by compiling the literary achievements of people of African descent. "I have prosecuted my researches," Murray stated, "in the same spirit animating Grégoire . . . to show to the world that the colored race . . . is entitled to greater credit than is now accorded to it by the American people." When, back in the summer of 1899, the *Colored American* referred to Murray writing a book, it is likely he had begun much the same work that he took up again in earnest two years later.

Murray revealed to George Myers that he "would indeed be glad to have a place that would enable me to have at command the money necessary to bring out such a book." He referred to the English tradition of giving literary men a "place under the Government to furnish sustenance while prosecuting their literary labors" and claimed that John Young had been made Librarian of Congress to enable him to prepare his biography of Ulysses S. Grant. To suggest such a far-flung possibility for himself, Murray must have composed this letter in a state of flush.[5]

Reality was not so rosy. Murray had to juggle his day-to-day responsibilities at the library with his special project. Devote himself to his project as he might on his own time, he had to angle for vacation approval in order to take research trips. As he explained to his supervisor, David Hutcheson, he had discovered that a personal appeal worked best. Such an approach was facilitated by letter, and Murray wrote four thousand tailored letters by October 1900, but also required on-the-ground research in cities such as New York, Boston, and Baltimore. Murray assured Hutcheson that his research was bearing fruit. He was gathering "proof that the Negro race possessed high intellectual capacity, and had produced literary works of an exalted character," pointedly adding, "It certainly is marvelous when the antecedent conditions are considered."

Daniel Murray had found his niche, not only a literary niche but, he reasoned, an antidote to troubled race relations. His list of 1,400 works authored by black Americans had "shocked the world." Believing that "the curse of prejudice is the hand-maid of ignorance," he would now expand his research and educate the world. "Since, as literature is the highest form of culture and the real test of the standing of a people in the ranks of civilization, this showing must undoubtedly raise the Negro to a plane previously denied him, but which, in spite of every drawback he has honestly won," he maintained. "No other test applied by the world at large is so fair and so conspicuously free from misconception." For daily inspiration, he could look to the words of Samuel Johnson inscribed on the Library of Congress wall above a second-floor window that looked out on the Capitol: "The chief glory of every people arises from its authors."

"I am bending my energies toward the completion of my book, which is probably somewhat more than half finished," Murray wrote to George Myers in December 1900. When the Union League Directory, compiled by Andrew Hilyer, came out in the new year, it carried an advertisement announcing that "Daniel Murray is preparing a very valuable book for publication, *Bibliographia Africana, or History of Afro-American Literature*, with sketches of 125 distinguished writers allied with the Negro race, to which will be appended a bibliography of 1600 books and pamphlets by Afro-American writers." By the time the *Washington Bee* interviewed Murray for an article published in its August 24, 1901, issue, his book encompassed Afro-Europeans as well and he had amassed nearly 250 sketches and 2,000 titles. "Mr. Murray's knowledge of modern languages and vast historical information so well fits him for the task that it is difficult to mention another person equally qualified," read the piece. "To insure thoroughness Mr. Murray expects to devote fully a year longer to the work, indeed, he says, he would rather delay it five years than have it full of errors when it does appear."[6]

Months before the Paris Exposition closed on November 12, 1900, the plan to install the American Negro Exhibit at the Pan-American Exposition in Buffalo, New York, was in the works. About eighty books that Murray had received too late to be shipped to Paris were added to the African American literary display in Buffalo in time for the exposition opening on May 1, 1901. As the summer proceeded, Murray planned a sojourn to the exposition and then "down the lake to Cleveland" to visit his friend George Myers. His trip was postponed because he was not granted vacation until the second week in September. He intended to take Harold, about to turn eight, who "is very anxious to come notwithstanding he made the Buffalo trip with his Mother" (Anna Murray may well have attended the National Association of Colored Women convention in Buffalo in July). "Harold wishes to wear his soldier suit, a sort of officer's fatigue dress. I wish him to appear in his velvet suit," Murray wrote to Myers on September 6, adding that Harold would have a "duck fit" were he not allowed to come. As he penned that letter, he had no inkling that September 6, 1901, was a date that would go down in history. President McKinley himself was visiting the fair in Buffalo, and late that afternoon he was laid low by an assassin's bullet. The Washington papers did not carry the news until evening.

Father and son traveled to Buffalo as the nation awaited word on the President's condition. He seemed to have gotten better by September 12, but the next evening at 9 p.m., the distressing news came that the President was unconscious and dying. Murray dashed off a postcard to Myers, writing, "My heart is so full I cannot enjoy myself here" and informing him that he and Harold would cut short their visit to Buffalo and leave for Cleveland in the morning. William McKinley died in the predawn hours of gangrene.

Murray's close friend Spencer Murray, had traveled to Buffalo with President McKinley. He'd had charge of the Pullman train cars that carried US presidents since the Cleveland administration. While Daniel Murray and George Myers had, no doubt, a somber reunion in Cleveland, Spencer Murray remained on the scene in Buffalo. It was he "who was sent to get McKinley's death-mask when his wounds resulted fatally, and subsequently he was in charge of the room in Buffalo in which [Theodore] Roosevelt took the oath of office." The remainder of the fair was rather a bust. Murray's book display was sent on to Charleston, South Carolina, where the Inter-State and West Indian Exposition took place from December 1901 to June 1902.[7]

Back in Washington, Daniel Murray, whom the *Colored American* dubbed the "Sage of Negro Bibliography," was called on to toast and to write and speak about "Our Literature." His added focus on biographical research was featured when, in May 1901, he addressed the Bethel Literary and Historical Association on "Eminent Negroes of Whom Little Is Known." Around the turn of the century, the country's black intelligentsia had formed several new scholarly organizations. The American Negro Historical Society of Philadelphia and the American Negro Academy were both launched in 1897. In February 1900, a nucleus of newspapermen founded the Pen and Pencil Club, an exclusive association for Washington's literati. Murray was invited to join this coterie of about forty men of the pen who shared "a common purpose, a common ambition and a common usefulness" and were prepared to "serve the race" by "concert of action" at critical moments. That organization, the *Indianapolis Freeman* pronounced, "gives promise of great influence in molding national sentiment."

On January 24, 1901, the club elected Lafayette M. Hershaw president, Daniel Murray first vice president, Henry P. Slaughter treasurer, and Paul Laurence Dunbar governing board chairman. Other members included John W. Cromwell, E. E. Cooper, Calvin Chase, Thomas Calloway, Kelly Miller, Richard W. Thompson, and Robert Terrell. There were also honorary members such as T. Thomas Fortune, who participated when in town. Meetings were held monthly at members' homes. Henry P. Slaughter hosted the elections meeting. In March the members gathered at Paul Laurence Dunbar's "cozy residence" in LeDroit Park. "The literary den of the famous poet was the scene of one of the most enjoyable and profitable meetings of the club."

In addition to literary development, the Pen and Pencil Club promoted "fellowship among congenial spirits." The annual banquet it hosted was always "a stellar event." In 1902, the club began the tradition of holding the affair on February 14 to honor Frederick Douglass. Douglass did not know the date of his birth but in later life celebrated it on February 14 (the colored public schools had been commemorating "Douglass Day" on that date for six years). Club members invited more than a hundred leading men to the banquet at Odd Fellows Hall, where Gray Brothers Caterers held sway. The chief speakers, all referencing various aspects of Douglass's legacy, included the recently appointed recorder of deeds, John C. Dancy, Register of the Treasury Judson W. Lyons, former governor Pinckney Pinchback, and former congressman George H. White. Given that the evening coincided with Valentine's Day, hearts and witty sentiments served as its motif, and once the speeches had transpired, the club's corresponding secretary, Robert Pelham, Jr., took over. Pelham engineered quite a show, most aspects of which were a surprise to the attendees, starting with the appearance of his six-year-old son, Fred, in the garb of Cupid. A four-foot-long pencil and fountain pen were unveiled, each filled with cigars and valentines. The audience laughed and applauded as little Fred delivered numerous valentines, with ditties tailored to each recipient. John R. Francis's, for example, noted that the doctor "had performed a surgical operation since he secured his automobile. He had 'cut' his horse." The pun in Murray's valentine revealed a familiarity with the abolitionist history of his wife's family: "We understand Capital is made of the fact that like one of the ancestors of your children, you're a good conductor of an underground system."

Advancement of the race through dissemination of knowledge may have been the club's calling card, but its "social standing" was clearly "18-karats fine." Murray's own standing was characterized as being much the same. According to the *Washington Bee*, "Daniel Murray is one of the best known social and literary lights in the United States." The *Colored American* did the *Bee* one better: "He is the authority peerless and undeniable as to the literary production of the Negro race. . . . In all social matters he is facile princeps. No social function is complete without his participation."[8]

The Pen and Pencil Club met so often at Henry P. Slaughter's bachelor apartments on 10th Street NW that they became "the club's regular headquarters." After serving as treasurer, Slaughter was elected president in May 1902, when Hershaw stepped away from the helm. Though Slaughter was a full twenty years younger than Murray, the two became steady friends. Both were devoted bibliophiles and collectors. Both worked for the advancement of African Americans through education and political action. For example, Slaughter, along with George White and Murray, had been on the committee appointed by the local NAAC in 1900 to testify before Congress's Industrial Commission on the black man's economic status.

Like Murray's friend Fred R. Moore, Slaughter had overcome

a hardscrabble early life as well as "bitter, unrelenting prejudice" to achieve success. As boys both had hustled newspapers on the street to help sustain their families; as men they became editors. Moore would take over *Colored American Magazine* in 1904 and later the *New York Age*. Slaughter had been associate editor of a newspaper in his home state of Kentucky, and eventually became editor of the *Odd Fellows Journal*. As a self-made man himself, Murray admired those colleagues who had carved their own paths out of a "mountain of opposition."

After high school, Slaughter had apprenticed as a printer, and in 1896 he landed a job in the nation's capital as compositor at the Government Printing Office. He combined that with studies at Howard University, earning two degrees. As a "a young man of unusual capacity and genius for work" and one of "Washington's most liberal entertainers," Slaughter took surprisingly little time to "know everybody worth knowing" and be welcomed among the capital's black elites. Like Murray, he was a social as well as political animal and a frequent host. One of Murray's first invitations to his place was for the stag party Slaughter threw in September 1899. Murray became so at home there that, while attending Slaughter's July 4 entertainment in 1901, he was induced to sing, no doubt influenced by Slaughter's "generous punch bowl, a la Kentucky." He offered up "In Happy Moments" and "Schneider, Don't You Want to Buy a Dog?" Murray was known for his own "famous punch" when he was host. The two men shared the same church. Slaughter was an active communicant at St. Luke's, and it was there, in 1904, that he gave up his bachelorhood.

At this time, Murray also formed a close association with his old friend Cyrus Field Adams. Adams, editor along with his brother John Q. Adams, of the midwestern *Appeal*, had moved to Washington once President McKinley had named him assistant register of the Treasury (directly under Register Judson Lyons) on January 4, 1901. "We Are at the Helm: The Appointment of Editor Adams as Assistant Register of the Treasury Places This Office in Charge of Afro-Americans" trumpeted the headline in the *Colored American*. Murray informed George Myers almost three weeks later that "Washington has still not recovered" from the surprise. In December 1901, Murray's biographical sketch of his friend was published in *The Colored American Magazine*. Adams possessed "an insatiable desire for reading," Murray wrote, "Dull encyclopedias had no terrors for him." Perhaps with that shared characteristic in mind, Murray welcomed Adams as a boarder. Adams took up residence with the Murrays by 1902 and remained there until at least 1910. His apartment in the Murrays' house was filled with "books, papers, and magazines. . . . His ample library contains everything worth reading—history, travel, biography, languages, poetry, fiction—all in beautiful binding, luxuriant in variety and scope. His big roll-top desk is a workshop . . . [that] may appear disordered to the critical housewife, but the owner knows where every scrap of paper is."

Adams was not sociable in the way that Murray and Slaughter were. He attended social functions, certainly, but was likely to be among the first to call it a night. He did not drink "spirituous liquors" or smoke cigars. Never married, his passion was philately, and his collection comprised six thousand stamp varieties by 1900. Although the president of the National Afro-American Press Association, he was not a member of the Pen and Pencil Club. Adams remained very active in the NAAC, even as Murray turned much of his attention elsewhere. The council's first lifetime member, he served as secretary from 1899 to 1907. In that capacity he published a history of the NAAC. It included a compiler's note dated July 1, 1902, wherein Adams disclosed that most of his work on the report had been done while he was "confined to a bed of sickness" at 934 S Street.[9]

COURTING CONTROVERSY

B ACK IN 1884, WHEN THERE WAS STILL HOPE THAT INTE-
gration might be the new order of things, Blanche Bruce had
assured those who had questioned a sequestered exhibit for African
Americans at the World's Industrial and Cotton Centennial Exposition in New Orleans that it "doubtless will be the last time" a
separate exhibit would be appropriate. But fifteen years later, the
organizers of the American Negro Exhibit in Paris could only la-
ment "the matter of drawing the color line at any time where it is
not already drawn by the other race." Such dilemmas, characterized by stark, reluctant choices, increasingly confronted African
Americans. Murray found himself in the middle of one in 1902.

Murray's Board of Trade friend and business mentor, Brainard H. Warner, was chairman of the citizen's committee in charge
of arrangements for the thirty-sixth annual encampment of the
Grand Army of the Republic (GAR), to be held in Washington
for the first time in a decade, in October 1902. The public comfort
committee fell under that umbrella. Its chairman, M. I. Weller, also
prominent on the Board of Trade, announced that he was forming
a special subcommittee to care for the needs and entertainment
of black veterans. March 15, 1902, was the date on Weller's letter

tendering Daniel Murray the position of subcommittee chairman, "with the privilege of selecting your own associates upon your committee."

Four days later a delegation from the Colored Ministerial Union met with Chairmen Warner and Weller to object to a separate committee. The formal protest letter they presented was signed by eight ministers, including Reverend Owen M. Waller of St. Luke's, Reverend Francis Grimké of 15th Street Presbyterian, and Reverend Sterling N. Brown of Lincoln Memorial Congregational Temple. "We the undersigned pastors of Washington, DC," began the letter, "earnestly protest against any arrangement that indicates an invidious distinction of treatment between old soldiers simply on account of color. Unless it is the policy of the managers to have special subcommittees and special consideration for every branch of our common humanity, let there be none for the battle-scarred, always loyal black soldier." The clergymen maintained that there had been no separate planning committee for previous encampments, that "every exigency in the case could be met by one committee rather than two," and that they "made no plea for any unreasonable social mingling."

After giving the delegates a "respectful hearing," the two officials indicated that they would consider melding the subcommittee with the general one and asked the ministers to compile a list of "representative colored men" they would like to see on a joint public comfort committee. They submitted their list the next day, but since the decision had been made before the *Evening Times* of that date was released, it was surely a foregone conclusion. "Complaint to be Ignored" ran the headline. "No action will be taken by Chairman B. H. Warner . . . on the complaint made yesterday by a number of colored ministers that the members of their race were being discriminated against in the making of arrangements for the gathering. After due consideration it was decided that the wisest course was to let the matter slumber as it appeared to those in charge of the arrangements that it was purely a factional disturbance among the negroes, some of whom would be dissatisfied whatever was done." Weller handed over the ministers' list (which included Murray's name) to Murray, as subcommittee chairman, for consideration as members. Weller wanted Murray, "in separate quarters, [to] manage by the aid of his committee the whole affair," he, Weller, "of course having the prerogative of oversight."

Covering the GAR encampment, the *Colored American* referred to the ministers' protest as a "hitch." The headline itself, "Mr. Daniel Murray, a Leading Citizen, to Direct the Labors of a Section of the Committee on Public Comfort—A Separation That Is Not Discrimination," revealed the paper's position. "The Negro visitors to this function in October will be numerous, and naturally the colored people of Washington are anxious to give the colored veterans and their friends a royal welcome to the nation's capital," the article read. "Mr. Weller's plan is not intended as an invidious distinction but as a means of avoiding the annoyance and embarrassment that would arise were the colored hotel and boarding house lists mixed up indiscriminately with those where only white guests would be welcome." The *Washington Bee* ran a letter to the editor written by Henry P. Slaughter that took a similar stance. "The only object was to have a committee of colored men who understood and appreciated existing conditions to so look after matters as to secure decent accommodations for people of color," which, Slaughter concluded, was "obviously necessary." Both pieces seemed to think that Murray needed defending and went out of their way to praise him, but the ministers consequently made clear that they had no objection to Murray per se.

"The incident may be considered closed," declared the *Colored American*, "and we can all get together and extend the hospitality of Washington to our friends, without the aid or consent of those who don't like our company." Murray and his committee went about the work of figuring expenses, preparing directions and "the list of available stopping places," and planning entertainments. The committee included twenty-three of the thirty men the ministers' union had suggested plus Reverend Sterling Brown himself. But the hubbub was in fact simmering and threatened to boil again come late summer.

It was Calvin Chase, the editor of the *Washington Bee* and himself a member of Murray's committee, who turned the heat up this time. The *Bee*'s slogan was "Honey for Friends, Stings for Enemies." If that were not unprofessional enough, the irascible Chase regularly vacillated on who were his friends and who his enemies. Now, writing in the August 30 edition of his paper, Chase stated that M. I. Weller had declared that "he did not propose to have colored men on committees with white people for the coming Encampment of the Grand Army of the Republic and if they want to serve they must be placed in a distinct committee." Although it seems surprising that such a remark would stun Chase, especially this late in the game, it set him off in a big way. He challenged the manhood of those who would subject themselves to such snubs rather than decline membership on "this 'Jim Crow' committee which must serve crow and see that it is well dished."

Murray sent out notifications to the members of his committee that a meeting would be held at his home on September 11 and that M. I. Weller would be present. If Murray sensed trouble brewing, he was right. Some of the men present at the well-attended meeting let Weller know they objected to being asked to serve on a separate committee because it amounted to a "badge of inferiority" and capitulation to being stigmatized. Weller tried to pacify them by offering to print their names along with those on the general public comfort committee in a single alphabetical list in the official program, a concession readily seen as too little, too late.

The *Washington Bee* that came out two days after that meeting was chock-full of dissent. Chase published his letter to Murray declining to serve on his committee, and again he called on others to show their "manhood" by doing the same. The issue carried an equally stinging letter from Lewis H. Douglass addressed to B. H. Warner, announcing his resignation from the subcommittee: "I protest against the action which 'Jim Crows' colored veterans and absolutely refuse to serve in a capacity which insults every man who took arms in defense of his country." It was followed a week later by a letter to the editor from Charles R. Douglass, who claimed that members of "this proscribed committee" were "leaving it like rats from a sinking ship."

Both these sons of Frederick Douglass had served with great distinction in the Civil War, and their open letters had to have affected Murray's sensibilities. Surely he appreciated that treating veterans of color differently from their former comrades in arms was shameful and hardly the equivalent of a segregated inaugural ball. Conflicting pressures cramped Murray between the proverbial rock and a hard place. Chase had declared, "Let the 'Jim Crow' Committee be abolished. There is but one flag." Chase might choose to stand on principle and urge others to follow his example, but someone had to do the work of assisting African American veterans and other visitors in a segregated city. Murray did not interpret his role as countenancing race prejudice. His point of view was projected in the *Colored American*'s columns: "We deplore the unfortunate social customs here, which cause embarrassment every time a public function has to be arranged," but "in the final analysis the care of the colored veterans would naturally devolve upon our people." The article concluded, "There is no reason why the plans of Mr. Murray may not be pushed to a successful conclusion."

And so they were. On the evening of October 3, committee members met at Murray's house, where badges were dispensed and assignments reviewed. The initial task was to meet veterans of color as they arrived on the trains and help them find lodging. The first day of festivities was Monday, October 6. The city was decorated in red, white, and blue, the sun's rays appeared on the heels of Sunday's rain, and great crowds attended outdoor events, including an automobile parade and a regatta race.

The main entertainment that Murray and his associates arranged took place on Thursday, October 9, a daylong excursion down the blue Potomac to the naval base in Maryland known as the Indian Head Proving Ground. Though the destination was an apt one for veterans and Murray had arranged with the secretary of war for the party to witness the testing of two large guns, the real fun took place on the boat. As it steamed along the river, passengers viewed points of interest and enjoyed the band and collation on board.

October 9 was also the date of the white folks' reception at Convention Hall. The thousand or more veterans assembled there were entertained not only by a military band but by African American performers hired to dance "an old Virginia catwalk" and sing plantation songs. The next night was the black folks' turn at staging a reception in the same facility. That opportunity to honor veterans was hosted by a new organization, the Native Washingtonians, and, according to the *Washington Bee*, "There never was a more brilliant ball and reception ever given in this city. . . . The ladies toilets were perfect dreams and the full dress attire of the gentlemen gave great dignity to the occasion."

For all the talk about equal treatment, it is notable that Thursday's excursion on the Potomac was by invitation, planned so that "The best people at home will have a chance to meet and entertain the best people attending the GAR." Tickets for the next night's reception had to be purchased directly from the organizers; none would be sold at the door, "to insure the high standing of the attendance." Of course only the elite graced the party that Pinckney Pinchback and his wife hosted at their posh new home (having finally moved to Washington altogether) during GAR week. Daniel and Anna Murray mingled among the Pinchbacks' many guests, among them Reverend Owen Waller, Charles Douglass, and others who had criticized Murray's committee. After a squabble like that attending the GAR reunion, the *Bee* liked to signal that all factions "smoked the pipe of peace."[1]

When the *Colored American*'s "man on the corner" responded to the question "Will it be pleasant for colored visitors to come to Washington for the Grand Army Encampment?" he answered with a follow-up query: "Do you want a bite to eat? You have a pocketful of money, but if you do not get someone to guide you to a Negro establishment, you might as well be in the Desert of Sahara." The address to the public that resulted from the meeting of the Washington branch of the NAAC that Murray conducted in early 1899 included an optimistic note: "Turning our faces toward the future, we close our eyes to the past and we hope that the beginning of the twentieth century will 'find us further than today.' " This hope was not realized. Ostracism, discrimination, and intimidation only increased in the new century. "The growth of color prejudice in Washington, the capital of the nation, is alarming," the February 1, 1902, *Colored American* declared. "Things have grown decidedly worse during the last few years." The article elaborated, "Now the 'Jim Crow cars' run right into our Sixth Street Station, the theaters either 'colonize' the colored people in some dark corner or refuse them altogether, not a restaurant or hotel will receive them as guests, the white churches, one and all, together with the Young Men's Unchristian Association, cast them out in utter darkness, they are separated and isolated in the City Lodging House, the Salvation Army Mission, the prison reformatories, insane asylum, hospitals and cemeteries."

In the following September 6 issue, a *Colored American* reporter described some of the prejudicial maneuvers that have "grown so notorious and disgusting." They included what today is called police profiling: "The appearance of a Negro in a Washington police court is a fair presumption of guilt." The writer detailed techniques proprietors used, when they bothered at all, to get around the local antidiscrimination laws, which had not been officially rescinded. At the theaters, "the ticket sellers tells you . . . parquet seats 'are all sold,' " but "a few seats are reserved in the rear of the balcony for colored folks." At restaurants and saloons, "unless you pick your places, there is a turndown in store for you. . . . They never give 'color' as the reason for refusing service. Some are 'just out' of every article that is called for." Department stores "object to showing their best lines to Negroes, especially in millinery and shoes . . . since these articles have to be tried on." More detrimental yet, "Not only is the opportunity to enjoy money in your own way denied, but the chance to earn it is meager indeed outside of the [government] departments and domestic service."

The writer drew glum conclusions: "The whites and the blacks of Washington live a separate existence . . . with two standards of treatment," and the coup de grâce, "Washington prejudice is more intense than is found in most of the cities in the South." So complete was the sequestration of the races that the McKinley National Memorial Association splintered off an "auxiliary" (Daniel Murray was its secretary) for African Americans wishing to help raise funds for a monument to the former President.

Pinckney Pinchback, speaking in February 1902, neatly summarized the situation: "The one time rebel has been restored to citizenship and is in control of Southern State governments and enjoying all the honors and emoluments of official station, while the colored men who fought to preserve the Union are being disfranchised by wholesale and humiliated by the most odious and unjust class legislation. . . . It is an act of injustice and an exhibition of ingratitude on the part of the nation without a parallel in the world's history." To add insult to injury, newly arrived European immigrants to America were accepted and assimilated in bold contrast to her native sons of color. Meanwhile, American blacks were treated better abroad than at home.

Daniel Murray and Cyrus Field Adams drew attention to diminished color prejudice in Europe when, in September 1901,
they initiated a drive for subscriptions to a testimonial honoring
the London hotel manager who, the month before, had declined
to draw the color line for American delegates to the International
Methodist Ecumenical Council. The American white conferees
asked the hotel manager to demand that their colleagues of color
leave the hotel, but he refused to go along, no matter that they
threatened to exit themselves. He expressed "surprise that a people
who boasted so much of their democracy should seek to draw such
a distinction between two sections of the human race." Adams and
Murray's stated purpose was not only to send a token of respect and
gratitude to the hotel manager but to gain press coverage for the
entire episode. Why let an opportunity to shame white Americans,
especially those nominally devoted to Christian precepts, go by?

When it came to African Americans being subject to stigmatiz-
ing and humiliating treatment, the most reputable among them were
not excepted—not even Booker T. Washington, the man with President Roosevelt's ear on all issues concerning black people. There was
a great hue and cry when newspapers disclosed that Florida's state
superintendent of education had invited Washington to speak at a
program in Gainesville scheduled for February 1903. Other education officials along with many town residents were incensed at the
idea of a black man addressing a white audience in a white school
auditorium. The *Washington Post* ran Daniel Murray's angry letter to
the editor. This insulting behavior, Murray wrote, "raising so forc-
ible and tangible a doubt as to the civilization of that section," had
been "prompted by the ignorance so inseparable from the exhibition of color prejudice." On another occasion in 1903, a young white
chambermaid refused to change the sheets of the bed Washington
had slept in at an Indianapolis hotel. When charged with being re-
miss, she indignantly responded, "I won't make up any nigger's bed."

Murray's close friend Dr. Charles E. Bentley, a leading member of Chicago's black elite, was forced to undergo a demeaning experience at the International Dental Congress that met in St. Louis in 1904. Although he was the sole black member, that was one too many for the southern delegates when it came to the conference banquet. "From the time they saw Dr. Bentley at the congress 'the social equality' idea flashed across their brains. . . . It was possible for Dr. Bentley to be at the banquet and what a horrible thought it was! The Southern delegates spent the week in lobbying and canvassing and agitating this matter." Bentley "gracefully stayed away from the banquet" but went back to the meeting the next day and introduced a resolution that stipulated that "at all future sessions of the International Dental Congress, all members shall be granted all privileges that pertain to the various activities of such congress regardless of race or creed." Bentley's opponents managed to subvert the challenge by continually shelving the resolution until it was too late for the full congress to vote.[2]

→ ←

IN 1901, MURRAY DRAFTED A PREFACE FOR HIS BOOK. "I HAVE assiduously treasured every notice of the literary kind tending to establish the equality of the Negro race and showing the rapid strides it has made according to its opportunities," he wrote of his years working at the library. "Its marvelous growth," he asserted, "has established indisputably, the anthropological dictum as to the equality of races, and verified the biblical statement that of one blood all men are made." But in the same year, he composed a forty-three-page essay entitled "The Power of Blood Inheritance," drawing sharp distinctions among subpopulations along racial lines. He laid out a theory of racial hierarchy positing that the majority of southern whites were genetically degenerate and that mixed-race Americans were superior to either whites or blacks.

A very different pseudoscientific theory of racial hierarchy held wide credence at that time. So-called Social Darwinists applied the concept of biological evolution to society, situating whites on the top rung as the most advanced and dark-skinned people on lower steps of development, thus appropriating a scientific gloss to claims of black inferiority. In asserting that "mixed-bloods" were superior to both whites and blacks, Murray argued that they were endowed with a sort of hybrid vigor. He was familiar with the principles of genetics established by Gregor Mendel (and rediscovered in 1900). Hybrid vigor is a true biological phenomenon, although it is applicable to humans only in the most general regard that large and varied genetic pools are advantageous. Nevertheless, in invoking it, Murray made more scientific sense than those who proffered the theory that mulattoes were feeble, infertile hybrids. Of course, many whites did not resort to this far-fetched notion; they merely dismissed any achievements by mixed-race people as due to their "white blood."

Murray contested such views. "The average number of children born to mulattoes exceeds by far those born to their white brothers and is not a whit behind their brother in black. These are indisputable facts, shown to be absolutely true by the census, and by all unprejudiced intelligent observers. I know it was urged by some theorists like Dr. Cartwright of Louisiana and accepted by others equally deficient in the matter of intelligent observation that the mulatto was a hybrid like a mule, and could not procreate his species, and was doomed to die out. . . . The reverse is true. The mulattoes are exceptionally prolific, more so than either white or black." Murray described his mixed-race countrymen as composites, "possessing all the mentality of his white progenitor, sustained by the stamina and endurance of his African." Indeed, he averred, they represented the beginning of a new race, the true American standard.

Murray disparaged whites from the South, characterizing that section historically as a "dumping ground for the thieves, respited murderers and prostitutes of Europe," citing the many "involuntary emigrants or transported convicts" England had sent to the southern colonies in the early eighteenth century. He continued:

Now take this fact and put it along side of the terrible massacre of inoffensive colored people in Wilmington, N.C., Nov. 1898, or the unprovoked murder of the Postmaster of Lake City, S.C., and the shooting of his baby in his wife's arms and the burning of his home. The criminal instincts of the people . . . [furnish] illustration of the power of blood inheritance. It is proper here to remark that I am mindful of the fact that not all the people in the Southern States are thus tainted in their blood through their ancestors, but those who are exhibit it in their acts and method of reasoning, in an absolute disregard for law. I am myself of Southern birth, but my ancestors were of gentle birth and came from Scotland. I stand to uphold the law and order and all my reasoning is in accord with my gentle blood. I venture to say, whenever you see a man or woman acting differently from this standard, you may safely affirm that the ancestral blood is asserting itself and register another witness for the theory "that blood will tell."

This essay was never published, but Murray covered its ideas in articles and in talks such as one he gave to the Bethel Literary and Historical Association in May 1901, claiming that "the greatest geniuses of any country were of mixed blood." His contention "that the mulatto, given an equal chance, will outstrip either of his ancestors" was first publicly revealed in the biographical sketch of Murray that appeared in *The Colored American Magazine* in October 1902:

That the Indian and the Jew who are singularly pure in their blood are deteriorating or standing still must be admitted by every truthful investigator. . . . Years ago, it was generally believed, the responsibility for such belief resting upon desire and ignorance, that the mulatto was a hybrid and was of weak physique and doomed to die out. . . . But they are not dying out; indeed, they have greater strength, larger families, more prolific in sexual union, greater mental power, and a larger percent of increase than either the white man or the black man.

The six-thousand-word sketch, under the byline Edwin Lee, in essence presents Murray's autobiography. The content clearly came directly from Murray with no indication that Lee had interviewed anyone else or explored any resource other than Murray. It may be that Murray actually wrote at least sections of the sketch. In 1915, Murray composed an article, "The Color Line Problem in the U.S.," that was published in C. V. Roman's *American Civilization and the Negro,* and a full page therein, including the above passage, is taken verbatim from *The Colored American Magazine* feature. Lee, Murray's white coworker at the Library of Congress, was not a journalist; no other piece attributed to him is known. Comparing Murray's writing style elsewhere to the sketch lends credence to the speculation that Murray was its ghostwriter. What one can conclude with certainty is that the 1915 article shows that Murray did not modify his controversial view over the years.[3]

There was a second element to Murray's focus on mixed-race people. On the one hand, he distanced "those allied with the Negro race" from the race as a whole. His growing list of titles, he conceded, "cannot strictly be called a bibliography of Negro authors, since the work and publications of all mulattoes, quadroons and octoroons are included" and "their status is open to revision." In accusing the dominant culture of "debasing the Negro and all allied to him, so that those allied may take their status from his lowly condition," he pointed out that "the whites and the mulattoes have a common father, and each is entitled to share the common heritage." But at the same time, he pursed a somewhat different tack: "I claim for the colored race whatever credit of an intellectual character an Octoroon, Quadroon, Mulatto, or Negro has won in the world of polite arts." He publicized this variation of his research in two articles published in 1904, "Bibliographia-Africania" in *The Voice of the Negro* and "The Color Problem in the United States" in *The Colored American Magazine.*

Murray initiated a new compilation: Americans and Europeans to "the remotest degree allied with the African race" who had made a name for themselves in the arts. Appropriating for his own use the "one-drop rule" that many whites subscribed to would surely draw attention. Murray hoped to "show that a strain of African blood was not to be despised since some of the world's elect carried such a mixture in their composition." Among them Murray named the American painter Henry O. Tanner; England's famed composer Samuel Coleridge-Taylor; the father of modern Russian literature, Alexander Pushkin; and the French writers Alexandre Dumas *père* and *fils*. These artists had not hidden their African ancestry, though not all who admired them were aware of their genetic background. As Murray wrote of Dumas *père*, "To thousands of intelligent Americans it would be news to learn that the world-renowned author of *The Count of Monte Cristo* and *The Three Musketeers* . . . was a man of mixed blood."

Murray took his research to the next level: "There are many instances, scattered through the annals of literature, of men identified with the African race in some degree, who have attained to high fame in the world of letters and in whose fame the African race is entitled to share, but who have lost by non-association their connection with the race, and people have either forgotten the facts or the principals have conspired to conceal it. Therefore, a systematic effort should be made to get this credit." He took on such an effort with dogged determination, remarking to one correspondent that it "gives me no little pleasure in its pursuit." The *Evening Star*, covering his research in 1905, quoted him on some of its results: "To the great mass of readers it will be news to learn that Robert Browning was an octoroon. It is an interesting story, and the details I have gathered with great care. The same may be said in the case of Alexander Hamilton, the American statesman, and Henry Timrod, the Southern poet." Murray had been "pressing the matter" of the English poet Robert Browning's background since September 1901, when he had been visiting George Myers and a fellow Clevelander, the fiction author Charles Chesnutt, had passed on "the hint about Browning."

In his "quest for information" Murray applied "unflagging zeal and great care," but, as might be expected with the investigative tools available to him, much of the genealogical and genetic intelligence he collected amounted to hearsay evidence. Later researchers found a mixed-race classification for Robert Browning inconclusive and for Alexander Hamilton altogether unsubstantiated, but with Henry Timrod, Murray was on the money. Murray was well aware that "In Charleston, S.C. there stands to-day a statue of Henry Timrod" and that his classification of the man known as the poet laureate of the Confederacy as a "mixed-blood" produced an "awkward situation." Also awkward was Murray's exchange of letters with a South Carolinian whom he queried on Timrod's genetic makeup. His correspondent fired back an indignant response. Referring to the state's monument to the memory of Timrod, the writer demanded to know, "Do you think for one moment that it would be done if one drop of such blood flowed in his veins?" That Timrod's fateful drop or more came from his mother's line is no longer contested.[4]

Murray tackled the issues of interracial sexual relations and amalgamation in his "Blood Inheritance" essay and published articles, in particular his 1906 piece in *The Colored American Magazine*, "Race Integrity—How to Preserve It in the South." Murray's answer to the question posed in the title was: *not* by laws preventing interracial marriage. The article began, "No man would do justice to his race who was so indifferent as to be unmoved at the prospect of preserving its integrity." That was Murray's jumping-off point for rebutting the white man's contention that preserving racial integrity was the intent of laws forbidding mixed marriage. Murray found that but a "specious cry," insisting that the true intent was to "foster a state of concubindage between white men and black women." Many white men, he maintained, "prefer the loose relation to the obligations and restraints of marriage, and without a shadow of fear seek the black women." If interracial marriage were legal, "it would remove the immunity from prosecution under the bastardy act, which the fornicators now enjoy, and impose the obligation upon them of supporting their illegitimate offspring. . . ."

"Thousands of white men threw race integrity to the winds and begot children by black women," noted Murray, further increasing the mixed-race population that, historically, the white southerner in his sexual exploitation of female slaves had engendered to begin with. "It was not in years past, the Negro who by giving rein to his passional inclinations broke down race lines," he pointed out. "It is not he now who begets mixed blood progeny." Restrictive marriage laws, he concluded, "instead of promoting [race integrity], have been . . . the most active and potent agent in defeating it."

But Murray did not stop with his analysis of laws forbidding interracial marriage. "We may as well look this matter full in the face and examine its every phase," he proposed. Not only is race integrity "difficult of maintenance," it must be conceded "that the constant inbreeding of a race invariably leads to deterioration" and might "ultimately lead to its extinction." European royalty had secured race integrity at the price of "propagating and foisting on the world a race of imbeciles." He continued, "The thousands of instances in sexual relations of departure from race lines have served to create a new race, neither Negro nor Caucasian. . . . Children born in defiance of law have inherited traits and mentality equal to, if not superior to those born in harmony with the law." He closed his article with the following statement: "From 1640 to the present time, amalgamation has produced over two millions of people of a new race, and as the foregoing conditions I have pointed out show no likelihood of a change, it will in time solve the race question by eliminating the Negro, the new race element filling the void. This may be God's solvent."

Murray muddied the swirling waters he intrepidly waded into. Distinctions based on color shade, interracial sexual relationships, biological amalgamation, passing for white: these were touchy issues, to say the least, from both black and white points of view. Most blacks agreed with Murray's arguments against laws forbidding mixed marriage. But not all favored full amalgamation, and at any rate, promoting the idea knowing it was anathema to white folks could only serve to inflame the already tense climate. As for Murray turning the tables on the "one-drop rule," white critics did not take to it, though as a supporter pointed out they "object to his doing what all prejudiced Americans do, to-wit: Classing every individual with a drop of 'colored' blood in his or her veins, as 'colored.' " Object they did. One wrote, "It is not necessary to remind Mr. Murray that though it is our habit in this country to class as a negro every person who has a perceptible trace of negro blood, when persons of mixed race show exceptional intelligence the custom is to credit it to the admixture of white blood, so that no amount of fame won by mulattoes and quadroons will be considered to demonstrate anything very significant about negro ability." Another critic thought Murray's work "of little historic value as it stands, because of the practice into which he fell of including as colored persons whom the world does not so regard. If Mr. Murray had heard that the blood of any writer of prominence contained a strain of the African, his works have been promptly included in the list, with the result that Murray's conclusions need to be taken with a grain of salt. But stripped of its superfluities, the fact remains that a surprisingly large amount of literary work has been done by mulattoes. The straight blacks appear to have done almost nothing."

Murray said he took pleasure in identifying notables who were mixed race. But in enabling a conclusion such as "Straight blacks appear to have done almost nothing," he clearly undermined the concept of disassociation of ability from skin color or ethnicity. He may have slammed the southern white man, but the absolute loser in Murray's calculation was the "undiluted" black man. In his foray into pseudoscience, he only substituted one hierarchy for another. Where, by Murray's lights, did that leave dark-skinned high achievers such as Paul Laurence Dunbar, Alexander Crummell, and Kelly Miller? Exceptions to the rule? Such a call would only feed into the "simply an exception" knee-jerk reaction from whites to all African American success stories. In proposing a biological explanation for the fact that mixed-race individuals accounted for a preponderance of men and women of distinction among African Americans, Murray ignored historical and sociological considerations.

Not only that; though he meant to "establish the high character" of all mixed-race Americans, by positing genetic inferiority in the southern white man and at the same time documenting the widespread dissemination of his "blood," the inescapable corollary (though Murray declined to draw it) is that his undesirable heritable traits can accompany whatever genetic benefit comes from race mixing. Murray was sure to except himself: his "white blood" had come from a Scottish gentleman, not a southern scoundrel. Yet he, in effect, disparaged every mixed-race person—including many friends and associates—who carried "blood" from white southerners not of the "gentle" type, who, Murray claimed, were "as common as Georgia watermelons."

Murray habitually used phrases such as "allied with the Negro race" in describing mixed-race people, essentially articulating a tri-racial division; hardly encouraging solidarity. Complexion was so complex an issue among African Americans that even as some were adjudged "too dark," others were "too light." That was the reason given for excluding Josephine Willson Bruce from consideration as president of the National Association of Colored Women at its

1906 meeting. When Cyrus Field Adams was spuriously accused of "masquerading as a white man," he lamented, "My trouble is, all my life I have been trying to pass for colored." Cases of color discrimination, or even distinction, among African Americans, much less Murray's ill-conceived hierarchy, were counterproductive to the goal of racial equality and justice and only obscured the focus of all eyes on the prize.

That, of course, was not Murray's intent. "What the Negro needs more than anything else is the facts at hand to refute such ignorant and prejudiced conclusions in regard to himself, and what I have gathered together will aid him in many instances. I claim for the colored race whatever credit of an intellectual character an Octoroon, Quadroon, Mulatto, or Negro has won in the world of polite arts, and believe a fair examination of the evidence I shall produce will remove no little prejudice against African blood." Murray found racially mixed people to be "the very crux of the race problem" and the key to its solution as well. He seemed to have the hope that racists would give way to reason through his efforts to obscure a delineation between who is white and who is not. "Who can explain," Murray queried, "why a mulatto is not a white man with Negro blood in him, rather than a Negro with white blood in him?" To be sure, he occasionally offered a sentiment such as the following: "No anthropologist to-day, worthy of the name, would dare assert a doctrine which denied the equality of races. There are many varieties of races, all of whom are susceptible of equal development with equal opportunities." But in all his writing, he never explained how his praise aimed at mixed-race Americans would encompass those without admixture in the estimation of the dominant culture.

If Daniel Murray was "in many respects the most influential Afro-American in this community" and "perhaps the very best informed colored man in the country," as the *Colored American* described him, his take on what he called "the vexatious color-line" bore weight. But his own statements were not self-consistent. Did he believe that mixed-race individuals were genetically superior, or did he embrace an "all one blood" concept that stipulated no correlation between ethnicity and ability? Studying all that he left behind on the subject, public and private, one is hard pressed to determine his bottom line. But there is no denying Murray's Sisyphian labors aimed at hastening the day "when the hysteria incident to the virus of race madness has been cured."[5]

12

STRUGGLING

M URRAY'S OFFICIAL ROLE WITH THE NAAC DIMINISHED
over time. The last-dated reference to his involvement with
the Louisiana test case is a December 13, 1900, notice on NAAC
letterhead in his papers. He was listed, along with his close friend,
Philadelphia Tribune editor Christopher Perry and Frederick Mc-
Ghee, on the three-man "executive committee on finance." The
letter concerned fund-raising for lawyers to challenge the Louisiana constitution suffrage restrictions before the US Supreme
Court. As it happened, the case never got that far. An illiterate
Louisianan was chosen as a test subject. When, as expected, his
attempt to register to vote was unsuccessful, the NAAC initiated a
suit in his name. After its dismissal in district court, an appeal was
made to the Louisiana Supreme Court. The higher court backed
the lower court's decision, affirming its argument that since both
white and black residents were subject to the literacy requirement,
rejection of the plaintiff's voter registration had been race neu-
tral. But the actual decision was based on the ruling that the court
lacked jurisdiction based on state law procedural grounds. The dismissal precluded appeal to the US Supreme Court, since that court
does not hear cases in which no question of federal law is presented.

Always supportive of the council's goals, Murray worked in earnest for a Freedmen's Inquiry Commission and against separate-car laws. Congressman Harvey S. Irwin of Kentucky learned of "my bill to create a commission to inquire into the condition of the Colored people" and, "having a large Colored constituency" asked to introduce it, Murray informed George Myers in May 1902. "I have been very busy indeed pressing this bill and the anti 'Jim Crow' amendment to the Interstate Commerce law," he confided. "I have strong hopes of seeing both become laws."

Murray was heartened when Representative Irwin took such interest in the measure he had originally drawn up back in 1899. Although the NAAC had included it in the resolutions of every annual national convention since that year, it was the first time a bill to provide for "a comprehensive investigation of the condition of the people of Negro origin under American jurisdiction" was introduced in Congress. The expectation was that the commission would be an integrated one. As the *Colored American* explained, "There are phases of the race problem which no one but a Negro can fully understand, and only from him can be expected a candid, unbiased report." At a mass meeting held by the NAAC at 19th Street Baptist Church on April 14, 1902, a resolution to support the Irwin bill was adopted and a committee to press for its passage before the House Committee on Labor formed. The committee, chaired by Jesse Lawson, included Daniel Murray, Henry P. Slaughter, George H. White, and Pinckney Pinchback. On Friday evening, April 18, the committee members met at Murray's house to confer with Representative Irwin and prepare for the congressional hearings on the bill three days hence.

Come Monday morning, they appeared before the Labor Subcommittee ready to push for the Irwin bill's passage "with all possible vigor." According to Murray, "The whole matter was carefully planned and carried out without a hitch." Immediately after the session, he reported to Booker T. Washington, "The subcommittee gave us a hearing this morning which was very effective. . . . The bill now goes to the full committee with a favorable recommendation and, as it has carefully been preserved from being denominated a political measure, there is a strong possibility of its passage." He assured the Tuskegeean that his name had not been mentioned at the hearings. On April 29, a delegation including Murray met with President Roosevelt to discuss the bill, had a "pleasant chat," and left with the "understanding that the President is favorable to the measure."

"By a strict party vote the republican members of the House committee on labor today authorized a favorable report on Mr. Irwin's bill," the *Evening Star* reported on May 15. "[T]he Inquiry is to be governed by the same rules as the late industrial commission." Murray referred to the measure as "my bill" when he informed George Myers that it had "now passed the committee stage but the democrats are to file a minority report." He later sent Myers a copy of that report, which, among other arguments, maintained that legislation giving a segment of the population "special footing" was inappropriate.

Notwithstanding strong Republican support, the bill did not pass. Its supporters hoped it might in the next congressional session, but as the *Colored American* conceded, "Just now the situation is not the brightest." By the start of 1903, it was clear that the legislative effort had fizzled out, not surprising given the Democrats' opposition and Congressman Irwin's exit from the scene when he had not been reelected the November before.[1]

As Murray wrote to Myers in May 1902, while pressing the Irwin bill, he was also working to reverse Jim Crow separate-car laws. At the same April 14 NAAC-sponsored meeting where the Irwin bill was endorsed, support was garnered for the bill introduced by Representative Edward Morrell of Pennsylvania "prohibiting railroad officials from separating passengers on account of race or color" under federal law.

Hearings on the bill were scheduled for May 9 before the House Committee on Interstate and Foreign Commerce. Since passage of the Morrell bill was a long shot, supporters wanted to hedge their bets on some effective action prevailing. So, in preparation for the hearings, Murray drew up a strongly worded amendment to the Interstate Commerce Law that would accomplish essentially the same purpose. It made discrimination related to interstate travel a crime, with stiff penalties of $500 to $5,000 imposed on offending rail or water transit companies, and called for passengers to be accommodated according to their ticket class. At the congressional hearings, a delegation including Murray, Cyrus Field Adams, Jesse Lawson, and George H. White testified in favor of Morrell's bill and Murray's amendment. George White was their principal speaker. "How can [segregation] humiliate you when you are simply associating with your own race?" one congressman wondered. White argued that the practice offended the entire race. It was against the fundamental principles of the Republic, and the squalid conditions assigned black travelers made the actual experience miserable.

The *Colored American* published Murray's amendment to the Interstate Commerce Law in full and urged its readers to "cut it out and send it" to every congressman who might be sympathetic. But a month later, September 13, the paper reported, "The status of this amendment at present is, that after an exhaustive hearing . . . in which Mr. Murray participated, his proposition was referred by the committee to the Interstate Commerce Commission for a report." The wait commenced, but neither the Morrell bill nor the Murray amendment ever advanced from committee.

Black citizens were not about to give up the fight. As one journalist observed, "No other point of race contact is so much and so bitterly discussed among Negroes as the Jim Crow car." So sensitive were elites in particular that a rumor that African Americans were to be excluded from Pullman car sleepers spread like wildfire.

Murray passed it on to George Myers, writing on December 8, 1903, that he had heard it from a Chicagoan and understood that it was also making the rounds in Atlanta. Myers acted immediately; the day after he received the letter, a large chunk of it was published in the *Cleveland Plain Dealer* (and shortly thereafter in the *Colored American*), reading in part, "The current rumor extensively circulated here [is] that the Pullman Car Co. would on the 1st day of January, 1904, exclude from the privileges of their cars, all persons of African descent. . . . To say that the anticipated order has caused consternation among the better element of the race but feebly expresses the condition here." As the *Plain Dealer* observed, "Leaders among the colored citizens" are "worked up over [this] persistent rumor." The paper did little to throw cold water on it, running the headline "Plan to Extend the Color Line" in a giant font. This in the face of the disclosure that "A special dispatch to the Plain Dealer last night from Chicago stated that General Manager Garcelon of the Pullman Co. emphatically denied the authenticity of the report and said it was untrue." Nevertheless, the article concluded, "Colored citizens are suspicious that such a move is in contemplation and steps are already being taken to contest any such possible action." Although this rumor was unfounded, there were individual cases of African Americans denied sleeping-car accommodations.

Vigilance was necessary to guard against public transportation status deteriorating in the nation's capital. "The Old Dominion electric line of Virginia is applying to Congress for a charter to run its cars through the streets of Washington," the *Indianapolis Freeman* reported in 1904. "This line carries jim crow cars, and the colored people of the District, under the leadership of Mr. Daniel Murray have taken pains to have the House and Senate committees on the District of Columbia, before whom the matter has been referred for consideration, insert in the charter a provision prohibiting the separations of passengers on account of race or color in the District." *The Colored American Magazine* assessed the situation of railway lines departing the nation's capital: "A separate or 'Jim Crowlean' law is not established or recognized by the laws of the District of Columbia, but the District authorities permit it to be in force." At the railroad terminus in Washington, "Colored passengers for the South are politely requested to go in 'the other end, please.' Should they refuse and insist on entering a car labeled 'White,' on reaching Alexandria, the first stop in Virginia, they are required, instead of requested, to go into the compartment marked 'colored.' . . . There is a general feeling of humiliation and when there are no trainmen present, there are often bitter denunciations against the law."

Many people did more than rail when it came to local streetcars. They resisted. In various southern cities black citizens launched boycotts and took to walking or riding hacks rather than patronize separate-car lines. In Nashville, African Americans established a company of their own. They began by using wagons, then "found that they owned among themselves seventy vehicles which they could use for the purpose." In Jacksonville, Jim Crow cars were "so objectionable to colored people that they built a street car line of their own and operated it with colored motormen and conductors." Another way of agitating the matter was by refusing to adhere to the segregation rules on streetcar or railway lines, which was almost always followed by arrest.

When that led to criminal prosecution and a guilty verdict, plaintiffs sometimes filed suits. Murray detailed one such case— *Hart v. State of Maryland*—in his *Voice of the Negro* article "The Overthrow of the 'Jim Crow' Car Laws." Murray's former Library of Congress colleague, lawyer William H. H. Hart, was a passenger on a through express from Boston to Washington on August 31, 1904. On reaching Maryland, he refused to be reseated in a Jim Crow compartment, as the separate-car law the state had passed earlier that year required. Arrested by a sheriff and jailed, Hart acted as his own lawyer when he faced the magistrate of the Cecil County grand jury. Found guilty as charged and fined, he appealed to the Maryland Court of Appeals. The higher court reversed the lower one, declaring that it had no right to fine Hart because the Jim Crow section of the Maryland statute did not apply to interstate railroad passengers. The verdict Hart won, as Murray explained in his article, was based on the interstate commerce clause of the US Constitution: Congress shall have exclusive power to regulate commerce between states. Murray wrote, "The railroads will not be able to enforce any of the 'Jim Crow' laws of the States, if they are engaged in any form of interstate commerce" in accord with previous US Supreme Court rulings that common carriers "are not subject to State legislation by way of freight, or passenger regulation." Although the Maryland statute could not be "sustained to the extent of making interstate passengers amenable to its provisions," the decision did not alter the legality of separate compartments for railways operating wholly within a state.[2]

> <

OVER THIS PERIOD, THE MURRAY FAMILY HAD THEIR UPS AND downs. Two days after Daniel Murray and his son returned from their visit to Buffalo and Cleveland in the fall of 1901, eight-year-old Harold was taken ill with sore throat and chills, followed by a fever so intense his mouth broke out in fever blisters. Though he recovered in a week or so, his parents were "constantly uneasy" because "he is never hearty and free from ailment, his appetite is so variable and he is so likely to be sick through indiscreet eating." On the heels of Harold's illness, the sister Murray was closest to, Ellen Butler, died of stomach cancer. She'd been suffering for months. By the first week in September, her state was so precarious that Murray anticipated that she "may drop off any moment." The end came on October 7. Ellen was survived by one child, Kate Proctor Jordan; her youngest daughter, Ella Butler Seville (for whom Murray had earlier served as guardian), had died the year before at thirty-eight. In her will Ellen bequeathed $250 to her brother Daniel "in satisfaction of my debt to him (which is less than that sum) and is a token of my affection for him."

Christmas 1901 brought a brighter day. The younger boys, Harold and three-year-old Paul, "had a merry time dealing with Santa Claus," their father recounted. "Harold had a Magic Lantern, which he proceeded to show Christmas night, the faint picture of which gave excellent play for one's imagination." Nat was completing his senior year at M Street High School. Come spring, he attended a surprise party for John W. Cromwell's daughter Fannie, who arrived home to find a "merry throng in the mazes of the dance." Two weeks later, on April Fools' Day, the Kappa Rho Tab Club, composed of M Street High School boys, gathered at the Murray home for their first party, a coed affair. After dancing, the young guests "marched in couples to the dining room, where a sumptuous repast was served and souvenirs of white and pink carnations were distributed." Thus were children of the black upper class familiarized to the kind of social activities their parents indulged in. When Harold was only fifteen, he would become a member of the Bon-Bon-Buddies; the club, made up of high school sons of "well-known families of Washington," held an afternoon "grand matinee," complete with band, at the True Reformer Building.

Nat turned eighteen on April 10, 1902. He graduated from high school in June and went on to Hampton Institute that September to begin a three years' postgraduate course in scientific agriculture. Henry, meanwhile, left Harvard after two years due to ill health. Thus, even as one son moved out of the S Street house, another returned home. Henry, having become familiar at Harvard with the newly popular game of football, taught it to his younger brother. Harold "is fairly crazy over the game," their father told George Myers, and likes to demonstrate how he "can 'hit the line' whatever that is." Henry was appointed a teacher in the Washington colored school system in September 1902, the month he turned twenty.[3]

Among their elite community of friends and associates, Anna and Daniel Murray were, like Robert and Mary Terrell, what today we call a power couple. In the same May 3, 1902, issue, *Colored American* ran a short piece on Anna's presentations at various literary societies and another on Daniel's progress with his colored authors project. Murray boasted, "My own wife is par excellence in domestic matters," while also supporting her activism outside the home. Each was committed to a specific approach to racial advancement. "The true test of the progress of a people is to be found in their literature," he declared, a complementary companion to her assertion that "It is the home which indicates the real elevation and substantial progress of any race." In July 1902, the couple attended the annual Hampton Negro Conference at their son Nat's soon-to-be school. Standing committees were formed, with Anna assigned to the domestic economy committee and her husband to business and labor.

Daniel Murray, who claimed he was "very susceptible to malarial influences," contracted a light fever and upon returning home was under the weather for more than two weeks. But the conference had done his mind good. As he told George Myers, there he had heard "evidence of the progress of the Negro" that "renewed hope that [he] will yet surmount the conditions that enthrall him and be emancipated indeed." He had expressed a similarly optimistic note to Myers the October before, when President Roosevelt had invited Booker T. Washington to dinner at the White House: "The world is moving."[4]

Murray had reason for satisfaction as he saw his aspirations for a manual training high school and a free public library come to fruition after years of effort. School officials expected the new building for Manual Training School No. 2, fronting P Street and stretching from 1st to 3rd streets, to be ready for pupils in September 1901. "To Mr. Murray is due the credit of our new manual training school," hailed the *Colored American* in August. "Year after year he continued to urge the matter until at last his efforts were crowned with success." Three months previously, the school board had appointed Murray's brother-in-law Dr. Wilson Bruce Evans principal of the new high school, a promotion from his principalship at Mott grade school. Murray had "brought along" his wife's brother Bruce, now thirty-eight, including him on many of the civic and social committees he had charge of. The press approved of Evans's appointment, the *Washington Bee* noting, "Dr. Evans comes naturally by his knowledge of manual work since his father was a cabinet maker and joiner and for several years had charge as foreman for Mr. Daniel Murray in all his building operations, during which time young Evans worked as assistant to his father."

Readying the school took a year longer than anticipated. The twenty-eight-room buff brick and stone building, designed for three hundred students, contained laboratories, workshops, a foundry, and classrooms for academic subjects. Outside were gardens for applied biology. The high school now had a name, Armstrong Manual Training School, honoring Samuel C. Armstrong, the white founder of Hampton Institute. Classes began on September 22, 1902. Among the twenty-four-member faculty was the principal's nephew George Henry Murray, a teacher of mechanical drawing and mathematics. Evans described the chief goals of the institution as "dignifying the work of the hand" and providing "training having a more marketable value" than classical studies alone. The chief speaker at the October 24 official dedication, "the apostle of industrial development," Booker T. Washington, agreed. During the exercises, held in the school's assembly hall, Bruce Evans, in a symbolic gesture, was presented with the key to the building.

At the annual meeting of the full Board of Trade, held in the

New Willard's ballroom on November 10, 1902, it was announced that "This city will soon be in possession of a beautiful, commodious, well located free public library." The Beaux-Arts white marble edifice sat on the low rise of Mount Vernon Square with the grand entrance facing K Street. Congress had provided the site and an appropriation for maintenance. Andrew Carnegie had donated a total of $375,000 for construction. In all, the steel magnate and philanthropist funded more than 1,500 libraries across the country, and he was quite serious about their being accessible to all. In 1901, it was reported that the white population of Richmond, Virginia, would not go along with Carnegie's condition, finding it "impossible to accept the gift unless the Negroes can be excluded from the library."

The Washington library would bear the name of its benefactor. It was dedicated and formally presented to the people of the District on January 7, 1903, in the presence of President Roosevelt and other dignitaries. In his comments, Carnegie declared, "The free library, maintained by all the people, for all the people, knows neither rank nor birth within its walls." Theodore Noyes, the associate editor of the *Evening Star* who chaired the Board of Trade library committee that Murray served on, was president of the library's board of trustees. Noyes, Murray, and their colleagues had worked assiduously for this red-letter day since 1894.[5]

The holiday season of 1902 brought unwelcome incidents for the Murray family. "My little boy Paul, not quite five years old, fell about three weeks ago from the bed and broke his arm," Murray informed George Myers on December 6. "Dr. Curtis set the limb." The fall may be related to the fact that Paul was epileptic. Although it is not known when the disorder first manifested, time would prove that Paul, not Harold, was the physically frail son.

The front page of the December 25 *Evening Star* blared, "Brutal Christmas Eve Murder at Hillsdale," the subheadline "Victim Clairvoyant." Said victim was Murray's niece Kate Proctor Jordan, the daughter of his late sister Ellen. Murray relayed the bloody tale to George Myers:

> On Christmas Eve a horrible tragedy was enacted at the lit-
> tle village of Anacostia, my niece, who lived alone on a piece
> of property belonging to my sister [Kate's aunt Catherine,
> who resided in Baltimore], was murdered. It happened about
> 7 o'clock in the evening Dec. 24th and up to this writing
> no definite clue has been received either as to the murderer
> or his motive. We cannot tell whether it was for the pur-
> pose of robbery or what? The only clue found is the knife,
> a poignard, with which a stab wound was inflicted, which
> caused death in twenty minutes. She was able to run into the
> lane running before her house and fell two doors below. The
> man was seen to come from the house and she following
> screaming at the top of her voice and yet he got away and no
> trace of him has thus far been found.

The papers were all over the sensational story. Robbery was not seen as the only possible motive as the murderer had been hidden in a closet when Kate arrived home from Christmas shopping but had not rifled through her belongings. The intruder had pounced on Kate and inflicted a three-inch-deep cut that "extended from in front of the left ear across and through the jugular vein." Another motive the authorities considered was revenge connected with Kate's being in the "fortune-telling line . . . furnishing 'conjura-tion' powders to some of [her patrons] and 'sprinkling fluid' to others." Some felt that "the crime may have been committed by some person who had a grievance on account of disappointment in the fortune telling business." Others speculated that the perpetra-tor was an escaped madman from St. Elizabeths, the government hospital for the insane just south of Hillsdale. Detectives pursued potential suspects in DC, Virginia, Maryland, and Pennsylvania, but the case remained unsolved. Murray, always the "go-to" relative, took charge of dealing with the house once it was no longer an active crime scene.

"My holidays have been rather sad days as you can infer," Murray wrote to Myers. The letter's date—January 5, 1903—was two days after the anniversary of the death of the Murrays' only daughter. The Christmas before Murray had confided in his friend how the memory of Helene dying during the holidays had subdued the season for him. Now this family tragedy would color future Christmases a deeper blue. All in all, 1902 was not the best of times for Daniel Murray. Although he did get to witness the opening of the manual training high school and anticipate the same for the public library that he championed, his niece's grisly death ended the calendar year that included the GAR controversy and failures with the Irwin bill, the Morrell bill, and the Murray amendment.[6]

The suspension and subsequent failure of the Capital Savings Bank induced Murray to write a series of letters on the subject to George Myers, beginning in December 1902: "I suppose you have heard the news of the suspension of the Capital Savings Bank. It is the talk of the town." He relayed that on November 24 the bank had opened with $50 on hand, commenting, "The fact that they closed their doors on a demand for $75 shows a bad state." Notification that the bank would remain shuttered for two months came as a shock to most Washingtonians. It had been operating for fourteen years, weathering economic downturns that had brought other banks down, and was considered a prime example of successful black enterprise.

The bank officers wanted an opportunity to regroup, but the courts decided otherwise. On January 9, 1903, bank receivers were appointed to administer the assets of the insolvent institution. The *Washington Bee*'s headline the next day announced, "The Capital Savings Bank No More." Murray took to the third person in informing Myers, "Your uncle Daniel is not affected, nor is he glad over its downfall, notwithstanding its officers constantly abused and opposed him in every way possible, simply because he did not deposit his hard earnings in their bank and had he done so would now be among the mourners." He went on, "The whole brunt of opposition to me in the GAR matter was centered in the bank, the same in the 'inaugural ball' when the bank people organized an opposition ball. . . . I do not know whether our friend Green was caught in the bank matter or not, but I am certain an effort was made to induce him to deposit because of race affinity." Murray claimed he had never had any confidence in the bank's methods, and anyway, "a most liberal spirit has always been shown by the white banks. . . . I have had every aid possible granted me." Andrew Hilyer, who documented the growth of black business in Washington, had warned, "The colored man who would succeed in business must meet the competition of his white neighbor . . . and also the distrust and jealousy of many of his own race."

"It is very disappointing, in fact disgraceful, that there is not likely to be realized more than three cents on each dollar" for depositors, Murray wrote Myers. "The bitterness of feeling is very great and will no doubt lead to attempts to hold the officers to criminal account." Some of the former officers went bankrupt. Some attempted to conceal assets. In the latter category Murray included Robert Terrell, Whitefield McKinlay, and others who he felt had opposed him because he had not patronized their bank. "There is one thing that must now come to an end," he asserted. "They will in the future be deprived of the satisfaction they used to gather, through boasting of their wealth." But Murray also had loyal friends among the disgraced bank directors. One of them was James T. Bradford, who in a state of depression closed his Washington house and returned to Baltimore. Murray expressed sorrow "for the unfortunate position of our friend Bradford whose entire fortune will be swept away."

The bank episode prompted Murray, in the same set of letters, to lend Myers financial advice, and here he really did sound like an uncle. He congratulated his friend on clearing his home of debt by "declining to yield to tempting invitations which if accepted would have postponed the day of your complete freedom." He advised him "not to let the one house be the end of your efforts, but seek to obtain a dozen because they are very handy things to have around on a rainy day," adding, "I hope you will realize all that your land is worth and that it will give you that ease in your declining years that has been my hope for myself for many years."[7]

In 1903, the Pen and Pencil Club was as active as ever, described by the *Colored American* at the time as "the most talked about, if not the most prominent club in the District, and by all odds the most representative colored club in the United States." The annual February 14 banquet fell on a Saturday, and corresponding secretary Robert Pelham, Jr., masterminded its theme, "A Train of Thought." He went all out, beginning with the invitations in the form of a railroad pass to ride the "The Pen and Pencil Club Special" to the Virginia waterfront resort of Grey's Point. Murray took his son Henry along. The hall the club rented at the destination, about 140 miles south of DC on the Rappahannock River, was outfitted as if it were a dining room of a railway station. From 7:30 p.m. until midnight, the club members and their guests feasted on fillet of beef and roast turkey, sipped punch, and listened to orations honoring Frederick Douglass. The Washington elite and literati were out in force.

"On last Tuesday Mch. 3rd I celebrated my 52nd birthday by inviting the Pen and Pencil club of which I am Vice-Pres. and a number of other friends," Murray informed George Myers. It was quite an affair, covered by the *Evening Star* on March 4, 1903, and by the *Colored American* in four consecutive issues. Murray's guests were "royally entertained" at his "palatial residence." The "parlors were well filled," and a repast was served in the dining room featuring pâté de foie gras. The invitees included Cyrus Field Adams,

Pinckney Pinchback, Jesse Lawson, George H. White, Christian Fleetwood, Wyatt Archer, John F. Cook, Charles R. Douglass, Judson Lyons, John C. Dancy, Kelly Miller, Edward E. Cooper, William H. H. Hart, Drs. John R. Francis and Austin M. Curtis, Lafayette M. Hershaw, John P. Green, and Bruce Evans, plus Murray's longtime Library of Congress colleague John F. N. Wilkinson and his old buddy Spencer Murray. While the company was in the dining room, "a telegram of congratulations was received from Hon. Fred R. Moore of New York, a lifelong friend of the host." A scrappy debate on who "had the honor of first capitalizing the word Negro" was one of the evening's lively discussions. "We would like to see," concluded E. E. Cooper, "Daniel Murray's birthday roll along oftener."

Some three weeks after the party, the *Colored American* ran biographical sketches of some of the "shining lights" of the Pen and Pencil Club, accompanied by pen-and-ink caricatures. Murray's showed his body shaped like a question mark because he "is a human interrogation point," and the article adjudged that "as a pencil pusher he stands at the head of the heap."[8]

The National Sociological Society, an organization "composed largely of educated negroes" but also including white members, was formed in Washington in the summer of 1903. The magazine *World Today* stated, "The society owes its origin to the earnest efforts of three prominent negroes," referring to Jesse Lawson, Daniel Murray, and Edward A. Johnson, "whose anxious thought for the present and future of their race has crystallized in this movement." Johnson, a North Carolinian, was best known as the author of a popular textbook, *A School History of the Negro Race in America*. The society organized a conference, "How to Solve the Race Problem," with sessions held at various African American churches in in the capital, from November 9 to 12, 1903. The society president, Jesse Lawson, called the conference to order on Monday afternoon, inviting the audience, "composed of men of both races, eminent in law, theology, medicine, literature, economics, and the science of statecraft," from across the country "to deliberate on the most serious phases of the race question, and to formulate plans for the relief of a strained situation." The conference opened for the transaction of business, and Murray, already a member of the society's executive committee, was elected to the five-person conference executive committee and appointed to the ten-person committee of resolutions. All these committees were interracial.

One of Monday's topics, segregation, "proved to be a bone of contention." The first speaker on the subject, Bishop Lucius Holsey of Georgia, endorsed a separatist approach, proposing that the "government set aside one or more states for the segregation of the Negro." The audience was shocked. All three of the city's mainstream newspapers, the *Evening Star*, the *Washington Post*, and the *Washington Times*, reported on the first day of the conference proceedings, and all led with the controversy, highlighting the prolonged "warm discussion" that followed Holsey's proposal. The conferees roundly rejected the idea and ultimately concluded that "colonization, expatriation, and segregation were unworthy of further consideration."

Although none was as heated as the segregation debate, spirited discussions with varying points of view fervently expressed, and even speakers interrupted, characterized subsequent topics over the following days. Murray's formal presentation, which took place on the conference's final day, centered on emigration from the South. "This Society will not have met public expectations unless it proposes, before closing its session, some practical solution," he began. "I believe the solution lies in the field of emigration; that is, induce those affected by unjust laws to seek those sections of the country that offer the greatest inducement in the matter of just treatment . . . where a higher appreciation is manifested for the principles of the Christian religion." He suggested that southern employers would feel this, or the threat of it, in their pocketbooks: "When confronted with the alternative of either dealing fairly with their laborers, the best in the world, or losing them, those who are largely now indifferent about the treatment accorded them will awaken by their own interest and insist that every just ground of complaint be remedied." His remarks would not have pleased Booker T. Washington, who had spoken two days before. He requested sympathy and help for "those who strive for better conditions right there in the south. There are some who under all conditions mean to remain there. If they suffer they mean to remain there, right there in the heart of the south, as long as the bulk of our people are there."

Following Murray's talk, the conferees adopted a series of resolutions based on the report of the committee on resolutions. Included were the following: that loyalty to the country is the first and highest duty of every American; that the duty of the government is to afford adequate and equal protection to all citizens; that every statute should apply to the whole people without discrimination by race or class; that mob violence destroys respect for orderly government and that crime of any character is most effectually prevented or punished by the processes of law; and that a commission of six be appointed by the conference "to consist of six experienced thinkers and workers on the race problem, three of the white and three of the negro race." This permanent commission was named and charged with carrying the conference's plans and conclusions into effect, presenting the resolutions before Congress, and keeping the general public aware of their efforts. The African American representatives were Jesse Lawson, Kelly Miller, and Daniel Murray. The three white men named had all participated in the conference: Dean R. Babbitt, a Brooklyn pastor; Amory D. Mayo, a Boston clergyman and educator; and George C. Gorham, a longtime California resident and former secretary of the US Senate.

On the same day the conference was concluded, November 12, thirty members of the National Sociological Society called on President Roosevelt at the White House. Roosevelt gave them but "a few minutes," barely enough time for introductions. "There was no discussion of the work of the convention or any other phase of the negro question." The conference was considered a success: it garnered plenty of press, the conference proceedings were published in short order, and by the end of the year the society had three thousand members. Yet, as it happened, over the next few years the National Sociological Society, like its representatives' meeting with President Roosevelt, petered out with no substantial outcomes.

On December 25, 1903, Murray informed George Myers that he was spending the day quietly at home with his family: "All my children are at home this Christmas, excepting eldest Dan, who is in New York. He wrote he could not come. Mrs. Murray has been as busy as a bee getting ready the Christmas dinner. . . . The children are happy over the visitation of Santa Claus. . . . Paul has thought of little else for a month. Harold I fear has a suspicion as to Santa Claus, gathered from his contact with older boys, and speaks of the matter with so much doubt that I am led to believe he has outgrown the fiction."

Murray had the opportunity to catch up with some of his closest friends that holiday season. Fred R. Moore, the newly elected national organizer of the National Negro Business League, was in town earlier in the month. A few days before Christmas, Murray entertained two of his friends, who, like his correspondent Myers, had been buddies since their shared childhood in Baltimore. "No Christmas nowadays seems like the time when I was a boy in Baltimore. The hearty good cheer of old Maryland hospitality is not known among the people of Washington, and it is only when a few get together that things are enlivened," Murray confided in a nostalgic vein. "Chris Perry was here Sunday and spent some time at my home. Spencer Murray also was along and you may judge things assumed a lively turn in a short time."[9]

→ ←

Murray's article "The Industrial Problem in the United States and the Negro's Relation to It" was published in *The Voice of the Negro* in 1904. Part I appeared in the September issue and part II in November. Murray claimed that in addition to the elective franchise, "There were other rights of equal importance that were not receiving the attention they should, and from which it was possible to gather benefits equal to what might be claimed on behalf of unobstructed suffrage . . . the right to unrestricted labor being one of them." He believed that "great as is the right of suffrage, it is secondary to the right to labor, the right to earn one's bread, which involves the right to live at all." Industrial emancipation offered the promising hope "that through it will come that permanent recognition of the Negro's right to vote, which all must regard as the right preservative of all rights."

Various labor unions "have scrupulously excluded all colored men from membership, and by the power of the organization have thus monopolized all the opportunities for profitable employment," he observed. "They have not only excluded the colored man as a participant, but have fixed the hours of their own employment, the amount the owner shall pay them, the number of hours he shall keep employed and whom he shall employ—in fact, they have, in a measure, excluded the employer from the control of his own business."

Even though employment opportunities were few, Murray maintained that "those few if embraced and a credible record made, will serve to open many others," and in order to "be ready to embrace an opportunity whenever such may come," it would be necessary "to equip ourselves for industrial places." He elaborated,

"It must be potent to all that such opportunities to be permanently employed in large numbers in the skilled labor lines would
do us no good, were not our boys and girls equipped in industrial
training. . . . The Negro has not been taught to labor scientifically;
he lacks the knowledge to interpret drawings or secure uniformity
of designs with tools."

In some lines of employment, such as agriculture, African
Americans were the relied-on laborers. "The cotton must be picked
and Negroes are needed to pick it." That suggested to Murray a
"practical solution to the 'Negro problem' in the South. . . . It indicates that just as soon as the white man's material interest is affected he will find a way to put down the element that is constantly
bringing forward propositions to humiliate the Negro. The colored men in this connection, standing as they would, between
these two forces, union labor and capital, would be advantageously
placed. . . . Prejudice cannot stand against self-interest. . . .

"If all the colored laborers of the South could be effectively
organized for protection on lines analogous to labor unions, they
could secure every right enjoyed by any other citizen irrespective
of color," he averred, calling for boycotts and work stoppages or
walkouts. "It involves no violence, no hot words, simply to stand
pat on every form of labor for a given time as a silent protest
against injustice." He was confident that "with this weapon," black
workers "could at any moment paralyze the industries of the South
and awaken such an interest in their cause, that the introduction of
[Jim Crow] bills would be stopped through a fear of their consequences to the industries of the South."

The solution Murray concentrated on here was different from
the emigration one he had extolled at the National Sociological
Society conference; here he was focused on Booker T. Washington's request to help the black man in place. In laying out
both alternatives—leave home for the unknown or stand pat in

refusal—he expressed little sympathetic appreciation for the magnitude of the sacrifice. He recommended fasting and prayer to sustain those in the process of resistance.

Because of his strong support for manual training, Murray is sometimes described as a Booker T. Washington partisan, but that is not accurate. Even as the Washington and DuBois camps became more defined, Murray's views, like those of many in his circle, were an amalgam of the philosophies of those standard-bearers. Unlike some of his colleagues, he was not beholden to Washington for patronage or financing and could thus afford to act according to his own lights. Certainly Washington did not approve of Murray's call for organized direct action. Indeed, even before part II of his article appeared, a Tuskegee Institute teacher, John W. Hubert, placed a letter of dissent in *The Voice of the Negro*. Though he confirmed Murray's "diagnosis," he abhorred his "antidote." He found strikes inadvisable and "a peaceful appeal to the enlightened conscience" more effective. "The race problems must be solved through patience and industry," he concluded, declaring thrice, "It takes time."

It is true that Murray hosted both Washington and his secretary, Emmett J. Scott, as overnight quests on separate occasions in 1899 and 1902, respectively, but he did the same for many friends and associates whom Washington would have considered radical. When, in 1903, Washington was the subject of a "spirited and hot" discussion at a Bethel Literary and Historical Association gathering, he, in his inimitable style, had Richard W. Thompson, who was beholden to the "Tuskegee Machine" for patronage, report back. Thompson named Anna Murray among the seven "heavyweights" present who had "maintained a silence rivalling that of the tomb" rather than defend Washington, and identified Lafayette M. Hershaw as one of the "antagonists" who had spoken out. Since Hershaw was the driving force of the Pen and Pencil Club and was a pronounced foe of the man he considered the "Great Accommodator," Washington was distrustful of the club (it is perhaps pertinent to point out that Thompson was a club member).

Meanwhile, Murray's article engendered a lot of response. One reviewer wanted to see the piece "put in pamphlet form and scattered broadcast among our laboring classes by the hundred thousand," and, referencing Murray's suggested tactics, advised, "DO IT." Another definitely disagreed, writing that Murray's "idea of vindication will work vastly more harm than good," because "all is against us should a strike be forced into combative spheres." But the response that got under Murray's skin was a sting from Calvin Chase in the *Washington Bee*. Though Chase acknowledged Murray as "a man of remarkable versatility of thought," he characterized the latest "emanation from the brain of Mr. Daniel Murray" as "ludicrous." Murray, he wrote, "takes his place in the ranks of the 'stand-patters,' by announcing that his remedy is to 'simply stand pat on every form of labor for a given time as a silent protest against injustice,' 'go on half rations,' and 'spend the time in earnest prayer to God to remove the threatening wrong.' " Chase did not leave it there. "We have never known him to 'stand pat,' and from his hospitable disposition, we think he has no predilection for 'half rations.' As for praying . . . we think Mr. Murray has no reputation as a man of prayer." Murray took extreme issue with the article. Chase claimed that he had but made "some playful and innocent observations" in "treating Mr. Murray's remedy with levity rather than with gravity." The outraged Murray, in a letter to the editor, described it as a "brutal, malignant and cruel tirade of personal abuse," wherein he "was held up to the public as a notorious hypocrite," and insisted that the editor had "done me, my wife and children an irreparable wrong." [10]

13

FATHER AND SONS

S AMUEL COLERIDGE-TAYLOR, CELEBRATED COMPOSER, PER-
former, and all-around musical genius, toured the United
States for the first time in 1904, making his initial appearance in
Washington, DC. As the *New York Tribune* announced, "Mr. Taylor is visiting the United States at the invitation of the Coleridge-
Taylor Society of Washington . . . a black choir which has taken his
name." The movement to form and train a chorus of two hundred
voices to render Coleridge-Taylor's acclaimed *Song of Hiawatha*,
with the hope that the composer himself might be induced to cross
the ocean and personally conduct his cantata, began in late 1901.
Among those actively involved in the effort were Daniel and Anna
Murray. Daniel Murray served on the society's board of managers
and was one of the signatories on the certificate of incorporation of
the Samuel Coleridge-Taylor Choral Society.

The society chorus practiced the *Song of Hiawatha* trilogy to
perfection. Coleridge-Taylor's cantata was inspired by the poem
of the same name written by American poet Henry Wadsworth
Longfellow. After almost three years of coaxing, the choral society
was thrilled and gratified to learn that the master had consented
to come to the nation's capital and conduct their rendition of his

work. The preparations were extensive. Daniel Murray served on the publicity and promotion committee and Anna Murray on the concerts and entertainment committee. Chorus rehearsals intensified, culminating in a splendidly received benefit performance at Metropolitan AME Church in April 1904.

The Samuel Coleridge-Taylor Society's dream of performing *Song of Hiawatha* with its composer at the podium was realized on November 16. As the *Evening Star* reported, "One of the most remarkable audiences ever assembled in Washington greeted Samuel Coleridge-Taylor, the eminent English composer. . . . Convention Hall was crowded, approximately three thousand persons being seated and many standing. As the chorus is composed exclusively of colored vocalists, led by a composer and conductor of their own race, the colored people were in the majority in the audience, but there were present also many prominent members of Washington social and official life, and nearly all the eminent local musicians. . . . The response tendered Mr. Taylor was as cordial and enthusiastic as ever greeted a composer of whatsoever creed or color."

Coleridge-Taylor's tour in America deepened his interest in his racial background. He collected African American spirituals and traditional African songs, and these served as the basis for his composition, *Twenty-Four Negro Melodies.* "I have tried to do for these Negro Melodies," he wrote, "what Brahms has done for the Hungarian folk music [and] Dvorak for the Bohemian."

Interest in the choral society was just one way in which the Murrays expressed their musical inclinations. Dannie chose the violin as his instrument, while his brothers Nat and Harold, like their mother, favored the keyboard. At ten Harold was taking piano lessons, and, according to his father, "promises to be a fine player on the piano; he also affects to sing." Anna was the most accomplished vocalist in the family, although her husband fancied himself a credible choral singer. Surely he was pleased when he was elected an honorary member of the Amphion Glee Club of Washington, the oldest and most prestigious African American male musical association in the city. The most musically talented member of the extended family would prove to be Anna's niece Lillian, the daughter of her brother Bruce. Lillian, destined to become a renowned opera singer with the stage name Madame Evanti, sang in her first public concert, a charity event, at age four, standing on a stool and dressed in a pinafore.

Lillian was fourteen and her brother, Joseph, a year or so younger when their parents bought a house at 1910 Vermont Avenue NW, just a few blocks from the Murray place on S Street. Bruce and Anna's mother, Henrietta, closed up the 12th Street home where Evanses had lived since 1870 and moved in with her son. The Evans and Murray families were always close, and now their houses were as well. Bruce called Anna "Sis," and his children called her "Aunt Sis."

Anna also remained close to her sibling Mary; the sisters visited between Washington and Boston regularly. Mary and Butler Wilson, married for ten years now, were parents to five children. Like Anna and Daniel Murray, the Wilsons were a dynamic couple, active in black elite circles, and in cultural, educational, civic, and political enterprises, especially those related to race.[1]

Theodore Roosevelt, elected president in his own right in an unprecedented landslide vote, took the oath of office for a full term on March 4, 1905. Preparations had begun months before. Once again M. I. Weller was public comfort committee chairman for a major capital occasion, and once again he tendered to Daniel Murray "the chairmanship of the sub-committee for colored visitors." There was a separate headquarters for the subcommittee, and its proposed members had to be "passed upon by Mr. Weller." George H. White and Jesse Lawson were selected as vice chairmen and Murray's son Henry as secretary. The makeup of the rest of the forty-member subcommittee included Henry Slaughter, John R.

Francis, and Bruce Evans, but not one of the dissenters from the GAR event. Nevertheless, Weller found it necessary to hold a special meeting of the subcommittee at Murray's house on February 3 to assure its members that "The colored visitors are entitled to the same courtesy as the white visitors when they come to attend the inaugural celebration, and they will be accorded that courtesy by the representative citizens of their own race," adding, "If they do not enjoy themselves, they themselves will be to blame." The next day's *Washington Post* headline proclaimed, "Colored Committee to Greet Inaugural Visitors Is No Race Discrimination." This, even as the *Post* stated, "Experience has proven the wisdom of the creation of this subcommittee, especially because of the knowledge on the part of the chairmen of certain existing social prejudices which debarred members of the negro race from entertainment at hotels or boarding houses patronized by white people."

In spite of white nearsightedness, African American Washingtonians and their visitors were determined to enjoy the inaugural festivities. For a week after Roosevelt's swearing-in ceremony, social functions of "brilliancy and enjoyment crowded upon each other's heels," recalled Mary Church Terrell. To those who "find it difficult to understand how it is possible for people who are handicapped . . . to give themselves over to pleasure and mirth," she explained, "People who insist upon smiling, no matter how often they have occasion to weep, can never be conquered by untoward circumstances or oppression." She reported on the great extravaganza of March 6, "Not one single, solitary ball, mind you, but three full-fledged bona-fide Inaugural affairs, all held on the same evening under three separate and distinct roofs." This was at a time when there was just one mainstream ball. One of the *Washington Bee*'s readers asked plaintively, "Is it possible that the colored society of this city cannot unite socially? Why should there be three inaugural balls?" Daniel Murray knew the answer: because there were cliques among DC's black elites. Again he took on the competition with relish, informing George Myers, "I am head and neck into it, but we have some little opposition. Thus far I have aided materially in breaking it down." Murray's challengers this year were the Native Washingtonians (the hosts of the grand reception during GAR week) and the Monacan Club (evolved from the Cosmos Club, the Inaugural Welcome Club's sole competitor four years earlier). Presumably all three balls were swell affairs, though Murray undoubtedly took pleasure in his club's garnering the largest attendance, with one thousand reveling at Convention Hall.[2]

About this time six-year-old Paul developed scarlet fever and Anna caught the infection. Both mother and son underwent surgery, probably to drain a throat abscess, and remained under treatment for weeks afterward. Anna was operated on a second time "in a more radical manner." She was better by May, but Murray was still "filled with deepest anxiety" over his wife's health.

Henry, the oldest son at home, was a mathematics instructor at Armstrong Manual Training School, specializing in remedial guidance for the slow learner. Active in extracurricular activities, he coached football and baseball and became an early leader in the Boy Scouts organization. He founded Camp Banneker, a segregated Boy Scout camp in Montgomery County, Maryland. Responding to a letter from George Myers wherein his old friend had boasted of his son's success, Daniel Murray wrote, "He is a 'Chip off the old block' and you may judge what we expect of the Chips." Certainly Henry could be described in the same way, not only in his industriousness but in the overly erudite writing style of the article he placed, at age twenty-two, in the February 1905 issue of *The Colored American Magazine*. Titled "Educated Colored Men and White Women," Henry's prose, like his father's, was forceful, indignant, and verbose. He was responding to a *Harper's Weekly* piece that had declared, "The educated colored man had not the feeling of 'reverence and awe' for white femininity held by his less fortunate brother." Though Henry did not disagree with that statement, he fearlessly offered his "view in which the subject criticized turned critic." The writer had implied, Henry maintained, "that women are not entitled to the chivalrous courtesy and deference of educated colored men because they are women, but only because they are white women" and that, by the writer's lights, it was better that all black men be left uneducated to ensure that they did not develop "a power of discrimination." Henry insisted that his respect for women was based on virtue and intelligence (although "we cannot set the same intellectual standard for them as we do for men") and those were "not the exclusive monopoly of any race of women."

Nathaniel Murray completed Hampton Institute's three-year course in scientific agriculture in May 1905. His mother attended the graduation exercises. His father did not make the trip but surely was proud of Nat, who he averred had "some good Maryland blood in him." Nat was scheduled to matriculate at Cornell University in the fall. One personal item in the Daniel A. P. Murray Pamphlet Collection at the Library of Congress is his son's 1906 copy of "Elegy Written in a Country Churchyard" by Thomas Gray. The title page displays not only Nat's signature in his large, loopy handwriting but also a sample of his doodling. Nat was nineteen when he entered Cornell, a second-year student in the College of Agriculture, slated to graduate in 1908. He sent his parents a photograph of himself in a flat straw hat on class registration day, with the walls of a university building, thickly covered in ivy, in the background. Nat roomed in Cascadilla Hall, a university-owned residence operated by a private contractor, part of his time in Ithaca, and part he boarded off campus.

Near the close of Nat's first year, Mary Church Terrell traveled to Cornell and presented a lecture before an audience that included "a large number of Southern-principled students and instructors." Her activities at the university were intended to "show just what education, refinement, and adaptability can do and is doing for the race." She took the time to meet with six young men, including Nat Murray, "representing the Afro-American student body of Cornell." All six were members of a literary and social club composed of black students, of whom there were only about fifteen, men and women, on campus. The club had been formed in response to their feeling isolated, Nat remembered. He was one of the members who favored the men taking it a step further by "banding ourselves into a fraternal organization, the same as the white boys on the hill." At a subsequent meeting, he recalled, "I offered the motion that I believed the time was ripe to disband the social club and organize a Negro College fraternity." In the fall term of 1906, Nat Murray and six other Cornell students founded the first black college fraternity. Its name, Alpha Phi Alpha, was selected at an October meeting in Nat's room. With the color line distinctly drawn, an independent parallel organization such as Alpha Phi Alpha promoted racial pride and bonding, a strong sense of manhood, and mutual support. "We helped," recalled Murray, "to prevent any of us from Busting Out by preserving all exam papers and filing them with our secretary to be gone over by any Brother who felt he was weak in any particular subject and wanted coaching." The official date of the fraternity's founding was December 4, 1906, but the first initiation of new members had taken place about a month earlier. Murray remembered it vividly. Masonic Hall was rented, and robes in the hall's lockers were "borrowed." The initiates "were led trembling into our midst" as Nat played the organ. A collegial banquet followed the ceremony.[3]

→ ←

THE NEWSPAPERS CONTINUED TO FOLLOW DANIEL MURRAY'S progress on his book. In 1902, "He is still at work on his book and hopes soon to be in a condition to announce a date for publication." His bibliography increased to more than 2,200 entries come May

1904, but "The listing of the books and gathering of biographical items is still incomplete, since the facts for such a work . . . can be gathered only after the most exhausting persistence of effort." He had lengthened the list to 3,000 by the end of the year when the *New York Tribune*, to Murray's delight, suggested that "my researches should be published as a public document for free distribution." The *Tribune* article, headlined "Negro Suffrage," quoted Murray at length. He identified his literary work as evidence of black men's "intellectual fitness for the ballot." Its examination, he said, "furnishes the best possible proof that they may be safely trusted with the ballot," especially given the restrictions against education prior to Emancipation.

By this time Murray had greatly extended his range from America and Europe to the full African diaspora (thus becoming an exponent of Pan-Africanism, the movement that recognized a common African heritage as a touchstone of black cultural identity); from starting with the early-modern period to reaching back to antiquity; and from literature and the polite arts to all fields of endeavor. For example, he revealed that "In my forthcoming book I have devoted a chapter to the subject of the 'Negro as an Inventor.' " He had been drawn into that particular topic in the press in 1904, after Democratic congressman J. Frederick Talbott of Maryland, on the stump for reelection, had declared that "No Negro was entitled to vote, since none had ever exhibited sufficient capacity to justify his exercising such a privilege. None had ever risen to the dignity of an inventor or architect." That drew a reader's response, which ran in the *Baltimore News*, claiming that a black man had invented the cotton gin. Murray, at the request of the *Afro-American Ledger* editor, weighed in with a piece that was published in that newspaper and then picked up by Georgia's *Augusta Chronicle*. Murray maintained that the credit staked by Eli Whitney had been "successfully disputed, and in the controversy the claim was made that he had imbibed the idea from a negro slave."

Although he was unable to "fully establish the negro's claim," the topic invited further research. The *Augusta Chronicle* article editorialized, "It will be seen that Murray, while discrediting Eli Whitney, or rather attempting to do so, admits that he cannot establish the negro's claim. . . . The whole world has practically agreed that the honor belongs to [Eli Whitney], and neither Murray nor anybody else with the evidence before him, can successfully wrest it away." Murray sought further references and published an article in the February 1905 *The Voice of the Negro*, "Who Invented the Cotton Gin?" While acknowledging that inventor's credit for a black man had to remain a matter of oral tradition, "the claim for Eli Whitney as originator of the idea," he insisted, "is inextricably clouded by much adverse testimony denying the same." He went on to detail the dispute and concluded that one "must ever set the seal of doubt on his claim as an inventor." Even as the *Chronicle* had admitted, that discourse represented the "revival of an ancient debate," and so it stands to this day.

By June 1907, having reached the milestone of 5,000 titles, Murray informed George Myers, "I am still writing on my history of the Colored race, but I am happy in being able to say that it is now practically finished . . . just think, I have been nearly eight years steadily gathering material and digesting the same. . . . I have received more than a thousand letters of inquiry as to when it would be ready." Murray's book was highly anticipated, especially because of its assertions of mixed-race ancestry for notables regarded as white. "The fact that it includes Alexander Hamilton and Robert Browning suggests animated discussion and protest, if the volume ever gets into print," pronounced *Harper's Weekly*. The *Colored American* chimed in, "The publication with his notes will likely produce something of a sensation."

As Murray told Myers, "I have now to seek a publisher." In fact, his first venture in that regard went back five years. The early responses set the tone for what would be an endless slog to secure a publisher. From Harper & Brothers in 1902: "May we inquire what measure you would propose to take to secure a subscription for five thousand copies of the work in advance?" From Funk & Wagnalls in 1903: "We should be pleased to have you submit the completed work as soon as it is ready." And from Hampton Institute in 1906, the standard "regret that I am returning the MS. which you kindly submitted."

In late 1901, Murray had been assigned to the Library of Congress's Capitol Station. Before 1905 was over, he was back in the main library reading room. In both locations, Murray was now the "go-to guy" on all things black history. The caption under his photograph in one of his *The Voice of the Negro* articles read, "Probably he knows more Negro History than any other man in America." His expertise was called on by senators and congressman, other patrons of the library, and friends and associates, just as when the *Afro-American Ledger* editor had consulted him in regard to African American inventors. Murray's papers are filled with inquiries from the public at large. If another library staff member received a relevant request, it would be passed on to him. Congressman Martin B. Madden of Illinois lauded Murray in the midst of his oration on black soldiers: "At this point I desire to state, Mr. Chairman, that I am indebted in a large degree to Mr. Daniel Murray, a representative of the Colored race, who has for many years been connected in an official way with our Congressional Library, for the many historical facts brought out by me." Of course Murray continued to assist lawmakers and library visitors with all topics. He saved the newspaper account of recognition of his "worth" to Democratic senator Joseph Blackburn of Kentucky's preparation of a speech: "Do you know how I gathered so much information on the subject? Well, I went over to Murray in the Library and asked him to select for me some books on the subject, and it was not long till he brought me a wheelbarrow load, all marked and turned down so that I needed only to open them to have before me just what I wanted."

Murray's longtime mentor, Ainsworth Spofford, died on August 11, 1908, in his home state of New Hampshire, having maintained his library position until the end. In his vision for an ever-growing national library with a dedicated grand building, the seasoned librarian's fidelity was described as "Spoffordian faith." His protégé was just as steadfast in pursuit of his vision. While his book remained "forthcoming," Murray published seven articles in *The Voice of the Negro* and four in *The Colored American Magazine* between 1904 and 1908. Some addressed race issues; others were biographical sketches, most on accomplished but obscure African Americans. He was determined that all data "previously overlooked in regard to the colored man should come to light, and be marshalled as testimony in favor of his intellectual equality with the races of mankind, and further proof that he has always been equal to his opportunities . . . deeper plowing will produce a more abundant crop." Meanwhile, plans were made for some of the books by black authors he had gathered to be transferred to Howard University and set aside at the Carnegie Public Library, to be designated the Murray Collection.[4]

The black history movement was gaining steam. The effort to preserve Frederick Douglass's home Cedar Hill in the Anacostia section of Southeast Washington originated at the Pen and Pencil Club's annual banquet honoring the famed agitator and orator on February 14, 1906. Daniel Murray was one of the twenty club members and Booker T. Washington one of the triple that number of guests gathered for an eight-course meal at Odd Fellows Hall that evening. After the cigars came out, President Henry Slaughter assumed the role of toastmaster. One toast honored Paul Laurence Dunbar, a former chair of the Pen and Pencil Club's governing board, who just five days earlier had succumbed to tuberculosis at age thirty-three. During Archibald Grimké's response to a toast to Frederick Douglass, the Bostonian suggested that his home Cedar Hill be preserved as a legacy. Booker Washington recalled, "It seemed to those of us who were present at the dinner . . . that the time had come when his memory should be preserved in something less perishable than after-dinner speeches, however elegant." The Tuskegee principal agreed to assist in the fund-raising effort. In a subsequent letter to Murray acknowledging his $10 gift to the Douglass Memorial Home Fund, Washington noted that the contribution "will serve to help us preserve Mr. Douglass' late home as a memorial in honor of himself, as well as a memorial to the Negro People," and added that Cedar Hill would, in time, "represent what Mount Vernon is to white Americans."

The next afternoon Washington was the guest of honor at a luncheon at the home of Richard R. Horner and his wife at their U Street residence. Horner, a Virginia educator and attorney, had moved to the District in 1900 and three years later established a law partnership with Robert J. Harlan. Covers were laid for twenty-five men, including Daniel Murray, Bruce Evans, Jesse Lawson, Kelly Miller, Charles R. Douglass, and Dr. John R. Francis, Sr.

Black elite occasions at this time not infrequently revolved around serious themes. The subject for discussion at a midsummer chautauqua held on the lawn of Kelly Miller's residence was "The Negro's part in making the history of the American nation" and included an address by Daniel Murray. When Bettie and John R. Francis hosted the Book Lovers and the Art Club for a travelogue of Europe in their parlor, the Murrays were among the guests. Other entertainments were purely social. Anna attended the "beautifully appointed luncheon" that Bettie Francis hosted for an out-of-town friend. "The table was tastefully decorated with sweet peas, and each lady guest was given a bunch of the same flower. A delightfully informal air pervaded the whole afternoon, interspersed with musical selections by a few of the guests."

The Murray and Francis couples socialized regularly. On the evening of December 28, 1906, the Francises celebrated their twenty-fifth wedding anniversary. Anna was among those helping "the bride and groom of a quarter of a century" receive "fully four hundred guests" at their fashionable residence on Pennsylvania Avenue adjoining Dr. Francis's private sanatorium. Just the month before, their dentist son, John R. Francis, Jr., had married Alice Wormely, connecting two families of Washington's "colored aristocracy." Intermarriage among those in the black elite was common. Alice Wormley's sister Edith married physician Henry McKee Minton, the scion of two of the most eminent African American Philadelphia families; Henry's father was Theophilus Minton, and his mother was the daughter of Colonel John McKee, a millionaire real estate mogul and philanthropist.[5]

Daniel Murray's devotion to his book project did not keep Anna Murray from her activism. Her article "In Behalf of the Negro Woman," published in *The Southern Workman* in April 1904, was a response to one entitled "The Negro Woman: Social and Moral Decadence," by Eleanor Tayleur, which had run in the high-circulation weekly *Outlook* three months earlier. Tayleur's blinkered view was that the sense of responsibility of the mass of black women had deteriorated since Emancipation because they were no longer daily exposed to the modest and moral model of white womanhood. "It was to have been expected that a childish race, suddenly freed from slavery, would mistake liberty for license," she wrote. "With the brains of a child and the passions of a woman . . . there she sits, unthinking, unknowing, with no desire save of the senses, no ambitions, no aspirations." Tayleur's tone was supercilious throughout. Anna Murray's, in her rejoinder, was measured; one imagines she must have restrained herself from sprinkling the vinegar that characterized Tayleur's diatribe. She agreed that "Womanhood is the measure of the potentialities of a race" but called Tayleur out on her historical interpretation and absence of commiseration. "Little consideration is given to the real reasons for such conditions," she pointed out. "Whatever may be said of the discipline of slavery no one will deny that while it existed home life and family sanctity were quite impossible for the slave. Is it, then, to be wondered at that after centuries of violation of the holiest instinct implanted in a human soul there should appear a vitiated sense of maternal responsibility?" She maintained that "The education of the Negro child should reach lower down, long before he reaches the age of six" and of course took the opportunity to promote kindergarten training as an antidote.

Anna continued her participation in the National Congress of Mothers. The organization held its national conference in Washington on March 10–17, 1905. Anna's paper, "The Negro Children of America," was subsequently published in *American Motherhood*. "In America there is a race problem, which will be solved aright only when the republic of all childhood is nurtured," she pronounced, calling for cooperation between white and black women to bring this about. Anna Murray "speaks with great precision, . . . Her presentation received high praise from the members of the congress," reported the *Evening Star*, adding, "Mrs. Murray is a tall, slender woman of creole appearance and has a crown of snow-white hair."

Motivated by their sense of parental and community responsibility, Anna and her husband took a deep interest in the District public school system. A structural reorganization that had gone into effect in September 1900 had replaced the two superintendents, one for white and one for black schools, with an overall superintendent, while reducing the former dual positions to assistant superintendents. In the words of the *Evening Star*, "In this way the colored schools were wiped out as an independent organization, and were merged into the general school system." Mary

Church Terrell described another aspect of the reorganization: "The directorships, without a single exception, were taken from colored teachers and given to the whites. . . . Now, no matter how competent or superior the colored teachers in our public schools may be, they know that they can never rise to the height of a directorship." Terrell was referring to directors of specialties such as music, art, and physical culture, the last the position that Anna's sister Mary had held before her marriage.

This loss of autonomy did not reduce infighting in the segregated schools. Few could argue with the *Indianapolis Freeman*'s pronouncement that "The colored schools of Washington, D.C., are always in a stew." The Murrays already had a reputation for inserting themselves into the mix when, in spring 1906, Anna provoked a stir. She testified at several points during the hearings on District school issues before a House of Representatives committee. Introduced as "the mother of the colored kindergarten of the United States," she identified herself as secretary of the National Kindergarten Association. On March 9, she contributed remarks on teacher pay, requesting "that the teachers of like qualifications, colored and white teachers, be given like compensation." She also objected to the current practice of awarding teachers raises as they moved from the lower to upper grades, since "many a fine woman who starts in the first grade, and who would be glad to remain with the little children, is forced onward and upward because she needs an increase in salary." As the *Evening Star* put it, "She thought a teacher who was specially qualified to teach younger children should be permitted to follow her natural bent, but not be barred from promotion."

On March 13, Anna Murray again spoke up at the hearings, this time alleging discrimination of colored kindergarten teachers by white supervisors. As the *Evening Star* reported, "Colored teachers in one instance, she said, were refused the opportunity to purchase tickets to a lecture which would have been of benefit to them. . . . On another occasion, she said, the supervisor of kindergartens on returning from a school convention at Boston had appointed a committee of six white teachers to consider some new kindergarten ideas and had absolutely ignored the colored teachers." Although Anna claimed that several black teachers had come to her to complain, as the matter flared into a brouhaha following the hearings, the assistant director of the colored kindergartens (herself African American) denied the allegations, asserting "that absolute harmony existed among the teachers of the schools." The *Washington Post* disclosed, "The situation developed into one of veracity as between the two women, and Mrs. Murray filed charges against the assistant director with the board." When the Board of Education met on March 28, a subcommittee that had investigated the matter reported "that no useful purpose could be served by further consideration," and the full board adopted its recommendation that the charges be dropped. Anna was present, and board member Bettie Francis requested that she be heard, but no one seconded the motion and Anna was silenced. Highly indignant that she had not been allowed to present her side before the matter was determined closed, Anna appeared at the meeting of the Board of Education on April 4, this time with a written letter insisting that the assistant director of the colored kindergartens prove her statements "and, on failing to do so, be required to withdraw them." The board president barred the communication from being read aloud or even entered into the minutes.

Perhaps not unconnected to her demeaning treatment at the hands of the board, the following June 4, Anna was publicly recognized for her kindergarten leadership on the tenth anniversary of the innovation in the nation's capital. Bettie Francis, Anna's loyal friend on the Board of Education, presided over the celebration. In Daniel Murray's papers is a note he penned referring to this "mark of esteem and high appreciation of Mrs. Murray's efforts to advance the system." Alongside he pasted a copy of the *Evening Star* article describing how "Mrs. Murray made a brief address after she had been presented with a large statute of Minerva by the colored kindergarten teachers of the District." He certainly took no notice of the letter of dissent from one teacher who was still smarting over what she saw as Anna's "attack" on the kindergarten administration; it ran in the *Star* a few days later, requesting the clarification that *some* of the teachers had made the presentation, claiming omission of that word represented "a vast difference."

Despite this unpleasantness, kudos for Anna flowed in. Senator William Allison, one of Anna's earliest allies in the effort to establish kindergartens in Washington, sent his congratulations on "your splendid and useful work." The *Washington Bee* enthused, "Mrs. Anna Murray has been enshrined in the hearts of her ex-pupils as the mother of kindergartens, since she was the originator of this movement in the city." In another article, enitled "Women Who Are Doing Something," the *Bee* singled out "Mrs. Anna Murray who belongs to the progressive class of women educators. She is the promoter of the kindergarten system. She is urged for the Board of Education. She is a woman of refinement and an honor to the race." Though the *Bee* claimed in March 1907 that "There is a monster petition being circulated asking for the appointment of Mrs. Anna Murray on the Board of Education," Anna either chose not to be considered or else, like her husband earlier, failed at the effort.[6]

The Jamestown Ter-Centennial Exposition took place from April 26 to November 30, 1907, near Norfolk, Virginia. "There will be held an Exposition in commemoration of the three hundredth anniversary of the landing of the first English-speaking people at Jamestown, Virginia," announced the newly formed Negro Development and Exposition Company for the Jamestown Exposition in 1906, holding that "we are an integral part of the nation and are bound to contribute to the same." The Jamestown Ter-Centennial Commission agreed, and Congress appropriated

$100,000 for a Negro Building and exhibits. On October 25 of that year, the Negro Development and Exposition Company held an open meeting in the nation's capital, recruiting Washingtonians to plan exhibits. A representative for the company assured his audience, "It was deemed wise by the leaders of our race to hold a separate and distinct exhibit in order to put upon view . . . what the race has made, produced, woven, carved, engraved, invented, written and published." Among those present and ready to volunteer their services were Daniel and Anna Murray, their son Henry, and Bruce Evans.

The headquarters of the Washington branch of the company, prepared to "handle and catalogue all articles that may be submitted," were established in the True Reformer Building at 12th and U Streets NW. The eighteen-member board of managers included Daniel Murray as fiscal agent, Anna Murray, and Bruce Evans. The goal was to "make a thorough canvass of Washington and secure the very best work of the race to be placed on exhibition in Jamestown." The classifications defined were fine arts, liberal arts, literature, education, domestic science, inventions, industrial arts, agricultural arts, and professional medical science. Anna Murray also served as chairman of the executive committee of the ladies' auxiliary club, in charge of domestic science. According to one participant, "Washington's branch is to be made the most important in the country."

The Negro Development and Exposition Company, facing various difficulties and setbacks by the start of 1907, drew on the expertise of Thomas J. Calloway and appointed him chairman of a new executive committee in charge of preparations and maintenance. The Negro Building was not expected to be ready until late May. When the exposition opened on April 26, it was just one of many elements not yet up and running. It was decided that June 10 would be considered the "real opening." President Theodore Roosevelt attended. He viewed just two attractions, the Georgia State

Building and the Negro Building. The Negro Building was sited on a reservation of six acres within sixty feet of one of the principal entrances. "Monumental in architectural proportions," it was 213 feet long, 129 feet wide, and two stories high.

The formal dedication of the Negro Building was purposefully set for Independence Day, with Kelly Miller the chief orator of the day. The Howard University professor delivered an eloquent speech. "A dozen years after the founding of the European population of Jamestown there came another bark from another continent with a human cargo of another color and clime. Europe and Africa have made America," he began. He closed, "How fitting, then, that the negro, too, should commemorate this time and place, which is intended to show something of the part which he has played in the general progress of the nation." As one journalist noted, "The opening of the $40,000 structure, designed by a Negro architect and erected by Negro contractors, filled from top to bottom with a choice collection of products indicative of Negro brain and brawn—the entire project conceived, planned and executed by Negroes—is bound to mark a distinct epoch in the history of the Republic."

With such a massive space, especially compared to that allotted at the Paris, Buffalo, or Charleston exhibitions, the scale of the exhibits was comprehensive—three thousand exhibitors displayed specimens of accomplishment—and represented "an accurate time-keeper of the progress of the race." Three-fourths of a million people visited the Negro Building before the exposition closed. Daniel Murray, in charge of the literary exhibit, was authorized by his Library of Congress superiors to display the books and materials shown at previous fairs, the assemblage "having been collected by him with the understanding that it would ever be available for exhibition purposes." Furthermore, "the suggestion made by Mr. Murray that he go to Jamestown to deliver the books and at the close of the Exposition go to bring them back seems a good one." One chronicler on the scene raved, "In complete and vivid fashion is shown the almost unbelievable rise of the race in the arenas of literature, music and art, including the exhibit of many books written by scholarly members of the race, and all of the four hundred or more current newspapers and periodicals published by Negroes." Three hundred books were arrayed alongside a card catalogue of five thousand works by authors of color. "Many rare books written by Negroes, some in the original manuscript and others touching the history of Negroes, are embraced in this fine collection gathered by Mr. Daniel Murray," commented another journalist. Indeed, some of the books and pamphlets were so valuable that they were locked in a safe between exhibition hours.

August 3 was set aside by the Jamestown Ter-Centennial Commission as Negro Day. Despite the "heated rays of the August sun," the event, featuring Booker T. Washington as keynote speaker and a performance by the Fisk Jubilee Singers, brought out ten thousand black visitors. "The restaurants and concessions on the Negro Reservation had their hands full of business and dollars," recorded the *Washington Bee*. The Jamestown exposition was very much a family affair for the Murrays. Dannie and Nat Murray acquired summer jobs as exposition attendants. Anna and the younger boys made a ten-day trip there, their dates flanking Negro Day, and at least on that special occasion, Daniel Murray joined his family.

Many of the country's African Americans were wary of the exposition because of its location in Jim Crow Virginia. One who spoke up early was Anna's brother-in-law, Butler R. Wilson. He and other "Boston radicals" objected to Massachusetts fabricating a state building at the exposition and led a large delegation in remonstration. "I would like to go down there and see the celebration of the settlement of Jamestown, but I don't want to go if I cannot be treated decently," he said. One of his colleagues, referring to the proposed appropriation for a Massachusetts Building, elaborated, "We as Negro citizens of this State will not get the benefit of our part of the appropriation. Under the laws of Virginia we must ride in separate compartments of the street and railroad cars, and very likely they will have a separate turnstile by which we must enter the grounds." Such uneasiness was not limited to northerners. One of Anna Murray's associates, a member of the ladies' auxiliary club, sent a letter to Thomas Calloway before the exposition opened, asking him "if the colored people are to be treated properly at Jamestown" and giving notice that "if there is to be any discrimination, her resignation was ready to be forwarded." Two days after that item appeared in the *Washington Bee*, Thomas Calloway's partner at the 1900 Paris Exposition, W. E. B. DuBois, published a letter, dated April 8, 1907, expressing his opposition to the Jamestown Exposition: "I do not like the treatment that they are going to accord Negroes. The Negroes are to be separate in practically all things and are to be treated as a separate caste and to that I am opposed." In the event, according to *The Colored American Magazine*, there were certainly instances of "discriminations that ought not to exist, and practices that can neither be defended nor condoned." However, steps were being taken to have offenders face exposition officials and be threatened with "having their concession privilege withdrawn in case of further violations of the order guaranteeing equitable treatment of all patrons of the Exposition, regardless of color." The magazine article continued, "While there are six acres of choice land set apart for the use of the colored people, on which are located the Negro building and a number of other well-constructed buildings for special exhibitions and concessions, they are by no means confined to this reservation." But some African American visitors chose to play it safe and not avail themselves of the midway and other mainstream attractions.[7]

In a June 23, 1907, letter to George Myers, Daniel Murray turned to politics: "I do not know where you stand on the political line, but my folks are rabid Forakerites." He was referring to

Joseph B. Foraker and no doubt admired the Republican senator from Ohio in particular because of his stand against President Roosevelt's handling of an incident that had transpired in Brownsville, Texas, the year before. Racial tensions were high in the Texas town, where African American infantrymen were stationed nearby. Just before midnight on April 13, 1906, gunshots rang out on a town street. One man was killed and a police officer injured. Local whites claimed to have seen uniformed black men on the streets, and shell casings that were produced, alleged the Brownsville mayor, matched those from the infantrymen's rifles. Without giving the soldiers a hearing, much less a trial, federal investigators concluded that they were guilty of a "conspiracy of silence," since they insisted they had been in their barracks at the time of the shooting and admitted to no crime nor fingered any of their fellows. On November 5, President Theodore Roosevelt ordered the entire battalion of 167 soldiers dishonorably discharged. The President exacerbated his blunder by sticking to his decision in the face of swift appeals from both black and white citizens. His only concession was to state that he would "reconsider the case of anyone who could present proof of his innocence."

Senator Foraker thought Roosevelt's actions patently unfair and fought for the soldiers' reinstatement. As a member of the Senate Military Affairs Committee, he conducted investigative hearings on the Brownsville matter from February to June 1907. Notwithstanding his masterful cross-examination of witnesses bent on promoting the soldiers' guilt, the Senate committee endorsed President Roosevelt's action by a 9–4 vote the following March. Foraker signed a separate report declaring that "the weight of the testimony shows that none of the soldiers of the Twenty-fifth U.S. Infantry participated in the shooting affray."

Although he knew his chances were slim, Foraker decided to run for president in 1908. Roosevelt, to his regret, had declared he would not seek reelection and had handpicked his secretary of war, William Howard Taft, as his successor. When it was time for would-be District delegates to June's Republican National Convention to reveal their candidacies, the *Washington Times* announced on February 23, 1908, that two pairs, each composed of one white man and one black man, as was the local custom, "will make the fight together for the respective places." Henry H. Flather, the cashier of Riggs National Bank, and Richard R. Horner, running for delegates, and Dr. William Tindall, secretary to the district commissioners, and Daniel Murray, running for alternate delegates, made up the ticket. In early March, the whole ticket was endorsed at a mass meeting of African American Republicans committed to Foraker. When the *Evening Star* looked to Daniel Murray to respond to rumors that Flather and Horner supported Taft, he gave assurances to the contrary, quoting Flather as saying, "If elected by the people whom [*sic*] I am satisfied desire the nomination of Senator Foraker, I will ratify their wish" and Horner, "first, last and all the time" for Foraker. Voting took place on April 28, and the foursome emerged victorious. As it turned out, the only final competition was for alternates, and Murray and Tindall easily took the majority of votes. Although Flather and Horner had time and again stated their support for Foraker, the week before the convention started both denied that they were pledged to either Foraker or Taft.

The Republican National Convention took place at the Chicago Coliseum on June 16–19, 1908. Richard Horner and Daniel Murray arrived on the fifteenth to a jam of "delegates, visitors, and newspaper men foregathered to exchange ideas and swap an astonishing amount of misinformation," while bands played and flags fluttered in the daylong breeze off Lake Michigan. Official proceedings began at noon the next day in the great coliseum on Wabash Avenue. "At either end of the hall an immense eagle, with twelve feet spread of wings, surmounted a mass of flags." Among the twelve thousand seats some were railed off up front for delegates and alternates. On June 18 at 4:45 p.m., following the first ballot, William Taft was nominated for president (and would go on to a landslide victory over the Democratic nominee). Flather voted for Taft, Horner for Foraker. That evening, Murray's longtime friend Colonel John R. Marshall and his 8th Illinois Regiment hosted a reception for the African American delegates and visitors to the convention that the *Washington Bee* described as possibly the "greatest social function in the history of the Negro race."

Foraker lost his Senate seat come March 1909, having tried to the end to pass the Foraker bill, which would have reinstated the dismissed infantryman upon oath that they had neither participated in the Brownsville incident nor had knowledge of any guilty party. Daniel Murray was treasurer of the fifteen-man committee formed to raise funds to honor the retiring senator. On March 6, in front of a packed auditorium at the Metropolitan AME Church, a massive solid silver loving cup was presented to Senator Foraker by "the colored citizens of Washington as a token of high esteem and in appreciation of his efforts in behalf of the discharged Brownsville battalion." In the gold lining of the bowl was inscribed a quotation from one of the senator's speeches: "They ask for no favors because they are Negroes, but only for justice because they are men."[8]

40. TOP LEFT: Blanche K. Bruce. Born a slave, Bruce had a fierce ambition. He served as a US senator and afterward as register of the treasury, with his signature imprinted on every bill of currency.

41. TOP RIGHT: Josephine Willson Bruce. Blanche Bruce married the daughter of Joseph Willson, author of the 1841 book *Sketches of the Higher Classes among the Colored Society in Philadelphia*. Josephine and Blanche Bruce were a fashionable couple in Washington's "colored aristocracy."

42. BOTTOM LEFT: Pinckney Pinchback. A governor of Louisiana, Pinchback was elected to the US Senate but never seated. He was a noted presence among black elites. The Murrays named one of their sons after him.

43. BOTTOM RIGHT: Paul Laurence Dunbar in his early years. Though most elites were of lighter complexion, Dunbar's very dark color was overlooked, given his prodigious talent as a poet. He lived in Washington for about four years, beginning in 1897, the first year or so working with Murray at the Library of Congress.

Four of Daniel Murray's best friends. 44. TOP LEFT: Fred R. Moore moved to New York after serving as confidential assistant to six sequential secretaries of the treasury. Murray's son Dannie boarded with the Moore family in Brooklyn when he first moved to the city.
45. TOP RIGHT: George A. Myers was a Republican Party politico who ran a first-class barbershop in Cleveland. He and Murray shared childhood roots in Baltimore and maintained a warm correspondence for decades.
46. BOTTOM LEFT: Cyrus Field Adams was a Midwest newspaper man active in the National Afro-American Council. He was appointed assistant register of the treasury in 1901, and boarded with the Murray family for close to a decade.
47. BOTTOM RIGHT: Dr. Charles E. Bentley was a formative figure in both the Niagara Movement and the NAACP. A Chicago dentist, he was a prominent member of that city's African American upper class. Black elites in about a dozen cities were part of a national network, and lodged in one another's homes when they traveled, thus avoiding potential rebuffs at hotels.

48. TOP LEFT: Henry P. Slaughter was another of Murray's closest friends, despite being twenty years younger. Both were bibliophiles and enjoyed the social circuit, these interests combining in "the Pen and Pencil Club," in which they were active.

49. TOP RIGHT: Arthur Schomburg was another bibliophile and collector. He, Murray, and Slaughter were founding members and officers of the Negro Book Collectors Exchange.

50. LEFT: William B. Allison, a senator from Iowa, was one of Daniel and Anna Murray's "white friends." The Murrays regularly cultivated influential contacts among national legislators and other Washington players.

Activist couples. Mary Church Terrell and Robert H. Terrell (51–52 TOP). Bettie Cox Francis and Dr. John R. Francis Sr. (53-54 BOTTOM). Like the Murrays, the Terrells and Francises energetically involved themselves in political and civic issues, and moved in black elite circles in Washington. One social chronicler identified Anna Murray, Bettie Francis, and Mary Terrell as a trio of ladies "prominent in the social world," who, "considering their cleverness and their activities along every line that makes for race progress, may be said to approach as near the ideal woman as one can find."

55. ABOVE: The wedding of Alice Wormley to John R. Francis Jr. brought together two of Washington's most prestigious African American families. Here the bride *(back row)* poses with her new husband *(back row, far right)* and his parents and siblings.

56. RIGHT: Edith Wormley Minton. Alice's sister Edith married Henry McKee Minton, a scion of the prominent Minton and McKee families of Philadelphia. Marriages within the black elite community were common.

Four prominent players in the National Afro-American Council (NAAC), a forerunner of the NAACP. 57. TOP LEFT: T. Thomas Fortune led the call for the first truly national civil rights organization in 1898.

58. TOP RIGHT: Bishop Alexander Walters served as the NAAC's first president.

59. BOTTOM LEFT: George H. White, US representative from 1897 to 1901, led the first effort in Congress to pass anti-lynching legislation.

60. BOTTOM RIGHT: Frederick McGhee succeeded Daniel Murray as director of the NAAC's legal and legislative bureau. He later disapproved of the undue influence that Booker T. Washington came to have in the organization, and was among the founders of the Niagara Movement.

Notable mixed-race artists. 61. TOP LEFT:
Henry O. Tanner, American painter.
62. TOP RIGHT: Samuel Coleridge-Taylor,
British composer and conductor.
63. LEFT: Henry Timrod, known as the Poet
of the Confederacy. Daniel Murray was
determined to identify and "claim for the
Negro race" any and all notable mixed-race
artists, including those commonly thought
to be white. Unlike Tanner and Coleridge-
Taylor, who gladly acknowledged their racial
background, Timrod's African ancestry was
hidden.

64. Daniel Murray at about age sixty. He sported a full mustache throughout his adulthood.

MURRAY'S HISTORICAL AND BIOGRAPHICAL ENCYCLOPEDIA

OF THE COLORED RACE THROUGHOUT THE WORLD

ITS PROGRESS AND ACHIEVEMENTS FROM THE EARLIEST PERIOD DOWN TO THE PRESENT TIME

EMBRACING

25,000 biographical sketches of men and women of the colored race in every age. A bibliography of over 6,000 titles of books and pamphlets, which represent their contribution to the world's literature. A synoptical list of all books of fiction by Caucasian authors that deal with the race question as a feature. Also a list of nearly 5,000 Musical Compositions by Colored Composers in every part of the World.

DANIEL MURRAY, Editor in Chief
(Forty-one years in the Library of Congress)

ASSISTED BY A CORPS OF THIRTY ASSISTANT EDITORS, INCLUDING

JOHN E. BRUCE, ARTHUR A SCHOMBURG, WM. C. BOLIVAR, REV. J. M. BODDY.
JOHN W. CROMWELL, L. M. HERSHAW, S. ROUZIER (HAITI), JAS. CAR-
MICHAEL SMITH (SIERRA LEONE), CHARLES ALEXANDER,
STANSBURY BOYCE, G. J. F. MADIOU (HAITI), BISHOP J.
ALBERT JOHNSON (SOUTH AFRICA), W. S. SCAR-
BOROUGH, R. R. WRIGHT, JR., HON. G. W.
GIBSON (LIBERIA).

IN SIX VOLUMES
Per Set, $24.00

1912

WORLD'S CYCLOPEDIA COMPANY
CHICAGO   WASHINGTON

65. Title page of *Murray's Historical and Biographical Encyclopedia of the Colored Race throughout the World*. This was part of a twelve-page prospectus that Murray had printed in 1912.

66. LEFT: Harold Murray's passport photo. At the same time that Harold graduated from Cornell and married Madrenne Powell, he secured a job in Cuba.

67. BELOW: Madrenne Powell Murray's passport photo with her daughter, Helene, on her lap. Helene, presumably named for her father's sister, was born in Cuba in 1887 and was Daniel and Anna Murray's first grandchild.

68. Helene and Harold Jr. Murray. Helene and her brother, nicknamed Bruzzy, were the first two of Harold and Madrenne's six children.

69. Walter F. White. Madrenne's twin sister, Gladys, was married to NAACP secretary Walter F. White. Their Sugar Hill apartment in upper Manhattan was a popular meeting place for luminaries of the Harlem Renaissance.

70–71. Granddaughters Pauline Murray Garcia *(top left)* and Constance Murray *(top middle)*. Nat and Mayme Murray had two daughters; only the elder is known to have married. Pauline's husband was Mexican national Cayetano Garcia; while he was serving in the Mexican army, Pauline gave birth to their first son at her parents' home on U Street.

72. TOP RIGHT: Grandson Jacques Murray, called Jack, was Harold and Madrenne's son, born in Harlem in 1922. He was the last of six grandchildren born before Daniel Murray died.

73. BOTTOM: Lillian Evans Tibbs, an acclaimed opera singer known professionally as Madame Evanti, with her son Thurlow Tibbs, photographed by Addison Scurlock.

74. ABOVE: The Ku Klux Klan—fifty thousand strong—marched along Pennsylvania Avenue in Washington, DC, on August 8, 1925, just a few months before Daniel Murray died at a segregated hospital and was buried in a segregated cemetery.

75. BELOW: St. Elizabeths Hospital. After his father's death, Paul Evans Murray was diagnosed with psychotic epilepsy and committed to this institution for the mentally ill, where he died in 1949.

76. LEFT: Grandson Marco Murray Lasso in 1940. Harold and his second wife, Olympia Lasso, a Mexican national, had four children. Marco Murray Lasso was the first direct descendant the author located in Mexico City and communicated with about family history.

77. BELOW: Granddaughters Elizabeth and Carmen Murray Lasso on the occasion of their First Communion. Though the Lassos were Catholic, Harold Murray followed the Baha'i faith, which teaches that all human beings are of a single race and all religions have true and valid origins.

78. ABOVE: Henry Murray and Lillian Evans Tibbs flank Harold, his wife, Olympia, and their four children visiting from Mexico in 1954 on the occasion of Carmen's *quinceañera*. FROM LEFT TO RIGHT: Henry, Elizabeth, Harold, Carmen, Marco, Olympia, Daniel, Lillian.

79. LEFT: Elderly Anna Evans Murray surrounded by Harold's children and Henry. Anna was dependent on a wheelchair during the last five years of her life. Henry moved into 934 S Street to care for her and continued to live there until his own death in 1965.

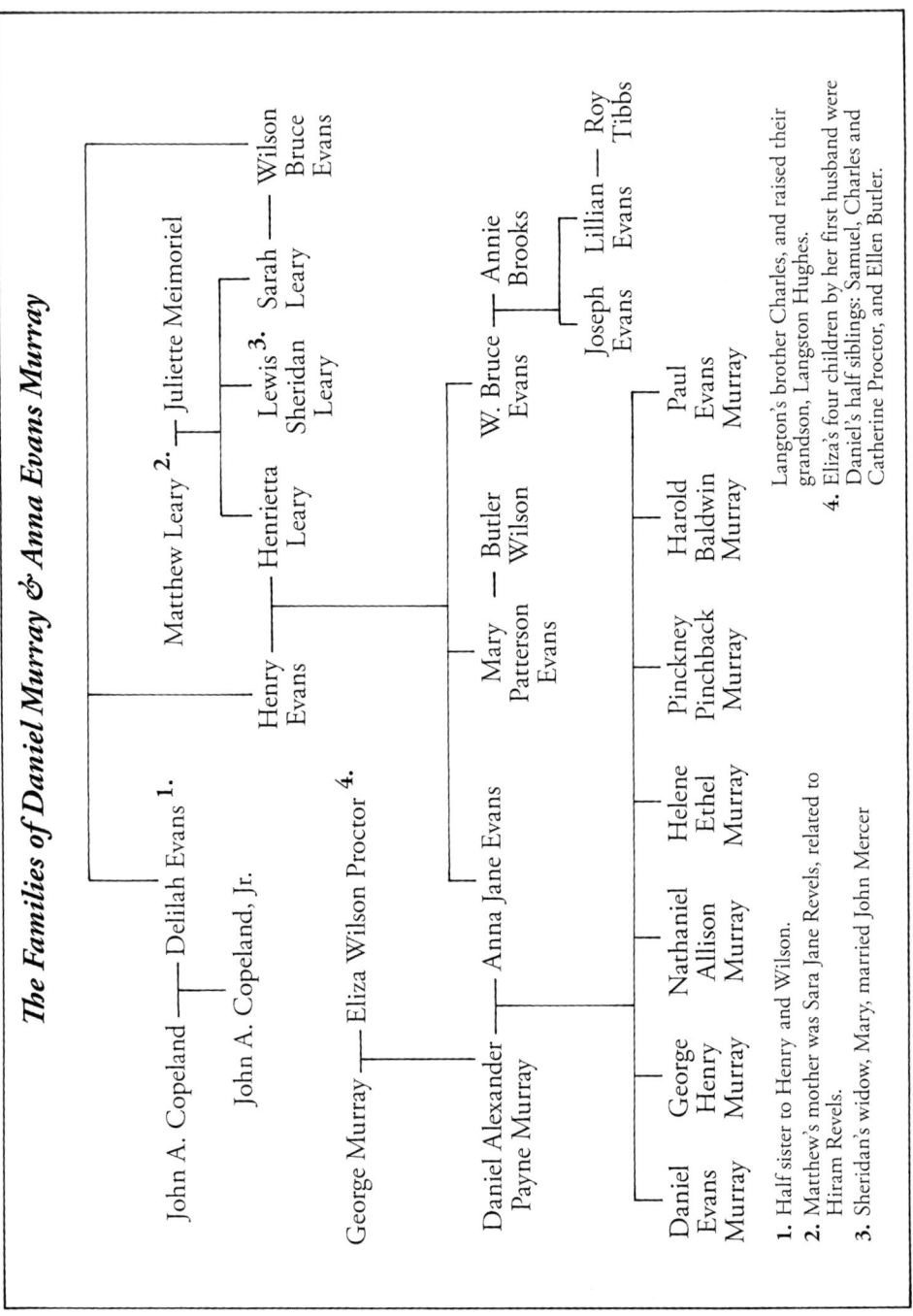

The Families of Daniel Murray & Anna Evans Murray

John A. Copeland —— Delilah Evans **1.**

John A. Copeland, Jr.

Matthew Leary **2.** —— Juliette Meimoriel

Henry Evans

Henrietta Leary

Lewis **3.** Sheridan Leary

Sarah Leary —— Wilson Bruce Evans

George Murray —— Eliza Wilson Proctor **4.**

Daniel Alexander Payne Murray —— Anna Jane Evans

Mary Patterson Evans —— Butler Wilson

W. Bruce Evans —— Annie Brooks

Joseph Evans

Lillian Evans —— Roy Tibbs

Daniel Evans Murray

George Henry Murray

Nathaniel Allison Murray

Helene Ethel Murray

Pinckney Pinchback Murray

Harold Baldwin Murray

Paul Evans Murray

1. Half sister to Henry and Wilson.
2. Matthew's mother was Sara Jane Revels, related to Hiram Revels.
3. Sheridan's widow, Mary, married John Mercer Langton's brother Charles, and raised their grandson, Langston Hughes.
4. Eliza's four children by her first husband were Daniel's half siblings: Samuel, Charles and Catherine Proctor, and Ellen Butler.

80. Family tree, depicting relevant connections in the Murray and Evans genealogies.

14

DISILLUSIONED

D ANIEL EVANS MURRAY, HAVING MOVED FROM BROOKLYN to midtown Manhattan, was on the program of a musicale presented at Odd Fellows Temple on West 29th Street on May 22, 1907. He performed a violin solo with piano accompaniment, Christian Sinding's Opus 30, "Romance in E Minor for Violin and Piano." Three years later, now thirty, his career took off. In June 1910, he organized the Port-Au Peck Quartette, named for its initial ten-week run at the Port-Au-Peck Hotel in Long Branch, New Jersey, "a summer colony where the wealthy are wont to spend the summer months." The walk from the hotel to the Shrewsbury River was just a hundred feet or so, and there local clams and ears of corn were steamed in a bed of seaweed. One guest recalled, "At 2:30 the dinner horn blew and all were ready to do their part. The vaudeville quartette from the Port-Au-Peck Hotel gave song, sound and broad darkey smiles to stimulate the excellent cheer furnished." The group also performed in private homes, as when some Trenton society trendsetters threw an entertainment with their dining space transformed into a French café, and "at one corner of the room was arranged, by the use of screens and palms, a stage, where the famous colored quartet from Port au Peck entertained the guests with clever songs and musical selections." The foursome was composed of James Reese Europe on piano, Arthur "Strut" Payne on cello, Tom Bethel on bass, and group manager Daniel Murray on violin. All were part of the community of African American musicians and other entertainers and artists whose lifestyle revolved around the dance halls, clubs, and cabarets that catered to them in that part of midtown Manhattan known then as "Black Bohemia." Marshall Hotel served as their unofficial headquarters. Home to Jim Europe, it was located a couple of blocks from Dannie's apartment, which was on West 52nd Street off Sixth Avenue.

Dannie Murray and Jim Europe had been born ten days apart, had grown up in Washington, DC, and had taken up the violin at an early age. Both had moved to the northern metropolis with the turn of the new century (the African American population of New York nearly tripled between 1890 and 1910). With gigs sporadic, most musicians could not afford to live on performing alone. Europe, a large man in more ways than one (he was six feet and 200 pounds), took the matter in hand. He was a founder and the first president of the Clef Club, a professional and fraternal organization, initiated in April 1910 to provide promotion as a booking agent and protection as a union for African American musicians and singers.

Europe organized the Clef Club Symphony Orchestra, including among its number Dannie Murray, "Strut" Payne, and Tom Bethel. On May 27, 1910, the orchestra debuted at the new Manhattan Casino, a huge dance space and beer garden located uptown at 155th Street and Eighth Avenue. Their next performance there in October filled the hall. The *New York Age* reporter observed "a sprinkling of white citizens, and they were quite a study, appearing very much surprised, with eyes, mouths and ears wide open, so absorbed were they in the work of the musicians." No wonder;

the ensemble, well over one hundred men strong, assembled and conducted by Europe, was unique. There were extensive sections of mandolins and upright pianos plus banjos, violins, cellos, and harp guitars; drums, timpani, and traps provided the percussion. The mix of instruments produced unusual, imposing modulations and expressive, evocative sounds and rhythms. The repertoire included rags, marches, vaudeville numbers, musical theater songs, and classical pieces. Over time, the orchestra added woodwinds and brass and developed a distinctive African American musical idiom featuring works by black composers such as Will Marion Cook (a Washington violinist, who had preceded Dannie Murray at Oberlin's Conservatory of Music), Samuel Coleridge-Taylor, and Europe himself.

The crowning coup for the Clef Club Orchestra came on May 2, 1912: a performance before an integrated audience at the famed Carnegie Hall. Billed as a "Unique Concert of Negro Music Composed and Rendered Exclusively by Colored Musicians," it marked a milestone, the first African American concert held at the iconic hall, which was "taxed to its utmost capacity, and a thousand people turned away." The diverse program included concert arias, popular ballads, dance hits, and slave spirituals. In the final piece, a march, all 125 performers on stage, dressed in black tuxedoes, sang out the "refrain on the last strain, surprising the audience with the sheer power of voice. . . . The audience sprang to its feet and cheered." Dannie Murray's hometown *Washington Bee* raved, "There was no one in that audience that did not feel that for once he had heard the 'real thing,' worked out with clever musicianship and general verve into a truly artistic manifestation." Europe and company had "stormed the bastion of the white musical establishment and made many members of New York's cultural elite aware of Negro music for the first time." The Carnegie Hall concert lent unprecedented validity to African American music, while the

Clef Club's collective voice paved the way for artistic collaboration among talented entertainers of color in the next decade's Harlem Renaissance.

In 1908, Henry Murray earned a diploma at Wood's Business School in New York City. Two years later he was given charge of Armstrong High School's business department. The business courses were conducted in "the old Mott School," and, with the support of Armstrong's principal, his uncle Bruce Evans, he pressed for a first-class location for "commercial training for colored youth." Starting in early 1911, there was a push for the Phelps School building on Vermont Avenue near U Street (across from Henry's elementary school, Garnet) to be "made a colored institution and used for the business department of the Armstrong Manual Training School," given that a new edifice was being constructed for the current occupants of the Phelps School. The school board approved the new use in late October 1911. Among the course offerings were business English, shorthand, typewriting, and bookkeeping. Though referred to as "the Colored Business High School," it remained under the auspices of Armstrong—at least it did until September 1912, when the school superintendent and the assistant superintendent for colored schools, Roscoe Bruce (the son of Blanche and Josephine Bruce), recommended that the Phelps School be transferred to the jurisdiction of the M Street High School and a member of its faculty placed at its head. That must have been a blow to Henry, since, as his father noted, the school "under his administration attained to high success." Henry was relegated to teaching in Armstrong's department of business practice. There he initiated a school savings bank to serve as an object lesson in practical banking and encourage thrift.

Meanwhile, Henry had become a married man, taking Emma Green, originally from North Carolina, as his wife on November 4, 1908. At the time of the 1910 census, Henry and Emma were part of her mother's household. Three years later they purchased a house on S Street just three doors down from his parents' home.

For reasons unknown and not particularly likely to be monetary, given his father's financial status, Nathaniel Murray broke up his years at Cornell. During the academic sessions of 1907–8 and 1908–9, he taught agriculture at Princess Anne Academy (now the University of Maryland Eastern Shore) in Somerset County, Maryland. He returned to Cornell as a junior and continued his studies and his involvement with Alpha Phi Alpha. The fraternity evolved through struggle and success. Its certificate of incorporation was recorded with New York's secretary of state in 1908 and four years later at the national level. Nat received his BS degree in agriculture in 1911. In April of the same year, he married Georgia-born Mary Louise Jordan, known as Mayme, in Washington.

Having worked in the school gardens for the District colored schools during summer vacation 1910, he applied for the same job the summer after he graduated. Assistant Superintendent Roscoe Bruce informed him that due to monetary considerations, no summer gardens work was available, nor were there "prospects as far as I know for permanent work with school gardens for the colored schools in this city." Suspecting that was not so, Daniel Murray and his wife zoomed into action on their son's behalf, and what followed, recalled Murray, was "a series of mendacious evasions on the part of the Asst. Supt. which ended in a direct falsehood." It turned out that a school garden would be open and Bruce was ready to offer the summer job to another candidate, one with no agricultural training but a large family to feed. Despite evidence, Bruce denied it to his supervisors. It was Nat Murray who, after the fuss made by his parents, received the appointment in late June. Telling the story eight years after it happened, Daniel Murray's anger still rankled. One wonders how riled up he would have been if the incident had not been decided in his son's favor.

According to the *Indianapolis Freeman*, at the end of the summer Nat was offered the directorship of the DC school gardens and a professorship at Tuskegee. Instead he took a position teaching horticulture at the Agriculture and Technology College of North Carolina in Greensboro. By 1913, he was assistant state agriculturist and a science teacher at West Virginia Collegiate Institute. Now West Virginia State University, this institution, like Princess Anne Academy and the A&T college in North Carolina, was one of the land-grant colleges established for African Americans in states where the education facilities were segregated. Cornell was a land-grant college as well, but in New York two separate schools were not necessary.

Nat left Ithaca a few months before his brother Harold made his way there. Harold had graduated from Armstrong High School in June 1911, the class valedictorian, and entered Cornell University in September. Harold felt "he was 'a cut above average' throughout his schooling." A mechanical engineering major at Cornell's Sibley School, Harold participated in extracurricular activities, including the university vesper club and the cosmopolitan club, composed of 250 Cornell men from twenty different nations, but never joined the Alpha Phi Alpha.

"Master Paul Murray," about to turn fourteen and preparing to start high school in September, spent a vacation with his parents at Cape May on the Jersey shore for a week in mid-August 1912. That December, he fell and broke his arm during a drill at Armstrong. His father raised a stink, demanding an investigation, and had to be satisfied with the official finding that the fall had been "entirely accidental." Three years later Paul did not make up for a missed assignment at the teacher's convenience, and Murray raised a stink again, maintaining it was the teacher's fault since the time he had elected was during regular classes. When Paul was found negligent and asked to drop the matter, Murray fired off a letter directly to the superintendent of schools, claiming it was "an unwarranted interference with my son's natural rights" and concluding, "Paul's feelings were greatly wounded by the incident and the humiliation gravely affected him and still affects him."[1]

→ ←

THE NATIONAL AFRO-AMERICAN COUNCIL, ACCORDING TO one critic, had been "Booker Washingtonized" by 1905, when Alexander Walters attempted to renew the interest of the organization's "Old Guard," naming Daniel Murray among many others in an open letter published on July 25 of that year in the *New York Age*. The prospects for African Americans were growing worse, and Walters "called loudly to the derelict members" of the council "to arouse themselves and do something to check this onslaught upon their civil and political rights." He wrote his letter just ten days after a new civil rights organization was formed at a Niagara Falls meeting. Although Booker T. Washington never held official office, he had become a powerful influence in the NAAC, rebuffing challenges to his accomodationist posture. W. E. B. DuBois, for one, was ready to counter the Tuskegeean's "nerveless acquiescence in wrong" with an activist agenda. Besides DuBois, the forces behind the initial impetus for what became known as the Niagara Movement were Frederick McGhee, who had succeeded Murray as director of the NAAC's legal and legislative bureau; Charles E. Bentley, Murray's dentist friend from Chicago, whom DuBois credited with "planning the method of organization"; and Boston militant William Monroe Trotter, the son of the recorder of deeds in the Cleveland administration and Washington's most open and bitter foe. Unlike Murray, McGhee had stayed active in the NAAC; he warned Walters that Washington's control had impelled the NAAC to lose faith with its preliminary goals and nonpartisan stance, thus forfeiting its effectiveness, and that the consequence would be an effort "to start anew with men who have not failed the people." He noted that even T. Thomas Fortune "sees no future for the council."

These four allies hand-selected a like-minded, articulate group of men who met with them on the Canada side of Niagara Falls. Twenty-nine in all, they named their association for the "mighty current" of protest they wished to see flow. The Niagara Movement's Declaration of Principles was eloquent and clear. It proclaimed that "persistent manly agitation is the way to liberty," that black citizens "should protest emphatically and continually against the curtailment of their political rights." Its leaders diplomatically insisted that their movement was not formed to strike at Booker T. Washington per se; rather, they "had gathered to consider principles and not men," but that smacked of semantics considering the declaration's statement: "We refuse to allow the impression to remain that the Negro-American assents to inferiority, is submissive under oppression and apologetic before insults."

The goals of the Niagara Movement—freedom of speech and criticism, manhood suffrage, the abolition of distinctions based on race, an unfettered and unsubsidized press, the recognition that advanced academic education was the monopoly of no race, support for the dignity of labor—were not different from those of the NAAC's original platform, nor were the strategies of pursuit, most notably through the courts system.

Washington had become paranoid over protecting his status and employed subversive methods to curb the efforts of those who threatened it. He expended what amounted to "hush money" to subsidize elements of the black press, pressuring certain journalists "hidebound" to his patronage into ignoring or criticizing the Niagara Movement. The Bookerites plotted against and harassed the new organization, planting rumors and disinformation, sending spies to their gatherings, and dissuading blacks from supporting them. The external opposition took a toll. The editor of *The Voice of the Negro* and one of the movement founders, J. Max Barber, was referring to Washington and those in his orbit when he decried "underhanded methods of strangling honest criticism, manipulating public opinion and centralizing political power by means of improper and corrupt use of money and influence." The Tuskegee Machine put a lot of effort into interfering with the Niagara Movement and its program, forcing the movement in turn to direct energy into fending off such intrusions.

The second annual Niagara Movement meeting took place August 15–18, 1906, in Harpers Ferry, West Virginia, a site chosen for its historic symbolism as well as the welcoming accommodations at Storer College. The meeting made history of its own. Speech after speech was riveting and ringing in content and tone. Many attendees to the public conference thought August 17, designated John Brown Day, the most interesting and inspiring of the whole four days. It started at 6 a.m. with a one-mile pilgrimage to John Brown's Fort. The participants formed a single-file procession, led by Reverend Owen M. Waller, "barefoot in true pilgrim style," and sang the "Battle Hymn of the Republic" as they circled the brick building.

The afternoon proceedings back at Storer College were equally moving. It is very likely that the Murrays, certainly Anna, were present. She and the younger children continued to spend their summers at the Ferry, with her husband joining them on weekends and for his two-week leave. Moreover, Anna's mother, seventy-nine-year-old Henrietta Leary Evans, whose brother, Sheridan Leary, and nephew-in-law, John A. Copeland, had been among the Harpers Ferry martyrs, was on the agenda. "The audience crowded forward as the venerable Mrs. Evans" spoke in a low voice. The "small, bent . . . very wrinkled" woman remained seated in her armchair on the platform as she shared her reminiscences.

Renewed interest in the history of the raid and in Henrietta Evans's recollections followed the conference. In late December

1907, Daniel Murray responded to a letter W. E. B. DuBois sent to Anna asking that her mother "detail again somewhat her recollections of the John Brown invasion." Murray wanted DuBois to understand, having debriefed his mother-in-law himself, that though her recollections were "in the main correct, they are slightly at variance with the facts." DuBois was planning a biography of John Brown, as was his close associate, civil rights activist Oswald Garrison Villard, the publisher of the *New York Evening Post* and a grandson of the abolitionist William Lloyd Garrison. On March 5, 1908, Villard's research assistant interviewed Henrietta Leary in her daughter's presence. The "aged woman" threaded out her memories, not only of her brother Sheridan but of a good deal of early family history.

Four months after that interview, the *Washington Bee* reported that "Bruce Evans and family and Mrs. Daniel Murray are rusticating at Harpers Ferry." Their mother was with them, and there, fittingly enough, Henrietta Leary Evans died on August 13. Both the *Evening Star* and the *Washington Post* ran extended obituaries, headlined "Venerable Colored Resident of This City Passes Away" and "Brother Aided John Brown," respectively. She was survived by five of her eleven children; her son Bruce traveled with her remains to Oberlin, where they were buried next to her husband's.

The possibility of the Niagara Movement and the NAAC merging was floated in the press now and again. The *Indianapolis Freeman* wondered, "Will the Afro-American Council absorb the Niagara Movement—or be absorbed by it?" At least two of the movement founders, Lafayette Hershaw and William H. H. Hart, remained NAAC members and were elected directors as late as 1907. But a marriage of the two organizations was not to be.

The NAAC did rally following Alexander Walter's plea, though Daniel Murray did not renew his involvement. The organization reasserted its direction and energy and reiterated its original action goals, in particular the legal fight against disenfranchisement and separate-car laws. Booker T. Washington lost influence generally, beginning in 1906 with his muted and nonconfrontational responses to the Brownsville injustice and to the Atlanta race riot that followed a month later, when a massive mob of white men surged through African American neighborhoods destroying businesses and assaulting black men, leaving scores dead or wounded. The resurgence of the NAAC was not enough to sustain the organization beyond 1908, however. The Niagara Movement faded as well, after only four years of existence, never reaching close to the peak membership of the NAAC nor achieving any milestone victories. If the original goals of the two organizations had been much the same, so were many of the reasons for their demise. Among them were chronic financial difficulties, the absence of regular paid staff, the inability to generate mass grassroots support due to organizational weaknesses and lack of sustained publicity, and failure to keep even the membership updated. Added to this were internal struggles, the clashing of personalities and ideologies, with Washington playing a foremost role. In the case of the Niagara Movement, there was a falling-out between DuBois and Trotter. (When Trotter made his exit, most of the other Boston radicals, including Butler R. Wilson, who served on the legal committee, remained.)

A new, interracial civil rights organization emerged in 1909. Offended by the injustice and violence aimed at African Americans, a group of white liberals, including Oswald Garrison Villard, proposed a conference on racial justice. Among those who signed the call, issued on February 12, the centennial of Lincoln's birth, were W. E. B. DuBois, Alexander Walters, Ida Wells-Barnett, Mary Church Terrell, and Francis Grimké. Echoing the focus of the NAAC and the Niagara Movement, the stated goal of the new organization, named the National Association for the Advancement of Colored People (NAACP), was to secure for all Americans the rights guaranteed in the Thirteenth, Fourteenth, and Fifteenth

Amendments of the Constitution. If the NAACP grew out of the failures of the NAAC and the Niagara Movement, it also profited by their examples—in platform, practice, and game plan.[2]

➤ ➤

DANIEL MURRAY DID NOT RALLY TO THE CALL FROM ALEXAN-der Walters, nor did he join the Niagara Movement or the nascent NAACP. He did offer his own "Race Solution Plan" in 1910, pub-lished in the *Evening Star* of March 27. It was provoked by a speech that Secretary of War Jacob M. Dickinson, a Mississippian, gave, appealing for "justice to the Negro compatible with white politi-cal control." Murray recognized that statement as slightly veiled support for political elimination, "an unjust proposition to make 10,000,000 loyal Americans pariahs in the land of their birth." He insisted, "All the people must join in the solution of the race prob-lem," and queried, "Why should I and my children be thus denied the right and protection by the ballot?" He suggested the creation of an interracial commission drawn from different sections of the country, concluding that "the solving of the problem consists in bringing those diverse elements together." He wanted the commis-sion to visit places outside the United States where "a measure of peace has been secured" between races. The article also ran in sev-eral other newspapers, and Murray sent copies to many associates. He garnered congratulations on his good idea, but it engendered nothing more. What did Murray realistically think might come of his proposal? After all, when the National Sociological Society, an interracial organization three thousand members strong, had called for the same approach and named such a committee, no ac-tion had followed. The *Macon Telegraph* had belittled that more concerted effort in a headline: "Solvers of Race Problem Make Usual Appeal."

The following month Murray demonstrated his overall frus-tration with the second-class status allotted to African Americans.

He led the Washington Civic Association, which he described as "an organization of colored people that undertakes to look after the affairs of the colored race in the District of Columbia." In December 1908, fourteen local civic associations met to combine forces in agitating for the restoration of home rule in Washington. Daniel Murray appeared at the meeting and, after a review of his credentials, was seated. He was the only African American representative at the convention that followed, during which the coalition adopted resolutions calling for substantial control of city governance. The resolutions were presented to Congress in the form of a memorial, but the timing for such changes, as passing decades would prove, was far from ripe.

Later in 1910, city civic organizations decided to formally coalesce to form the Federation of Citizens' Associations of the District of Columbia. A constitution was drafted that defined the federation as consisting of "all eligible civic associations and societies of white citizens of the National Capital." When a secretary sent out invitations to an April 30 meeting to ratify the constitution, he worked from an inclusive list of local civic groups. Thus, that evening representatives from five associations of black citizens, Daniel Murray among them, arrived to the surprise of the organizers, one of whom declared the federation "a white man's movement" that ought to proceed "without race entanglement." The delegates from the black civic groups "failed to see how one-third of the population could be left out" and wanted to know why they had been invited, only to be insulted. "It is not an insult," they were told. "It is a mistake." When the constitution was read, Murray stood up to object to the word "white," requesting it be stricken. "The colored associations of Washington can be of great benefit to the federation, and I see no reason why they should not be admitted," he stated. "We are all striving for the betterment of conditions, so why shouldn't the Negro assist." A heated debate followed. The chairman of the constitution committee insisted, "The taking in of Negro associations would kill this movement. . . . The races have been segregated in Washington, and I see no need for an alliance in citizens' associations." With that, Murray turned on his heels and walked out, and one by one the other black representatives followed. The last one waited on the vote, 11–10, to adopt the constitution with the word "white" intact.

Daniel Murray was disillusioned. He remained a lifelong community activist but only rarely ventured onto the national political stage again. His deflating experiences in 1910 were followed by total absorption in his writing project. Still determined to contribute something of "lasting benefit to my race," he narrowed his scope to black history while enlarging his vision to monumental proportions. It could not be contained in "a book." Daniel Murray set his sights on a multivolume encyclopedia.[3]

15

LIFE'S WORK

Daniel Murray was as a man possessed, juggling daily library duties with his own project, to which he devoted himself after the library closed and on his days off. He obsessively grew a mountain of biographical sketches that he hoped to see incorporated into a multivolume monumental work. Anna remembered that the family "dinner table talk for a quarter of a century was always on that portion of the current work" her husband was engaged in. "Prejudice," Murray averred, was "the screen behind which ignorance seeks to entrench itself." Understanding that education was race activism and believing that truth examined would break down stereotypes, he aimed for "perfection and completeness." The words he had written back in 1901 still applied: "As the material increased upon my hands and the necessity for giving to the world the result of my research, I was obliged to redouble my efforts to bring it to an end."

On October 29, 1910, Murray sent a letter to about forty friends and associates of the black intelligentsia: "I am pleased to tell you that the work—the encyclopedia of the colored race—upon which as you know I have been actively engaged in for the past fifteen years is now about to be published. . . . I am inviting a few gentlemen to cooperate as associate editors, each of a small and compact section, and am seeking as allies those whose scholarship and fitness suggest them as exponents of the high principles for which the work so earnestly stands." Consisting of five volumes and featuring "over 20,000 biographical sketches and a bibliography of over 6,000 books," the work, entitled *Murray's Historical and Biographical Encyclopedia of the Colored Race Throughout the World*, was being published by World's Cyclopedia Company. Both Booker T. Washington and W. E. B DuBois were included in the mailing. Washington declined ("I am simply overwhelmed with matters . . . which will absolutely preclude my taking part in any way") while DuBois was tentative, responding, "If you will kindly let me know the names of the other persons who are going to cooperate with you, I think that probably I shall be willing to help."

To those who answered in the affirmative Murray sent a second letter: "I am conscious that this effort will be scanned in many quarters most minutely for errors of fact and ill-considered statements." To "reduce to a minimum all adverse criticism . . . I propose to advance to you for advanced review, those matters on which the country regards you as the best obtainable authority." One respondent congratulated Murray that his "arduous labor . . . is about to see the light of public day. I am frank to say, when you first conversed with me about the work, it looked so ponderous, arduous and far-reaching, I could not then see how you would ever reach your goal."[1]

The word was out that Murray, yet again, was close to completing his long-maturing project. The *Boston Colored Citizen*, in an article entitled "The Noble Service of a Noble Man," expressed "profound satisfaction that the master work of his life is about completed, and that at no distant day we will all have the pleasure of enjoying it." The *Cleveland Gazette* anticipated that "Mr. Murray's promised work will prove monumental for he has devoted practically all of twenty years in its preparation." A year later, Murray had amassed five thousand additional sketches and his goal had expanded to an encyclopedia of six volumes, each of 800 pages. According to the *Evening Star*, "Four volumes were to be devoted to articles of encyclopedic length only, one to longer articles on individuals and events of racial interest, one volume to bibliography alone."

By this time Murray had acknowledged the extreme unlikelihood of finding a publisher to undertake financial responsibility for publishing his encyclopedia. He thus fabricated his own publishing house with himself as the sole staff, named it World's Cyclopedia Company, and solicited bids from printing establishments. The *Washington Bee* identified Murray as "one of the wealthiest colored men in the community," due to his accumulated assets invested in land, stocks, and bonds. In 1910, perhaps with an eye to the expenses he would incur in publishing his encyclopedia, he added to his realty ventures in partnership with his close friend Reverend John Hurst. Born in Haiti, Hurst had graduated from Wilberforce University with a divinity degree and joined the Baltimore Annual Conference in 1882 under Bishop Daniel Alexander Payne; he would himself be elected an AME bishop in 1912. Murray and Hurst took over the $5,500 mortgage on Cherry Heights, "a new suburb for colored people" on the eastern edge of Baltimore, in October 1910. When the city streetcar line was extended along Belair Road to that rural setting of high-lying farmland, it became an attractive location. In 1909, an effort to establish the first subdivision for black families there was undertaken by enterprising African American realtors. But the following year the white men who held the mortgage were on the verge of foreclosing on them. That was when Murray and Hurst stepped in to save the community. Cherry Heights was divided into 156 lots. The *Baltimore Afro-American* advertisements for this "first-class settlement," just thirty minutes from the city's center, promoted the lots as investments, promising an annual increase in worth greater than 10 percent. In addition

to holding the mortgage, Murray and Hurst themselves later purchased, in partnership, seventy-five building lots for $9,000.

Certainly Murray could not rely on his Library of Congress
salary. Herbert Putnam remained the Librarian of Congress
throughout Murray's career, while his direct supervisor, beginning in 1909, was the new superintendent of the reading room,
William W. Bishop. John Morrison and Hugh Morrison held the
two chief assistant titles. They would go on to make $1,800 annu-
ally, while Murray's salary stayed stuck at $1,200, one-third less.
When John F. N. Wilkinson died at age eighty-one in October
1912, "performing his duties even on the day of his death," Murray
became the longest-serving assistant at the library.[2]

In late 1911, Murray began what would turn out to be years of
correspondence with R. R. Donnelly and Sons, a Chicago printing and binding company that served as the US printers of the
Encyclopaedia Britannica. Most of the correspondence naturally focused on the specifications and pricing of the six volumes. Since
even the preparatory work would cost the company money, assurances that Murray could afford to follow through were sought before executing a contract. He was informed that "a report from our
commercial agency which indicates that you are financially able
to carry out any contract which you might enter into with us" had
been conducted. A 10,000-copy run per volume would cost about
$11,500. That was the price without illustrations, but Murray was
determined to include 1,200 "rare illustrations in half tone." The
books would be royal octavo (10 by 6.25 inches), bound in half
morocco, with title and ornamentation in gilt. One thousand dollars was due at the time of contract signing, and Murray would be
billed for 2,000 copies of volume one before any production commenced; after that "considerable payment on this contract as we go
along" would be expected.

Murray sent content copy to the company, from which it
worked in creating a twelve-page prospectus in 1912. Printing

5,000 copies cost Murray $175. The title page bore the following title and description:

MURRAY'S HISTORICAL AND BIOGRAPHICAL
ENCYCLOPEDIA OF THE COLORED RACE
THROUGHOUT THE WORLD

*Its Progress and Achievements from the Earliest Period
down to the Present Time Embracing*

*25,000 biographical sketches of men and women of the colored
race in every age. A bibliography of over 6,000 titles of
books and pamphlets, which represent their contribution to
the world's literature. A synoptical list of all books of fiction
by Caucasian authors that deal with the race question as a
feature. Also a list of nearly 5,000 musical compositions by
colored composers in every part of the world.*

The same page featured a list of assistant editors including John E. Bruce, John W. Cromwell, Lafayette M. Hershaw, bibliophiles and collectors Arthur A. Schomburg and William Carl Bolivar, and the president of Wilberforce University, William S. Scarborough. DuBois had apparently decided not to participate.

Murray might have been well-off, given his investments, but he did not have the kind of ready money needed to ensure a production run. Looking to the model used with other encyclopedias or serial works, he set into motion a subscription process, whereby individuals order a set via advance sale with the option to pay by installment, to garner the necessary cash. The prospectus, which included a variety of sample pages, began with a lengthy introduction. Murray announced that "my legacy to the colored race," with which he "had so many years been engaged, was at last complete. . . . The issuance of the first volume of this Encyclopedia will, indeed, mark an epoch . . . the greatest step toward fixing the race's status among the peoples of the world, that has been taken since emancipation." He "planned to sell the Encyclopedia as near cost as possible, hoping through increased sales to equalize the cost." The *Boston Colored Citizen* article noted, "One of the most interesting features in connection with this work is that Mr. Murray is understood to have no idea of personal gain in connection with it. He is purely altruistic, as much as his means will permit."

Murray, not Donnelly and Sons, was responsible for advertising and marketing, and setting the price was his choice. He decided on $24 per set of six volumes, with terms of $2 down and the balance due in monthly installments of $2 each. At the bottom of the last page of the prospectus was a subscription form to be cut out and sent to World's Cyclopedia Company with payment. The volumes were to be released serially over 1912 and 1913.

Murray sent a tailored letter with the prospectus to libraries, offering a discounted price of $20 for a full set. He tried to interest newspaper editors in serving as agents to secure subscribers by their printing a notice of the work along with the subscriber form in their papers in return for 10 percent of the resultant intake. "I am not able to pay for the service asked at advertising rates," Murray explained, "but by actively aiding the publication you will pay yourself." Murray followed up with another idea for newspaper editors: "The proposition I herewith submit, is to publish simultaneously in about a dozen selected papers throughout the country, a series of numbered articles. . . . The articles will be copyrighted and their use prohibited to all papers not members of the syndicate, so that all who join will secure the exclusive right of publication." His hope, of course, was that that would serve as a stimulant to lengthen the subscriber list.

Murray conceived of a special scheme for "high-class student canvassers." He sent flyers to the editors of college gazettes at fourteen institutions, including Harvard, Yale, Cornell, Howard, Fisk, and Atlanta. "Go to College at our Expense!" the flyer's headline read, promising that high tuition fees need not be an impediment for those who earned a year's tuition by selling subscriptions to Murray's encyclopedia. The advertisement he ran in the NAACP's *The Crisis* magazine explained that those in college or college bound who sold 150 subscriptions to the encyclopedia would be awarded a scholarship of $150. That would be a bonus in addition to a 10 percent commission on each subscription sold, which for students who sold 150 would mean $510 total. Murray fashioned a letterhead for his World's Cyclopedia Company, and the sheets customized for students were designated "Scholarship Department."

Once the prospectus was issued, newspapers from New York to Texas and from Baltimore to Illinois ran features announcing that Murray's encyclopedia was ready for distribution and commending the work, "the most thorough and comprehensive publication of the kind ever presented to the public," according to the *Baltimore Afro-American*.

Murray was off and running, or so he hoped. Would-be editor agents and student canvassers did not exactly line up, nor did subscriptions pour in. Murray wrote to his loyal friend George Myers on November 23, 1912, "I was indeed greatly pleased to receive your letter and the order to enroll your name as a subscriber with your check. I have received many letters of praise, but few of them contain any money. They don't seem to realize that an Encyclopedia planned on the scale of this one requires a vast amount of capital to launch it. . . . I will need 5000 advance subscribers and upon getting them will depend the issuance of the Encyclopedia."[3]

➔ ❤

"OUR SCHOOLS IN WASHINGTON, D.C. DO NOT SEEM TO BE happy unless they have a fight of some kind on their hands," declared the *Cleveland Gazette*. "Now it's the Prof. Bruce Evans case." On November 6, 1912, Bruce Evans was suddenly dismissed from the public school system by the Board of Education, effective immediately, because, it was alleged, he had been "found lacking in the necessary academic, pedagogic and administrative qualifications of a competent high school teacher or principal." The board's precipitous action was based on the recommendation of the superintendent of schools, the *Evening Star* reported, who had "followed the request of Roscoe Conkling Bruce, assistant superintendent of colored public schools." Evans, present at the board meeting, was dumbstruck. He had been with the school system since 1885 and principal of Armstrong High School since 1901. Earlier that year, he and his high school had been highly praised in a government report. Richard R. Horner, one of the three African Americans on the board of seven, made a motion that Evans be allowed to speak in his defense, but it was voted down. Nor was Horner, himself outraged, allowed to question Assistant Superintendent Bruce about the specific reasons behind the firing.

Evans's brother-in-law lost no time in launching a counteraction. Daniel Murray went right to the top, the President of the United States, to protest the unwarranted dismissal (not surprisingly, Taft's secretary rejoined that it was "a matter over which the President has no jurisdiction"). Small wonder Murray felt some responsibility for Evans's predicament. There can be little doubt that Bruce's action in dismissing Evans was personal, but probably aimed as much at Murray as at the principal himself. Murray had been harassing Roscoe Bruce for two years. Bruce had plenty of naysayers—many black parents felt he ignored their concerns while kowtowing to his white superiors—but Murray took a lead role.

In June 1910, the *Washington Bee* described Bruce as a "lickspittle Negro" who "runs things with a high hand in the schools here, except when called down by the superintendent," and promised that "Mr. Daniel Murray and other prominent citizens are preparing to look after Bruce and something will be doing soon." The following year Murray headed the "anti-Bruce element" that attended a Board of Education meeting and called for the assistant supervisor's removal, but their concerns were left out of the formal proceedings. When the barrage of criticism did not let up over the following months, the superintendent, claiming to have investigated the various allegations made against Bruce, presented a report to the board on March 20, 1912, supporting Bruce's retention. Before the vote was taken, vigorous protests were voiced by the three black board members, Horner in particular, who "asserted that the case had been insufficiently investigated and that the adoption of the report would discredit colored members of the board." At the start of the meeting Murray placed a circular on the desk of each board member outlining the charges against Bruce, but Horner's request that at least some of the contents be read aloud was opposed. The superintendent's recommendation that Bruce be retained was sustained by a vote of 5–3. On April 3, a mass protest meeting was held at an African American church. When Murray was introduced and told he had fifteen minutes to speak, the *Washington Bee* reported that it "greatly displeased Citizen Dan, who had come prepared to speak from five to fifteen hours."[4]

Murray wrote an article at that time describing Bruce, a Harvard graduate and former academic department director at Tuskegee, as "deficient in requisite qualifications" and "not equal to the job." Those words perhaps came back to him when his brother-in-law was dismissed by Bruce for a similarly nonspecific cause come November. Indeed, getting Bruce to articulate any solid charge against Evans would prove to be like pulling teeth. Evans, whom the *Washington Bee*, at least, referred to as "Old White Top," was only forty-five, and under the shock of his peremptory dismissal, he traveled to his sister Mary's home in Boston to weigh his options. He received job offers that would entail his family's relocation but rejected them in favor of fighting his dismissal. The *Bee* reported that Evans considered his having been "put on the toboggan slide" a frame-up and that he would demand to know what the charges were, and that Daniel Murray was "rummaging the Congressional Library for facts against Roscoe." Evans's repeated efforts to get a public hearing before the school board on why he had been summarily fired without a chance to defend himself were repeatedly denied. In the summer of 1913, the board resolved that no injustice had been done to Evans and no further communications from him would be considered. Daniel Murray had had enough. It was time for his brother-in-law's day in court, facing his accusers with counsel at his side. On October 27, 1915, nearly three years after his termination, Bruce Evans filed suit against the Board of Education, and the next day Circuit Division Justice Wendell P. Stafford directed members of the board to show cause why a writ of mandamus should not be issued requiring Evans to be reinstated in his former position. Daniel Murray informed George Myers a week later that "Mrs. Murray is like myself very busy on her brother's case." Meanwhile, in April, Roscoe Bruce was seriously injured in an automobile accident, occasioning John P. Green to remark in a letter to Murray, "They tell me that when Bruce got hurt, Doc Evans got up and walked around, repeating to friends whom he met, 'Vengeance is mine, saith the Lord.' " Indeed, when Bruce relapsed with a sudden brain concussion in July, the *Bee* maintained that there was little sympathy for "the most despised man in the city."

The trial began on December 6, with Evans represented by Arthur A. Birney, a prominent white attorney who taught law at Howard University and who had been retained by the NAAC in the Louisiana disenfranchisement case. The courtroom was packed to overflowing, and the five days of testimony covered 280 pages. Anna and Daniel Murray and Evans himself were among the witnesses. When Roscoe Bruce was finally put on the stand, the only charges he came up with were weak transgressions such as tardiness in turning in certain forms. There being no jury, the decision fell to Justice Stafford, who issued his ruling on May 8, 1916. He dismissed Evans's case, holding that the district court "has no au-

thority to act as a court of appeals from a decision of the board"
and that "the board, having reached the decision in good faith, its
action, even if mistaken, cannot be overruled." Evans retreated,
"his life mission having been shunted out of his hands," but Daniel
and Anna Murray were not finished with Roscoe Bruce.[5]

→ ←

"THE 900 BLOCK OF S STREET IS RAPIDLY PASSING INTO THE
hands of colored owners and tenants," announced the *Washington
Bee* in June 1912. "Up to two years ago, and for many years previous, there was but one colored family in this handsome square—
that of Daniel Murray. Benjamin Washington broke the ice by
purchasing the property adjoining that of Mr. Murray. Then the
exodus of the whites began, and when their places were taken by
additional colored families, a regular panic ensued, and it is now
only a question of time when the block will be solely colored." That
time arrived before the next census. Emma Murray, Henry's wife,
was the census taker in 1920, and she noted all residents as either
mulatto or black (predominantly "mu") as she walked the block
of brick row houses featuring an assortment of bay windows, tur-
rets, fancy brickwork, decorated cornices, and other architectural
flourishes. As color prejudice crested, rampant "white flight" from
the U Street neighborhood progressively turned the mixed-race
area all black. When whites fled, it was often to newer suburbs farther from downtown, which became practicable as more and more
families bought automobiles.

Flight was not the only reaction of whites determined to foster
racial homogeneity in a given neighborhood. Rather than exiting
themselves, they often stood their ground and used race-restrictive
covenants to keep out black families. Those were contracts that
barred owners from selling or renting to African Americans. They
applied either for a specified period of years or in perpetuity. Sometimes riders were attached to individual house deeds. Sometimes

neighbors came together and drew up agreements that were then filed with the recorder of deeds. That was the pattern followed farther west on S Street, just outside the U Street neighborhood. Sixteenth Street served as an unofficial black/white dividing line. The residents on the 1700 block of S Street signed a contract "for their mutual benefit as well as for the best interests of said community." The parties, it read, "do hereby mutually covenant, promise and agree each with the other and for their respective heirs and assigns that no part of the land now owned by the parties . . . shall ever be used or occupied by, or sold conveyed, leased rented, or given to Negroes or any person or persons of the Negro race or blood." When legally challenged, as in this case, the courts held such documents to be enforceable by law. White home owners, realtors, developers, and banks conspired to put up obstacles affecting both housing availability and pricing. African Americans were overcharged for the few housing options open to them and often denied loans.

Among the Murrays' new neighbors on S Street was William H. Grimshaw, who lived at 924 S Street, next door to Henry and Emma Murray. Grimshaw had been Daniel Murray's coworker at the Library of Congress since 1897. As the *Washington Bee* reported in January 1915, "For a long time he was in charge of the Senate Reading Room at the Congressional Library, holding that position until during the current administration he was changed to another place in the same building."[6]

The administration referred to was that of Democrat Woodrow Wilson, President of the United States from 1913 to 1921. Notwithstanding Wilson's achievements with his "New Freedom" agenda, his administration was a bitter disappointment for the African Americans who had voted for him, relying on his campaign guarantee for "absolute fair dealing," and a disaster for those employed by the federal government. Two days after Wilson's inauguration, the highest-ranking black government official, Assistant

Attorney General William H. Lewis, was forced to resign. Segregation by color in federal offices was introduced a month later.
Cabinet members who, like Wilson, were southern-bred, thought
it "intolerable" that whites not only had to work with blacks but
were forced to use the same washrooms, towels, and drinking
glasses. African Americans in federal departments, including the
Post Office and Treasury, were moved to separate or screened-off
work areas and required to use "colored only" lavatories and eating
spaces. Wilson defended such segregation, claiming it was simply a
way of avoiding "friction." Photographs were now required of civil
service job applicants, an obvious mechanism for excluding blacks.
Even those positions traditionally held by African Americans were
consigned to whites, including register of the Treasury, recorder
of deeds, and minister to Haiti. Thousands of black government
employees were demoted, displaced by whites, or contended with
stalled careers.

Following segregation in federal departments came discrimination in government public places. Even before the Wilson administration, when Register of the Treasury William T. Vernon
had eaten his lunch in the House of Representatives restaurant in
1909, it had precipitated "indignation expressed by five southern
congressmen, because they were compelled to take lunch in the
house office dining room when the Hon. W. T. Vernon was oc-
cupying a table in the same room." By 1917, the mixing of colors
in Capitol restaurants was no longer tolerated. That summer, the
Washington Bee relayed, "Certain gentlemen who were at the Capitol on business went into the Senate restaurant for lunch and were
denied service there on the ground of color, the waiter who came
to them stating that he could not take their order for the reason
that direction had been given by Senator Overman, under whose
control the Senate restaurant comes, not to serve colored people."
Lee S. Overman, a Democratic senator from North Carolina, when
queried, responded, contrary to fact, that his "personal opinion"

was that the dining room was private and that even if there was no official rule prohibiting blacks, senators "had the right to exclude whomever they liked." That must have struck Daniel Murray, who had held the job of waiter there without ever being compelled to refuse service to African Americans, but such strictures hit even closer to home when, in 1919, the superintendent of buildings and grounds at the Library of Congress sequestered the library's black employees in the staff lunchroom and excluded blacks, staff and visitors alike, from the public cafeteria. And how humiliating it must have been for Murray when a separate "colored men's locker room" was installed.

African Americans and their solid supporters did not take these setbacks lying down. The NAACP, Oswald Garrison Villard and W. E. B. DuBois in particular, jumped on Wilson early on. William Monroe Trotter was especially aggressive. In November 1914, he met with Wilson at the White House and demanded answers. "Have you a 'new freedom' for white Americans and a new slavery for your Afro-American fellow citizens?" he demanded. The President lost his composure after Trotter repeatedly interrupted him and snapped, "Your manner offends me. . . . I am the one to do the interrupting, not you." He assured Trotter that he would not deal with him again as spokesman and declared the interview over.

Persistent pushback resulted in curbing but not reversing the administration's actions, although protesting activists kept them from being codified by law. On September 19, 1916, Murray complained to his friend George Myers, "The segregation order issued last Aug. has been revoked, it should never have been issued. The intent is the thing. Says Juvenal, 'In the eye of heaven, a wicked deed intended is done.' " He may have been referring to the just-rescinded segregation order issued by Wilson's military aide for the State, War, and Navy Building. Murray continued, "No self respecting Man of Color could support a party that is constantly bringing to the front these hellish devices designed to humiliate the Man of Color . . . treating the colored American as an alien in the land of his birth." But the Republican Party, to which Murray was always faithful despite his regular plugs for political independence, could not be absolved. As the *Washington Bee* noted in January 1920, "The Republicans have shown no disposition to challenge segregation in the departments in Washington . . . [and] they have refused to lift the ban against colored people in the House and Senate Restaurants."[7]

Instances of discrimination evolved into a way of life in Washington. Strict segregation was the pervasive policy. Gone was any negotiable color line that accounted for class. Even the formerly inviting St. John's Church on Lafayette Square lost faith. In 1913, the *Bee* reported that "a prominent colored society woman . . . was told when she visited St. John's Church that colored communicants were not desired, that St. John's communicants were largely southerners, to whom colored communicants were odious." Historians consider the first part of the twentieth century the "nadir" for African Americans' prospects in their native land. "Not since the emancipation of the colored race, has there been so much discrimination and prejudice," concluded the *Bee*. An English visitor to the capital described "the cruel and deplorable incidents in the every-day life of the streets" with which Americans of African descent contended in a *Washington Post* article that Murray cut out and saved. Querying a former Confederate, the Englishman was told, "The Washington negro is particularly bumptious and intolerable. Immediately after the war Washington was the black man's paradise. They flocked there in their thousands, thinking that the government was going to do everything for them, and that there was nothing they had not a right to expect. That spirit still survives and makes trouble."

Black Washingtonians had their own take on the obsolete epithet once the twentieth century was well under way. "It would be difficult to find a worse misnomer for Washington than 'The

Colored Man's Paradise,'" Mary Church Terrell maintained. Her article "What It Means to Be Colored in the Capital of the United States" was published in 1907. History teacher and political activist Neval H. Thomas authored an article in the next decade with the title "The District of Columbia—a Paradise of Paradoxes." Terrell, who had first arrived in Washington in 1891, declared that the capital "has been doing its level best ever since to make conditions for us intolerable." She detailed how a black visitor looking for lodging could "spend the entire night wandering about" while foreign visitors easily found hotel accommodations, or "walk from the Capitol to the White House . . . without finding a place to eat, unless willing to sit behind a screen." Residents found themselves kept from securing jobs due solely to "a fatal drop of African blood." Black people, she concluded, "are sacrificed on the altar of prejudice in the Capital of the United States." She closed her essay: "The chasm between the principles upon which this Government was founded, in which it still professes to believe, and those which are daily practiced under the protection of the flag, yawns wide and deep."

In view of the persecutions, rebuffs, and depressing and cruel conditions, Neval Thomas described "a scene of sorrows" in the capital in his essay. "Even now at this very hour the ghost of the slave power is stalking about seeking to perpetuate the aged master-and-slave scheme of society. The more cultured and ambitious the Negro, the greater is the delight in humiliating him, and in forestalling his progress." The public library had turned out not to be for all classes after all when it came to employment. "In our city library there is not a single colored employee," lamented Thomas, "and the librarian, a native of Rochester, N.Y., told me plainly in reply to one of my protests that he would employ no colored person there save in the capacity of charwoman." In February 1922, there was a hue and cry when it was announced that branch libraries in public schools would open to all students irrespective of color. A white citizens' association decried the action "as vicious and detrimental," threatening that "any attempt to put this order into effect would be provocative of violent dissentions and disorder."

A highly symbolic blow followed on May 30, 1922, on the occasion of the dedication of the Lincoln Memorial, nearly sixty years after the Emancipation Proclamation. By order of the Washington superintendent of public buildings and grounds, marines with bayonets, characterized as "distasteful, discourteous and abusive," were placed at the entrance to force black citizens into a roped-off section behind the chairs reserved for white people. It was a block away from the memorial, with rough-hewn benches the only seating. As one disgusted American of color declared, "The conditions which confronted us as a race were the most shameful and disgraceful in the annals of history."[8]

16

IRONIC FRUITS

IN AN APRIL 1909 *COLORED AMERICAN MAGAZINE* ARTICLE, Ralph W. Tyler, the auditor for the Navy Department (until 1913, when he was replaced by a white appointee under the Wilson administration) and himself a member of Washington's black elite, identified Anna Evans Murray, Bettie Cox Francis, and Mary Church Terrell as a trio of ladies "prominent in the social world," who, "considering their cleverness and their activities along every line that makes for race progress, may be said to approach as near the ideal woman as one can find." They "not only grace and dominate the social circles, but they devote much time and money to the many colored charity institutions that abound in Washington." He continued, "These three women are quite dissimilar in their temperament, figure and face, but all three are voted clever and interesting matrons, and handsome matrons, too. While they are dissimilar in a few points they are decidedly similar in their desire for race uplift along every possible line. All three are charming hostesses. In fact Madame de Staël never presided over her salon with more grace than these three matrons preside over social affairs at their homes. And all three are public-spirited women, quite as well versed in affairs of state and as well informed on all public questions as many men. Much more so than the average man."

Anna Murray did indeed keep up a full schedule with her kindergarten promotion, charity and civic work, speaking engagements, and social activities while managing a home and family. A partial accounting for one twelve-month period shows just how busy she stayed. In October 1910, she made an address at the opening of the National Training School for Women and Girls, founded by Nannie H. Burroughs. That December, she attended a ladies' luncheon hosted by Ralph Tyler's wife. The following February she was seated on the rostrum along with Bettie Francis, Mary Church Terrell, and Josephine Bruce at a YWCA program (it was Washington's first YWCA and the nation's only independent black YWCA). April brought her son Nathaniel's wedding to Mayme Jordan. She attended the Fifteenth Annual Convention of the National Congress of Mothers, held in the capital April 25–May 2. On the evening of May 3, she joined other elite women at "one of the most brilliant gatherings of the season," a home entertainment in honor of Georgia Douglas Johnson, the wife of the new recorder of deeds, Henry Lincoln Johnson. In late May, she traveled to Georgia, where she was one of the principal speakers at the Sixteenth Annual Conference for the Study of the Negro Problems, at Atlanta University, directed by W. E. B. DuBois (the conference theme was "The Common School and the Negro American"). In June, she had the pleasure of seeing one son, Harold, graduate from high school as class valedictorian at the same time that another, Nat, received a BS degree from Cornell University. The next month she made a monetary contribution to Camp Pleasant, a summer respite for poor African American children. Along with her sons and husband as available, she spent the steamy season, August to early September, at the family's Harpers Ferry cottage. She saw Harold off to Ithaca to enter Cornell in late September and then left Washington herself to spend three weeks in Chicago.

By the next year Anna was advocating for yet another cause: women's suffrage. The first national parade of the National Woman Suffrage Association took place in Washington, DC, on March 3, 1913. It was the day before Woodrow Wilson's inauguration, so the city streets were crowded with visitors as well as residents. Many lined Pennsylvania Avenue to witness the procession of more than a thousand determined suffragettes waving "Votes for Women" banners, led by one of the movement's standard-bearers astride a white horse. Some onlookers cheered, but they were drowned out by the many who rudely jeered. The NAACP journal, *The Crisis*, identified Anna Murray as one of about forty-five African American women who marched that day. Others included Mary Church Terrell, Ida Wells-Barnett, twenty-five Howard University students in caps and gowns, and "an old mammy" who had been brought down from Delaware. "The women all report most courteous treatment on the part of the marshals of the parade, and no worse treatment from bystanders than was accorded white women," reported *The Crisis*. "In spite of the apparent reluctance of the local suffrage committee to encourage the colored women to participate, and in spite of the conflicting rumors that were circulated and which disheartened many of the colored women from taking part, they are to be congratulated that so many of them had the courage of their convictions and that they made such an admirable showing in the first great national parade."[1]

George Henry Murray earned an LLB degree from Howard University Law School in 1914 and, while maintaining his full-time teaching job, occasionally took on cases connected with family or civil rights. More than any of the other sons, he followed in Daniel Murray's footsteps, though his 1905 article for *The Colored American Magazine*, "Educated Colored Men and White Women," would be his only foray into writing. In one *Washington Bee* article, Henry was identified simply as "young Murray." Like his father, he was a joiner and a doer. He was active in clubs and causes and dabbled in real estate. He joined the Inaugural Welcome Club, working alongside his father to plan events, and the Mu-So-Lit Club, cofounded by his uncle Bruce Evans in 1905. "Mu-So-Lit" was derived from the first syllables of "music, social, literary," though "Po" might have been added for "political." The club's "monthly meetings are the rallying point for the best men in the capital," noted the *Indianapolis Freeman*. Bruce Evans was elected president in 1909, and Henry would later win that role. Daniel Murray's favored club became the Oldest Inhabitants Association, modeled after the white association of the same name and restricted to "Old Citz." Many attracted to the club, formed in 1912, the outgrowth of the Native Washingtonians, held familiar old District names such as Cook, Brent, Muse, and Wormley. The organizational goal was "the preservation of the valuable personal and racial history, touching more than a century of Negro residence at the Capital of the Nation, which might otherwise be lost." Daniel Murray, of course, had a lot of research to share in addition to personal memories. For example, at the April 1915 meeting he told the story of Paul Jennings, James Madison's enslaved manservant who later became a leader in Washington's free black community and in 1848 served as Underground Railroad operative in the largest-scale attempted-slave escape in American history.[2]

Dannie Murray came home in 1914. He was, his father noted, "invited by Mr. Preston Gibson, a society leader of Wash. D.C. and Newport, to furnish the dance music for several society functions in Washington," but he also acknowledged that his son's health was poor. Dannie secured steady work as "leader and director of the orchestra in Washington's leading and most popular winter garden," Geyer's Restaurant, located on 14th Street just below U Street. Remodeled in early 1914, Geyer's was considered "the dandy of all beer gardens." According to the *Washington Post*, "A band played away while waiters rushed to and fro with seidels, steins, and schooners. Geyer's was the Mecca for young love; for the young blades of the day. It was packed and jammed nightly."

The U Street neighborhood (roughly covering the area from S Street to Florida Avenue and from 7th Street to 16th Street, in later decades designated "Shaw") became the very "heart of black Washington," its commercial, cultural, and social center. Disenfranchised, precluded from most federal and District government positions, barred from public and private services and accommodations, partitioned into residential enclaves, black citizens, though never abandoning avenues of protest, fashioned a separate economic and recreational community that was largely self-sufficient. Without unduly romanticizing segregated black life, a vital and vibrant culture flourished in the U Street neighborhood, and so did racial pride: ironic fruits of exclusion. It evolved into a community in which residents could patronize a full range of black-owned businesses, three hundred of them by 1920, that met essentially all their needs. There were restaurants, pharmacies, barbershops, groceries, funeral homes, printers, photographers, doctors, dentists, lawyers, and community meeting and recreation centers. Most of them were located on the major commercial corridors of U, 7th, and 14th streets. U Street was a wide boulevard lined with shade trees; getting "dressed up" to go there was the rule, not the exception. Noted landmarks included the True Reformer Building, Odd Fellows Hall, YMCA and YWCA, Industrial Savings Bank, Whitelaw Hotel, Ware's Department Store, Griffith Stadium, St. Luke's and other churches, Freedmen's Hospital, and Howard University. Howard and the two main high schools nearby, Dunbar (M Street High School had been transferred to a new building in 1916 and renamed to honor the poet) and Armstrong, were among the best educational facilities Washington had to offer students of any color. There was street life that included parades and annual cadet drills and other competitions between

Dunbar and Armstrong. Residents took pride in the community's entrepreneurial spirit and the achievements of its individual members. Parents appreciated the opportunity to raise their children in a place where they were protected from ostracism and racism on a daily basis. The neighborhood thrived beginning in the 1910s and for decades to come. Here African Americans enjoyed living in a city within a city, away from the restrictive, repressive environment of whites. Working people with modest incomes and middle-class professionals shared the community. Certainly there were divisions among residents based on class and complexion, but bonding in the face of common adversity prevailed.

Geyer's was just one of many places of entertainment. Clubs and cabarets, ballrooms and theaters, juke joints and pool halls made for a lively, when not boisterous, nightlife. The U Street thoroughfare became the capital city's own "Black Broadway." Howard Theater was the focal point of it all. The 1,500-seat theater had a broad and magnificent lobby and was divided into an orchestra section and a balcony with eight proscenium boxes. The building occupied an entire block at 7th and T streets. One of the first theaters erected specifically for African Americans, it was their premier entertainment venue in the country throughout the 1920s. Howard Theater first opened its doors on August 22, 1910. "The orchestra was monopolized with the social elite of Washington, gayly and gorgeously dressed" on opening night. "Beyond all doubt it is the finest theater in the city," the *Washington Bee* proclaimed, expressing confidence that "the people of Washington will support a first-class theater." Indeed they did; patrons lined up around the corner to see the popular shows. And the theater manager supported them. All kinds of shows were booked, from vaudeville to musicals to highbrow fare, employing local and national talent. The neighborhood residents were permitted to use the theater for local programs and organizational meetings between professional engagements. For example, in February 1915, a gathering was held in the theater to protest a bill in Congress proposing separate streetcar accommodations for white and black Washingtonians. Henry Murray presided, and to add to the event's appeal, "Daniel Murray, Jr. of New York rendered a violin solo."[3]

Two months later, Dannie Murray performed at a Howard Theater concert described as "one of the truly 'society' events of the season." Others on the bill included Will Marion Cook and Dannie's cousin Lillian. Lillian Evans, tall and slender, was a dark-eyed beauty who became an accomplished performer while still in her teens. She often performed at churches and theaters, many of them benefit shows, sharing the program with others. Before 1915 was out, she was ready to carry a solo concert. On November 5, "Mr. George Henry Murray announced the premier recital of Miss Lillian Evans, a young coloratura soprano, who has made a splendid reputation here and elsewhere as a musical genius." It was the first but not the last time Henry Murray managed his cousin's concerts.

Dannie and his brother Harold, in Washington before returning to Cornell for his senior year, formed a quartet with Eubie Blake and Noble Sissle at Howard Theater on September 26, 1915. Eubie Blake grew up in the same Baltimore neighborhood near Belair Market that Daniel Murray had a generation earlier and displayed his genius for ragtime piano as a young boy. In 1905, he was part of the same music scene in Manhattan as Dannie Murray, and certainly the two may have already been acquaintances. Blake was in Baltimore when he met Noble Sissle in May 1915. They were a brand-new piano and singing act, just beginning to write popular tunes together. In fact, they had come to Washington to try them out. The house was packed. As reported by the *Indianapolis Free-man*, "The stellar piece of the day was the rendition by Sissle of the new song written by Sissle, with the music by Blake, entitled 'It's All Your Fault.'" As Sissle rendered the number in his flexible tenor voice, "Daniel Murray, a violinist of more than local fame, accompanied by Harold Murray, played the selection from the fashion box." The *Freeman* concluded, "The quartette, Sissle-Blake and the Murrays, showed themselves to be entertainers of class and the afternoon was one of the most enjoyable Washington's musical and dramatic lovers have experienced in a long time." Dannie and Harold must have had the time of their lives, the memory only enhanced looking back. Dannie resumed his engagement at Geyer's and Harold his studies at Cornell. Noble and Sissle went on to play with James Reese Europe orchestras beginning in 1916, and in March 1921 their musical, *Shuffle Along*, was tried out at Howard Theater before opening in New York in May. It was the first box-office hit musical on Broadway written by and about African Americans.

Making the Washington entertainment scene at the time was the composer, pianist, and bandleader Edward "Duke" Ellington, who would become the most famous of DC's homegrown stars. He had grown up in the same U Street neighborhood as the Murray brothers and was one year younger than Paul Murray. The two had attended Armstrong High School together. Ellington had dropped out three months before graduation, determined to make a living as a musician. He had been called Eddie until 1913, when a friend, observing his polished manners, dubbed him "Duke" and the nickname stuck. Ellington worked as a soda jerk and played piano at various joints in the neighborhood to begin with. In 1917, he formed his first band, the Duke's Serenaders. Six years later, he moved to New York City, renaming his band the Washingtonians. He "remained a strong presence in the neighborhood" and returned often to visit and perform.[4]

→ ←

THE AMERICAN NEGRO HISTORICAL SOCIETY OF PHILADELphia, inaugurated in 1897, was the first organization founded with the specific objective of compiling, preserving, and sharing books and materials documenting African American history. Daniel Murray, who had a close relationship with charter member William Carl Bolivar, was a participant. Bolivar, a journalist as well as a devoted bibliophile and collector, signed his column in the *Philadelphia Tribune* "Pencil Pusher." In 1910, the society launched an annual lecture series. Murray was among the presenters noted for "fidelity to historical endeavor." His topic in May 1911 was Philadelphia's relation to the Haitian Revolution. The *Philadelphia Item* adjudged it "a brilliant historical lecture" and Murray "a gentleman of the highest character and culture." Murray was a solid link in the network of bibliophiles in New York, Philadelphia, and Washington who recognized the importance of preserving African American works and whose efforts were integral to the development of African diaspora studies.

In 1911, the Negro Society for Historical Research (NSHR) was created by John E. Bruce and Arthur Schomburg, both of whom, like Bolivar, were assistant editors for Murray's encyclopedia. The former, who had long been a friend and supporter of Murray, was a journalist who went by the pen name "Bruce Grit." His close associate Schomburg had been born in Puerto Rico and immigrated to New York in 1891. A self-schooled historian, he was a major collector of not only books but documents, prints, and memorabilia as well. The NSHR was anchored in Bruce's home in Yonkers, New York. It aimed to enlighten all people's understanding of black history and achievement by collecting books and other materials and by initiating a circulating library and bureau of race information. Qualification for membership was "Race love and a strong desire to know its history." Daniel Murray, William Carl Bolivar, W. E. B. DuBois, John W. Cromwell, and Howard professor Alain Locke were all corresponding members. The NSHR published occasional papers, sponsored speakers, and encouraged the teaching of African American and Pan-African history.

Murray participated in celebrations of the fiftieth anniversary

of the Emancipation Proclamation as curator of literary exhibits
in at least three cities. He was the chairman of the racial literature
committee for the event in Washington, the start date of which
was scheduled to fall on September 22, 1912, in commemoration
of the day Lincoln issued the Preliminary Emancipation Proclamation. African Americans had hoped for a full-scale national
celebration to eclipse all others, but states stepped in to plan their
own celebrations when Congress declined to appropriate the required funding. The Pennsylvania Emancipation Exposition
opened on September 15, 1913, in South Philadelphia. Murray
provided nearly seven hundred Library of Congress books written by colored authors and advised organizers to seek others from
private collectors. Along with the books he shipped 170 charts and
a bronze statue of Frederick Douglass to sit on a pedestal in front
of the exhibit, which was housed in the main exposition building,
a two-story Beaux-Arts edifice designed by an African American
architect.

New York's was the grandest of all the semicentennial celebrations. It ran from October 22 to 31 in the 12th Regiment
Armory on Columbus Avenue, in the heart of New York City.
W. E. B. DuBois was programming chairman and called on Murray to "come and act as Curator" for the literary exhibit, offering
him a $50 honorarium. To the Library of Congress's loan collec-
tion Murray added titles from his personal library. The books "fill
quite a good sized library and appear to cover every phase of Negro history and life," the New York Age reported, adding that they
were displayed "in a wire screened case to prevent damage from
promiscuous handling." Murray also supplied Library of Congress
images of artists and scholars of African descent from the medieval
period. Those helped lend the exposition a Pan-African flavor, as
did other elements evoking African and Egyptian cultural roots.
A highlight of the festival was an elaborate pageant, "The Star of
Ethiopia," written and directed by DuBois. Illustrating the history

of the race and featuring 250 actors and a live orchestra, the pageant was staged four times during the ten-day exposition.

A major player had joined Washington's literati by this time, the man who would ultimately win the epithet "Father of Black History." His name was Carter G. Woodson. Woodson must have met Daniel Murray as early as 1909, when he was doing research on his Harvard PhD dissertation at the Library of Congress, but there is no evidence of a meaningful relationship between the two. Many of Woodson's associates found his independent streak difficult. A man married to his work, he was characterized as stubborn and erratic, and he tended not to share credit where it was due. In 1915, he incorporated his Association for the Study of Negro Life and History (ASNLH) in Washington. A year later he created *The Journal of Negro History*. Murray was a dues-paying member of the ASNLH but was never called on to submit an article to the journal. Woodson was voted into the American Negro Academy in 1914.

The American Negro Academy (ANA) was launched in 1897, just after the American Negro Historical Society of Philadelphia. Its objective was more about promoting scholarly publication and higher education than about book collecting. It was the most prestigious organization of its kind and very selective, limited to fifty members elected by ballot. The founding president was former St. Luke's pastor Alexander Crummell. W. E. B. DuBois and Archibald Grimké followed in succession. The ANA held its annual meetings in Washington, and Murray attended sessions and participated in discussions, but he was never invited to join the academy, even though many of his fellow bibliophiles were, both college degree holders such as John W. Cromwell and Henry P. Slaughter, and self-trained historians such as John E. Bruce and Arthur Schomburg.

Between sessions of the ANA's 20th Annual Convention in Washington, December 26–27, 1916, John W. Cromwell hosted a dinner party for a half dozen or so book lovers, including Murray, at his home in the U Street neighborhood. That evening, after considerable discussion, they formed a new coalition of dedicated bibliophiles—the Negro Book Collectors Exchange—with the goal of centralizing a compilation of African American literature. They planned to contact collectors throughout the United States, Africa, the West Indies, South America, and Europe and request copies of books (or at least details thereof) written by authors of color. They hoped to have all collectors register themselves and their collections to allow for a master bibliography and clearinghouse for materials related to the African diaspora and to facilitate the trading of duplicate copies among collectors. Officers were elected before the night was over: Henry P. Slaughter president, John Cromwell vice president, Arthur Schomburg secretary-treasurer, John E. Bruce publicity agent, and Daniel Murray registrar. The Des Moines, Iowa, *Bystander* relayed their wish that "citizens having old books and pamphlets by race authors will perform a patriotic duty" by communicating with the exchange, adding, "No better disposition of these old books stored in closets and garrets when not on the library shelves of colored citizens could be made than by sending them either to the exchange or to the Library of Congress."

Henry Slaughter, one of Murray's closest friends, was now widowed. Slaughter's town house overflowed with his ever-expanding collections, and he invited researchers recommended through the Library of Congress or Howard University to make use of it. This quintessential bookworm compiled more than 10,000 volumes, 100,000 newspaper clippings, and 3,000 pamphlets plus manuscripts, engravings, and curios. They filled the three stories and basement of the town house that he shared for at least twenty years with the same housekeeper. "His rare books occupied the tops of dressers and small bookcases in all his bedrooms," recalled one visitor. "His book stacks, specially built on the top floor, held in classified arrangement his slavery and Civil War books." Slaughter purchased books from William Carl Bolivar and from English booksellers, carefully tucking the sales slip into each volume. Although a very social individual, he was quoted as saying, "My books are my best friends and I would furnish a house with books rather than with furniture." Those in the Negro Book Collectors Exchange remained devoted to their avocation, but their shared objectives continued on a more informal basis than that implied by the organizational structure set into motion at Cromwell's gathering. Largely self-funded, they endured personal deprivations to feed their collections. As Schomburg averred, "History must restore what slavery took away."[5]

By the 1910s, with its membership rolls ever rising, headquarters in New York replete with paid staff, financial stability, a popular monthly journal (*The Crisis*, edited by DuBois), and constant vigilance of and response to racial issues, it was clear that the NAACP was the nation's foremost civil rights organization. While highly centralized, the national body nevertheless made branch associations an important organizational element. Membership in a branch included membership in the national organization. The Washington branch was organized in early 1912, thanks to the leadership of Mary Church Terrell, Lafayette M. Hershaw, and Bishop John Hurst, among others. On March 19 DuBois addressed a mass recruiting meeting held at Metropolitan AME Church. The next year Archibald Grimké, who had moved from Boston to Washington and was living with his brother, Reverend Francis Grimké, was elected branch president. In the fall of 1915, the national board of directors voted to present a trophy to the branch in recognition of its development. It was the largest branch, with an enrollment of 1,500. The national association then had a total membership of 8,266.

Scores of Daniel Murray's associates joined the NAACP, and several served as local branch officers. It is more than likely that he signed up as well. Harold became a member while at Cornell. Anna not only joined but was a speaker at the May 1917 NAACP annual meeting. There is no evidence to suggest that her husband was particularly active in the organization, unlike two of his dearest friends, Bishop John Hurst of Baltimore and Charles E. Bentley of Chicago, who were major forces at both the national and branch levels.

John Hurst owned a house in Northwest Washington at this time and in 1912 was an executive committee member of the DC branch. He was also active in the Baltimore branch, chartered in April 1912, right after Washington's. By 1916, he sat on the national board of directors. Charles E. Bentley was a founding member of the national board. He was a "Niagara Man," who, like DuBois, Hershaw, and others, had moved seamlessly on to the NAACP. He, Ida Wells-Barnett, and the white social reformer Jane Addams were among those who established the Chicago branch, one of the first to form. Bentley, who ran a very successful dental practice in the Marshall Field Building, was "a man of learning, polished in manner, having entre to the highest social circles, and," concluded the *St. Paul Appeal*, "has been able to do effective work in fighting prejudice against the colored people."

Anna Murray's brother-in-law and sister, Butler and Mary Evans Wilson, were founders of the NAACP Boston branch. A dynamic husband-and-wife team and the parents of five children, both became famed civil rights activists. The Boston branch was the first chartered, formally established in 1911. Among the fifty-six original members were offspring of notable abolitionist leaders. One of them was William Lloyd Garrison's son, Francis Jackson Garrison, who claimed that the Wilsons were the "real life" of the branch. Butler Wilson was executive secretary from 1912 to 1926 and by 1916 also sat on the national board of directors. The Wilsons were not only the chief organizers and directors of the Boston branch's early activity but also top recruiters, Mary in particular.

She paid her own expenses to travel to New Jersey, Pennsylvania, Ohio, and upstate New York. She recruited thousands of members and laid the groundwork for additional branch associations. In 1915 alone, she held 150 parlor meetings in her Rutland Square home to raise money. Like her husband, she often spoke publicly. The duo participated in many antisegregation struggles in the Boston area, agitating against race-limited education and employment opportunities.

Butler Wilson was one of the most determined among NAACP leaders who protested exhibition of the influential, race-baiting movie *The Birth of a Nation*, directed by the innovative filmmaker D. W. Griffith. He tried to suppress its showing in Boston but managed just to get one of the most offensive scenes cut. Appeals such as Butler's only increased publicity for the film, with its harmful and absurdly inaccurate portrayal of blacks. In the words of *The Crisis*, the film depicted the black American as an "ignorant fool, a vicious rapist, a venal and unscrupulous politician, or a faithful but doddering idiot." In the movie, released in 1915, freedmen were depraved villains and the heroes who saved the day, garbed in flowing white, were Ku Klux Klan members. It was "history upside down, a complete inversion of the historical truth," lamented one NAACP leader. Protestors in other parts of the country were fiercely opposed as well and contrived to get the film banned in the state of Ohio, and in cities including Chicago, St. Louis, and Denver. Where the film's run could not be curtailed, techniques such as calls for boycotts and distribution of counterpropaganda leaflets at theaters were employed.

But the damage was done. *The Birth of a Nation* was a terrific box-office success, and most filmgoers accepted it as valid history. Generations of Americans, deprived of an unbiased accounting of the Reconstruction era in their schooling, absorbed lasting images from the film, such as the scene where duly elected African American representatives were rendered as buffoonish rubes in the state legislative chamber. In one screen shot, a legislator's bare feet up on his desk loomed enormous in close-up, while the background revealed his colleague gnawing on a chicken leg.

Before 1917 was over, the NAACP won two court cases representing major breakthroughs. In *Guinn v. United States* (1915), the Supreme Court found the grandfather clause enacted by the Oklahoma State Legislature a violation of the Fifteenth Amendment. In a case brought by two Kentuckians, *Buchanan v. Warley* (1917), the Supreme Court upheld, by unanimous decision, the right of all people to buy and sell residential property unimpeded by color. It was the first high court decision to strike at the state segregation laws sanctioned under *Plessy v. Ferguson*. Those triumphs propelled the NAACP's growth. By the end of 1918, membership was at 43,994, with Washington still the largest branch, at 6,843.[6]

→ ←

ON JUNE 15, 1916 DANIEL ALEXANDER PAYNE MURRAY received an honorary Doctor of Laws (LLD) degree from Wilberforce University in recognition of his "extensive research work in the history and progress of the Colored race." It held special meaning for him as the namesake of the institution's founder and longtime president, Bishop Daniel Alexander Payne. The invitation was extended by current president, William S. Scarborough, a Greek scholar and one of the intellectuals Murray had enlisted as an assistant editor for his encyclopedia. "Of course, you will be my guest," Scarborough wrote. Murray embraced the offer but was disappointed that he was unable to visit George Myers while in Ohio. He had to turn his friend's invitation down because Cleveland was two hundred miles north and he had barely been able to get the necessary days off from work to accept his honorary degree. On Monday evening, June 12, he delivered a lecture before the university's literary societies on "some early illustrations on behalf of the African, confirming the intellectual equality of all races." He received his honorary degree three days later, conferred during commencement exercises by President Scarborough. On the platform sat "a host of distinguished people from all parts of the country," including the fifteen active bishops of the AME Church. Among them was Murray's friend John Hurst, who offered the invocation. Murray's hometown paper was impressed. The *Washington Bee* adjudged the awarding of Murray's honorary degree "The event of the month, the one that has caused the greatest amount of local gossip." His paper to the literary societies had "produced a profound sensation." The article went on, "Deep research was evident in every line and justified the assertion often made that Mr. Murray is today's authority concerning the history of the colored throughout the world." Murray experimented with adding the Dr. prefix to his name, at least in his own papers, overdoing it in one instance where he referred to himself as "Dr. Daniel Murray LL.D."[7]

On June 20, 1916, Anna Murray with son Paul traveled to Ithaca, New York, to attend Harold's graduation from Cornell and enter Paul at the university. Harold graduated with honors the next day with a degree in mechanical engineering, "the first colored student to complete the course of that institution." Paul was a fresh graduate of Armstrong High School. According to his father, he was class valedictorian, though the local newspaper account of the graduation exercises does not bear that out. Paul's senior year report card showed his grades, deportment, and attendance as being all good to excellent, but he was required to take summer courses at Cornell in order to matriculate in the fall. His mother remained with him not only in the summer, "to prepare her son to enter Cornell," but throughout the winter. His mother's hovering must have been due to Paul's frailties given his epileptic disorder.

Murray wrote his friend Myers in September 1916 that "Harold is playing every night with Dan and making over 20.00 per week but seems bent on going back to Cuba. He spent his vacation there in 1914." Harold had enjoyed that summer job in Havana and was interested in finding a permanent position there. But he also had other business to attend to. Her name was Madrenne Powell. She was a local Ithaca girl who worked as a hairdresser, and she met Harold in 1913 and dated him for the remainder of his college tenure. Local blacks made up only a small fraction of Ithaca's townspeople. They often referred with deference to the African American Cornellians they encountered as "Prof," and that was Harold's nickname. On the second day of November 1916, Harold Murray married Madrenne Powell at her parents' home in Ithaca. Her twin sister, Gladys, served as bridesmaid. Observers regularly marveled at the sisters' good looks. Elaborated one, "They were the most beautiful women I had ever seen—identical twins with glorious deep bronze complexions and both of them wearing white satin evening dresses. This beauty in duplicate more than doubled its startling character. They were breathtaking." On the same day as his wedding Harold landed a job in Havana. The President of Cuba, Mario García Menocal, who had himself earned an engineering degree from Cornell, wanted a graduate from Cornell's Sibley School to work out some issues in his sugar mill industry. Two days after the wedding, the newlyweds sailed from New York, arriving in Cuba four days later. Madrenne was in the family way and gave birth three months later to a girl, whom the new parents named Helene.[8]

A family tragedy closed out 1916. On the late afternoon of Wednesday, November 22, Daniel Evans Murray died of tuberculosis. He was thirty-six. He had recently married, and his wife, Pearl Calloway, was at his bedside along with his parents when he succumbed. Earlier in the month, he had left his engagement at Geyer's because of acute throat trouble. Obituaries described him as "fondly known among the music loving public of Washington, Baltimore, Philadelphia, New York and Boston" and "one of the leading violinists of the country." Floral tributes, in addition to those from relatives, were sent by Pinckney Pinchback, Spencer

Murray, John G. Morrison of the Library of Congress, and Dannie's employer, Fred Geyer. The day after Dannie's death was Thanksgiving, and it must have been a sad occasion for the family, as was the Saturday to follow, when they escorted his body that morning from the house on S Street to Woodlawn Cemetery. Arrangements had been made with McGuire's Funeral Home. The procession, six carriages following the hearse, made its way across the Anacostia River to Southeast Washington. On an earlier winter day a few years after Helene and Pinckney had been reinterred at Woodlawn, Daniel Murray had traveled to the cemetery and paid cash for six more plots adjoining theirs. Now, as Daniel Evans Murray was laid to rest next to his siblings, the mourners stood bundled against the city's cold snap. The family tradition is that Anna blamed Dannie's death on his Bohemian lifestyle and shut closed the piano to dissuade Harold from following in his brother's footsteps. Anna tended to be strict and stern in complement to her husband's more placid and peaceful disposition when it came to child rearing.[9]

Henry Murray was the only one of the four surviving Murray sons to serve during World War I, and he never saw action in the conflict. The United States joined the Great War, under way since 1914, in April 1917. Secretary of War Newton D. Baker contended that reports of race discrimination in the military were due to "overworked hysteria," even as blacks were almost entirely excluded from leading men in battle or engaging in frontline combat. "When we are waging a war 'to make the world safe for democracy,' we plead that this American democracy be made safe for us," reasoned Cleveland's *Plain Dealer*. To rectify the paucity of African American officers in the US Army, NAACP leaders called for an all-black officer training camp, given that blacks were barred from mainstream officer training camps. Some African Americans (including Butler Wilson) rejected the idea of a "Jim Crow Training Camp," but most came around to accepting that the "choice is as

clear as noonday" as W. E. B. DuBois maintained: "It is a case of
camp or no officers." In May 1917, the War Department established the Fort Des Moines Training Camp for Colored Officers.
Fort Des Moines was a military base and training facility on the
south side of Iowa's capital city.

The War Department wanted mature men between the ages
of twenty-five and forty-four enrolled for the first officer candidate class of African Americans in US military history, designated
the 17th Provisional Training Regiment. Its 1,250 officer candidates comprised 1,000 recruits and 250 noncommissioned officers. Henry Murray reported for training at the 400-acre camp
on June 15. Most of his fellow cadets were, like himself, college
educated (40 percent had earned degrees) and held professional,
skilled jobs. The class was described by their white commander
as "remarkably strong, earnest, and well-educated." The 17th Provisional Training Regiment was divided into fourteen companies.
Henry was in Company 5, known familiarly as the "Washington
Company" because many of its members lived in the capital or
attended Howard University. Henry completed the three-month
prescribed course, which entailed grueling 5:30 a.m. to 10:45 p.m.
days. To their surprise and disappointment, the cadets learned four
days before the close of camp in mid-September that a deferral
order meant their commissions were postponed. Their term of
service having expired, Henry was among those who chose to be
honorably discharged. His discharge paper, issued on his thirty-
fifth birthday, described him as "honest and faithful" and "entitled
to travel pay." He returned to Washington. About half the cadets
cooled their heels in Iowa and a month later were awarded commissions ranging in rank from second lieutenant to captain.[10]

On February 28, 1918, Wilson Bruce Evans died at his residence on Vermont Avenue at the age of fifty. His last job was in
the signal bureau of the War Department. In a family photograph
taken in his last years he sat in a chair surrounded by his wife and

two children, looking haggard and old before his time, a cane by his side. He died a broken man, according to his daughter Lillian, who later wrote that it brought tears to her eyes to remember "the five years my father suffered with heart trouble [caused by] the mental anguish of injustice." He was buried at Woodlawn Cemetery on March 3, Daniel Murray's sixty-seventh birthday, after a service at St. Luke's. A few days after the burial, Harold and his wife arrived from Cuba with one-year-old Helene. Madrenne was about to give birth to a second child. By this time Harold was working for Havana Marine Company, furnishers of gas and oil, and making $175 a month ("A Washington Boy Strikes It Rich" ran a local headline). Anna and Daniel Murray's second grandchild, Harold B. Murray, Jr.—nicknamed Bruzzy—was born at their home in the wee hours of March 12, 1918. Madrenne showed off her two children to her parents in Ithaca before the family of four returned to Havana.

While advancing her career in music, Lillian Evans was teaching kindergarten in the public schools, having taken the two-year kindergarten course at Miner Teachers College after high school, undoubtedly influenced by "Aunt Sis." Subsequently she earned a bachelor of music degree from Howard University. On September 10, 1918, about six months after her father died, she married her Howard music teacher, Roy W. Tibbs. They lived in the family home on Vermont Avenue and in 1919 presented their first joint recital, she the soprano and he the pianist.[11]

Anna and Daniel Murray had not given up their struggle to oust Roscoe Bruce from the school system. Some of their charges can only be characterized as nitpicking, as when Daniel Murray complained that Bruce had allowed a certain teacher to exceed her Easter vacation by one week with the result that taxpayers had been "grievously injured." The Murrays were far from alone in their determination to see Bruce fired. In 1919, a major issue came to the fore that focused the assistant superintendent's detractors.

The public discovered that school officials had allowed a Dutch man who went by the name of Professor Herman Moens to photograph teenage girls from the colored high schools in various stages of undress or altogether naked. The officials had been duped into believing that Moens was conducting an anthropological study. The imposter was indicted by a grand jury on a charge of taking, possessing, and exhibiting indecent photographs. Tried by the District courts, he was found guilty in March 1919, although he managed to avoid imprisonment on a technicality. Assistant Superintendent Bruce was implicated because he had allowed the improprieties. That was the contention of the Parents' League, formed in disgust and indignation the same month as Moens's conviction. Speaking for the league, Anna Murray claimed that Bruce had been guilty of "great negligence" in that he "took no action in the matter whatever," even after he was made aware that girls from the high schools were being taken to Moen's studio to be improperly photographed. The league held one mass meeting after another at various churches. In no time there were more than twenty thousand members (the *Washington Bee* even ran a handy form to sign up). Anna addressed a number of the gatherings; on one occasion she delivered "one of the most eloquent and sensible speeches that one would care to listen to," according to the *Bee*, which styled her "a most forceful speaker and a woman of remarkable intellect."

The league's mission became synonymous with toppling Roscoe Bruce. Though they held him responsible for the Moens debacle, they held the Board of Education responsible for not removing him. By the end of May the league decided to file charges against Bruce with the Board of Education. Richard R. Horner served as one of the league's lawyers (Horner, a widower, was living in Henry Murray's household at the time). The board referred the matter to corporate counsel for the District of Columbia, but he held that there was no basis for legal action, that the board had legal jurisdiction in matters of hiring and firing, and that "this controversy should terminate." It did not. In the words of the *Washington Bee* headline: "The Parents' League Has Declared War on the Board of Education." At the end of July, the board resolved to appoint a committee of three to investigate the charges against Bruce. The Parents' League was incensed upon learning that testimony would be restricted to questions of Bruce's educational and administrative efficiency. Members had counted on presenting their main thesis: that Bruce's moral laxity made him unfit to head the colored schools. The committee ignored entirely, deplored Anna, the offer of her husband "to place before said committee documentary matter proving beyond a doubt the untruthful character of the assistant superintendent." Daniel Murray was beside himself that he would not be allowed to testify to Bruce's "moral delinquencies." He wrote a letter to the school official in charge of the committee on August 15, 1919, in a full steam of heat over the "fake investigation," whose purpose, he purported, was "to sustain a preconceived verdict." Convinced of a disappointing outcome, he warned, "This failure to call me will serve to reopen the case. I am not satisfied." Sure enough, on October 8, 1919, the board adopted a resolution based on a preliminary majority report from the investigating committee that "Mr. Bruce was competent to be assistant supervisor of colored schools." As anticipated, it did not touch upon his moral unfitness. To the league's mind, the resolution was, as Anna commented, "in full keeping with [the board's] policy of covering up and condoning every species of disgraceful conduct charged against their favorites."

The ruling only spurred the Parents' League to renewed action, its clamor reaching a fever pitch. Members continued to protest on a daily basis outside the school administration building, chanting, "Roscoe C. Bruce must go." As Anna put it, "There was only one recourse left: to come to Congress and try to get some redress." Confronting the unceasing agitation, a Senate select committee held hearings in the spring of 1920 to investigate the deteriorating school situation. Anna, representing the Parents' League as a member of its executive committee, testified at length and submitted the league's "monster petition." It was signed by twenty thousand citizens insisting that the Board of Education remove Roscoe Bruce, "who by his acts of omission and commission has lost the confidence and respect of the people." Letters and statements from Daniel Murray were also entered into the record. At the end of 1920, Bruce groused that the school board had kept him from suing the Parents' League and others who had attacked him: "I should have entered suit—for example against Daniel Murray—but my official supervisors advised not to go to court. . . . I must rely on my official superiors to safeguard my good name and they promised to do so." But the ruckus finally wore the school authorities down. They'd had enough of Roscoe Bruce, the "storm center" of endless troubles, and in June 1921 they appointed a replacement assistant superintendent and sent Bruce packing on "indefinite leave." He left the city, and his career and reputation spiraled further downhill.[12]

17

NEW NEGRO/OLD CIT

RACIAL TENSION AND ANTAGONISM IN WASHINGTON peaked in the sweltering summer of 1919. The Great War had ended, and the city was crowded with returning soldiers. Many were competing for work, and their prospects were not auspicious given that the government was dismantling wartime agencies. Young men of both races were jobless, restless, and ready to act out. African American military men returning to Washington found that prejudicial practices had only proliferated under the Wilson administration in their absence. Already disadvantaged in the job market, they were treated with disdain and disrespect, notwithstanding the fact that five thousand of them had served in the military during the war and had hoped that their duty fulfilled would earn them a fair shake. Manifestations varied from the experience of one Washington veteran who approached a theater in uniform only to have the ticket seller shake his head "no" before he even reached the booth, to lynchings of black men in uniform elsewhere.

The racial tinderbox that was the nation's capital was fueled by lurid headlines of "Negro crime," as likely to be groundless as not, and certainly exaggerated and biased, running almost daily in the mainstream newspapers. The series of sensational stories included unsubstantiated accounts of alleged sex crimes against white women by "Negro fiends" at loose in the city. They left the impression that a "Negro crime wave" was overspreading the area. Archibald Grimké, the president of the NAACP Washington branch, wrote to city newspaper editors on July 9, pleading that they tone down such reports because they were "sowing the seeds of a race riot by their inflammatory headlines." No preventive measures followed.

The explosive situation did indeed blow up, ignited by an incident on the evening of Friday, July 18. A white woman, returning to her Southwest home about 10 p.m., was confronted by two black men, who jostled her as they tried to take her umbrella but ran off when she screamed and whites nearby intervened. News of that latest "outrage" immediately circulated with the *Washington Post*'s morning headline "Negroes Attack Girl." All Saturday, rumors proliferated without constraint, more hysterical with each retelling. Word spread on the streets and in bars and pool halls where young men were drinking near beer and airing grievances that two black men had attempted to sexually assault a sailor's wife. In a mood for revenge, a throng of military men, some still in uniform, and civilians headed out for the Southwest quadrant that evening. Drawing strength in numbers as they went along, several hundred men wielding clubs, lead pipes, and pieces of lumber attacked blacks at random, fracturing the skull of one with a brick.

With Sunday, the weather hot and humid, came the unleashing of a wave of white on black violence as mobs, emboldened by the limited police response, roamed the city. African Americans were chased, dragged, and pummeled, two of them directly in front of the White House. Roving bands of white men in the hundreds pulled blacks, women as well as men, off streetcars and beat them. That night Carter Woodson, newly appointed a Howard University professor, witnessed a "most horrifying spectacle." He was walking home when a white mob materialized and he was forced to hide in the recess of a storefront. "They had caught a Negro and deliberately held him up as one would a beef for slaughter, and when they had conveniently adjusted him for lynching they shot him," he recalled. "I heard him groaning in his struggle as I hurried away as fast as I could without running, expecting every moment to be lynched myself."

July 20, a steamy Monday, proved to be the peak day of an outright race war. The morning edition of the *Washington Post* blared "Mobilization for Tonight," giving instructions on where white combatants should meet at 9 p.m. for "a 'clean up' that will cause the events of the last two evenings to pale into insignificance." As on Sunday, white mobs attacked blacks in several locations throughout the city. An African American boy was knocked off his bicycle in front of the Carnegie Public Library, and cries of "Lynch him!" and "Who's got the rope?" followed. Before the threats could be carried out, the boy was rescued by police.

But that night, African Americans were ready to retaliate. Hundreds had bought guns from pawnshops or gun dealers during the day (secondhand pistols went for as much as fifty dollars apiece) or pulled out the military rifles they had brought home from the war. The city was a battleground. Both sides—each two thousand or more in number—fought with fists, bricks, bats, razor blades, knives, and firearms. In addition to street brawling, blacks turned the tables on their adversaries by employing their methods of revenge. They beat up whites pulled off streetcars and shot at them from drive-by vehicles known as "terror cars."

One of the areas white mobs targeted was the Murrays' Northwest neighborhood. Residents there stood armed and ready to guard their families and property. Anna Murray's Parents' League distributed 50,000 copies of a handbill that advised "our people, in the interest of law and order and to avoid the loss of life and injury, to go home before dark and to remain quietly and to protect ourselves." Neighbors mobilized in self-defense, erecting crude barricades around the perimeter of their community. More than a thousand armed residents manned U and 7th streets. Sharpshooters waited tensely on the roof of Howard Theater, the tallest building in the area. White mobs did advance and were met by armed resistance. There were several clashes at 7th and T streets, just a few blocks from the Murrays' house. The city did not quiet down until 3 a.m. Overall, whites fared as badly as or worse than blacks.

Reaction by the authorities was slow. The police were ineffectual, given the scope of the violence, and not until Tuesday were a thousand or more federal troops employed to restore law and order. A summer rainstorm helped them dissipate the excitement and clear the streets. Unlike in earlier race riots, African Americans had vigorously fought back at their persecutors, heeding the advice W. E. B. DuBois had given in May 1919:

> We are cowards and jackasses if now that that war is over, we do not marshal every ounce of our brain and brawn to fight a sterner, longer, more unbending battle against the forces of hell in our own land.
> We *return*.
> We *return from fighting*.
> We *return fighting*.
> Make way for democracy!

Four days and nights of armed conflict in the nation's capital resulted in the deaths of approximately 30 Washingtonians, with 150 or more injured. The precise numbers are unknown because a thorough investigation was blocked by southern congressmen. There were race riots incited by white against black violence in at least twenty cities during the summer of 1919. The season of bloodshed came to be known as Red Summer.[1]

Notwithstanding the prominence and success of the NAACP,

other civil rights organizations came and went. One was the Colored American Council, incorporated in Washington in 1919, its purpose to serve as a watchdog over the merits and demerits of proposed national legislation affecting African Americans. Lafayette Hershaw was the organization's vice chairman, Daniel Murray the treasurer, and Henry Murray the general counsel. The Colored American Council managed to arrange hearings in early September 1919 before the House Committee on Interstate and Foreign Commerce. Under discussion was an amendment introduced by Martin B. Madden, a Republican representative from Illinois, calling for the abolition of Jim Crow cars in interstate commerce. It was a proposal black Washingtonians were pleased to advocate. More often they were required to combat strenuous efforts by southern lawmakers to introduce separate streetcar accommodations in the national capital. So persistent were such efforts that African Americans had to bird-dog the matter and regularly re-fight the same battle. The *Washington Bee* found the city's elites self-centered in their fixation on issues "where the shoe pinches them," separate-car laws in particular: "The high brow is fond of travel, hence he is interested primarily in doing away with jim-crow discrimination on passenger coaches and sleeping cars."

Henry Murray, representing the Colored American Council, gave testimony at the House hearings in support of the Madden amendment. He provided a plethora of arguments both ethical and practical and referenced many points and precedents of law, including the *Hart v. Maryland* case. "For forty-five minutes the committee listened with the closest attention to his vigorous attack upon the jim-crow car system, and at the close joined in the spontaneous applause," lauded the black press. Daniel Murray had to be very proud of his son's thorough and erudite presentation. During Representative Madden's own remarks at the hearing, he was interrupted by congressmen from Texas and Louisiana who "seemed to take a delight" in injecting references to "our niggers" and the

"good treatment" shown them. After the hearings white supremacist lobbyists immediately set to work to counteract the proposal's
momentum. The following November 16, the Madden amendment
was defeated by a House vote of 142–12.

The Eighteenth Amendment to the Constitution, decreeing
that the manufacture, sale, and transportation of intoxicating liquors was prohibited, became effective in January 1920. So did the
Volstead Act, passed by Congress to enforce it. But prohibition had
an earlier history in the District of Columbia, thanks to Congress's
control of the city. Yet again, the District had served as an experimental arena for the politicians. During the period in 1916 when
Congress, backed by the Anti-Saloon League, was considering local prohibition, Washingtonians had pressed for a residents' referendum. Daniel and Henry Murray had both spoken in favor of the
referendum at a meeting of black citizens' associations in March.
It was not to be. Washington went dry at midnight on Halloween
1917. The Murrays were among the "wets" who enjoyed alcoholic
beverages, and the private imbibing of them was not proscribed
by law. Daniel Murray informed George Myers in August 1920,
"The Volstead has played havoc with sociability in this old town,
for sure, but your humble servant is still on deck and has a little
hay, made while the sun was shining. They will need to get up long
before day to catch an old Marylander like myself napping."

Nathaniel Murray spent the last years of the 1910s teaching in
West Virginia, New Jersey, and North Carolina. In the fall of 1919
he and Mayme's first daughter, the senior Murrays' third grandchild, Pauline Leary Murray, was born in Washington. By that
date, Daniel Murray owned a substantial working farm with multiple cottages in Dorsey, Maryland, a community in eastern Howard County. Nat moved there with his small family and worked
the farm "that he might have a more intimate contact" with the
subjects he taught. He penned a long letter to "My dear Father"
on August 28, 1920, reporting on the status of the farm and its

bills since "you were last here." He wrote about horse shoeing and poultry supplies and apple, corn, and potato crops. Mayme and the baby, who "is 11 mos. old today and is beginning to learn to walk," were well. Nat claimed that he was working hard while Henry, visiting at the farm, was "continuing his policy of sitting around." In 1921, Nat returned to Washington and began a twenty-eight-year tenure teaching biology, botany, and agriculture at Dunbar and Armstrong High Schools. He purchased a house at 150 U Street.

The Dorsey property as well as the Cherry Heights lots would remain in the Murray family for many decades to come. Daniel Murray wrote his friend Myers about the latter in the summer of 1920: "I have not been to Baltimore for a long time and yet I have considerable interests there. I own one-half of a subdivision there, Cherry Heights. The recent extension of the city of Baltimore placed our property right on the line. Bishop John Hurst is my partner. My son George looks after it. My idea is to hold it and allow it to grow for the benefit of my grandchildren. I have three."

Henry and Emma Murray had no children but did care for a number of cats in their S Street home. Paul Murray, too, though briefly married, never had children. He had dropped out of Cornell University's school of arts and sciences after a year. Back in Washington he worked as a messenger in the Bureau of Engraving and Printing. He then tried another go at Cornell, attending the summer session of 1919. But when the census taker came around to the Murrays' house in January 1920, Paul was included, described as having no occupation and married, though no wife was listed. But that May, according to his father, Paul was certified to the census office with a high mark from the Civil Service Commission, and in July he was named chief of his section.[2]

Aaron Bradshaw, a lawyer and politico, and Daniel Murray were elected District delegates to the 1920 Republican National Convention at a March 30 meeting of twenty-two Republican clubs. The pair pledged to support suffrage for women, as well as a series of resolutions promoting "the Americanization of the National Capital," including a delegate in the House of Representatives, no increase in taxes, direct popular election of Board of Education members, and a substantial raise for public school employees. However, other city Republicans declared the balloting unauthorized, and over the following weeks two other white/black delegate pairs emerged via voting by other of the District's Republican factions. The national convention was slated to start on June 8 at the Chicago Coliseum. A week before, all three sets of Washington's would-be delegates, along with their alternates, traveled to Chicago to stake their claims before the national committee. The committee (which had fifteen other cases of contesting delegates to decide on), despite the "stiff fight" put up by Bradshaw and Murray, chose one of the other pairs to represent the District of Columbia. On June 19, inside the overheated coliseum, Ohio senator Warren G. Harding was declared the Republican nominee on the tenth ballot. His Democratic challenger took the solid South (except for Tennessee) in November, but Harding was the victor in every other state and won the election in a landslide.

Woodrow Wilson had forgone an inaugural ball for both his terms and Harding followed suit, setting an example of austerity. That did not stop Washington's black elite from pulling out all the stops for an inaugural ball of their own. The Oldest Inhabitants Association sponsored the March 7, 1921, event at Convention Hall. It was a family affair for the Murrays. Daniel served on the reception committee, Henry on the press committee, and Anna was chosen to lead the grand march on the arm of the association's president, Eugene Brooks. According to the *Washington Bee*, "One of the most striking figures on this occasion was that of the tall and graceful form of Mrs. Anna Murray, attired in black beaded net, trimmed with green ostrich plumes, with diamond jewelry." The *Baltimore Afro-American* noticed that her silver hair was the perfect complement to her black spangled gown. The revelers danced from nine in the evening to three in the morning to the strains of an eighteen-piece band. "The reception of the Oldest Inhabitants was indeed an occasion long to be remembered," raved one. "I thought when I entered the hall last Monday night that every person whom I knew was in attendance."[3]

To be sure, by this time many in Washington's "colored aristocracy" had seen their fortunes and careers diminished and their entitlement to respect belittled. But the black elite was still the black elite, living the high life folded in on themselves. As a group, they were disillusioned but not decimated. When Langston Hughes lived in the District in the 1920s, he found "it had all the prejudices and Jim Crow customs of any Southern town. . . . I asked some of the leading Washington Negroes about this, and they loftily said that they had their own society and their own culture." According to family members, Anna carried herself with a superior—even "haughty"—air; others took notice when she entered a room.

One ladies' luncheon Anna attended was described as "informal," although it was served by Jules Demonet, one of Washington's best caterers, and included a receiving line and a color scheme. At another "beautifully appointed luncheon," presided over by Bettie Francis and her daughter-in-law, Alice Wormley Francis, the table was decorated with sweet peas, and Anna and the other guests each received a nosegay of the same flower. When Anna visited friends in Chicago, she was characterized as "the society leader from the Capital of the nation" and elaborately entertained by Florence and Charles E. Bentley, Colonel John R. Marshall's wife, and others of that city's elite with dinners, receptions, and theater parties. The Bentleys, in whose home she stayed, hosted a musicale in her honor, and a columnist who covered the event said she "looked very regal in her exquisite gown of white satin and rare lace, with jewels flashing in her beautiful white hair."

On January 3, 1913, the "flower of Washington's social life," including Daniel and Anna Murray, attended a reception hosted by Register of the Treasury James C. Napier and his wife that "opened the social season of the New Year most auspiciously." The journalist Richard W. Thompson gushed:

> The elaborate function took place at the historic "Hillside Cottage," 2225 Fourth Street, near Howard University, for many years the home of famous Congress-man John Mercer Langston, of Virginia. In this picturesque mansion Mr. Langston's widow has continued to reside, and with her for the past three years have lived Register and Mrs. Napier, the latter being her daughter. The reception was attended by upwards of a hundred of the flower of Washington's social and intellectual life, and at no similar entertainment within memory has there been brought together a more representative assembly of the race. . . . The flawless appointments, the personnel of the party, the elegance of the ladies' toilettes and the courtliness of the gentlemen suggested the stately functions of the White House.

The Murrays never missed a season rusticating at the "the Ferry," playing cards and croquet, and fishing and boating with other elites summering there. From Harpers Ferry on July 1, 1914, the *Washington Bee* reported, "Mrs. Daniel Murray arrived last Saturday and opened her cottage for the summer. Mrs. Murray has done the same thing thirty-five times and her cottage is as nice and comfortable as her beautiful mansion on S Street is grand and massive."[4]

→ ←

DANIEL MURRAY, FAR FROM HIS GOAL OF SIGNING UP FIVE thousand initial subscribers to his encyclopedia, asked Donnelly and Sons to help underwrite its publication in 1914. Given that "publishers are our customers," they were shocked at the request: "We could not assume any financial responsibility in connection with it; nor could we undertake the selling of the finished product." They were on the mark in suggesting that what Murray was really seeking was "a publisher who would take the entire burden on his shoulders." Indeed, at this same time he was fashioning a multipronged approach to the Carnegie Institution of Washington, established by Andrew Carnegie in 1902 "to encourage in the broadest and most liberal manner investigation, research, and discovery, and the application of knowledge to the improvement of mankind." Murray requested funding for his project and lined up a series of friends and associates, including William Carl Bolivar and John Hurst, to lend their support. For their convenience, he even composed a letter to which they needed only to add a signature. All to no avail. The institution president turned Murray down in a flash. Referring to the copy of the prospectus Murray had sent, he pointed out that World's Cyclopedia Company had "already undertaken the publication of your works" and the institution "never subsidizes commercial agencies." Murray's posing as World's Cyclopedia Company worked against him in this instance.

The last correspondence in Murray's papers from Donnelly and Sons (still willing to negotiate "the manufacturing feature of this job") was dated September 22, 1914: "It has been a long time since we have had any word from you in regard to the Encyclopedia. Are you expecting to do anything with it in the near future?" Instead, in 1915, Murray opened negotiations with another printing and bookbinding company, Trow Press in New York City. But with the war under way the cost of publication had risen sharply. Trow wanted $5,000 with the order, $10,000 more within sixty days, and another $10,000 once the electrotyping was complete, and that did not include the cost of binding! Between that and other attendant vicissitudes of war, Murray suspended the publication venture for a time.

His publication prospects may have been held in abeyance, but he pushed on as always. He added to his bibliographical compilation and his biographical sketches, which ran anywhere from fifty to five thousand words in length. He drafted essays on a broad range of topics; examples are Egyptians' Alphabet, African Civilization, AME Church, Revolution in Haiti and San Domingo, Missouri Compromise, Nat Turner Insurrection, Anti-Slavery Struggle in Congress, Jim Crow Laws, and Brownsville Affair.

Murray remarked on his "years of unremitting labor." For all his references to bringing the project to a close, at no point did he cease his research to concentrate on birthing the baby. In 1910, he identified an experienced managing editor he had hired, but there was never a second mention of a professional like that who might have whipped his manuscripts into shape. Plus it seems that the assistant editors he recruited did little or nothing. He may have appreciated their names as window dressing for the cover page, but there is no evidence that he delegated assignments to them. Murray, with his own unceasing additions to the work, had allowed himself to be overwhelmed by the burden of the message. No encyclopedia can ever be absolutely complete and up to date if it is to see the light of day in print. Rather sadly, he would periodically go through manuscript drafts wherein he had referred to the number of years he had been at his project or connected with the Library of Congress, cross out the number, and insert a larger one.

Searching for a way to publish his tome for more than a dozen years, Murray had amassed piles of ultimately fruitless correspondence, but the number of actual subscribers was negligible. He had informed George Myers in 1912 that he needed five thousand advance subscribers to proceed and that "Failing in getting them I will return to each person the amount subscribed in full." In 1916, he did just that, while at the same time writing to Myers that he was diligently working on his encyclopedia "night and day." Four years later, still keeping the faith, he wrote his friend, "I have strong hopes that Congress will publish for the race my encyclopedia. I stand to give the material. At times when I view what I have gathered I am myself amazed at the results of my researches." It is not known what transactions transpired to give Murray such hope, but government publication was never a serious possibility.

In that same letter, Murray expressed some bitterness toward Carter G. Woodson: "In regard to the MSS. I hardly care to offer it to the 'Negro Journal.' They never invited me to contribute an article and I scarcely care to ask the privilege." One of the items in the Daniel Murray Papers is a short letter from Woodson dated May 22, 1922, notifying Murray that his active membership in the Association for the Study of Negro Life and History was expired. According to one of Murray's associates, the journalist Walter J. Singleton, "At first Mr. Murray was quite generous with the use of his material but later was forced to assume a different attitude when he found his work was being pirated by persons who sold the information as original."

In November 1922, Murray and W. E. B. DuBois exchanged a series of letters on the forever forthcoming encyclopedia. DuBois advised, "I think that you would find that the only feasible way of getting a large work printed would be to print parts of it so that people could see its interest." He would, he said, be happy for Murray to furnish an article to *The Crisis*. It would "let our large circle of readers know that such a body of knowledge exists and that you are master of it." When Murray demurred, DuBois immediately wrote again with a tone of increased urgency: "You have got to face the facts. You have reached the allotted span of human life in the ordinary course of events. You cannot hope for much further time to work. If you should die before the publication of any part of your work, what would become of it? Is it in such shape that it could be published? Have you funds to insure its publication?" DuBois concluded that if the work were not disseminated, it "would mean the practical loss to the world of your long and arduous labors" and "this would be a calamity to the Negro race." Although Murray himself had conceived of a scheme similar to DuBois's in 1912, in cooperation with a select group of newspaper editors, he now stubbornly refused to break up his opus.[5]

→ ←

IN 1920, HAROLD AND MADRENNE MURRAY MOVED TO NEW York City's Harlem, just as the cultural flowering famously known as the Harlem Renaissance was beginning to unfold. Their apartment building was on 137th Street, but Harold made his way each day to the financial district on Manhattan's southern tip, where he worked for the Island Oil Company of New York as a purchasing agent. Anna Murray traveled to Harlem in October 1921 to visit her son's family and, in particular, to see the new baby, eight-month-old Valerie. Madrenne had given birth to Ritzi, as she was called, in her hometown of Ithaca, and it was there, a year later, that Madrenne's twin sister, Gladys, married Walter F. White. The two had met at the NAACP national headquarters in New York, where he was the organization's assistant field secretary and she was a stenographer. White was blue-eyed and golden-haired, only 1/64th black, but every inch a race man. Before moving to New York City in 1918, he was one of the founders of the NAACP branch in his hometown of Atlanta.

Harold and Madrenne's fourth child, Jacques, Jack for short, was born in Harlem in July 1922. The next year, Harold accepted a temporary position in Mexico City. His wife traveled there with the children for a prolonged visit but returned to New York and established a new household at 76 Edgecombe Avenue, where Harold rejoined his family in 1925. Their apartment building, located at the southern edge of Harlem's fashionable Sugar Hill neighborhood, was just a block or so from Walter and Gladys White's at 90 Edgecombe Avenue. The Harold Murray family would soon emigrate permanently to Mexico City. In 1929, the same year Duke Ellington moved into 379 Edgecombe ("Take the A train to go to Sugar Hill way up in Harlem"), the Whites relocated to a top-floor apartment at 409 Edgecombe. That architecturally splendid building, sited on a bluff high above the Harlem River and served by uniformed doormen and elevator operators, was Sugar Hill's most prestigious address and home to many African American elites. White, a political and cultural leader, was a seminal figure in the Harlem Renaissance. A novelist himself, he enthusiastically promoted the work of talented writers, artists, and performers. He and Gladys turned their spacious apartment into a salon for Harlem literati and other notables. Though short and slender, White was a dapper dresser and a congenial personality. Gladys was a glamorous hostess and, as adjudged by Langston Hughes, "the most beautiful brown woman in New York." As the Whites' daughter, Jane, recalled, "The parties in Daddy's and Mother's apartment were formidable."[6]

The cultural flowering in Northwest Washington in the 1920s rivaled that in Harlem. Black Washingtonians made up more than a quarter of the overall number of city residents. Only New York and Chicago had larger African American populations. The U Street neighborhood was the locus of African American intellectual, literary, and artistic life, bringing forth an outpouring of talented and inventive writers, artists, and performers. Poet Georgia Douglas Johnson, the wife of Henry "Link" Johnson, the former recorder of deeds (he had been replaced by a white appointee under Woodrow Wilson's administration), held a stimulating weekly literary salon at her 1461 S Street home, where a rose-lined walk welcomed visitors. Many who would go on to participate in the full bloom of the Harlem Renaissance had earlier lived in Washington and taken advantage of Johnson's gifts as creative nurturer and gracious hostess. Examples are Zora Neale Hurston, Jessie Fauset, Langston Hughes, and Jean Toomer. It was the last who inspired Georgia Douglas Johnson to commence her literary gatherings.

Jean Toomer was born Nathan Eugene Pinchback Toomer. He grew up in the Washington home of his grandfather Pinckney Pinchback, and returned to the capital in 1920 to live in his grandparents' U Street apartment. He was writing his innovative novel combining prose and poetry, *Cane*, and looking for intellectual companionship when he approached Johnson about housing "weekly conversations among the writers here in Washington." Johnson opened her home to writers, artists, scholars, and politicos to come together as a community to discuss and read from their works, to exchange criticism and views on literature, art, and politics, to encourage one another and hone their craft, and to celebrate black culture. The gatherings took place every Saturday night and became one of the most influential forums of the Harlem Renaissance period. Many of the participants were young and ambitious, and they appreciated the support they found for lonely artists striving in the milieu of a segregated society to express their truest selves.

Langston Hughes was one such "Saturday Nighter," as those in Johnson's circle were called. Hughes had moved to Washington in 1924 to join his mother, who was living with their Langston relatives in tony LeDroit Park. Like Jean Toomer, Hughes was critical of the black elite that included his own family members. He found them boorish and mocked their pompous performance, as he saw it. He met some of the "best people" in the city, who, he wrote, "themselves assured me they were the best people. . . . Negro society in Washington, they assured me, was the finest in the country, the richest, the most cultured, the most worthy. In no other city were there so many splendid homes, so many cars, so many A.B. degrees, or so many persons with 'family background.' " Again like

Toomer, Langston preferred the "sweet relief" of 7th Street, with its bars, street life, and storefront churches, "where the ordinary Negroes hang out, folks with practically no family tree at all, folks who draw no color line between mulattoes and deep dark-browns, folks who work hard for a living with their hands. On Seventh Street in 1924 they played the blues, ate watermelon, barbeque, and fish sandwiches, shot pool, told tall tales, looked at the dome of the Capitol and laughed out loud." Hughes relocated to an un-heated, two-room apartment on S Street not far from Johnson's home. There, in some of his happiest times in Washington, he would "eat Mrs. J's cake and drink her wine and talk poetry and books and plays." He wrote his first volume of poems, *Weary Blues*, in Washington. It was published in 1926, the same year he exited the capital.

Writers and activists from the New York contingent of the Harlem Renaissance such as Countee Cullen, Claude McKay, and W. E. B. DuBois took in Johnson's Saturday-night soirees when in town. Washington residents associated with Howard University who attended the salon, in addition to Zora Neale Hurston, in-cluded Kelly Miller, Carter G. Woodson, and Alain Locke. Locke, a philosophy professor (and the first African American Rhodes Scholar), was advancing the concept of the "New Negro." The epithet referred to African Americans interested in crafting new images to subvert and challenge old stereotypes, recognizing that art and literature were forms of protest in the fight for full citizen-ship rights. Locke published a major Black Renaissance work, *The New Negro: An Interpretation*, an anthology of essays, poems, plays, and short stories. Johnson's home, one salon goer noted, "was a house of ideas." Johnson took responsibility for the stimulating mood, ample refreshments, and medley of attendees. "If dull ones come, she weeds them out, gently, effectively," recalled one of the regulars.

Lillian Evans Tibbs was among those who mingled with other

up-and-coming creative talents on Saturday nights at 1461 S Street. She was good friends with Georgia Douglas Johnson as well as the novelist Jessie Fauset, a Phi Beta Kappa Cornell University graduate. All three had taught in the District colored school system. Lillian was perfecting her own art form, leading the way for black opera divas to follow. She traveled to Paris in 1924 to study voice, acting, and French and to seek professional opportunities, less limited as they were by color prejudice in Europe than in her home country. There, at the suggestion of Jessie Fauset, who was in Paris at the same time, she changed her name to Lillian Evanti and began using the stage name Madame Evanti.

Daniel Murray, on the other hand, was not a "New Negro" but rather an "Old Cit" or, as Locke would have it, "Old Negro," in contrast to the newer, younger version self-confidently asserting themselves in the years following World War I. Though he lived five blocks from Johnson's home, Murray was not included in the select group of salon attendees. "The conditions that are molding a New Negro are molding a new American attitude," wrote Locke. Of course, the ultimate goals were the same as they were for Murray and his peers, and race pride had been a major theme in literary and political self-expression in Murray's heyday among Washington's black intelligentsia. So in many ways this represented a generational shift whereby those associated with the New Negro Renaissance found a renewed purpose and definition in fiction, poetry, journalism, music, and painting. The younger writers and artists sought to break free of restrictions imposed on their expressive forms, not just to liberate the individual but to demonstrate that art could create community and serve black protest ideology.[7]

It was time for "Old Citz" such as Murray to think about retirement. "I am now looking forward to retiring in 1921 and then I will be free and can take up some of my leisure in visiting my friends," he informed George Myers in August 1920. He had worked hard throughout his adult life to ensure financial stability.

He advised his friend to be conservative in his prosperity, "since my observation has been that nine of every ten Colored men who attain to a certain height come down again before they die to the point of beginning." He continued, "I have kept very clear of speculation now I am old, believing that I have received what fate has in store for me in that respect. I have paid up everything and am free from encumbrances besides having about $12,000 in mortgages. It is indeed remarkable that we two Baltimore boys should each have started out in life about the same time and accumulated over $10,000 each."

In the event, Murray waited until the last day of 1922 to retire. There was confusion about his birth date in the Library of Congress records, and no wonder; he was as likely as not to erroneously state his birth year as 1852. He had begun working at the library when there was a staff of twelve and left with that number over five hundred. Acquisitions had grown from a quarter of a million volumes to five million and the institution from cramped quarters in the Capitol with masses of unwieldy materials to a highly efficient operation in one of the grandest library buildings in the world. Murray received a special citation from Librarian Herbert Putnam on his retirement for faithful and efficient service. His pension, $720 annually, commenced on January 1, 1923.[8]

Daniel and Anna Murray had six grandchildren before 1922 was over, Nat and Mayme having had a second daughter, Constance Vivian, in April of that year, two months before baby Jack was born. Although four of their grandchildren lived in New York, the eldest, Helene, now five, they were able to see Pauline and Constance on a regular basis. The Murrays' son Paul rallied in 1924, when, in June of that year, he graduated from Howard University's School of Law with an LLB degree. It is not clear if he ever had a stable marriage, but he and his wife divorced. He took a messenger job in the Department of Justice, but it did not last long. That his parents recognized that their son would only become further debilitated is clear from the will Daniel Murray prepared in March 1924, three months before Paul's Howard graduation. It provided a special annual outlay from his estate for Paul's "maintenance." Paul would eventually be diagnosed as a psychotic epileptic. Unable to work at all by 1931, two years later he began what would turn out to be a lifelong stay as a "mental health case" at St. Elizabeths Hospital.[9]

Notwithstanding the glory of the Harlem Renaissance and the confidence embedded in the "New Negro" concept, the offspring of the "colored aristocracy" faced diminished vistas relative to their parents' prospects. The rise the earlier generation had enjoyed in the Reconstruction period was just a memory. If a major element of the American Dream is seeing one's children do better than their progenitors, both the older and younger generations had ample reason to be disillusioned. Black elites could organize social clubs and throw elaborate parties for their children, they could summer with them at exclusive vacation enclaves, and they could bring them up to be cultured and well schooled. But they could not promise them an easier or more auspicious time of it than they had experienced, given an environment increasingly hostile and humiliating for African Americans. "It now looks as though our children must go through in a large measure at least, the same fire of proscription that our fathers had to endure," opined the *Colored American*. Daniel Murray memorialized hard-won African American success stories in his mammoth literary endeavor, believing that "such biographical illustrations should be kept before our youth, who are often disheartened by the mountain of opposition that obstructs every path."

African Americans were not accepted at any white colleges in the District except for Catholic University. Daniel Murray described "a terrible row" at Howard University itself in 1905, when its white president, Reverend John Gordon, had been "seen as lacking in sympathy and respect for the students and colored members of the faculty and being averse to colored and white being together on social terms of equality." Many of the universities in the North, including Cornell and Harvard, became increasingly inhospitable to blacks. Segregation in dormitories and dining halls and on sports teams was introduced. The reason often given was that more young southerners were attending the institutions and school officials could not afford to offend their sensibilities. When Butler and Mary Wilson's son Edward was admitted to Harvard in 1921, its president, A. Lawrence Lowell, barred black students from the freshman dorm. Response to the new policy included a petition of protest from the NAACP. The next year, Lowell came to loggerheads with Roscoe Bruce, whose son was planning to enter Harvard. Bruce made public his outrage that, unlike his own Harvard experience, his son was to be excluded from the dormitories. Following his letter to Walter F. White, the NAACP amplified its effort and gathered protest letters from prominent African American alumni, including Robert Terrell, Archibald Grimké, William Henry Lewis, and W. E. B. DuBois. The day had arrived, wrote DuBois in *The Crisis,* "when the grandson of a slave has to teach democracy to a president of Harvard." A national debate ensued. Franklin D. Roosevelt, who had been in the same Harvard class as Henry Murray, weighed in, remembering that when he attended the university, "no question ever arose" relating to segregation of black students. The Harvard Board of Overseers bowed to pressure and tactfully reversed Lowell's call. African Americans would be allowed in the dormitories, but to avoid pairing racists with their black fellows, students would be permitted to select their own roommates. Oberlin College, no less, also transitioned from welcoming to intolerant. One student there, who wrote her master's thesis on "The Negro in Oberlin" in 1925, commented, "The constant northward-drifting race-prejudice has brought about a change that it is no longer possible to ignore even in Oberlin."

When the children of elites toughed it out at these educational institutions in spite of the drawbacks, they faced severely limited job prospects. Educator and activist Nannie H. Burroughs declared that young African Americans were "suffering for the need of vocational freedom," forced "to follow the trades or professions that are 'open to Negroes.' " Instead of choosing a career by following one's natural bent, "color prejudice chooses for them." One major reason that the colored schools in the District were superior was the excellence of the faculties. Many instructors held degrees, even PhDs, from the best universities in the country but had not been allowed to compete for the variety of positions that their white counterparts could. Indeed, so restricted were their career choices that there was ongoing competition for places in the public schools. That was the experience of Henry and Nathaniel Murray. Harold Murray achieved terrific business success, but he had to move to another country to do so. The same with Lillian Evanti, who performed with opera companies all over Europe but because of her color was unable to fulfill her dream of being the first African American to sing with the Metropolitan Opera of New York. Some in the next generation, including scions of the Wall, Greener, Bruce, and Syphax families, decided to melt into the white world rather than accept society's dregs as African Americans.[10]

Murray's dear old friend Spencer Murray died on November 23, 1925. Murray made a note of it in his papers, having no idea he would join him in the beyond a month later. Daniel Murray died on December 31—New Year's Eve—three years to the day after he retired. He drew his last breath on a Thursday night at Freedmen's Hospital, succumbing to Bright's disease, an operation on his inflamed kidneys having failed to save him. Funeral services were conducted at St. Luke's, where Bishop John Hurst offered an estimate of the value of Murray's services "to the negro race and to the world." He was buried at Woodlawn Cemetery on the third day of January, the anniversary of his only daughter's death. He was laid to rest near her remains and those of his two sons who had preceded him to the grave. His death certificate listed his true birthday, March 3, 1851. He would have turned seventy-five in 1926. Last born, he was the final one of the Murray and Proctor siblings to die.

At Murray's funeral "a special tribute" sent by Herbert Putnam was read. When Murray had retired, Putnam had mentioned his lengthy years of service in the Annual Report of the Librarian of Congress and had gone on at rather great length to applaud the "extraordinary regularity of his attendance." Certainly Putnam might have credited Murray with more than an extended tenure and admirable attendance record or for that matter, made it to his funeral in person. Murray remembered the great institution where he had worked for fifty-two years (without a raise for the last twenty-five) in his will: "All the books forming my collection of Colored authors I direct to be given to the Library of Congress to be part of the 'Loan Collection,' gathered therein by me for exhibition purposes."

By the terms of Murray's will, Anna was made executrix of his substantial estate. She was designated sole beneficiary until her death, at which time the trusteeship would pass to son Henry, then to Harold, and ultimately to the grandchildren. Murray instructed that Nathaniel's and Harold's children were to be the final beneficiaries and that distribution to them was to take place twenty-one years after the deaths of all his sons. Murray identified six close friends in the will he had drawn in 1924—Spencer Murray, George Myers, John Hurst, Charles Bentley, Richard Horner, and Fred R. Moore—and to each he left a personal remembrance. They encompassed "my brace of dueling pistols" and "my elaborately carved Filipino cane," as well as books and paintings. He noted that these were the men whom he trusted to advise his sons in case of dispute.

Daniel Murray's bibliography peaked at 7,500 titles. "His Encyclopedia of the Colored Race, the crowning achievement of his life, presents to the world for the first time the only authoritative and complete history of the achievement of colored people and their contributions to culture and civilization." Thus wrote Anna Murray to W. E. B. DuBois, at his request for obituary details for *The Crisis*, three months after her husband's death. She continued, "Mr. Murray continued his research into the literary fecundity of the colored race until his death and now his manuscripts contain over 250,000 indexed cards giving titles and condensed biographical sketches of all notable persons who were in blood related to the African race. In addition Mr. Murray had over 250 manuscripts giving complete and authentic biographies of the outstanding men of color. All this has been compiled in a great encyclopedia going back to the earliest period of Ismael . . . up to the present day."

Daniel Murray lived just long enough to be aware of the shameful spectacle of the Ku Klux Klan marching down Pennsylvania Avenue and circling the Washington Monument, waving American flags, in August 1925. The Klan had experienced a revival ten years earlier, following the popularity of *The Birth of a Nation*, and peaked at a membership of around four million. With government sanction, both men and women, fifty thousand strong, led by "Uncle Sam," paraded in full regalia in the nation's capital. Murray, ever the hopeful integrationist, remained on the Board of Trade until his demise, the last African American participant, though its overall membership had grown exponentially. A final effort at passing anti-lynching legislation through Congress had failed in 1922. There was not one African American in the US Congress, nor had Howard University yet been administered by a black president, when Daniel Murray died in a segregated hospital and was buried in a segregated graveyard. Woodlawn Cemetery, the African American burial ground that served as the final resting place for many in the black elite, is defunct and forlorn today. The finely crafted tombstones, obscured by overgrown weeds, are lonely reminders of the rise and disillusionment of Washington's "colored aristocrats."[11]

Epilogue

The slave went free;
stood a brief moment in the sun;
then moved back again toward slavery.

—W. E. B. DUBOIS

Before March 1926 was over, Daniel Murray's personal collection of books and pamphlets was, as directed in his will, presented to the Library of Congress by his widow. Librarian Herbert Putnam accepted the fund of 1,448 books and pamphlets, fourteen broadsides, and one map "with the idea that it should form part of the material especially selected by him for exhibit purposes." Putnam added the Murray bequest to the books and pamphlets gathered by him while assistant librarian and kept this special collection as a unit, according to Murray's wish. However, at some point after Putnam's tenure ended in 1939, its contents were interspersed onto the shelves of the library's general holdings. Only a subset of 351 pamphlets was held back, and today they are in the Rare Books Division (designated the Daniel A. P. Murray Pamphlet Collection, they have been digitized and are accessible on the Library of Congress website).

As for the materials Murray amassed for his encyclopedia, "the famous Murray manuscripts," as the *Pittsburgh Courier* called them, "No policy has been decided upon by the heirs of the late literateur. They were gathered in anticipation of a six volume encyclopedia. . . . It is now probable a syndicate will be formed by the heirs and the work published posthumously. Mr. Murray's will provides that the copyright income shall accrue to his estate."

Assessing the quality and quantity of the Daniel Murray Papers is a complicated undertaking. To start with the latter, descriptions both contemporary and recent deviate rather wildly. Chroniclers variously enlisted the descriptors "manuscript," "essay," and "sketch," and the numbers given range from 250 to 700. All evaluations referred to the enormous reservoir of catalogue cards that Murray wrote or typed on (often in series, often on both sides), and those totals range from 35,000 to 250,000. Accounts of just what the cards cover differ as well. The only chronicler who mentioned the bibliography per se does so apart from the volume of cards (which he estimated at the maximum number). The difficulty lies in the unorganized state of the papers. Whether one designates a given item a sketch, essay, manuscript, or card series is an individual call.

As to quality, one certainly cannot conclude that Murray's papers represented an encyclopedia waiting to be published. Murray desperately needed the strong hand of an editor both to organize and improve the material he drafted. Truth be told, he was an ace collector but neither a gifted writer nor a trained historian.

As a writer, Murray was verbose, ponderous, and overly academic, his work full of classical and other allusions. His essays went off on tangents at the drop of a hat. For example, in one he wrote entitled "Civil Rights in London," he started off by describing a race-related incident at the International Methodist Ecumenical Conference in 1901 (see chapter 11). Less than halfway through the six-page composition, at a mere reference to "the President," he changed course, and the rest of the piece is entirely about the assassination of William McKinley. In his biographical sketch of Ida Wells-Barnett he compared her as an agitator to Anne Hutchinson and then veered off for six pages with a sketch of the New Englander before returning to the subject at hand. Murray never had the gift of the pen or tongue when it came to inspirational expression that Jesse Lawson and W. E. B. DuBois, for example, had. In the midst of ringing speeches at one National Afro-American Council mass gathering, Murray, in pedagogical mode, described the nuanced Rochdale system of cooperation to advance the movement's goals.

As a historian, William W. Bishop, Library of Congress superintendent of the reading room and Murray's boss from 1907 to 1915, made a fair assessment. Murray, he wrote, "enjoyed a high reputation among his associates as a person of erudition. He was, unfortunately, only half-trained and had very little discrimination. On the other hand, he collected assiduously the writings of the people of his own race. . . . The Library of Congress has never attempted to exploit this material, largely, I suppose, because it was gathered without that type of scholarly discrimination." W. E. B. DuBois was no less forthcoming in his evaluation. He informed the librarian at Tuskegee Institute, "The so-called Murray Encyclopedia is not an encyclopedia. It is a very interesting and voluminous series of notes made by the late Daniel Murray. . . . It is quite unorganized and not scientifically done. It could be used to great advantage in the making of a real encyclopedia, and we shall make every effort so to use it." Howard University historian Rayford Logan, upon inspecting the papers at 934 S Street, noted, "In many instances the source of the information is given neither at the upper right hand corner nor at the end of the material."

Be that as it may, the data Murray gathered was of encyclopedic proportions, and scholars from far and wide sought access to his papers. W. E. B. DuBois was one of them. He was planning an *Encyclopedia Africana* of his own. In reply to a letter from him on the topic, Georgia Douglas Johnson advised DuBois in November 1935, "Dr. Daniel Murray's collection would be a wonderful source of data. Most of this material is in his late home in a room set aside for it. . . . It may be that Mrs. Murray may have to be approached very diplomatically to obtain this, but there are various ways of managing this that you might consider." She added that a portion of the material had been stolen. Anna kept the bulk of the collection in a small spare room located under the first-floor stairs; there was also material on shelves and in pigeonholes elsewhere. Anna confessed that she was torn between sharing and protecting the collection.

An *Evening Star* reporter who interviewed Anna in October 1935 wrote that with her husband's death, she had been "left the burden of trying all over again to interest a publisher and, at the same time, keep up with the increasing activities of her people. This she has done, devoting a number of hours each day to it." She was at present, the reporter noted, working up an entry on "ring idol Joe Louis Barrow." Ironically, historians' use of the Daniel Murray Papers today is hampered by Anna Murray's "help," given her unattributed inclusions. She even wrote historical essays of her own, including the tale of Phoebe Fraunces and her lifesaving aid to General George Washington during the Revolutionary War, which is now considered an unsubstantiated legend. On the other hand, at the request of historian Pearl Graham, researching, for the first time in 150 years, the "old chestnut" that Thomas Jefferson had fathered children with his slave Sally Hemings, she supplied notes on Jefferson's mulatto children from her husband's papers, and eventually what had been dismissed as a legend for more than two centuries was confirmed by circumstantial evidence, oral testimony, and DNA analysis.

Anna applied herself throughout the decade of the 1930s to the goal of seeing her husband's opus published, but the hurdles were only ratcheted up due to the Depression. Rayford Logan, who visited Anna at DuBois's request in 1937, reported that she wanted $60,000 for the papers, a sum regarded as unreasonable. No buyer for the whole collection materialized, and, like her husband before her, she resisted offers to break up the work.[1]

Though a pioneer in the black history movement, Daniel Murray would not be celebrated as the Father of Black History. That honor went to Carter G. Woodson. He established Associated Publishers in 1920 to bring black history books to print. His own *The Negro in Our History*, published in 1922, was the top text in black studies until John Hope Franklin's *From Slavery to Freedom* was released in 1947. He founded Negro History Week in 1926. The *New York Amsterdam News* presented a chronological review of 1926, and interestingly enough, the first item listed was the death and burial of Daniel Murray, while under February was this item: "Negro History Week observed. Carter G. Woodson was instrumental in making this celebration successful." The annual commemoration of Negro History Week proved to be an influential vehicle for sharing African American heritage; it was later expanded and renamed Black History Month. Although he laid the groundwork, Daniel Murray would not publish the first *Encyclopedia Africana*; neither would DuBois. Woodson, too, failed at the attempt. All ran up against the insurmountable odds involved in funding an encyclopedic history of black people. The distinction finally fell to Kwame Anthony Appiah and Henry Louis Gates, Jr., and not until the last year of the twentieth century.[2]

"Anna Murray Nears Her 80th Birthday Still Aiding Her Race," ran the *Evening Star* headline for a three-column story on August 15, 1937. "Alert brown eyes that seemingly have lost none of the eagerness of youth look out from under snowy white hair as she reminisces," observed the interviewer. Anna remained a dedicated child welfare activist well into her eighties. The day her husband died, she was scheduled to speak on behalf of the Parents' League at a Board of Education meeting but dispatched a substitute once his condition turned critical. That July, she traveled to Oakland, California, as a District delegate for the annual convention of the Federation of Colored Women's Clubs. Her range of activities over the ensuing period encompassed participating, along with her brother's widow, in the dedication of the new home of the W. Bruce Evans Elks Lodge, discussing Carl Van Vechten's new book, *Nigger Heaven*, at the Literature Lovers Club, speaking at a Mu-So-Lit Club program on John Brown and his band, entertaining houseguests, and enjoying the company of family in the neighborhood, including her granddaughters Pauline and Constance.

Anna gave testimony before Congress promoting "colored improvements" on a number of occasions. For instance, she was a spokesperson at Senate Appropriations Committee hearings in February 1929, part of a delegation of African American District residents. They succeeded in securing increased funding for colored schools but were stymied in their effort to acquire a health center for black children. They protested that the owners of several potential sites refused to sell or rent to African Americans, only to have the committee sanction race-restrictive covenants. In 1935, and again four years later, Anna was elected second vice president of the District Public School Association, an integrated organization with which she had been active since 1923. She pushed for hot lunches and for playgrounds and other recreational facilities, concerned that "thousands of colored children were forced to depend entirely on the streets for recreation." By 1937, she was the head of the Parent-Teacher Association or PTA (evolved from the National Congress of Mothers) at Morse School, a grade school near her home. She worked for improved housing and schools in Southeast Washington and was a speaker at the dedication of a housing development for low-income families there in 1940.

Several other events over this period stand out. In July 1930, Anna traveled to New York City for a reception at the 135th Street Branch of the Public Library, where she and W. E. B. DuBois were two of four speakers, while Arthur Schomburg, Jessie Fauset, Wallace Thurman, and the Walter Whites were among the attendees. That November, President Herbert Hoover sponsored a White House Conference on Child Health and Protection. Secretary of the Interior Ray Lyman Wilbur, a medical doctor and Stanford University president, was in charge. His planning committee involved leading African American educators from the start. "The work of the conference," he asserted, "has been strengthened by the membership of many Negro experts in child care." Anna Murray served on the Family and Parent Education Committee. At the White House on November 20, President Hoover shook the hands of 2,500 conferees as they filed by him, there "to battle for the inherent rights of 43,000,000 American children for health, proper upbringing, education and opportunity in life." Black newspapers were well pleased with the results. "Devoid of all racial discrimination throughout the three days of the conference, both at the White House and at the receptions at the Willard and Washington Hotels, President Hoover's child welfare confab proved to be a huge success here last week," applauded one. "The Negro child came into its own at President Hoover's White House Conference on Child Health and Protection," opined another. "The 1930 conference marks the first time that Negroes have served both as members of the committee personnel and as delegates. As a general result of this participation due recognition was given to the problems of Negro children heretofore overlooked."

The tide turned back when the opera singer Marian Anderson was refused the opportunity to perform at Constitution Hall. The venue was controlled by the Daughters of the American Revolution (DAR), and their use contracts banned black artists. Objections came fast and furious. In February 1939, Anna Murray submitted an editorial to the *Evening Star*. Referring to Crispus Attucks, she began, "Have the Daughters of the American Revolution forgotten that it was a man of Marian Anderson's race who in a few minutes accomplished for American liberty what years of correspondence with England had failed to do?" The piece closed, "This is no time for either expression or act of racial discrimination against a woman who has been recently characterized as the 'proudest ornament of the American concert stage.' The eyes of the world are trained upon American democracy." First Lady Eleanor Roosevelt pointedly dropped her membership in the DAR, but no plea or protest budged the staid organization. It was NAACP executive secretary Walter White who came up with the suggestion that Marian Anderson sing in the open air in front of the Lincoln Memorial. What would have been a travesty turned into a triumph come Easter Sunday, April 9, 1939. The renowned contralto took to the makeshift stage before an integrated audience of 75,000 and, with the iconic seated statue of Abraham Lincoln looming behind her, began a magnificent performance with "My Country 'Tis of Thee."[3]

Paul Murray lived on and off with his mother until, on January 12, 1933, he was admitted to St. Elizabeths Hospital, "overtaken by poor health," as Anna put it. Paul was a patient at St. Elizabeths, with occasional visits home, for sixteen years. Psychotic manifestations accompanying adult epilepsy are not uncommon, but Paul's situation was sadder yet. African American patients at St. Elizabeths were segregated into lodges, treated as alien and inferior, and expected to display deferential dependence on their white doctors, who often assumed that common labor was the most appropriate form of therapy for them. Paul Murray died at St. Elizabeths at age fifty. His mother updated the alumni office at Cornell, reporting that her son had "passed to his eternal reward on April 30th, 1949." Anna's will was drafted well before Paul's death, and in it she bequeathed to him one of her most prized possessions, her piano.

In her will, Anna requested that her sons sell a particular English pastoral painting and "apply the proceeds to the purchase of etchings of myself to be placed in the kindergarten rooms of the D. C. public schools." Praise for her lengthy and fruitful tenure of voluntary service was not lacking. The seventy-fifth anniversary of public education for black youth in the District of Columbia was observed over a six-month period in 1939 with a wide variety of programs, among them a conference on "Enriched Learning Experiences in the Home," during which Anna was celebrated at an evening event. She was honored by a new generation of female race activists, including Mary McLeod Bethune, Nannie H. Burroughs, and Dorothy Height when the National Council of Negro Women (founded by Bethune in 1935) held its annual conference in Washington in October 1941. Six years later, she was recognized by both the National Association of Colored Women and the Association for Childhood Education for her many years of outstanding service.

After Anna took a fall in 1950 at age ninety-two, she depended on a wheelchair for the rest of her days. Basically an invalid, even forced to dictate letters, she hired a full-time nurse. Henry (and his cats) moved in with his mother after his wife died in September 1950, renting out his house three doors down. By 1952, he was permanent conservator of his mother's estate and she his adult ward. Henry set up living quarters for Anna in the warm basement. The kitchen was on that level, and he had a bathroom installed there. Anna spent much of her time scanning resources to supplement her husband's research, sitting in her favorite chair near the front window of the English basement, where she could see passersby on S Street. She valued her tooled, leather-bound copy of the Jefferson Bible, Thomas Jefferson's compilation of the Gospel teachings of Jesus with religious dogma and supernatural elements excised.

Anna Evans Murray died at home on May 5, 1955. A year earlier she had been described by a grandson as "in good mental condition . . . very sharp in her mind." In retrospect, Daniel Murray made an awful lot of comments on his wife's ill health for a woman whose activities never slowed and who lived to ninety-seven. That was long enough for Anna to see color bars lowered in Washington's public places, hail Mary Church Terrell, who led the fight to force the courts' acknowledgment that the city antidiscrimination laws of the 1870s, the so-called lost laws, were enforceable. The black press was jubilant. One 1953 headline blared, "In Nation's Capital You Can Now Eat Anywhere," and another, "Color Bar Ends as D.C. Theatres See the Light." Survived by two sons, ten grandchildren (of twelve total), four great-grandchildren, and her niece, Lillian Evans Tibbs (the last of her many siblings, Mary Evans Wilson, had died in 1928), Anna Murray was laid to rest at Woodlawn Cemetery.[4]

Like many highly educated African Americans, her sons Henry and Nathaniel served long tenures in District colored high schools, fifty and twenty-eight years respectively. A case of exclusion in the high schools came to the fore in 1928. The *Evening Star* sponsored an annual local oratory competition, the winner of which would compete in the National Oratorical Contest, but that year the individual in charge declared that it was not his "intent to enter Race youths in competition with whites." School leaders at Dunbar and Armstrong expressed their disapproval by pulling out of the "Jim Crow contest." Henry Murray came to the rescue by taking up the matter directly with his father's old friend, *Star* editor Theodore Noyes. He reported back to the Dunbar-Armstrong joint committee that Noyes knew nothing about an effort to separate black students from white, and in the end all of the District high schools were handled identically.

That same year, school authorities established a black high school specializing in business practice. In 1936, Henry was transferred to Cardozo Business High School, where he taught mathematics, English, and business courses until his retirement. He remained active with the Mu-So-Lit Club. In 1928, he was elected president, and for many years after his term expired, he was chairman of the executive committee. A very special event came along in 1934. President Franklin D. Roosevelt and the First Lady hosted a late-afternoon reception on the White House lawn for all the men who had been in Roosevelt's 1904 Harvard class, along with their families. Henry and Emma Murray were among the approximately three hundred people who were served lunch and enjoyed music provided by the Marine Band on Saturday, April 21, 1934. Afterward, the Murrays threw a party of their own for a few of Henry's old classmates at their S Street home.

When Henry turned seventy in 1952, he was retired from the school system as required. He had worked his way up from an annual salary of $550 to one of $5,313. In January 1955, he applied for a military veteran's pension and described himself as totally disabled, although elsewhere he admitted that any physical problems amounted to general old age. According to Harold's son Marco, who spent summers living with Henry when he was in middle school in the United States, his uncle Henry was fond of betting on horse races and frequented the track during his retirement. Henry rented out the three houses on 12th Street that his father had built back in the 1880s and managed the Dorsey and Cherry Heights properties in Maryland.

Henry was a litigious individual. Those he brought suit against included the heirs of his father's close friend John Hurst and some of his own family members. In 1931, he filed a suit against Hurst's widow and son, the executors of the late prelate's estate, in connection with the Cherry Heights development. The case was litigated, and the verdict was returned against him. In August 1936, Anna Murray (one readily imagines at Henry's instigation) sued her niece, Lillian Evans Tibbs, because payment of a $50 loan was seven weeks overdue. In December of that year, Henry filed a petition in District Court for construction of Bruce Evans's will, of which he was executor. The defendants named were Evans's widow, Annie, and her children, Lillian and Joseph. Henry objected to the sale of a property owned by the estate. The Evans heirs countered his interpretation of the will, asserting that they were legally qualified to put the sale through. Moreover, they motioned that the suit be dismissed because Henry Murray's executorship had terminated in 1919 and the will had granted him no role as ongoing trustee. Indeed, they charged that the sole reason for the suit was "to have the proceeds from the sale pass through his hands so as to claim a commission for services." For all that, the evidence is that any bad feeling between Anna's family and that of her brother was overcome, though perhaps not before 1936 ended. That was the year Anna's will was drawn and the clause bequeathing her wearing apparel to her niece, Lillian, was crossed out; her granddaughter Helene's name was inserted in ink script in its place. In 1952, three years after Paul Murray's death, Henry hired counsel to conduct a protracted battle in probate court with St. Elizabeths Hospital over his brother's estate. And the year he died, he initiated suit against his nieces and nephews, seeking an interpretation of Daniel Murray's will in regard to the estate's lands in the District and the Cherry Heights development in Baltimore.[5]

Nathaniel Murray spent most of his teaching career at Armstrong High School, where he successfully combined his academic training and practical know-how. His daughter Pauline earned a degree in Spanish from the University of Mexico and in 1942 married Cayetano García in Mexico City. While her husband was serving in the Mexican Army, Pauline gave birth to their first son in Washington, a happy event that great-grandmother Anna Murray lived to witness. The Garcías later moved to Los Angeles. Constance, who remained single, relocated to Los Angeles as well, and in 1949, Nat and Mayme followed their daughters to California's City of Angels when Nat retired from the school system at age sixty-five.

Nat clung to his status as one of Alpha Phi Alpha's "Jewels," as the seven founders came to be known beginning in 1929. Looking back, he realized that initiating the country's first black college fraternity had been a highlight of his life. The fraternity honored its charter members—looking to them "for inspiration and guidance"—and that provided Nat with needed ego gratification.

One of the fraternity's founders was uncomfortable with the title, but Nat relished signing "Jewel" after his name. He faithfully attended the annual conventions and was always pleased to present a founder's address.

Nat experienced severe financial difficulties during his retirement. Like their father, both Henry and Nat knew how to rub two pennies together. Once Nat sent Henry two pairs of his shoes to be resoled in his old neighborhood because "the cost even with the parcel post is less in DC . . . than it is here in Los Angeles." Unlike his father and brother, Nat was not a good manager of his money, although as a teacher his salary was more than double what Daniel Murray's was at the Library of Congress and he was receiving a pension. In a series of letters to Henry and his mother (on Alpha Phi Alpha Fraternity letterhead) in 1952–53, he seemed desperate for their assistance in keeping up with expenses as basic as taxes. He even asked the fraternity for financial help. Nat had bulked up and walked with a cane due to arthritis when he died of a heart attack in Los Angeles in December 1959 at the age of seventy-five. He was survived by his wife, two daughters, and two grandsons, and by two of the seven Jewels and 24,700 Alpha Phi Alpha fraternity members.[6]

Harold Murray pursued a prosperous engineering career in Mexico City as the cofounder and vice president of Maricopa Trading Company, importers of exclusive papers from the United States and Europe. At one point the firm employed three hundred people and represented twenty-five of the world's leading paper mills. In his adopted country he was perceived as an "American," not an "Afro-American." He and Madrenne had two more daughters but later divorced. Some years later, Harold married a Mexican woman, Olympia Lasso, and they had four children. Harold became an ardent follower of the Baha'i faith, which preaches that all human beings are of a single race and all religions have true and valid origins. He played the piano daily. His daughter Ritzi manifested autistic behaviors; though normally uncommunicative, she always responded when her father played piano in his emotive fashion. Like Dannie before him, Harold was a composer of popular songs. Among the tunes he copyrighted were "No One After You" and "Embers of Romance." His daughter Carmen remembers her father as having a "tranquil, smooth" character generally but as being a "fighter" when necessary. He was a confident man; in his words, "I've never been a 'rubber stamp' or a 'yes-man.'" Perhaps one can discern a metaphorical demonstration in his shoes. A granddaughter recalled, "From an early age I remember listening to my grandfather's footsteps. He screwed 'estoperoles' or metal studs to his shoes, always Bostonian type of shoes. The studs were placed on the bottom of the front part of the soles and made a click click sound against the floor every time he walked around the house."

Harold, Olympia, and their children—Daniel, Marco, Carmen, and Bessy—visited their Washington family from time to time. While at boarding school in New York, the two boys spent their summers living on S Street. Marco took after his cousin Lillian and called his grandmother "Aunt Sis." To his younger sister Carmen she was her "Abuelita," although all spoke English while in Washington. Since Anna could move around only in a wheelchair by that time, the family visited with her in her lower-floor quarters. Her grandchildren recalled books, magazines, and family photographs filling the house; in the backyard, a little patio garden; at the street corner, a place to buy ten-cent ice cream sandwiches. One visit of note occurred during the winter holiday of 1953–54. It coincided with Carmen's fifteenth birthday, and her parents hosted a coming-out reception "to meet Señorita Maria del Carmen" at 934 S Street on her January 18 birthday. Carmen was a vision of young beauty in her strapless gown and gossamer wrap. It was the custom in Mexico to celebrate a girl's *quinceañera* with a party to introduce her into society and toast her passage into womanhood.

Madrenne remained in Mexico with her children after her divorce from Harold. Her sister, Gladys White, visited for two months in 1936, and four years later Madrenne, accompanied by her young daughter Anita, returned the favor in New York. On the same trip she stopped in with her former in-laws in Washington. It was in Mexico in 1949 that Gladys formally ended her twenty-seven-year marriage to Walter F. White, who scandalized both his family and the NAACP by taking up with, and immediately after his divorce marrying, a white South African. "From coast-to-coast they're talking these days about two things," gossiped the *New York Age* of July 16, 1949. "The Mexican divorce Mrs. Gladys Powell White now admits she was granted on June 30 . . . [and] the linking of Walter White's name in an interracial romance with Mrs. Poppy Cannon, divorcee and well-known freelance writer." Gladys had dedicated herself to her husband and children's well-being and was devastated when her husband told her he wanted a divorce. "As long as I live I shall remember the stricken ashen look on her face," revealed White. Gladys spent many weeks commis-erating with her twin sister in Mexico City after going to Juárez to obtain divorce papers on the grounds of incompatibility.

A Brooklyn friend of Madrenne named Estelle Leslie traveled to Mexico and was her houseguest in 1944. She was gratified to find "a great deal of freedom from the color line," in Mexico, mar-veling that "the most unusual experience I had was the feeling of freedom which was with me during the whole time I was there." There was no question of race in going into a hotel, in choosing a place to eat, or in preparing to travel about the country. It was a revelation to participate in a way of life "where at no time was she made conscious of the fact that she was a Negro, but rather was treated simply as an individual." She longed to return: "I felt like a new person there and I want that feeling again."

When Harold Murray traveled to Washington in October 1957, the local black press dubbed him a "top-notcher," hosting a gathering at Longchamps, a downtown restaurant: "Setting the stage in the style to which he's accustomed, Harold Baldwin Murray, big business man of Mexico, entertained a group at dinner the other eve." Cousin Lillian, who at the time was teaching a six-week course on "The Art and Charm of Gracious Living," was one of his guests. Harold's family always spent time with Lillian when they visited from Mexico. She would take his children to museums in the capital. Her career thrived at the expense of a happy marriage. She spent a lot of time traveling, but the house on Vermont Avenue, her home base, was "my anchor through all my life." There, the piano took center stage, just as it did in most of the Murray and Evans households. She displayed original African American art, including a work by Henry O. Tanner that she had acquired directly from the painter. She hosted salons for artists, scholars, politicos, and other elites that were just as stimulating as earlier ones at Georgia Douglas Johnson's house.[7]

George Henry Murray, eighty-three, died at Freedman's Hospital on December 7, 1965, following a brief illness. His was the last burial in the Murray family lot at Woodlawn (Nathaniel was interred in Los Angeles, and Harold would be in Mexico City). Henry had followed through on the instructions in his father's will: "Erect in our family burial lot . . . a monument not to exceed in cost the sum of five hundred dollars." The author visited Woodlawn Cemetery in September 2013 and found the burial ground in sad disarray. The Murray family monument, ample but simpler than many, inscribed only MURRAY, was in place. The remains of Daniel and Anna Murray and five of their seven children rested underground in close vicinity to the marker, but the individual headstones were missing. Helene's was discovered in a pile of broken stones off to the edge of the cemetery.

Anna Murray lived long enough to see the beginning of the deterioration of Shaw, as the U Street neighborhood came to be officially designated, but it was Henry who witnessed its escalation during the decade between his mother's and his own death. The area had been named after Shaw Junior High School, itself named for Colonel Robert Gould Shaw, the white commander of the famous all-black 54th Massachusetts Volunteer Infantry during the Civil War. Although desegregation of the public schools had transpired in the mid-1950s in accordance with Supreme Court rulings declaring segregated schools unconstitutional, the neighborhood schools were still predominantly African American because of residential patterns. Shaw Junior High School became overcrowded, and as the building itself degenerated, it was referred to as "Shameful Shaw," a sobriquet that spread to describe the entire sector. In a story full of ironies, one of the strangest is that desegregation led to a downward spiral in school quality and an overall decline in community spirit and functioning. Restrictive real estate covenants were no longer legal, and scores of well-to-do black families moved to outlying regions. Many single-family homes were divided into rental units. The neighborhood's economic well-being disintegrated when local businesses no longer had a cornered market or when shoppers gained access to downtown stores. By 1965, poverty, crime, and drug use had multiplied. The area was transformed from a safe, stable community to a seedy, scary neighborhood where a child walking home from school might crush a used hypodermic needle underfoot on the sidewalk.

After his brother Henry's death, Harold emptied the family house at 934 S Street. Out from the room under the stairs came Daniel Murray's life work, forty years after his death, dusty and brittle. Harold made a stab at trying to get the papers published but met with the same obstacles that his father, then his mother, had experienced. He next offered to donate the collection to the Library of Congress but was turned down. Through a friend Harold was put in touch with Leslie H. Fishel, Jr., the director of the State Historical Society of Wisconsin. Fishel was overseeing a collection of civil rights materials at the time and convinced Harold that the society would be a well-suited home. Harold donated the material in 1966, sending four locked file cabinets containing papers, broadsides, clippings, cards, photographs, maps, and a few larger visual items relating to Lincoln, McKinley, and Harpers Ferry. The papers were catalogued but unfortunately, due to their frail condition, were destroyed after being microfilmed. (Copies of the twenty-seven microfilm reels are available at several universities and the Library of Congress.)

As for the house itself, just as Harold was cleaning it out, the Department of Housing and Urban Development (HUD) declared Shaw an urban renewal area. Before the massive plan for redevelopment could be implemented, the community was rocked by days of rioting, burning, and looting that erupted following the news on April 4, 1968, that Martin Luther King, Jr., had been assassinated. With federal funding, the city's urban renewers, the Redevelopment Land Agency (RLA), began the slow rehabilitation process in 1969. As time went by, the unoccupied structures were vandalized, ransacked, and squatted in. Six hundred rehabilitation projects were targeted in Shaw, including the former Murray house at 934 S Street, now boarded up due to a fire. In many cases, including that one, the process was one of "gut rehabilitation." Only the shell of outside walls and sound structural beams remained. Everything else was newly built. The gut rehabilitation approach was more cost efficient than a painstaking restoration that would have preserved the fine interior features—marble fireplaces, classical moldings, and decorative elements such as stained glass, frescoing, and artistic tiling. Instead, those artifacts were piled high in the street and neighbors who recognized their value picked them over.

The house at 934 S Street was one of about seventy-five that the RLA renovated using hired contractors. The process of final inspection of this group of houses was stalled by bickering between bureaucrats and contractors. When the DC government finally put the Murray house up for sale in 1978, it was purchased for $37,000 by Godfrey and Jacqueline Kilkenny, the same family that still occupies it. Improvements were made in the neighborhood: sidewalks were paved in brick, trees were planted, and new lampposts and curb gutters were installed. Today the house is worth well over a million dollars.

On March 30, 1977, Harold Murray died in Mexico City, leaving many offspring centered there to this day. Those in the recent generations of Murray, Evans, Tibbs, Wilson, and Leary descendants have expressed fierce pride in their ancestors' race activism. Lillian Evanti's grandson Thurlow Evans Tibbs, Jr., remembered his grandmother impressing on him, "We were in the John Brown Raid." Anna and Daniel Murray's granddaughter Carmen identified just as strongly. She traveled from Mexico to West Virginia with her family to see Harpers Ferry, remarking, "It's in our blood."[8]

→ ←

THIS IS A STORY ABOUT CHANGE OVER TIME, PERSONALIZED BY couching the narrative in the lived experiences of one man and his family. It is the story of the rise and disillusionment of a subset of the American population, the black elite centered in Washington, DC. Shaking the dirt loose from historical roots laid down from 1851 to 1925, Murray's life span, brings light to the account of the emergence of a black elite, the rise of prospects with Reconstruction, and the reversal leading to the nadir in the early twentieth century. It is an era that has not gotten the attention that American slavery before it and the modern civil rights movement after it have. The former has been well depicted in hundreds of books in the last forty years, and the tendency has been to fast-forward from there to the civil rights struggles of the 1950s to 1970s, also a favorite subject for authors.

One commonly hears or reads reference made to "the black

community" today as if 42 million Americans form an indistinguishable block. There is no one black community that speaks for or represents all African Americans. Today's African Americans are decidedly not a homogeneous population. Nor were they in the nineteenth century. In our national dialogue the phrase "the black community" is often used as code to reference a supposedly monolithic population of poor, marginalized inner-city residents. To say that black stereotyping is unreasonable is not to deny that there is a sizable populace of black Americans who are struggling in inner cities, stuck in cycles of poverty, lacking access to middle-class education and opportunity. But that is far from the experience of all African Americans. Many Americans are unaware that a class of black elites stretches back to the time before the Civil War. The keener our understanding of the historical roots of America's race-related issues, the more considered the solutions can be.

Disillusionment came to all African Americans, but the black elite had farther to fall when the rug was pulled out from under them. As W. E. B. DuBois noted, "The Nation has not yet found peace from its sins; the freedman has not yet found in freedom his promised land. Whatever of good may have come in these years of change, the shadow of a deep disappointment rests upon the Negro people." Many African Americans who fostered high hopes during Reconstruction faced bitter disappointment because of rising exclusion. Careers were lost or stalled. Incomes were decimated or irregular.

The original black elite formed, according to Jean Toomer, "an aristocracy—such as never existed before and perhaps never will exist again in America—midway between the white and black world." Without minimizing the profound decline experienced by many individuals in the original generation, as a group the black elite endured. Disillusioned they may have been, but they did not "fall" as in disappear. Many continued to lead the high life and, having lost faith in assimilation, nurtured their exclusiveness among themselves. As late as 1917, the *Washington Bee* accused the elite of promoting "caste based on complexion . . . [and] caste based on book learning and professional career."

The black elite flourishes to this day. They favor certain insular clubs, sororities and fraternities, and vacation spots such as Oak Bluffs on Martha's Vineyard, and they talk about Boule, Jack and Jill, and other points of reference unique to them. Many of the movers and shakers in our common culture are members of today's black elite group, the heirs of DuBois's "talented tenth" concept. DuBois called on the talented tenth not to belittle the other 90 percent but to motivate those who were educated and able to step up to leadership positions. As Gerri Major, a principal chronicler of black society, put it in describing the generations that followed the original black elite, "What has remained is what there has always been: A class of people, who are as large, perhaps, as ten percent of the total black population, and who are and have been in the vanguard of their people. They provide the leadership, the role models."

The focus in this narrative is on the black elite not only to highlight the heterogeneity of the black experience but to put into highest relief the absurdity of the notion of white supremacy. Too often whites in power pretended that equality was all well and good but only once black people were "civilized" enough, educated enough—in short, "ready." Ready compared to whom? And who decides when that time has arrived? This was a smokescreen, a ruse. The true roadblock was not lack of ability but lack of autonomy and opportunity.

The story of Daniel Murray and his associates counters the false narrative that progress for African Americans was incumbent on white largesse, however slow in coming, as if blacks sat back and bit their nails waiting. The National Afro-American Council, the country's first truly national civil rights organization, zoomed into action before the 1890s were over. According to historian Rayford

Logan, "Walters and the Afro-American Council, which had a wider following than did the Niagara Movement, have not received the credit which they deserve as precursors of the NAACP." Alexander Walters, the NAAC's most persistent single force, stated in 1906, "If I were asked today, What is the most important thing for the Negro to do to secure his civil and political rights, I would answer without hesitation, 'Go into the courts and fight it out.' " He noted that the NAAC had been "first in the field to test in the courts, the discriminatory laws of the Southern States." The NAACP was modeled on the structure and strategies of the earlier organization, including test case litigation, national legislative reform, and direct-action protest.

Most Americans take pride in the ideals embedded in the Declaration of Independence and the US Constitution: respect for individual rights, opportunity to rise, equal protection under the law. These are values we honor, and if they were not equally applied to all creeds, colors, and genders at the start, we take comfort in believing that the American master narrative is one of increasing freedoms over time. On the very day the author composed this section of the epilogue (July 1, 2016), she perused a local newspaper article that included the following sentence: "In our struggle, we have always moved toward this idea of greater liberty." The "our" and "we" referred to Americans collectively. That statement is false. The master narrative is not unidirectional. The single greatest reversal in our history was the disregard of black citizens' newly won rights when Reconstruction was peremptorily abandoned. Worse yet, here was a case where the Constitution spoke loud and clear but was discounted. Worst of all, though we tout our being—first and foremost—a nation of laws, violent crimes such as arson and lynching were ignored or even tacitly condoned. It is a part of our history many Americans do not want to hear about, much less own. Yet only by remembering, and determining to respect the rights of all henceforth, can we redeem ourselves as a nation for shameful chapters in our past. Americans recognize, even as James Madison did, that slavery was "a blot on our Republican character," but too many think that prospects for African Americans grew continually from the day the Emancipation Proclamation was released, and if progress was slow, well, maybe blacks tended not to be go-getters, rather preferring to languish in the victim role. The historical reality reveals a temporary rise in status followed by a disastrous suppression, forced by white supremacists and reinforced by government. Blame-the-victim characterizations of black struggles do not take into account the full historical evolution. Unrealized black advancement is America's problem, and our government and society are rightly tasked with fixing it.

We can find gratification in recognizing that there was not a black hole between Reconstruction and the modern civil rights era. There were literally countless men and women such as Daniel and Anna Murray who refused to knuckle under in the face of setbacks to the newly secured rights of African Americans. Gaining equal rights for all proved an excruciatingly slow and torturous climb. The early twentieth century may have been the nadir for the African American plight and for violence, but American apartheid—de jure in the South and de facto in the North—persisted decade after decade. The failure of governance at the federal level in refusing to enforce those articles of faith—the Fourteenth and Fifteenth Amendments to the Constitution—only began to be remedied in the 1950s.

The American master narrative of increasing freedoms can reverse direction at any time again. The lessons from the past are obvious. Will we, even in times of overhyped fear, dare to risk upholding our ideals? We grapple with the debate between national security and individual rights and must be exceedingly careful how much of the latter we are willing to give up to fortify the former. Recent terrorist incidents as well as systemic racial bias in law enforcement have brought this debate to the fore and highlighted inequities such as facial, ethnic, and religious profiling. We can never take our freedoms for granted. The founders never expected us to. They understood that for representative self-government to be successful, not only is a free press necessary but an informed and vigilant citizenry as well. Rights won must be rights guarded and, if necessary, rewon.[9]

→ ←

"THE GIFT OF EXPRESSION, WHEN FIXED IN INK, IS THE ONLY lasting thing," William Carl Bolivar stated. For all of Daniel Murray's unremitting labor, the only "book" of his ever published was the eight-page *Preliminary List of Books and Pamphlets by Negro Authors*. No one understood the primacy of "printer's ink" better than Daniel Murray:

> It has ever been so, those who would rob the darker peoples of their rights or property begin by systematically writing them down. The Negro has suffered more in this respect than any other people. But because he has neglected to use the white man's weapon—printer's ink—in the past, need he forever be negligent in this respect? No. Let the whole race rise up as if it were one man, resolved to put forth to the world the achievements of its kind by magazines, books and encyclopedias, to the end that the world shall no longer be in ignorance of the black man's past history.

Murray noted that one would not expect a Roman to produce an accurate history of Greece or rely upon an Englishman for a full history of France. Likewise, American blacks and whites tended to present conflicting versions of historical memory. For example, to hear early-twentieth-century white historians tell it, "Reconstruction was widely viewed as little more than a regrettable detour on the road to reunion," as a leading historian of the period, Eric Foner, noted.

Murray never lost faith in the primacy of reason and education. He had an abiding belief in the power of truth to dispel prejudice. He believed that this along with recourse to the spirit of justice and Christian character would eventually usher in a new and enduring day in the sun. "It is coming," former US congressman Robert Smalls wrote to Murray, "whether you and I live to see it or not."

Daniel Murray's support for the integration of blacks into American society did not entail the idea that they lose their identity as a people. Though always embracing racial consciousness, he sought assimilation as the signal that advancement was not race-based, that there was room for cultural pluralism. Murray and others in the "colored aristocracy" believed their function was to serve as a bridge or broker between the black and white worlds of their day, that that was a natural way to break down barriers of ignorance. Their determination to prove their right to be acknowledged as full citizens contributed to the stress the black elite placed upon exemplary behavior. But whites became increasingly prone to make no distinction between genteel high achievers and the mass of less fortunate black Americans.

Daniel Murray was a man of parts. He tended to overextend credit to himself and his family members. He indulged from time to time in jealous, petty, petulant factionalism. In many ways he had a thin skin and a big ego. That was just one of many conflicting pressures he wrestled with on a daily basis, forced to live in a world where blacks were belittled on a daily basis, forced to live in two worlds. He and others in the black elite were initially ready to think of themselves as "American first" (or "class first"), but mainstream society forced them to think "black first." W. E. B. DuBois described the sensation of "double consciousness" in *The Souls of Black Folk*: "One ever feels his two-ness—an American, a Negro; two souls, two thoughts, two unreconciled strivings; two warring ideas in one dark body." It was tiresome to have to "measure one's soul by the tape of a world that looks on in amused contempt." One hungered "To be a co-worker in the kingdom of culture . . . to husband and use his best powers and his latent genius." Daniel Murray, too, longed to "merge his double self into a better and truer self."

Murray responded to the call for leadership. He deserves to be lauded for his contributions to the black history movement and other race issues. He is also entitled to admiration as an exemplar of the ideal American citizen, active in civic and political life at every level decade after decade. How many give civic or political activism a try and conclude it is like banging one's head against the wall, not to mention that the endless meetings and minutia get so boring? Not Daniel Murray. He did not just dip a toe into the water. He waded in. He stayed in through numerous betrayals, through the hollow rhetoric of one President after another, when the prize seemed increasingly illusory. Of the NAAC issues that Murray worked so hard on—anti-lynching, representative reduction, Freedmen's Commission, court challenge to Louisiana's grandfather clause, insufficient representation in District governance, anti–Jim Crow legislation—virtually none was successful. Still he kept on.

Black Americans generally displayed unwavering loyalty to the high ideals of the nation, despite their profoundly shameful treatment in return. The South basically committed treason but took the upper hand again, while blacks who had bravely fought for union were relegated to second-class citizenship and worse. Southern whites may have lost the Civil War, but with the end of Reconstruction, it was clear that they had been the political victors of that historical phase.

As for his own lasting legacy, Daniel Murray professed not to care. "A niche in the temple of fame has not been the secret of my determination to give to the world what I have gleaned," he wrote.

He claimed he would be satisfied if he succeeded at "removing the moss and lichen of neglect from the monument of one excellent name." The obliterating hand of time has only lessened the recognition that Murray himself deserves for his roles in the black history movement and the first national civil rights organization. A race man to the core, he did not live to see the fruits of his labors. Not until the 1970s would African Americans approach the legal status, merit-based recognition, and cultural assimilation that Daniel Murray had anticipated to be just around the corner almost a full century earlier.[10]

Acknowledgments

I START WITH A DEEP BOW TO MY AGENT, MICHELLE TESSLER. In the course of laboring over my first book, I often wondered how anyone, having endured the concentrated effort entailed in birthing a book, could ever contemplate starting all over again. Without a doubt I would be a one-book author if not for Michelle's persuasive pushes. Amistad's editorial director, Tracy Sherrod, recognized the promise in my book proposal; I am forever obliged to her for taking on the project.

At the Virginia Foundation for the Humanities in Charlottesville I was sustained by fellowship in both senses of the word, which meant the world to me during what would otherwise have been solitary years of research and writing. Thank you to foundation president Robert Vaughn and all the staff, especially Jeanne Siler, and to the other fellows. I eagerly take this opportunity to sing the praises of the University of Virginia's extraordinary interlibrary services.

The Library of Congress has long been a special place to me, as of course it was for my biographical subject, Daniel Murray. I was encouraged early on to pursue Murray's story by the former director of the library's Center for the Book, John Cole, and by

Jurretta Hecksher. Jurretta kindly connected me with Cheryl Fox and Adrienne Canon, and both were extremely helpful in sharing documents related to Murray's employment. Staffers at many other research institutions and libraries liberally lent their time and expertise. My experience at Anacostia Community Museum stands out as one of my best research days ever. Curator Jennifer Morris cordially shared with me binder after binder of photographs from the Evans-Tibbs Collection, and I was like a kid in a candy shop discovering likenesses of the Murray and Evans family members whom I felt I had gotten to know through my research. Happily, many of those photographs are included in the book.

I heartily commend the services of my friend Rick Britton, talented cartographer and graphic artist. The two-page map, "Daniel Murray's Washington," is his handiwork, along with the diagrams in the illustrations sections.

It is with profound pleasure and appreciation that I identify the many individuals to whom I am eternally indebted because they freely rendered the gift of time from their busy schedules to focus attention on my project out of a spirit of intellectual fellowship. Hail to the readers of my manuscript (in part or full): Shawn Alexander, Edward Ayers, Michael Benjamin, Adrienne Canon, Patsy Fletcher, Cheryl Fox, Don Graves, Sr., Robert L. Harris, Jr., Maurice Jackson, Margaret Jordan, Andrew Kahrl, Deborah Lee, David Levering Lewis, Kim Roberts, Blair Ruble, Kay Springwater, John M. Taylor, Luke Taylor, and Eric Yellin. I am humbly and abundantly grateful to each one of them. Hail to those, too, who generously provided information, photographs, or other assistance and support: Adele Logan Alexander, Michael Dickens, Jan Fontaine, David Fox, Edwin Henderson and Dena Sewell, Tony Horwitz, Niani Kilkenny, Jonathan Nelson, Jack Robertson, and Riley Temple.

It was my great good fortune to locate and communicate with

direct descendants of Daniel and Anna Murray. I extend a warm thank-you to Marco Murray Lasso, Maria del Carmen Murray de Bondi, Mari Carmen Bondi Murray, Gregory Lopez-Bondi, and Harold Murray Walpole for sharing family stories with me. I close with gratitude to my own loving family and blow a kiss to my son Luke, who is, and always will be, my inspiration.

Notes

My understanding of the history of the black elite was initially informed by the work of the late Willard B. Gatewood, in particular his seminal book on the subject, *Aristocrats of Color: The Black Elite, 1880–20.* It is with gratitude and admiration that I acknowledge that base of knowledge with which I commenced my research. I consider my own study of primary sources an exhaustive one, yet I found little to contradict Gatewood's conclusions. If his name appears less often in the notes than I would have predicted, it is only because his influence was as much pervasive as specific.

Prologue

1. Frederick Douglass, quoted in Adele Logan Alexander, *Parallel Worlds* (Charlottesville: University of Virginia Press, 2010), 44; *Times* (Washington, DC), Sept. 28, Oct. 1, 2, 1899; *Washington Post*, Sept. 30, Oct. 2, 1899; Daniel Murray will (box 879), DC Archives; *The Elite List: A Compilation of Selected Names of Residents of Washington, D.C.* (Washington, DC: Elite Publishing Co., 1886); *Evening Star* (Washington, DC), Sept. 27, 1899.

2. *Colored American*, Oct. 7, 1899; J. Max Barber, *How They Became Distinguished: To Accompany the Picture "101 Prominent Colored People"* (Atlanta:

Hertel, Jenkins, and Co., 1905), 62–63; *Times* (Washington, DC), Jan. 30, 1899; *Colored American*, March 29, 1902.

3. *Evening Star*, Sept. 27, Oct. 3, 1899; Official Program, Admiral Dewey Reception, Oct. 2 and 3, 1899, Washington, DC; *Times* (Washington, DC), Aug. 5, Sept. 28, 30, Oct. 2, 3, 1899.

4. Daniel Murray Papers, State Historical Society of Wisconsin, microfilm reel 27; F. Thomas Hewin, "The Separate Car Law in Virginia," *The Colored American Magazine* 1 (1900): 30; Edwin A. Lee, "Daniel Murray," *The Colored American Magazine* 5 (1902): 436; Daniel Murray, "Color Problem in the United States," *The Colored American Magazine* 7 (1904): 724.

1: Up and Coming

1. Some sources give 1852 as Murray's birth year, but the most reliable evidence supports the year 1851. That evidence includes Murray's application for hire at the Library of Congress in 1871, the 1900 federal census with year and month of birth listed, his March 1903 letter to George Myers wherein he notes his fifty-second birthday just past, and his death certificate; Daniel Murray Miscellaneous Personnel Files, Library of Congress Archives, Manuscript Division, Library of Congress; George A. Myers Papers, Ohio Historical Society, microfilm edition; Daniel Murray 1925 death certificate (record no. 295964), DC Archives; Christopher Phillips, *Freedom's Port: The African American Community of Baltimore, 1790–60* (Urbana: University of Illinois Press, 1997), 145; Daniel Murray Papers, State Historical Society of Wisconsin, microfilm reel 2.

2. *Baltimore Sun*, Aug. 11, 1890; Edwin A. Lee, "Daniel Murray," *The Colored American Magazine* 5 (1902): 432–33; *Baltimore Sun*, Dec. 27, 1883; Edward C. Papenfuse et al., *A Biographical Dictionary of the Maryland Legislature, 1635–1789*, vol. 1 (Baltimore: Johns Hopkins University Press, 1985), 460–61; National Register of Historic Places for Centreville Historic District, National Park Service; State Historic Sites Survey for Wharf House, QA-196, Maryland Historic Trust; Manumission deed for George Murray, 1810 (STW 9/208), manumission deed for Bill Murray, 1822 (TM 3/10), and manumission deed for Tom Murray and sister Mary, 1822 (TM 2/535 and 536), land records, Maryland State Archives; Baltimore directories for 1831 (first appear-

ance), 1856–57, 1860; Arthur B. Caldwell, *History of the American Negro and His Institutions*, vol. 6 (Atlanta: A. B. Caldwell Publishing Co., 1922), 26; Daniel Murray Papers, reel 2; *Evening Star* (Washington, DC), Dec. 1, 1883.

3. Lee, "Daniel Murray," 433, 435; Daniel Murray, "The Power of Blood Inheritance," unpublished c. 1901 essay in Daniel Murray Papers, reel 2; Caldwell, *History of the American Negro*, 26; Ellen Butler 1901 death certificate (record no. 139475) and will (box 205), DC Archives; Eliza Murray 1897 death certificate (no. 93451), Maryland State Archives; Maryland Marriages, 1655–1850; Baltimore directory for 1881; *Baltimore Sun*, Dec. 27, 1883 (George Murray's death notice, Aug. 11, 1890 *Sun*, stated that he had fathered six children, but in the earlier article George was responding directly to an interviewer); Alexander W. Wayman, *Cyclopedia of African Methodism* (Baltimore: Methodist Episcopal Book Depository, 1882), 115; *Baltimore Sun*, Aug. 12, 1890; *Washington Bee*, Jan. 23, 1897.

4. Some sources claim that George Murray participated in bringing Daniel Coker to Baltimore and founding Bethel Church, but all that happened well before his Baltimore residency. Indeed, Coker left for Liberia a decade before George Murray moved to Baltimore. Daniel Murray (Daniel Murray Papers, reel 2) credits Alexander Murray, with whom he mentions no kinship, with playing the role that some later sources ascribed to George Murray, and early histories of the AME Church are in accord; David Smith, *Biography of David Smith of the A.M.E. Church* (Gloucestershire, UK: Dodo Press, modern reprint, original published in 1881), 7, 11–13, 16–17; *Federal Gazette and Baltimore Daily Advertiser*, July 25, 1815; Phillips, *Freedom's Port*, 133–40; Nina Honemond Clarke, *History of the Nineteenth-Century Black Churches in Maryland and Washington, D.C.* (New York: Vantage Press, 1983), 19; *Baltimore Sun*, Feb. 5, 1847; Wayman, *Cyclopedia of African Methodism*, 4–5; Baltimore Architecture Foundation, baltimorearchitecture.org/biographies/robert-cary-long/jr/; *Baltimore Clipper*, June 17, 1840; Daniel Alexander Payne, *Recollections of Seventy Years* (New York: Arno Press and the *New York Times*, 1968), foreword by Benjamin Quarles, 77–81, 93–94, 234–35, 256.

5. *Evening Star*, Dec. 1, 1883; Daniel Murray Papers, reel 2; The Baltimore directory of 1851 lists the address for George Murray as "74 Bank

Lane or McElderry Street continued." Bank Lane would be renamed Little McElderry Street. See Thomas P. Bocek, *Baltimore Street Name Changes, 1730 to 2000* (Baltimore: Historyk Press, 2007), 10. Eliza may have maintained a place there; in 1881 she is double listed in the Baltimore directory at both Forrest and Little McElderry Streets; Lee, "Daniel Murray," 435; Wayman, *Cyclopedia of African Methodism*, 7–8; *Colored American*, April 28, 1900; Daniel Murray, "Three New Folk-Lore Stories," *The Colored American Magazine* 14 (1908): 104; Daniel Murray to George Myers, June 3, 1905, and Dec. 25, 1903; J. F. Weishampel, Jr., comp., *The Stranger in Baltimore, a New Handbook* (Baltimore: J. F. Weishampel, Jr., 1866), 140–42; *American Republican and Baltimore Daily Clipper*, Dec. 3, 1844.

6. Lee, "Daniel Murray," 433, 435–36; federal census and Baltimore directory data; *National Republican*, Dec. 27, 1862; *Evening Star*, Dec. 29, 1862; *Colored American*, April 28, 1900 (the story of Murray being kissed by Lincoln was picked up by other newspapers, including the Kansas City *Star*, Chicago *Daily Tribune*, and Biloxi, Mississippi, *Daily Herald*); Miscellaneous Personnel Files, Library of Congress Archives; William E. Matthews, *John F. W. Ware and His Work for the Freedmen* (Boston: Press of George H. Ellis, 1881), 11–12, 18; *Baltimore Sun*, April 21, 1881, May 17, 1870, Aug. 11, 1890; George Murray always lived in the same Forrest Street house, but the number changed over time from 39 to 37 (after 1855 but before 1886) to 311, see Bocek, *Baltimore Street Name Changes*, iii.

7. Federal census and Washington directory data; Ellen Butler 1901 death certificate (record no. 139475) and will (box 205), DC Archives; Samuel Proctor 1887 death certificate (record no. 58276), DC Archives; Charles W. Proctor 1909 death certificate (record no. 187695), DC Archives; *Washington Bee*, Jan. 23, 1897; Murray, "The Power of Blood Inheritance." Interestingly, both Daniel Murray and his mother are double listed in the 1870 federal census: they are both at the Forrest Street house with George, plus each is listed in DC, Daniel with his sister Ellen and Eliza with her daughter Catherine Proctor; *Evening Star*, April 18, 1866; *National Republican*, Feb. 3, 1873; Sept. 24, 1887; Diane Dale, *The Village That Shaped Us* (Lanham, MD: Dale Publishing, 2011), xvii–xviii, xlii–xliii.

8. Constance McLaughlin Green, *The Secret City: A History of Race Rela-*

tions in the Nation's Capital (Princeton, NJ: Princeton University Press, 1967), 33, 75–77, 80; Elizabeth Clark-Lewis, *First Freed: Washington, D.C. in the Emancipation Era* (Washington, DC: Howard University Press, 2002), 47; *Evening Star,* July 28, 1865; March 11, April 16, May 7, 1868.

9. Lee, "Daniel Murray," 436 (Lee states that the Senate restaurant was known as the "Hole in the Wall," but see *U.S. Senate Catalogue of Graphic Arts,* 2008, 65, for identification of the "Hole in the Wall" as a small circular room in the preextensions Capitol where Senators Clay, Webster, and Calhoun conferred over meals); John B. Ellis, *The Sights and Sounds of the National Capital* (Chicago: Jones, Junkin and Co., 1869), 56ff, 86, 112; Proctor's advertisements for the Senate Saloon ran repeatedly in the *Critic-Record* in 1869 and 1870; example, Nov. 25, 1869; Daniel Murray Miscellaneous Personal Files, Library of Congress Archives; Congressional Directory for 1869; *Miscellaneous Documents of the Senate of the United States* (Washington, DC: GPO, 1875), 8; *Annual Report of the Architect of the U.S. Capitol* (Washington, DC: GPO, 1901), 18; *Evening Star,* April 22, 1870; May 17, 1872; John Willis Menard was the first African American elected to the U.S. Congress, but due to a dispute over election results, he was not seated.

10. Ellis, *The Sights and Sounds of the National Capital,* 66, 68–69, 71–73, 75–80, 82–83, 86, 90, 94; Lee, "Daniel Murray," 435–36; *Times* (Washington, DC), Aug. 22, 1897; Congressional Directory for 1869 and 1870; Daniel Murray Miscellaneous Personnel Files, Library of Congress Archives; David C. Mearns, *The Story Up to Now: The Library of Congress, 1800–1946* (Washington, DC: Library of Congress, 1947), 75–76, 82, 84–89; Ainsworth Spofford, "Government Library at Washington," *International Review* 5 (1878): 755, 757, 759–60.

11. Mearns, *The Story Up to Now,* 73, 75–76, 84–89, 108, 116; Spofford, "Government Library at Washington," 760, 762–66; Congressional Directory for 1869; *Evening Star,* Aug. 23, 1853; *National Republican,* March 18, 1869; *Annual Report of the Librarian of Congress* (Washington, DC: GPO, 1871), 3–6.

12. *National Republican,* Sept. 24, 1887; Franklin T. Howe, "The Board of Public Works," *Records of the Columbia Historical Society* 3 (1900):

259–60, 274; *Evening Star*, Feb. 18, 20, 21, 22, 1871; Feb. 13, 1873; *New National Era*, Feb. 20, 1873.

13. *Revised Statutes of the United States, 1873–74*, vol. 18, appendix (Washington, DC: GPO, 1878), 109; *Annual Report of the Librarian of Congress* (Washington, DC: GPO, 1912), 13; U.S. Official Register for 1869, 1871, 1879, and 1887; The federal census of 1880 gives Murray's occupation as messenger in the Capitol, and since the 1879 Official Register staff list for the Library of Congress does not break down into assistant librarians, messengers, and laborers as in some years, it may be that Murray secured the assistant librarian title in 1880; Congressional directory for 1872; *Washington Bee*, June 15, 1901; U.S. Congress Joint Committee on the Library, *Condition of the Library of Congress, March 3, 1897*, 54th Congress, 2nd Session, Senate Report 1573, (Washington, DC: GPO, 1897), 42, 46, 48; *Who's Who of the Colored Race*, vol. 1 (Chicago: Half-Century Anniversary of Negro Freedom in the U.S. Memento Edition, 1915), 203; Lee, "Daniel Murray," 434, 436–37; John Y. Cole, "Ainsworth Spofford and the 'National Library' " (PhD dissertation, George Washington University, 1971), 31, 36; Mearns, *The Story Up to Now*, 76, 82, 115; *Washington Bee*, June 22, 1812; John Y. Cole, "Daniel Alexander Payne Murray," Dictionary of American Library Biography (Littleton, CO: Libraries Unlimited, 1978), 381; Amherst College conferred an honorary LLD degree on Ainsworth Spofford in 1882; for Murray's honorary degree, see chapter 16.

14. Passbook, Freedman's Savings Bank, Daniel Murray Papers, reel 4; *Evening Star*, Oct. 12, 26; Nov. 5, 1875; Dec. 6, 1878; March 10, 1880; *Washington Post*, April 6, 1878; *People's Advocate*, April 2, 1881; *Colored American*, April 28, 1900.

15. www.culturaltourismdc.org/portal/; www.stlukes.org/about; Olive A. Taylor, "The Protestant Episcopal Church and the Negro in Washington," (PhD dissertation, Howard University, 1874), 223–25; John W. Cromwell, "The First Negro Churches in the District of Columbia," *Journal of Negro History* 7 (1922): 101–02; *National Republican*, May 12, July 22, 1874; June 8, 1876; Jan. 10, 1877; *Evening Star*, April 18, 1876; April 14, 1879; federal census and Washington directory data. For quote on historical assessment of Crummell, see Rayford W. Logan and Michael R. Winston, eds., *Dictionary of American Negro Biography* (New York: W. W. Norton and Co., 1982), 145–47.

16. *Evening Star*, April 3, 1877; Another vestryman at St. Luke's was Charles F. Murray, his relationship to Daniel, if any, unknown. Neither he nor his parents were born in Maryland, yet his will reveals, intriguingly, that he had an aunt named Catherine Proctor, who was born in DC and was a longtime resident of Rhode Island. Except for the common church, there is no evidence that he socialized with Daniel or his brothers. Federal census data, Charles F. Murray 1903 death certificate (record no. 147501) and will (box 250), DC Archives; *Colored American*, Feb. 28, 1903; *National Republican*, April 10, 1874.

17. John W. Cromwell et al., "Adjourned Meeting of the Negro Society," *Journal of Negro History* 64 (1979): 63–64; *Evening Star*, Oct. 25, 1877; March 6, 1878; for an article on Syphax, see E. Delorus Preston, Jr., "William Syphax, a Pioneer in Negro Education in the District of Columbia," *Journal of Negro History*, 20 (1935): 448–76.

2: The Good Wife

1. Federal census data; "The Leary Family," *Negro History Bulletin* 10 (1946): 27; Katherine Mayo, interview with Henrietta Leary Evans, March 5, 1908, Box 12, John Brown-Oswald Villard Papers, Columbia University Rare Book and Manuscript Library; Malinda Maynor Lowery, *Lumbee Indians in the Jim Crow South: Race, Identity, and the Making of a Nation* (Chapel Hill: University of North Carolina Press, 2010), preface and chaps. 1–3; Glenn Ellen Starr Stilling, "Lumbee Indians," in *Encyclopedia of North Carolina*, ed. William Powell (Chapel Hill: University of North Carolina Press, 2006), 699–700; George E. Butler, *The Croatan Indians of Samson County, North Carolina* (Durham, NC: Seeman Printery, 1916), including, p. 21, an 1891 letter from Matthew Leary's son, John S. Leary, accessed at http://docsouth.unc .edu/nc/butler/butler.html; Rose Leary Love [John S. Leary's daughter], *Plum Thickets and Field Daisies* (Charlotte, NC: Public Library of Charlotte and Mecklenburg County, 1996), 74; *Daily News* (Frederick, MD), July 2, 1887. Although the claim that the Lumbees are descended in part from Lost Colony survivors has never been proved, it remains current and DNA analysis that might provide evidence is under way; *Charlotte* [NC] *Observer*, Aug. 3, 1900.

2. "The Leary Family," 28; Federal census data; North Carolina marriage bonds, 1741–1868; Love, *Plum Thickets and Field Daisies*, 74–75;

Auguste Levasseur, *Lafayette in America in 1824 and 1825*, trans. Alan R. Hoffman (Manchester, NH: Lafayette Press, 2006), 306; *Fayetteville Observer*, Aug. 25, 1897.

3. Federal census data; Emily Farrington Smith, *Fayetteville, North Carolina: An All-American History* (Charleston, SC: History Press, 2011), 63–64; *Raleigh News and Observer*, May 29, 2006; *Oberlin News*, Oct. 13, 1909; Katherine Mayo, interview with Henrietta Leary Evans; the spelling of Sheridan Leary's first name in almost all records is "Lewis," but in the only letter of Leary's that has been reproduced he uses the same spelling as his namesake, "Louis"; Claude A. Clegg III, *The Price of Liberty: African Americans and the Making of Liberia* (Chapel Hill: University of North Carolina Press, 2004), 156; Robert Ewell Greene, *The Leary-Evans, Ohio's Free People of Color* (Washington, DC: Keitt Printing Co., 1979), 46; Rose Leary Love, "A Few Facts About Lewis Sheridan Leary Who Was Killed at Harpers Ferry in John Brown's Raid," *Negro History Bulletin* 6 (1943): 198; William E. Bigglestone, *They Stopped in Oberlin* (Scottsdale, AZ: Innovation Group, 1981), 71; Love, *Plum Thickets and Field Daisies*, 76.

4. Ibid., 75; One apprentice in Matthew Leary's shop was John H. Scott, who would later move to Oberlin and participate in the Oberlin-Wellington Rescue; Mayo, interview with Henrietta Leary Evans; Henrietta said that her father stopped buying slaves after manumissions became problematic, but the 1850 slave schedule shows Leary owning three slaves; according to Rose Leary Love, he did continue teaching slaves to read and write after it became illegal; John Hope Franklin, "Slaves Virtually Free in Ante-Bellum North Carolina," *Journal of Negro History* 28 (1943): 289, 291, 300; "The Leary Family," 27; Federal census data.

5. Ibid., North Carolina marriage bonds, 1741–1868; Greene, *The Leary-Evans*, 16, 33; *Fayetteville Observer*, Oct. 4, 2009.

6. Federal census data; www2.census.gov/prod2/decennial/documents/1850a-13.pdf; note: Elizabeth Keckley lived in Hillsborough from 1835 until about 1842, an abused slave working for the Alexander Kirkland family, www.stmatthewshillsborough.org; Patricia Phillips Marshall and Jo Ramsay Leimenstoll, *Thomas Day: Master Craftsman and Free Man of Color* (Chapel Hill: University of North Carolina Press, 2010), 35; Henry Evans's advertisements ran in the *Hillsborough Recorder*, e.g.,

on Sept. 27, 1848, and Nov. 28, 1849; North Carolina marriage bonds, 1741–1868.

7. *Washington Post*, May 7, 1955; Marjorie Lockett, "His Own Man," *Mexican-American Review* 9 (1971): 29; Greene, *The Leary-Evans*, 7, 46–47; federal census data; William E. Bigglestone, *They Stopped in Oberlin*, xiii, xix, 70.

8. www.Oberlinheritage.org was helpful throughout this section; *Oberlin Weekly News*, Aug. 19, 1881; Bigglestone, *They Stopped in Oberlin*, xiii, xix, 70; Denton J. Snider, *A Writer of Books in His Genesis* (reprint London: Forgotten Books, 2013), 99; Oberlin directory, 1859–60; federal census data; www.oberlin.edu/archive/resources/photoguide/walton_hall.html; Wilbur H. Phillips, *Oberlin Colony: The Story of a Century* (Oberlin: Oberlin Printing Company, 1933), 37, 42; Allan Patterson, ed., *Oberlin Community History* (State College, PA: Josten's Publications, 1981), 18; Oberlin City Directory; as with Daniel Murray, the confusion surrounding Anna Murray's correct birth date is partly of her own making. After her eightieth birthday in 1938, some articles, including her obituary, name a birth year of 1857. However, a birth date of February 1858 is supported by her Oberlin College records, by her husband's brief sketch of her in his papers, and by the 1900 federal census, in which a birth date citing month and year was asked for.

9. Cally Lyn Waite, *Permission to Remain Among Us: Education for Blacks in Oberlin, Ohio, 1880–1914* (Westport, CT: Praeger, 2002), 27; William C. Nell, "Gleanings at Oberlin," *Liberator*, Oct. 9, 1856; Bigglestone, *They Stopped in Oberlin*, xv, 163–64, 183; William Cheek and Aimee Lee Cheek, *John Mercer Langston and the Fight for Black Freedom, 1829–1865* (Urbana: University of Illinois Press, 1996), 280; William C. Nell, "John Brown's Men: Louis Sherrard [*sic*] Leary," *The Pine and Palm*, July 27, 1861; Katherine Mayo, interview with Henrietta Leary Evans; Katherine Mayo, interview with Mary Leary Langston, July 27, 1909, Box 12, John Brown-Oswald Villard Papers; Love, "A Few Facts About Lewis Sheridan Leary"; Oberlin directory, 1859–60.

10. John Mercer Langston, *From the Virginia Plantation to the National Capital* (Hartford, CT: American Publishing Co., 1894, reprint New York: Arno Press and the *New York Times*, 1969), 157–58, 162, 168, 195; Cheek and Cheek, *John Mercer Langston*, 252, 278–81, 285 (twelve leaders based on frequency and prominence of mention in newspapers and

records), 287, 290, 293; Oberlin College data; Patterson, *Oberlin Community History*, 25–26; Bigglestone, *They Stopped in Oberlin*, xviii, 126, 206–07; Phillips, *Oberlin Colony*, 68–69, 77; J. Brent Morris, *Oberlin, Hotbed of Abolitionism* (Chapel Hill: University of North Carolina Press, 2014), 164–65, 188–89; Lida Rose McCabe, "The Oberlin-Wellington Rescue: An Antislavery Crisis Which Almost Precipitated the Civil War in 1859 Through the Secession of the North," *Godey's Magazine*, Oct. 1896, 363–64.

11. Clayton Sumner Ellsworth, "Oberlin and the Anti-Slavery Movement up to the Civil War," (PhD dissertation, Cornell University, 1930), 25; William C. Nell, "John Brown's Men: John Anthony Copeland," *The Pine and Palm*, July 20, 1861; Nell, "John Brown's Men: Louis Sherrard [*sic*] Leary"; *Cleveland Morning Leader*, Dec. 16, 1859; Wilbur Greeley Burroughs, "Oberlin's Part in the Slavery Conflict," *Ohio Archaeological and Historical Quarterly* 20, no. 1 (1911): 289–330.

12. For the most complete contemporary account of the rescue and trials, see Jacob R. Shipherd, *History of the Oberlin-Wellington Rescue* (Boston: John P. Jewett and Co., 1859), citations here at 104–09, 126; for the fullest secondary source, see Nat Brandt, *The Town That Started the Civil War* (Syracuse, NY: Syracuse University Press, 1990), citations here at 78–79, 103–4, 117–24, 149, 160; *Oberlin News*, Oct. 13, 1909; Morris, *Oberlin, Hotbed of Abolitionism*, 210; McCabe, "The Oberlin-Wellington Rescue," 365, 367, 369, 370, 376; Langston, *From the Virginia Plantation*, 184; Burroughs, "Oberlin's Part in the Slavery Conflict," 302–06; Nell, "John Brown's Men: Louis Sherrard [*sic*] Leary"; Nell, "John Brown's Men: John Anthony Copeland"; Ronald Shannon, *Profiles in Ohio History: A Legacy of African American Achievement* (New York: iUniverse, 2008), 42; *Cleveland Plain Dealer*, Dec. 7, 1858; April 7, 1859; *Cleveland Leader*, Dec. 10, 1858; Jan. 13, April 6, 1859; *Oberlin Evangelist*, Dec. 22, 1858; Jan. 19, 1859.

13. Morris, *Oberlin, Hotbed of Abolitionism*, 220–21, 223; Burroughs, "Oberlin's Part in the Slavery Conflict," 307, 310–15; *Cleveland Leader*, May 14, July 7, 1859; McCabe, "The Oberlin-Wellington Rescue," 370, 372–74; Shipherd, *History of the Oberlin-Wellington Rescue*, 89–94, 113, 261–63, 266, 273; *Oberlin Evangelist*, May 25, July 13, 1859; two prisoners whose names had been misspelled in the indictment were released (Wall was one of them; his first name was incorrectly given as "Oliver" on the bill

of indictment), as were several of the Wellington men after pleading *nolo contendere*. Twelve men were released on July 6 (the exceptions were Simeon Bushnell, who stayed five more days to complete his sentence, and Charles Langston, who was released on June 1, having completed his shorter sentence).

14. Leary's daughter's name is spelled variously as Loise and Lois as well as Louise; Morris, *Hotbed*, 226, 229; Cheek and Cheek, *John Mercer Langston*, 338; Langston, *From the Virginia Plantation*, 191–93; *Cleveland Plain Dealer*, Oct. 27, Nov. 1, 1859; Nell, "John Brown's Men: Louis Sherrard [*sic*] Leary"; Clegg, *The Price of Liberty*, 158; Love, "A Few Facts About Lewis Sheridan Leary," 198; Katherine Mayo, interview with Henrietta Leary Evans; Katherine Mayo, interview with Mary Leary Langston; Katherine Mayo, interview with John H. Scott, Dec. 7, 1908, Box 12, John Brown-Oswald Villard Papers.

15. For a full account of John Brown's Raid, see Tony Horwitz, *Midnight Rising: John Brown and the Raid That Sparked the Civil War* (New York: Henry Holt and Company, 2011), citations here at 124, 129, 161–63, 265–66, 289; Katherine Mayo, interview with Henrietta Leary Evans; *Cleveland Morning Leader*, Nov. 1, 1859; Nell, "John Brown's Men: John Anthony Copeland"; *New York Tribune*, Jan. 6, 1860; *Sunday Evening Star*, Washington, DC, Aug. 15, 1937; *Fayetteville Carolinian*, quoted in the *Southerner* (Edgecombe County, NC), Nov. 26, 1859; "The John Brown Letters Found in the Virginia State Library in 1901 (Continued)," *Virginia Magazine of History and Biography* 10, no. 4 (1903): 384.

16. Federal census data; Lockett, "His Own Man, 29"; Phillips, *Oberlin Colony*, 63, 104, 106–09; Patterson, *Oberlin Community History*, 18, 34–35; Oberlin and Russia Township directories; Cheek and Cheek, *John Mercer Langston*, 285–86, 289, 390–93, 409; Brandt, *The Town That Started the Civil War*, 252; Bigglestone, *They Stopped in Oberlin*, xx–xxi, 70, 208, 222; Langston, *From the Virginia Plantation*, 202, 219; *Lorain County News*, Jan. 23, 1861; March 22, 1865.

17. Benjamin Quarles, *Allies for Freedom: Blacks and John Brown* (New York: Oxford University Press, 1974), 150–52; Richard B. Sheridan, "Charles Henry Langston and the African American Struggle in Kansas," *Kansas History* 22 (Winter 1999–2000), 273, 280; federal census data; *Washington Bee*, June 1, 1901; Cheek and Cheek, *John Mercer Langston*, 290;

Phillips, *Oberlin Colony*, 63–64, 112–15, 118, 120, 122–23; Patterson, *Oberlin Community History*, 34–35, 46.

18. Federal census data; "Anna Evans Murray" in *Notable Black American Women*, ed. Jessie Carney Smith, book II (New York: Gale Research, ITP, 1996), 492; Phillips, *Oberlin Colony*, 57, 122, 126, 129; Patterson, *Oberlin Community History*, 32, 63; Bigglestone, *They Stopped in Oberlin*, xix; *General Catalogue of Oberlin College, 1833–1908* (Oberlin: Oberlin College, 1989), intro 116, intro 117, 309; *Oberlin Alumni Magazine* (1955), 31; Oberlin College records for Anna Evans Murray.

19. *Washington Bee*, June 1, 1901; Freedman's Bank records; federal census and Washington city directories data; *Cleveland Gazette*, Feb. 23, 1884; *Evening Star*, Jan. 30, 1886; Bigglestone, *They Stopped in Oberlin*, 165; Brandt, *The Town That Started the Civil War*, 19; the identities of Mary S. Patterson Leary Langston and Mary Jane Patterson are sometimes confused—they were first cousins, and both attended Oberlin College; Oberlin College records for Anna Evans Murray; United States Official Register for 1871, 1873, and 1877; Daniel Murray Papers, reel 2; *Fourth Report of the Board of Trustees of Public Schools of the District of Columbia, 1877–78* (Washington, DC: Gibson Brothers, 1878), 153, 215; *National Republican* (Washington, DC), March 10, 1875; *Evening Star*, March 10, 1875; June 23, 1877; March 6, 1878; June 21, 1879; Oct. 16, 1885; *One Hundred Years: St. Luke's Episcopal Church, 1873–1973* (Washington, DC: St. Luke's Episcopal Church, 1873), 78.

3: The Black Elite

1. Marriage record, book 13, p. 121, DC Archives; Edwin A. Lee, "Daniel Murray," *The Colored American Magazine* 5 (1902): 435; *Evening Star* (Washington, DC), Jan. 30, 1886; Aug. 15, 1937; Alice Birney, "First National Congress of Mothers," *The Kindergarten Primary Magazine* 9 (1896–97): 673.

2. *Evening Star*, Dec. 19, 1883; Jan. 30, 1886; Willard B. Gatewood, *Aristocrats of Color: The Black Elite, 1880–1920* (Bloomington: Indiana University Press, 1990), 39.

3. Rayford W. Logan and Michael R. Winston, eds., *Dictionary of American Negro Biography* (New York: W. W. Norton and Co., 1982), 123, 125–27; Carol Gelderman, *A Free Man of Color and His Hotel: Race, Re-*

construction, and the Role of the Federal Government (Washington, DC: Potomac Books, 2012), 13, 21, 46; *New York Globe*, Oct. 18, 1884.

4. Logan and Winston, *Dictionary of American Negro Biography*, 382–84, 507–08.

5. Gelderman, *A Free Man of Color and His Hotel*, 105–09; H. C. Bruce, *The New Man* (York, PA: P. Anstat and Sons, 1895), iii; Lawrence Otis Graham, *The Senator and the Socialite: The True Story of America's First Black Dynasty* (New York: HarperPerennial, 2006) 29, 94–95, 97–102; Logan and Winston, *Dictionary of American Negro Biography*, 74–76; Joseph Willson, *Sketches of the Higher Classes of Colored Society in Philadelphia* (Philadelphia: Merrihew and Thompson, 1841); *Washington Post*, Nov. 16, 1890.

6. Logan and Winston, *Dictionary of American Negro Biography*, 267–68, 273–74.

7. Gatewood, *Aristocrats of Color*, 7–29, 238; Paul Laurence Dunbar, "Negro Society in Washington," *Saturday Evening Post* 174 (Dec. 14, 1901): 9.

8. Logan and Winston, *Dictionary of American Negro Biography*, 508; *New Era* (Washington, DC), Feb. 22, 1870; Daniel J. Sharfstein, *The Invisible Line* (New York: Penguin Press, 2011), 157.

9. *Indianapolis Freeman*, Dec. 25, 1897; Langston, quoted in William Cheek and Aimee Lee Cheek, *John Mercer Langston and the Fight for Black Freedom, 1829–1865* (Urbana: University of Illinois Press, 1996), 291; Grimké, quoted in Gilderman, *A Free Man of Color*, 19.

10. Willson, *Sketches of the Higher Classes*, 13; Dunbar, "Negro Society in Washington," 9.

11. Gatewood, *Aristocrats of Color*, 173; Henry Loomis Nelson, "The Washington Negro," *Harper's Weekly* 36 (July 9, 1892): 654.

12. *Baltimore Afro-American*, June 4, 1898; *National Republican*, Sept. 11, 1879; *Weekly Louisianian* (New Orleans), Sept. 20, 27, 1879; *People's Advocate*, Sept. 20, 1879; *Washington Bee*, June 14, 1884.

13. *Weekly Louisianian*, Nov. 1, 1879; *New York Globe*, Jan. 12, 1884; Cheek and Cheek, *John Mercer Langston*, 399–402; *People's Advocate*, Sept. 27, 1879; Nov. 20, 1880; *National Republican*, May 30, 1879; June 5, 1882; *Washington Post*, Nov. 13, 1878.

14. *Weekly Louisianan*, Sept. 27, Dec. 13, 1879; Marilyn J. Chiat, *America's*

Religious Architecture: Sacred Places for Every Community (New York: Wiley, 1997), 218; Saint Luke's Episcopal Church, Historic American Buildings Survey (HABS) no. DC-359; *National Republican*, Nov. 27, 29, 1879.

15. *Evening Star*, Dec. 20, 27, 1879; Jan. 9, 1880; *Weekly Louisianian*, Jan. 10, 17, 1880; *People's Advocate*, Jan. 10, 1880.

16. Federal census and Washington directory data; Daniel Murray Papers, State Historical Society of Wisconsin, microfilm reel 2; Philadelphia, PA, death certificate index for Samuel W. Proctor; *People's Advocate*, Dec. 13, 1879; July 18, 31, Aug. 21, Sept. 11, 1880; May 21, 1881; *Evening Star*, Nov. 29, 1879; *National Republican*, Dec. 1, 1879; Gatewood, *Aristocrats of Color*, 27.

17. *People's Advocate*, Jan. 17, Aug. 14, 1880; April 9, Dec. 31, 1881; *Indianapolis Freeman*, Dec. 7, 1889; *National Republican*, April 29, 1876; April 6, 1881; *Evening Star*, April 3, 1877; www.syphaxfamilyreunion.com/tree.html.

4: The Good Life

1. Edwin A. Lee, "Daniel Murray," *The Colored American Magazine* 5 (1902): 435; *Evening Star* (Washington, DC), Dec. 24, 1877; Jan. 22, 1881; *People's Advocate*, Feb. 14, 1880; *Weekly Louisianian* (New Orleans), Aug. 20, 1881.

2. *People's Advocate*, Sept. 10, Nov. 19, Dec. 10, 1881; *Evening Times* (Washington, DC), Sept. 5, 1895; *Washington Post*, Nov. 24, 1881; March 11, 1882; March 27, 1883; Dec. 12, 1884; *National Republican*, Dec. 10, 1879; May 16, Aug. 6, Nov. 25, 1881; March 16, 1882; March 27, April 4, 9, 1883; Dec. 12, 1884; *Critic-Record* (Washington, DC), Nov. 24, 1881; *Weekly Louisianian*, April 3, 1880; *Evening Critic*, March 10, 1882; *Evening Star*, March 10, 27, 1883; Wilson Jeremiah Moses, *Alexander Crummell: A Study of Civilization and Discontent* (New York: Oxford University Press, 1989), 201–07.

3. *Evening Critic*, June 19, 1883; *New York Globe*, June 23, 1883; *Cleveland Gazette*, Aug. 10, 1912; August Meier, "Negro Class Structure and Ideology in the Age of Booker T. Washington," *Phylon* 23 (1962): 262–63; Lee, "Daniel Murray," 439; *Times* (Washington, DC), Aug. 22, 1897; *Washington Bee*, June 1, 1901; Washington city directory data; *Evening Star*, May 2, 1895; *Colored American* (Washington, DC), April 28, 1900.

4. *Washington Post*, April 7, 1882; *Evening Star*, Feb. 17, March 31, 1883;

George Henry Murray birth certificate (box 35, no. 31002), DC Archives; Daniel Murray Papers, State Historical Society of Wisconsin, microfilm reel 2.

5. United States Official Register for 1883; Congressional Directory for 1883; *Annual Report of the Librarian of Congress* (Washington, DC: GPO), 1871, 5, 1884, 5–6; David C. Mearns, *The Story Up to Now: The Library of Congress, 1800–1946* (Washington, DC: Library of Congress, 1947), 89–90, 97, 108, 113–19; *Evening Star,* Dec. 22, 1881; Sept. 13, Dec. 10, 1883.

6. Robert A. Toomey, "The Brighton of America," *The Colored American Magazine* 3 (1901): 206; *New York Age,* Aug. 2, 1890; *People's Advocate,* July 26, Sept. 13, 1879; Sept. 17, 1881; Aug. 25, 1883; Andrew W. Kahrl, "The Political Work of Leisure: Class, Recreation, and African American Commemoration at Harpers Ferry, West Virginia, 1881–1931," *Journal of Social History* 42, Fall 2008: 57, 59, 64; *Washington Bee,* July 24, 1886.

7. *Evening Star,* June 6, Dec. 1, 1883; *Baltimore Sun,* Dec. 27, 1883.

8. *People's Advocate,* Jan. 1, 1881; Lawrence Otis Graham, *The Senator and the Socialite: The True Story of America's First Black Dynasty* (New York: HarperPerennial, 2006), 128, 154, 161; *Washington Critic-Record,* Aug. 22, 1887; *Washington Bee,* March 20, 1886; *New York Freeman,* March 20, 1886.

9. *Washington Critic-Record,* Aug. 22, 1887; *Washington Evening Critic,* March 15, 1882; *Washington Bee,* May 31, 1884; May 9, June 20, 1885; *Cleveland Gazette,* April 18, 1885; *National Republican,* March 14, 1884; Nov. 14, 1885.

10. Federal census data; *Evening Star,* Sept. 29, 1884; June 8, 1886; *Washington Bee,* Nov. 22, 1884; June 20, 1885; July 24, 1886; *Cleveland Gazette,* Nov. 7, 1885; *New York Freeman,* March 20, 1886; *The Elite List: A Compilation of Selected Names of Residents of Washington, D.C.* (Washington, DC: Elite Publishing Co., 1888).

11. Mearns, *The Story Up to Now,* 125; United States Official Register for 1885 and 1887; *Annual Report of the Librarian of Congress* (Washington, DC: GPO, 1887), 6–7; *Evening Star,* Jan. 23, April 10, 1886; *Washington Bee,* March 12, 1887; Daniel Murray, "Cyrus Field Adams," *The Colored American Magazine* 4 (1901): 151; *Washington Times,* Aug. 22, 1897.

12. *Cleveland Gazette,* Aug. 28, 1886 (note: there is no death certificate for

Henry Evans in the DC Archives); Henry Evans, Westwood Cemetery C-036-04; *People's Advocate*, July 26, 1879; *Washington Bee*, June 1, 1901; federal census and Washington city directory data; Samuel Proctor 1887 death certificate (record no. 58276) and will (box), DC Archives; *National Republican*, Sept. 24, 1887; *Washington Critic-Record*, Sept. 24, 1887; *Evening Star*, Nov. 17, 1880; Feb. 5, 1881; Feb. 6, 1885; Oct. 10, 1901; Dec. 26, Dec. 31, 1902; Jan. 2, 1903; *Washington Times*, Dec. 26, 1902; Aug. 22, 1903; equity case file 4657, May–July 1881, Record Group 21, NARA.

13. *Washington Critic*, March 2, 5, 1889; *New York Age*, March 16, 1889; *Washington Bee*, March 16, 1889.

14. *Leader* (Washington, DC), Dec. 8, 1888; Constance Green, *Secret City: A History of Race Relations in the Nation's Capital* (Princeton: Princeton University Press, 1967), 123; *New York Age*, March 16, 1889; Nov. 22, 1890; Jan. 10, Feb. 28, 1891; *Washington Bee*, March 16, 1889; Willard B. Gatewood, *Aristocrats of Color: The Black Elite* (Bloomington, Indiana University Press, 1900), 226–27, 233.

15. *Washington Critic*, March 15, 1889; Pinckney Murray birth certificate, no. 54331, DC Archives.

16. Pinckney Murray death certificate, box 94, no. 72391, DC Archives; *Evening Star*, Aug. 9, 1890; George Murray death certificate, no. 29873, Maryland State Archives; *Baltimore Sun*, Aug. 11, 12, 1890; Jan. 16, 1897; Eliza Murray death certificate, no. 93451, Maryland State Archives; Baltimore city directory data; *Washington Bee*, Jan. 23, 1897; Laurel Cemetery was also the final resting place of Bishop Daniel Payne, who died after George and before Eliza Murray and who was eulogized at his burial site by Frederick Douglass.

17. *New York Age*, April 25, May 2, 1891; Hollis R. Lynch, *Edward Wilmot Blyden* (London: Oxford University Press, 1967), 138–39; Paul Laurence Dunbar, "Negro Society in Washington," *Saturday Evening Post* 174 (Dec. 14, 1901): 9; Rayford W. Logan and Michael R. Winston, eds., *Dictionary of American Negro Biography*, (New York: W. W. Norton and Co., 1982), 446–48.

18. *Washington Post*, May 30, 31, June 9, 10, 1891; *Washington Bee*, June 6, 20, July 18, Aug. 1, 1891; *Evening Star*, May 29, June 15, 1891; Murray inexplicably revived his accusations against Gregory in 1896. This time the professor responded with a $50,000 lawsuit for libel, eventually settling

out of court, with Murray submitting a public retraction and apology. See *Evening Star*, April 9, 1896; *Washington Bee*, April 10, 1897.

19. *Appeal* (St. Paul, MN), Dec. 5, 1891; David V. Taylor, "John Quincy Adams, St. Paul Editor and Black Leader," *Minnesota History* 43 (Winter 1973): 286; *New York Age*, Jan. 18, 1890; *Colored American*, April 28, 1900; May 31, 1902; *Washington Bee*, June 12, 1901; Daniel Murray will, box 879, Anna Evans Murray will, box 2411, DC Archives.

20. *Evening Star*, Dec. 23, 1892; March 29, 1893; Helene Ethel Murray death certificate (box 115, no. 87931), DC Archives; Daniel Murray to George A. Myers, Dec. 28, 1901, George A. Myers Papers, Ohio Historical Society microfilm edition.

5: The Good Citizen

1. Daniel Murray Papers, State Historical Society of Wisconsin, microfilm reel 2; *Washington Bee*, Sept. 17, 1892.

2. United States Official Register for 1993; *Annual Report of the Librarian of Congress* (Washington, DC: GPO, 1893), 3; *Evening Star*, Feb. 27, 1894.

3. *Evening Star*, Nov. 18, 25, 1893; Jan. 12, 13, March 10, 15, 1894; *Washington Post*, Nov. 12, 13, 1889; Edwin A. Lee, "Daniel Murray," *The Colored American Magazine* 5 (1902): 437–39; Daniel Murray Papers, reel 27; Rayford W. Logan, *Howard University: The First Hundred Years, 1867–1967* (New York: New York University Press, 1969); 137; *Washington Bee*, June 22, 1912; *Indianapolis Freeman*, June 15, 1895.

4. *Evening Star*, Jan. 8, 1891; April 11, 1894; Nov. 12, 19, 1895; Nov. 12, 1896; Jan. 1, 1897; June 30, 1898; Feb. 24, 1899; *Washington Post*, March 23, 1894.

5. Lee, "Daniel Murray," 439; *Evening Star*, Jan. 23, March 2, April 9, 1895; April 22, Dec. 9, 10, 1896; Feb. 5, July 2, Nov. 22, 1898; Jan. 7, May 2, 1899; *Colored American*, Aug. 10, 1901; *Washington Times*, Jan. 23, 1895; "Educators of the First Half Century of Public Schools in the District of Columbia," *Journal of Negro History*, 17 (1932): 134.

6. *Evening Star*, May 14, 17, 18, 1894; Jan. 23, May 11, June 6, 1895; Feb. 10, 1896; Feb. 10, March 27, May 2, Dec. 1, 1897; Jan. 21, Feb. 25, May 12, 21, 1898; Feb. 24, 1899; *Colored American*, Nov. 19, 1898; *Evening Times* (Washington, DC), Oct. 26, 1895; *Washington Post*, Feb. 24, 1899.

7. *Evening Star*, May 8, Nov. 21, 1894; Dec. 14, 1895; April 21, May 21, 1896;

March 5, April 12, 1897; Dec. 3, 1904; *Washington Times*, May 9, 1894; Aug. 22, 1897; David E. Lewis, *The Politics of Presidential Appointments* (Princeton, NJ: Princeton University Press, 2008), 17–18; *Washington Bee*, May 8, 1897.

8. *Evening Star*, Oct. 19, 1893; June 27, 1894; Feb. 11, 1895; *Report of the Board of Trustees of Public Schools of the District of Columbia, 1892–93*, 181–82; *The Woman's Era* 1, no. 4 (July 1894); Rayford W. Logan and Michael R. Winston, eds., *Dictionary of American Negro Biography* (New York: W. W. Norton and Co., 1982), 662–63; federal census data; Daniel Murray Papers, reels 2, 27; *Washington Bee*, Feb. 16, 1895; Daniel Murray, "Three New Folk-Lore Stories," *The Colored American Magazine* 14 (1908), 104; Marjorie Lockett, "His Own Man," *Mexican-American Review* 9 (1971): 29.

9. Daniel Murray Papers, reels 2, 27 (note: Murray was incorrect on the start date for Henry at Cambridge; it was not 1894 but rather 1895); *Washington Bee*, July 14, 1883; Aug. 24, Sept. 7 (note: reference confuses the boys' schooling), 14, 1895; John Langone, *The Cambridge Rindge and Latin School Yesterday and Today* (Cambridge, MA: Cambridge Historical Society, 1998), 28–34, 36; Arthur Gilman, ed., *The Cambridge of 1896: A Picture of the City and Its Industries Fifty Years After Its Incorporation* (Cambridge, MA: Riverside Press, 1896), 225–26; Isabel C. Barrows, ed., *A Conference on Manual Training, Held at Boston, April 8–11, 1891* (Boston: New England Conference Educational Workers, c. 1891), 5–8, 101–03; *Annual Report of the School Committee for the City of Cambridge, 1895* (Cambridge, MA: Cambridge Cooperative Press, 1896), 11, 43; Paul E. Bierley, *John Philip Sousa: American Phenomenon*, rev. ed. (Columbus, OH: Integrity Press, 1973), 244; *Afro-American* (Baltimore), May 30, 1896; *Cleveland Gazette*, Sept. 24, 1898.

10. Lee, "Daniel Murray," 439; *Washington Post*, Dec. 10, 1894; April 20, 1897; *Evening Star*, Dec. 11, 1894; April 16, Sept. 4, 7, 1895; April 7, 1896; *Indianapolis Freeman*, June 5, 1897.

6: Activist Couple

1. *Evening Star*, Jan. 25, 1894; April 1, 6, 1895; June 16, July 4, 7, 14, 16, 21, 22, Dec. 30, 1896; Aug. 15, 1937; *Baltimore Sun*, Feb. 20, 1897; *Colored American*, Feb. 25, 1899; May 19, 1900; *Washington Bee*, July 25, 1896; *Washington Post*, July 25, 1896; Jessie Carney Smith, ed., *Notable Black*

American Women, Book II (New York: Gale Research, 1996), 137–39, 492–93; program, First Annual Convention of the National League of Colored Women, Daniel Murray Papers, State Historical Society of Wisconsin, microfilm reel 27; *Fourth Annual Report of the Colored Woman's League of Washington, D.C. for the Year Ending January 1, 1897,* Daniel Murray Pamphlet Collection, Library of Congress; *Iowa State Bystander* (Des Moines), May 25, 1900; Anna J. Murray, "A Key to the Situation," *Southern Workman* 29 (1900), 504–05.

2. *Evening Star,* Feb. 17, 19, 20, June 7, 1897; *Baltimore Sun,* Feb. 20, 1897; *Colored American,* July 22, 1899; *Kindergarten Primary Magazine* 9 (1896–97): 673; *Kansas City Star,* May 23, 1898; Anna J. Murray, "A Key to the Situation," 505–06; "The Kindergarten from Different Points of View," *Southern Workman,* 30 (1901): 360–61; *Kindergarten News* (April 1897): 391–92; *Times* (Washington, DC), March 17, 19, June 8, 1897; *Washington Bee,* June 12, 1897; *Iowa State Bystander,* May 25, 1900; *Fourth Annual Report of the Colored Woman's League of Washington, D.C. for the Year Ending January 1, 1897,* Daniel Murray Pamphlet Collection, Library of Congress; *Indianapolis Freeman,* March 13 and 27, 1897.

3. Jean Marie Robbins, "Black Club Women's Purpose for Establishing Kindergartens in the Progressive Era, 1890–1910" (dissertation, Loyola University, Chicago, 2011), 186, 196; Daniel Murray Papers, reel 2; *Kindergarten News* (Apr. 1, 1897): 392; *Kindergarten Primary Magazine* 9 (1896–97): 673; Anna J. Murray, "A Key to the Situation," 506; Daniel Murray to George Myers, July 14, 1899 George A. Myers Papers, Ohio Historical Society, microfilm edition; *Evening Star,* Oct. 4, 1897; Feb. 26, June 10, 25, 27, July 2, 1898; Aug. 15, Oct. 4, 1937; *Kindergarten Magazine* 11 (September 1898): 58–59; *Colored American,* June 25, 1898.

4. *Evening Star,* June 30, July 1, 1896; *Evening Times,* Oct. 17, 1896; *Thirty-second Annual Report of the National Association for the Relief of Destitute Colored Women and Children for the Year Ending January 1, 1895,* Daniel Murray Pamphlet Collection, Library of Congress; Sharon Harley, "Beyond the Classroom: The Organizational Lives of Black Female Educators in the District of Columbia, 1890–1930," *Journal of Negro Education* 51, no. 3 (1982): 260; *Colored American,* Nov. 25, 1899; *Plain Dealer* (Topeka, KS), Dec. 8, 1899; *Washington Bee,* April 10, 1897.

5. *Washington Bee,* Sept. 7, 21, Oct. 12, 19, 26, Nov. 9, 1895; Aug. 29,

Nov. 28, 1896; *Evening Star,* Sept. 10, 16, Oct. 19, Nov. 1, 9, 1895; Jan. 29, 30, May 4, June 16, Sept. 2, Nov. 16, 1896; *Times* (Washington, DC), Oct. 19, Dec. 4, 1895; Jan. 28, 29, June 15, 1896; *Washington Post,* Nov. 29, 1895; Jan. 21, 1896; *Indianapolis Freeman,* Jan. 18, Oct. 3, 1896; Daniel Murray Papers, reel 1; *Repository* (Canton, Ohio), Aug. 18, 1896; *Chicago Tribune,* Aug. 22, 1896.

6. *Washington Bee,* Dec. 25, 1896; Jan. 1, 16, 1897; Mary Church Terrell, "Society Among the Colored People of Washington," *The Voice of the Negro* 1 (1904): 152; *Evening Star,* Jan. 15, 20, 23, 1897; *Indianapolis Freeman,* Feb. 6, 1897.

7. *Idaho Statesman* (Boise, Idaho), Dec. 16, 1896; *Leavenworth Herald* (Leavenworth, KS), Dec. 19, 1896; *Washington Bee,* March 6, 1897; *Afro-American* (Baltimore), Feb. 1, 1941; *Evening Star,* Feb. 9, March 4, 8, 22, 1897; *Iowa State Bystander* (Des Moines), March 12, 1897; *Indianapolis Freeman,* March 13, 1897.

8. David C. Mearns, *The Story Up to Now: The Library of Congress, 1800–1946* (Washington, DC: Library of Congress, 1947), 125–26, 130, 134, 136–37, 139–41; U.S. Congress Joint Committee on the Library, *Condition of the Library of Congress, March 3, 1897,* 54th Congress, 2nd Session, Senate Report 1573 (Washington, DC: GPO, 1897), 33, 37–38, 40–42, 45; *Morning Times* (Washington, DC), Dec. 4, 1895 (note: the newspaper account erroneously identified the site of the accident as the attic of the new library; also see Mearns, *The Story Up to Now,* p. 139); *United States Official Register,* July 1895 and other years; *Report of the Librarian of Congress for the Calendar Year 1895* (Washington, DC: GPO, 1896); *Evening Star,* June 30, July 2, 1897; *New York Tribune,* July 2, 1897; *Washington Post,* July 12, 1897; *Library Journal* 22, no. 7 (July 1897): 366; John Y. Cole, *Jefferson's Legacy: A Brief History of the Library of Congress* (Washington, DC: Library of Congress, 1993), 26; James Conaway, *America's Library: The Story of the Library of Congress, 1800–2000* (New Haven, CT: Yale University Press, 2000), 90; Josephus Nelson and Judith Farley, *Full Circle: Ninety Years of Service in the Main Reading Room* (Washington, DC: Library of Congress, 1991), 12, 15.

9. Mearns, *The Story Up to Now,* 134, 138–40; U.S. Congress Joint Committee, *Condition of the Library of Congress,* 57, 62; *Library Journal* 22, no. 8 (August 1897): 414; *Library Journal* 22, no. 9 (September 1897): 453; *Library Journal* 22, no. 11 (November 1897): 230: Spofford, "The

Nation's Library," *Century Magazine* 53 (1897): 691–92; Herbert Small, comp., *Handbook of the New Library of Congress* (Boston: Curtis and Cameron, 1897), 127; *Idaho Stateman*, Dec. 16, 1896; *Evening Times* (Washington, DC), Dec. 18, 1896; *Washington Post*, July 12, 1897; *Washington Bee*, July 31, 1897; Daniel Murray Miscellaneous Personnel Files, Library of Congress Archives, Manuscript Division, Library of Congress; *Evening Star*, Nov. 26, 1896; Sept. 18, 1897.

10. U.S. Congress Joint Committee, *Condition of the Library of Congress*, 7, 8, 18, 28; Spofford, "The Nation's Library," 683–87; *Handbook of the New Library of Congress*, 128; *Evening Star*, Feb. 17, 1894; Feb. 10, Sept. 18, 1897; June 4, 1905; *Idaho Stateman*, Dec. 16, 1896; *Annual Report of the Librarian of Congress* (Washington, DC: GPO, 1897), 6, 9; "Book Delivery System at the Congressional Library, Washington," *Harper's Magazine*, Aug. 14, 1897, 804; *Washington Post*, Oct. 28, 1897; *Washington Bee*, July 10, 1897; Angela Jones, *African American Civil Rights: Early Activism and the Niagara Movement* (Santa Barbara, CA: Praeger, 2011), 216; *Cleveland Gazette*, Aug. 7, 1897; *Indianapolis Freeman*, Aug. 21, 1897; *Times* (Washington, DC), Aug. 22, 1897; *Seattle Republican*, Aug. 23, 1901.

7: Backsliding

1. Daniel Murray Miscellaneous Personnel Files, Library of Congress Archives Manuscript Division, Library of Congress; Edwin A. Lee, "Daniel Murray," *The Colored American Magazine* 5 (1902): 436; *Washington Times*, Aug. 22, 1897; *Evening Star* (Washington, DC), July 8, Aug. 24, 28, Sept. 1, 1897; *Washington Bee*, July 31, 1897; *Oregonian* (Portland), Jan. 20, 1939.

2. *Annual Report of the Librarian of Congress* (Washington, DC: GPO, 1897), 11; *Washington Bee*, Oct. 23, 1897; Adelaide M. Cromwell, *Unveiled Voices, Unvarnished Memories* (Columbia: University of Missouri Press, 2007), 226–27; *Evening Star*, Feb. 17, 1894; Aug. 28, Nov. 6, 23, Dec. 23, 1897; Dec. 6, 1908; United States Official Register for 1895, 1897, 1899; Sylvia Lyons Render, "The Black Presence at the Library of Congress," *Library Lectures* (nos. 21–28, 1975), 66–67; *Digest of Appropriations for the Support of the Government of the United States for the Fiscal Year Ending June 30, 1921* (Washington, DC: GPO, 1920), 29–30; *The First Colored Professsional, Clerical, Skilled, and Business Directory of Baltimore City (with Washington*

Annex), 9th Annual Edition, 1921–22, 101; Peter Armenti, "The Caged Bird Sings: Paul Laurence Dunbar at the Library of Congress," posted June 27, 2013, blogs.loc.gov/catbird/2013/06/the-caged-bird-sings-paul-laurence-dunbar-at-the-library-of-congress; *New York Tribune*, Dec. 8, 1897; Lida Keck Wiggins, *The Life and Works of Paul Laurence Dunbar* (Naperville, IL: J. L. Nichols and Company, 1907), 73; David C. Mearns, *The Story Up to Now: The Library of Congress 1800–1946* (Washington, DC: Library of Congress, 1947), 134; Josephus Nelson and Judith Farley, *Full Circle: Ninety Years of Service in the Main Reading Room* (Washington, DC: Library of Congress, 1991), 19; Lee, "Daniel Murray," 436; U.S. Congress Joint Committee on the Library, *Condition of the Library of Congress, March 3, 1897*, 54th Congress, 2nd Session, Senate Report 1573, (Washington, DC: GPO, 1897), 272.

3. Daniel Murray Miscellaneous Personnel Files, Library of Congress Archives; *Evening Star*, Aug. 24, Nov. 1, 2, 23, Dec. 23, 1897; Nov. 2, 1898; *Washington Times*, Jan. 19, 1897; Daniel Murray Papers, State Historical Society of Wisconsin, microfilm reel 27; Harriet Pierson, *Rosemary: Reminiscences of the Library of Congress* (Washington, DC: n.p., 1943), 14; *New York Tribune*, Dec. 8, 1897; Armenti, "The Caged Bird Sings"; Alice M. Dunbar, "The Poet and His Song," *AME Review* 12 (October 1914), 129; *Annual Report of the Librarian of Congress* (Washington, DC: GPO, 1899), 30.

4. *Colored American*, Feb. 1, 1902; *Weekly Louisianan*, Aug. 20, 1881; *People's Advocate*, Aug. 6, 1881; *Critic-Record* (Washington, DC), Feb. 12, 13, 1890; *Evening Star*, June 27, July 18, 1889; Feb. 12, 15, 1890; Edward Ingle, "The Negro in the District of Columbia," *Johns Hopkins University Studies in Historical and Political Science*, 11th series, ed. Herbert B. Adams (Baltimore: Johns Hopkins University Press, 1893), 47; Andrew W. Kahrl, *The Land Was Ours: African American Beaches from Jim Crow to the Sunbelt South* (Cambridge, MA: Harvard University Press, 2010), 88–89.

5. *Washington Bee*, July 30, 1887; Feb. 15, 1890; *Evening Star*, May 9, Dec. 10, 11, 1891; July 24, Aug. 27, Sept. 6, 24, 1895; Ingle, "The Negro in the District of Columbia," 55; Mary Church Terrell, *A Colored Woman in a White World* (Washington, DC: Ransdell, 1940), 113–14, 119; Ronald M. Johnson, "From Romantic Suburb to Racial Enclave: LeDroit Park, Washington, D.C., 1880–1920," *Phylon* 45, no. 4 (1984):

264–66; *National Republican,* June 13, 1873; *Washington Post,* July 24, Aug. 28, 1895; *Morning Times* (Washington, DC), Sept. 24, Oct. 13, 1895; Record Group 21 (Records of the District Courts), equity case file 16730, NARA; Paul E. Sluby, Sr., *Graceland Cemetery: Brief History and Records of Interments, 1872–1894* (Temple Hills, MD: Comprehensive Research, 2010), 190–91 in original ledger book.

6. *Washington Post,* Nov. 18, 1891; March 23, Oct. 31, 1892; May 19, 1894; *Evening Star,* July 7, 1896; May 6, 7, June 2, 3, 11, 1897; *Washington Bee,* Aug. 4, 1883; March 26, 1892; April 10, 1897; *Report of the Committee on Interstate and Foreign Commerce of the House of Representatives* (Washington, DC: GPO, 1902), 446–47.

8: Confronting Lost Ground

1. *Washington Bee,* May 31, 1890; Dec. 19, 1891; March 26, 1892; Dec. 25, 1896; *Washington Post,* Dec. 11, 1891; March 23, Oct. 31, 1892; *Evening Star,* (Washington, DC) Dec. 14, 1887; Edward Ingle, "The Negro in the District of Columbia," Johns Hopkins University Studies in Historical and Political Science, 11th series, ed. Herbert B. Adams (Baltimore: Johns Hopkins University Press), 57. Three helpful books on Washington and DuBois include: Jacqueline M. Moore, *Booker T. Washington, W. E. B. DuBois, and the Struggle for Racial Uplift* (Wilmington, DE: Scholarly Resources Books, 2003); David Levering Lewis, *W. E. B. DuBois, Biography of a Race, 1868–1919* (New York: Henry Holt, 1993); Louis R. Harlan, *Booker T. Washington: The Making of a Black Leader, 1856–1901* (New York: Oxford University Press, 1972).

2. Three useful books on the NAAC in general are Shawn Leigh Alexander, *An Army of Lions: The Civil Rights Struggle Before the NAACP* (Philadelphia: University of Pennsylvania Press, 2012); Susan D. Carle, *Defining the Struggle: National Organizing for Racial Justice* (Oxford, UK: Oxford University Press, 2013); and Benjamin R. Justesen, *Broken Brotherhood: The Rise and Fall of the National Afro-American Council* (Carbondale: Southern Illinois University Press, 2008); Alexander Walters, *My Life and Work* (New York: Fleming H. Revell Company, c. 1917), 98, 103–14; *Colored American,* Dec. 17, 24, 1898; Jan. 7, 1899; *Evening Star,* Dec. 24, 28, 1898; Jan. 3, 16, 1899; *Times* (Washington, DC), Dec. 28, 29, 30, 1898; *Daily Press* (Newport News, VA), Dec. 23, 1898; *Official Programme: First Annual Meeting of the Afro-American Council*

at the Metropolitan Baptist Church, Daniel Murray pamphlet collection, Library of Congress; *New York Sun*, Dec. 30, 1898; *Appeal* (St. Paul, MN), Jan. 14, 1899.

3. *Evening Star*, Dec. 29, 1898; Jan. 25, 30, April 6, 10, 1899; *Times* (Washington, DC), Dec. 29, 1898; Jan. 4, 30, 1899; *Colored American*, Dec. 17, 1898; Jan. 14, March 11, 25, April 1, 22, 1899; May 24, 1902; Daniel Murray, *Report of the Legal and Legislative Bureau*, March 1899, Daniel Murray Papers, State Historical Society of Wisconsin, microfilm reel 1; *Denver Post* (Denver, CO), Feb. 5, 1899; *New York Evening Post*, Feb. 21, 1899; Alexander Walters to Daniel Murray, Feb. 25, 1899, Daniel Murray Papers, reel 1; Edwin Lee, "Daniel Murray," *The Colored American Magazine* 5 (1902): 435–36, 440; Daniel Murray to George Myers, Aug. 11, 1899, George A. Myers Papers, Ohio Historical Society, microfilm edition; Daniel Murray to John E. Bruce, quoted in William Seraile, *Bruce Grit: The Black Nationalist Writings of John Edward Bruce* (Knoxville: University of Tennessee Press, 2003), 61.

4. *Colored American*, Dec. 24, 1898; Feb. 25, July 15, 22, 1899; June 23, 1900; Paul Evans Murray birth certificate, DC Archives; *Evening Star*, Feb. 11, 13, 15, 1899; *Kindergarten Magazine*, 11, no 7 (March 1899), 462; Venice Johnson, *Heart Full of Grace: A Thousand Years of Black Wisdom* (New York: Touchstone, 1997), 221; Mary Church Terrell, "The Duty of the National Association of Colored Women to the Race," *AME Church Review* (January 1900): 347; Anna J. Murray, "A New Key to the Situation," *Southern Workman* 29, no. 9 (September 1900): 504, 506; "The Kindergarten from Different Points of View," *Southern Workman* 30, no. 9 (June 1901): 361; *Daily American Citizen* (Kansas City), April 8, 1900; *Iowa State Bystander* (Des Moines), May 25, 1900; *Des Moines Daily News*, May 24, 1900.

5. *Colored American*, Feb. 3, 25, July 22, 1899; June 23, 30, July 28, Aug. 4, Sept. 14, Oct. 27, 1900; *Evening Times* (Washington, DC), June 6, 1900; Pauline E. Hopkins, "Famous Women of the Negro Race," *The Colored American Magazine* 5, no. 2 (1902): 274; *Omaha Daily Bee*, June 7, 1900; Rayford W. Logan, *The Betrayal of the Negro from Rutherford B. Hayes to Woodrow Wilson* (New York: Collier Books, 1954), 239–41; *Baltimore Sun*, July 19, 1900; Murray, "A New Key to the Situation," 503, 506–07; *Washington Post*, April 4, 1901; *Indianapolis Freeman*, June 29, 1901; Anna Evans Murray Oberlin College records; *Iowa State Bystander*,

June 1, 8, 1900; Daniel Murray to George A. Myers, July 14, 1899; Daniel Murray Papers, reel 2.

9: National Afro-American Council

1. Piero Gleijeses, "African Americans and the War Against Spain," in *A Question of Manhood: A Reader in U.S. Black Men's History and Masculinity*, eds. Earnestine Jenkins and Darlene Clark Hine (Bloomington: Indiana University Press, 2001), 322; *Indianapolis Freeman*, March 13, 1897; *Evening Star*, Jan. 17, 25, June 7, July 26, 27, Aug. 2, Dec. 24, 1898; Jan. 25, 1899; *New York Sun*, Dec. 30, 1898; *Washington Bee*, March 19, 1898; *Colored American*, May 28, 1898; Daniel Murray to George Myers, June 28, July 11, 1899, Aug. 11, Aug. 19, 1900; George A. Myers to Daniel Murray, Aug. 14, 1899, George A. Myers Papers, Ohio Historical Society microfilm edition; Daniel Murray Papers, State Historical Society of Wisconsin, microfilm reel 1; Ruth Martin, "Defending the Reconstruction: George A. Myers, Racism, Patronage, and Corruption in Ohio, 1879–1930," in *Before Obama: A Reappraisal of Black Reconstruction Era Politicians*, vol. 1, Matthew Lynch, ed. (Santa Barbara, CA: Praeger, 2012), 194–95, 198–99.

2. Gleijeses, "African Americans and the War against Spain," 323–24, 326, 335–38; *Evening Star*, May 30, July 11, 1898; Feb. 28, March 7, 8, Nov. 24, 1899; *Colored American*, May 28, 1898; June 24, July 15, Nov. 11, 1899; Edwin A. Lee, "Daniel Murray," *The Colored American Magazine* 5: 437–38; Daniel Murray to George Myers, July 14, July 29, Aug. 11, 1899; May 10, 19, 1900; *Tacoma Daily News* (Tacoma, WA), June 3, 1898; *New York Times*, June 22, 1898; George B. Cortelyou to Daniel Murray, Aug. 11, 1899, Daniel Murray Papers, reel 1; *Santa Fe Daily New Mexican*, Sept. 9, 1899; *Cleveland Gazette*, Dec. 2, 1899.

3. *Colored American*, May 6, June 24, Aug. 19, 26, Oct. 21, Dec. 2, 1899; Daniel Murray to George Myers, July 14, Aug. 11, 1899; *Iowa State Bystander* (Des Moines), Aug. 4, 1899; *Broad Ax* (Salt Lake City, UT), Aug. 26, 1899; *Evening Bulletin* (Maysville, KY), Aug. 23, 1899; Shawn Leigh Alexander, *An Army of Lions: The Civil Rights Struggle Before the NAACP* (Philadelphia: University of Pennsylvania Press, 2012), 109–10; *Baltimore Sun*, Aug. 18, 1899; *Appeal* (St. Paul, MN), Aug. 26, Oct. 7, 1899; *Indianapolis Freeman*, Sept. 2, 1899; *Washington Post*, Sept. 8, 1899;

New York Tribune, Oct. 3, 1899; *Evening Star*, Oct. 13, 1899; *Plain Dealer* (Topeka, KS), Oct. 12, 20, 1899.

4. *Colored American*, Nov. 25, Dec. 2, 9, 16, 1899; Jan. 6, 13, 27, March 3, April 28, 1900; Shawn Leigh Alexander, "The Afro-American Council and Its Challenge of Louisiana's Grandfather's Clause," in *Radicalism in the South Since Reconstruction*, eds. Chris Green et al. (New York: Palgrave Macmillan, 2006), 17–21; Benjamin R. Justesen, *George Henry White: An Even Chance in the Race of Life* (Baton Rouge: Louisiana State University Press, 2001), 270, 273, 279, 285–86, 293; *New York Times*, March 5, 1900; Booker T. Washington to Emmett Scott, March 11, 1900, in Booker T. Washington, *Booker T. Washington Papers*, vol. 5, eds. Louis R. Harlan and Raymond W. Smock (Champaign: University of Illinois Press, 1977), 457; *Washington Post*, March 13, 1898; June 5, 1900; Daniel Murray to George Myers, May 10, 14, 19, 26, undated (c. June 23), June 25, 1900.

5. *Colored American*, Dec. 9, 1899; Jan. 13, Feb. 10, June 30, Sept. 8, 1900; *New York Times*, June 18, 1900; Daniel Murray to George Myers, May 6, July 6, 1900; *Washington Bee*, June 23, 1900; *Washington Post*, Oct. 31, 1892; Justesen, *George Henry White*, 293; *Indianapolis Freeman*, Aug. 4, Sept. 1, 1900; *Appeal* (St. Paul, MN), Aug. 25, 1900; *Cleveland Gazette*, Sept. 8, 1900; Edwin A. Lee, "Daniel Murray," *The Colored American Magazine* 5: 440; Mitch Kachun, "A Beacon to Oppressed Peoples Everywhere: Major Richard R. Wright Sr., National Freedom Day, and the Rhetoric of Freedom in the 1940s," *Pennsylvania Magazine of History and Biography* 128, no. 3 (July 2004), 285–86.

6. Daniel Murray Papers, reels 2, 27; Harvard University Catalogue, 1900–1901; *Colored American*, Nov. 4, 25, 1899; Dec. 8, 15, 1900; June 11, 1904; federal census for 1900; Daniel Murray to George Myers, Dec. 9, 22, 30, 1900; For an overall review of the exhumation and reinterment of John Brown's raiders, see Gordon L. Iseminger, "The Second Raid on Harpers Ferry, July 29, 1899: The Other Bodies That Lay A'mouldering in Their Graves," *Pennsylvania History* 71 (2004); *Washington Post*, Nov. 13, 1898; Thomas Featherstonhaugh, "John Brown's Men: The Lives of Those Killed at Harpers Ferry," *Publications of the Southern History Association* 3 (1899): 17, 21–23; Thomas Featherstonhaugh, "The Final Burial of the Followers of John Brown," *New England Magazine* 24 (1901): 133–34; *New York Tribune*, Aug. 31,

Sept. 18, 21, 1899; *Kansas Semi-Weekly Capital* (Topeka), Jan. 9, 1900; Langston Hughes, *The Big Sea: An Autobiography* (New York: Alfred A. Knopf, 1940), 9, 12; Benjamin Quarles, *Allies for Freedom: Blacks and John Brown* (New York: Oxford University Press, 1974) 173–74; Curator's file on Langston blanket shawl, Ohio Historical Society.

7. Daniel Murray Papers, reel 27; *Evening Star*, Oct. 26, 27, 1897, March 2, 1901; *Washington Bee*, Aug. 31, 1895; Oct. 30, 1897; *Washington Post*, Nov. 16, 1890; March 23, 1892; Sept. 12, 1900; Daniel Murray to George Myers, Jan. 21, Dec. 28, 1901; Mary Church Terrell, "The Duty of the National Association of Colored Women to the Race," *AME Church Review* (January 1900): 346; *Colored American*, Sept. 30, 1899; Sept. 6, 1902; Andrew W. Kahrl, *The Land Was Ours: African American Beaches from Jim Crow to the Sunbelt South* (Cambridge, MA: Harvard University Press, 2010), 89; Audrey Elisa Kerr, *The Paper Bag Principle: Class, Colorism, and Rumor and the Case of Black Washington, D.C.* (Knoxville: University of Tennessee Press, 2006), xi, xiv, 60.

8. *Colored American*, Dec. 8, 1900; Jan. 12, Feb. 16, March 16, 1901; Daniel Murray to George Myers, Dec. 2, 22, 30, 1900; Jan. 21, Feb. 23, March 16, 1901; Daniel Murray Papers, reel 27; *Evening Star*, Dec. 24, 1900; *Appeal* (St. Paul, MN), March 9, 1901; *Plain Dealer* (Topeka, KS), March 15, 1901; Paul Laurence Dunbar, "Negro Society in Washington," *Saturday Evening Post*, Dec. 14, 1901, 9.

9. Justesen, *George Henry White*, 307–11 (White's farewell speech was delivered on January 29, 1901); Alexander, "The Afro-American Council and Its Challenge of Louisiana's Grandfather's Clause," 21–25.

10: Black History Pioneer

1. Alexander Walters, *My Life and Work* (New York: Fleming H. Revell Company, c. 1917), 108–09; *New York Times*, July 31, 1898; *Evening Star*, Jan. 30, 1899; Daniel Murray to George Myers, May 10, 1900, George A. Myers Papers, Ohio Historical Society microfilm edition; *Times* (Washington, DC), Nov. 3, 4, 1899; *Colored American*, Nov. 3, 1900; Daniel Murray Miscellaneous Personnel Files, Library of Congress Archives, Manuscript Division, Library of Congress.

2. Daniel Murray Papers, State Historical Society of Wisconsin, microfilm reel 1; Daniel Murray Miscellaneous Personnel Files, Library of Congress Archives; *Washington Post*, Jan. 22, 1900; *Colored American*,

March 31, Nov. 3, 1900; *Bureau of Education Report for the Year of 1893–94*, vol. 1 (Washington, DC: GPO, 1896), 1056–61; Michael Benjamin, "A 'Colored Authors Collection' to Exhibit to the World and Educate a Race," in *Education and the Culture of Print in Modern America*, eds. Adam N. Nelson and John L. Randolph (Madison: University of Wisconsin Press, 2010), 44–45.

3. Daniel Murray Papers, reel 1; Daniel Murray Miscellaneous Personnel Files, Library of Congress Archives; Daniel Murray to George Myers, April 23, May 10, 1900; *Colored American*, March 10, Nov. 3, 1900; *New York Times*, Paris Exposition Edition, Oct. 9, 1900; Miles Everett Travis, "Mixed Messages: Thomas Calloway and the 'American Negro Exhibit' of 1900" (master's thesis, Montana State University, 2004), 19–21, 45–47, 63; Thomas Calloway, "The American Negro Exhibit at the Paris Exposition," *Hampton Negro Conference* 5 (1901), 78; W. E. B. DuBois, "The American Negro at Paris," *American Monthly Review of Reviews* 22 (1900): 576–77.

4. *New York Times*, May 12, 1900; *Colored American*, March 31, Sept. 15, 1900; *Washington Bee*, Sept. 28, 1901; *Daily Herald* (Biloxi, MS), June 22, 1900; Daniel Murray Papers, reel 1; Daniel Murray to George Myers, May 6, 1900; Daniel Murray, "Bibliographia-Africania," *The Voice of the Negro* 1 (1904): 190–91; Daniel Murray, *Preliminary List of Books and Pamphlets by Negro Authors* (Washington, DC: Library of Congress, 1900); *Annual Report of the Librarian of Congress* (Washington, DC: GPO, 1900, 1901), 18, 365, respectively.

5. Daniel Murray Papers, reels 1, 24; Daniel Murray Miscellaneous Personnel Files, Library of Congress Archives; Daniel Murray to George Myers, April 23, July 6, 1900; Murray, "Bibliographia-Africania," 186–87; *Colored American*, June 24, 1899: May 5, 1900; *Evening Star*, Feb. 15, 1905.

6. Daniel Murray Papers, reels 1, 2, 24; Daniel Murray Miscellaneous Personnel Files, Library of Congress Archives; Daniel Murray to George Myers, Dec. 2, 1900; Andrew F. Hilyer, ed., *The Twentieth Century Union League Directory* (Washington, DC, The Union League 1901); *Washington Bee*, Aug. 24, 1901.

7. *New York Times*, May 12, 1900; Daniel Murray to George Myers, June 23, 30, Aug. 21, Sept. 6, 13, 1901; *Chicago Broad Ax*, Dec. 12, 1925; Travis, "Mixed Messages," 75.

8. *Colored American*, Feb. 24, March 13, 1900; Jan. 26, March 16, May 18, Aug. 10, 1901; Feb. 22, Sept. 13, 1902; *Evening Star*, April 19, May 11, 1900; Feb. 15, 1902; *Indianapolis Freeman*, Jan. 26, 1901; *Plain Dealer* (Topeka, KS), March 15, 1901; *Washington Bee*, Dec. 22, 1900; Feb. 15, 22, 1902.

9. *Colored American*, Sept. 30, 1899; Jan. 12, May 18, 1901; May 10, May 31, 1902; July 25, 1903; *Evening Star*, April 29, 1904; Daniel Murray Papers, reel 1; Daniel Murray to George Myers, Jan. 21, 1901; Daniel Murray, "Cyrus Field Adams: Assistant Register of the United States Treasury," *The Colored American Magazine* 4 (1901): 149–53; Federal census and Washington city directory data; Cyrus Field Adams, *National Afro-American Council* (Washington, DC, NAAC, 1902).

11: Courting Controversy

1. Lawrence Otis Graham, *The Senator and the Socialite: The True Story of America's First Black Dynasty* (New York: HarperPerennial, 2006), 142; *Colored American*, Nov. 3, 1900; March 29, April 12, 26, Sept. 20, Oct. 4, 18, 1902; Daniel Murray Papers, State Historical Society of Wisconsin, microfilm reels 1, 27; *Evening Times* (Washington, DC), March 20, Oct. 6, 1902; *Washington Bee*, March 29, April 5, Aug. 30, Sept. 13, 20, Oct. 18, 1902; *Washington Post*, Aug. 20, Sept. 12, 1902; *Evening Star*, Oct. 7, 10, 1902.

2. *Colored American*, Sept. 21, 1901; Feb. 1, 22, Sept. 6, 1902; *Evening Star*, Jan. 30, 1899; Sept. 14, 1901; *Washington Post*, Aug. 7, 1902; Feb. 2, 1903; Arthur O. White, "Booker T. Washington's Florida Incident," *The Florida Historical Quarterly* 51 (1973), 231–32; *Grand Rapids Press* (Grand Rapids, MI), May 9, 1903; "Dr. Bentley at the Dentists' Congress," *The Voice of the Negro* 1 (1904): 443–44.

3. Daniel Murray Papers, reels 1, 2 ("The Power of Blood Inheritance" essay); Edwin Lee, "Daniel Murray," *The Colored American Magazine* 5 (1902): 432–33; *Colored American*, May 18, 1901; Daniel Murray, "The Color Line Problem in the United States," *The Colored American Magazine* 7 (1904): 719–23; C. V. Roman, *American Civilization and the Negro* (Philadelphia: F. A. Davis, 1921), 399–400.

4. Daniel Murray, "Bibliographia-Africania," *The Voice of the Negro* 1 (1904): 187; Murray, "The Color Line Problem," 719–20, 722–24; Daniel Murray, "Struggling to Rise; Or the Handicaps of the Colored Race:

Just and Unjust," *AME Church Review* 29 (1913): 247; Daniel Murray Papers, reels 1, 2; *Evening Star*, Feb. 15, 1905; Daniel Murray to George Myers, Oct. 6, 1901 Ohio Historical Society, microfilm edition; Thomas J. Brown, *Civil War Canon: Sites of Confederate Memory in South Carolina* (Chapel Hill: University of North Carolina Press, 2015), 21–23.

5. Daniel Murray Papers, reel 2; Daniel Murray, "Race Integrity—How to Preserve It in the South," *The Colored American Magazine* 11 (1906): 369–73, 375–77; Daniel Murray, "Struggling to Rise," 252; *Cleveland Gazette*, March 25, 1905; *Harper's Weekly*, March 11, 1905; *Indianapolis Recorder*, Dec. 27, 1902; *Afro-American Ledger* (Baltimore), June 29, 1907; Willard Gatewood, *Aristocrats of Color: The Black Elite, 1880–1920* (Bloomington: Indiana University Press, 1990), 142, 173; *New York Times*, June 11, 1907; Murray, "The Color Line Problem," 724; *Colored American*, March 29, Sept 13, 1902.

12: Struggling

1. Murray Papers, State Historical Society of Wisconsin, microfilm reels 1, 27; Shawn Leigh Alexander, "The Afro-American Council and Its Challenge of Louisiana's Grandfather's Clause," in *Radicalism in the South Since Reconstruction*, eds. Chris Green et al. (New York: Palgrave Macmillan, 2006), 28–33; Susan D. Carle, *Defining the Struggle: National Organizing for Racial Justice, 1880–1915* (Oxford, UK: Oxford University Press, 2013), 128; Shawn Leigh Alexander, *An Army of Lions: The Civil Rights Struggle Before the NAACP* (Philadelphia: University of Pennsylvania Press, 2012), 180–82; Daniel Murray to George Myers, May 24, June 27, 1902, George A. Myers Papers, Ohio Historical Society, microfilm edition; *Evening Star*, March 25, May 15, 1902; *Colored American*, April 5, May 3, 10, June 21, Oct. 4, 1902; *Washington Post*, April 15, 1902; Booker T. Washington, *Booker T. Washington Papers*, vol. 6, eds. Louis R. Harlan and Raymond W. Smock (Champaign: University of Illinois Press, 1977), 446–47.

2. Daniel Murray to George Myers, May 24, 1902, Dec. 8, 1903; Alexander, *An Army of Lions*, 182–83; *Washington Post*, April 15, 1902; *Washington Times*, May 10, 1902; *Report of the Committee of Interstate and Foreign Commerce of the House of Representatives* (Washington, DC: GPO, 1902), 444; *Colored American*, May 24, Sept. 13, 1902; Jan. 2, 1904; Glen Feldman, *Before Brown: Civil Rights and White Backlash in the Modern*

South (Tuscaloosa: University of Alabama Press, 2004), 25; *Plain Dealer* (Cleveland, OH), Dec. 10, 1903; *Indianapolis Freeman*, May 7, 1904; "The Aggressiveness of Jim-Crowism," *The Voice of the Negro* 1 (1904): 217; *Macon* (Georgia) *Telegraph*, Sept. 15, 1905; Daniel Murray, "The Overthrow of 'Jim Crow' Car Laws," *The Voice of the Negro* 2 (1906): 520–21; *Patriot* (Harrisburg, PA), Sept. 24, 1904; *Baltimore Sun*, Oct. 5, 1904.

3. Daniel Murray to George Myers, Sept. 6, Oct. 6, Dec. 28, 1901; Dec. 6, 1902; Daniel Murray Papers, reels 1, 2, 27; Federal census data; Ellen Butler 1901 death certificate (record no. 139475) and will (box 205), DC Archives; *Washington Bee*, March 31, 1900; Oct. 17, 1908; *Evening Star*, March 17, April 2, 1902.

4. *Colored American*, May 3, 1902; Daniel Murray to George Myers, Oct. 6, 19, 1901; Aug. 14, 1902; Daniel Murray, "Bibliographia-Africania," 187; Anna Murray, "In Behalf of the Negro Woman," *Southern Workman* 33 (1904), 232; *Afro-American Ledger* (Baltimore, MD), July 19, 1902.

5. *Colored American*, May 18, June 15, Aug. 10, 1901; Aug. 30, Nov. 1, 1902; *Washington Bee*, June 1, 1901; Daniel Murray to George Myers, Dec. 6, 1902; Wilson Bruce Evans, "Armstrong Manual Training School," *The Colored American Magazine* 7 (1904), 535; *Evening Star*, Nov. 11, 1902; Jan. 7, 1903; *Plain Dealer* (Topeka, KS), March 15, 1901; Allan B. Slauson, ed., *A History of the City of Washington* (Washington, DC: Washington Post, 1903), 102.

6. Daniel Murray to George Myers, Dec. 28, 1901; Dec. 6, 1902; Jan. 5, 1903; *Evening Star*, Dec. 25, 26, 27, 1902; *Washington Post*, Dec. 30, 1902.

7. Daniel Murray to George Myers, Aug. 14, Dec. 6, 1902; Jan. 5, March 10, 1903; June 3, 1905; *Washington Bee*, Jan. 10, 1903; Andrew F. Hilyer, ed., *The Twentieth Century Union League Directory* (Washington, DC, The Union League 1901), 12, 16.

8. *Colored American*, Feb. 21, March 7, 14, and 21, 1903; Daniel Murray Papers, reel 4; Daniel Murray to George Myers, March 10, 1903; *Evening Star*, March 4, 1903.

9. "A Movement for Race Harmony," *World Today* 6 (1904): 15, 17; *How to Solve the Race Problem: The Proceedings of the Washington Conference on the Race Problem in the United States* (Washington, DC: Beresford Printers, 1904), 3, 7, 23, 38, 252–55; *Evening Star*, Nov. 10, 11, 1903;

Washington Post, Nov. 10, 13, 1903; *Washington Times*, Nov. 10, 1903; *Charlotte* (North Carolina) *Daily Observer*, Nov. 13, 1903; *Colored American*, Sept. 19, Dec. 19, 1903; Daniel Murray to George Myers, Dec. 25, 1903.

10. Daniel Murray, "The Industrial Problem in the United States and the Negro's Relation to It," *The Voice of the Negro* 1 (part I, no. 9, September 1904; part II, no. 11, November 1904), part I, 403–06, part II, 548, 551–52; Robert L. Harris, Jr., "Daniel Murray and the Encyclopedia of the Colored Race," *Phylon* 37 (1976): 276–78; *Colored American*, Oct. 7, 14, 1899; May 24, 1902; Louis R. Harlan and Raymond W. Smock, eds., *Booker T. Washington Papers*, vol. 7 (Champaign: University of Illinois Press, 1977), 33–35; *Washington Bee*, Feb. 7, 1903; Dec. 10, 17, 1904; "Strong Words on 'The Industrial Problem,' " *The Voice of the Negro* 1 (1904): 489; "Still After Murray," *The Voice of the Negro* 2 (1905): 95.

13: Father and Sons

1. *New York Tribune*, Oct. 19, 1904; *Colored American*, Oct. 19, Dec. 7, 1901; June 14, 1902; Jan. 10, June 7, 1903; *Washington Times*, May 27, 1903; *Evening Star*, April 13, Nov. 17, 1904; Jeffrey Green, *Samuel Coleridge-Taylor, a Musical Life* (New York: Routledge, 2011), 130–31; Daniel Murray to George Myers, May 4, 1905, George A. Myers Papers, Ohio Historical Society, microfilm edition; Andrew F. Hilyer, ed., *The Twentieth Century Union League Directory* (Washington, DC, 1901), 153; Eric Ledell Smith "Lillian Evanti: Washington's African-American Diva," *Washington History* 11 (1999): 26–29; federal census and city directory data.

2. Daniel Murray Papers, State Historical Society of Wisconsin, microfilm reel 1; *Washington Post*, Jan. 3, March 4, 1905; *Evening Star*, Jan. 26, 1905; Mary Church Terrell, "The Social Functions During Inauguration Week," *The Voice of the Negro* 2 (1905): 237–38, 241–42; *Washington Bee*, Dec. 24, 1904; Daniel Murray to George Myers, undated but from internal evidence late February 1905.

3. Daniel Murray to George Myers, undated but from internal evidence late February 1905, May 4, June 3, 1905; Daniel Murray Papers, reel 27; *Washington Post*, Dec. 14, 1965; George Henry Murray, "Educated Colored Men and White Women," *The Colored American Magazine* 8

(1905): 93–95; Nathaniel Murray alumni file, Cornell University Archives; Daniel A. P. Murray Pamphlet Collection, Library of Congress; Hallie E. Queen, "Mrs. Mary Church Terrell at Cornell University," *The Voice of the Negro* 3 (1906): 639–40; Herman "Skip" Mason, Jr., *The Talented Tenth: The Founders and Presidents of Alpha* (Winter Park, FL: Four-G Publishers, 1999), 99–100, 370–71; Charles H. Wesley, *The History of Alpha Phi Alpha* (Chicago: Foundation Publishers, 1929, 1950), 19–21; Carol Kammen, *Part and Apart: The Black Experience at Cornell, 1865–1945* (Ithaca, NY: Cornell University Library, 2009), xii, 15; April 2016 email communication with Alpha Phi Alpha historian Robert L. Harris, Jr.

4. *Colored American*, Aug. 10, 1901; Sept. 13, 1902; Murray, "Bibliographia-Africania," *The Voice of the Negro* 1 (1904): 187, 191; *New York Tribune*, Dec. 29, 1904; Daniel Murray, "Who Invented the Cotton Gin?," *The Voice of the Negro* 1 (1905): 97–98, 101; For more on the Eli Whitney debate, see Angela Lakwete, *Inventing the Cotton Gin: Machine and Myth in Antebellum America* (Baltimore: Johns Hopkins University Press, 2003); *Indianapolis Recorder*, June 29, 1907; Daniel Murray to George Myers, undated but from internal evidence late February 1905, June 23, 1907; *Harper's Weekly*, March 11, 1905; Daniel Murray Papers, reels 1, 2, 24; David C. Mearns, *The Story Up to Now: the Library of Congress 1800–1946* (Washington, DC: Library of Congress, 1947), 85; *Broad Ax* (Salt Lake City, Utah), Sept. 5, 1914.

5. *Washington Bee*, Feb. 26, 1906; March 28, 1908; Aug. 7, 1909; April 23, 1910; Daniel Murray Papers, reel 1; *Washington Post*, Feb. 16, 1906; *Colored American*, March 28, 1903; *Evening Star*, Nov. 19, 1905; Dec. 29, 1906; federal census data; Carter G. Woodson, "The Wormley Family," *Negro History Bulletin* 11 (1948), 78–80.

6. Anna Murray, "In Behalf of the Negro Woman," *Southern Workman* 33 (1904): 232–33; Eleanor Tayleur, "The Negro Woman: Social and Moral Decadence," *Outlook* 76 (1904): 266–68, 270; Anna E. Murray, "The Negro Children of America," *American Motherhood* 21 (1905): 19; *Evening Star*, Jan. 1, 1901; March 17, 1905; March 13, June 3, 5, 10, 1906; Mary Church Terrell, "What It Means to Be Colored in the Capital of the United States," *Independent* 62 (1907): 210; *House Committee on the District of Columbia Report of Hearings before the Subcommittee on the Several School Bills Relating to the Reorganization of the Schools of the District*

of Columbia (Washington, DC: GPO, 1906), 247–48; *Washington Post,* March 29, April 5, 1906; Daniel Murray Papers, reels 1, 2; *Washington Bee,* March 18, April 6, 1907; June 12, 1909.

7. *Final Report of the Jamestown Ter-Centennial Commission Embodying Reports of the Various Officers of the Jamestown Exposition* (Washington, DC: GPO, 1909), 138–43, 147–49, 152; *Evening Star,* Oct. 26, Nov. 9, Dec. 23, 1906; *Washington Post,* Dec. 23, 1906; *Washington Bee,* March 17, Dec. 29, 1906; April 6, July 6, Aug. 10, Sept. 7, 1907; *Duluth* (Minnesota) *News-Tribune,* June 11, 1907; R. W. Thompson, "The Negro Exhibit at Jamestown," *The Colored American Magazine* 13 (1907): 27–28, 30–33; Daniel Murray Miscellaneous Personnel Files, Library of Congress Archives Manuscript Division, Library of Congress; Daniel Murray to George Myers, June 23, 1907; Daniel Murray Papers, reel 1; W. E. B. DuBois to *Appeal to Reason* (Girard, KS), April 8, 1907.

8. Daniel Murray to George Myers, June 23, 1907; John D. Weave, *The Brownsville Raid* (College Station: Texas A&M University Press, 1992), 66, 71, 114, 116–17, 182–85; *Washington Times,* Feb. 23, 1908; *Washington Herald,* March 6, 1908; *Evening Star,* March 15, June 11, 15, 16, 21, 1908; *Washington Post,* April 29, 1908; March 3, 1909; *Indianapolis Freeman,* May 2, 1908; *Washington Bee,* May 23, 1908; March 13, 1909; *Emporia* [Kansas] *Gazette,* June 18, 1908; Daniel Murray Papers, reel 27.

14: Disillusioned

1. Daniel Murray Papers, State Historical Society of Wisconsin, microfilm reels 1, 2, 27; *Washington Bee,* Nov. 9, 1910; March 18, 1911; *New York Age,* June 30, Oct. 27, 1910; *Acetylene Journal* 15 (1913): 113; *Trenton Evening Times,* Jan. 25, 1912; R. Reid Badger, "James Reese Europe and the Prehistory of Jazz," *American Music* 7 (1989): 48, 50–51; David Gilbert, *The Product of Our Souls: Ragtime, Race, and the Birth of the Manhattan Musical Marketplace* (Chapel Hill: University of North Carolina Press, 2015), 2, 105–06, 134, 136–37, 153; *Washington Bee,* Oct. 12, 1912; *Evening Star,* Nov. 4, 1908; Aug. 26, Oct. 23, 1911; Sept. 21, Oct. 4, 1912; *Indianapolis Freeman,* July 22, Aug. 25, 1911; Aug. 17, 1912; July 3, 1915; federal census and city directory data; Nathaniel Murray and Harold Murray alumni files, Cornell University Archives; Charles H. Wesley, *The History of Alpha Phi Alpha* (Chicago: Foundation Publishers, 1929, 1950), 25, 39, 82; *Southern Workman* 46 (1917): 249–50, and 48 (1919):

512; Marjorie Lockett, "His Own Man," *Mexican-American Review* 9 (1971), 30; *New York Times*, Nov. 10, 1912; *Washington Post*, Jan. 9, 1913.

2. *Cleveland Gazette*, Aug. 12, 1905; *New York Age*, July 27, 1905; Aug. 29, 1908; *Washington Bee*, Aug. 12, 1905; Aug. 25, 1906; July 6, 1907; July 18, 1908; Shawn Leigh Alexander, *An Army of Lions: The Civil Rights Struggle Before the NAACP* (Philadelphia: University of Pennsylvania Press, 2012), 244–45, 260, 278, 290, 293–95; J. Max Barber, "The Significance of the Niagara Movement," *The Voice of the Negro* 2 (1905): 600–603; W. E. B. DuBois, "The Niagara Movement," *The Voice of the Negro* 2 (1905): 619–21; Christopher E. Forth, "Booker T. Washington and the 1905 Niagara Movement Conference," *Journal of Negro History* 72 (1987): 46–47, 51–52, 54; J. Max Barber, "The Niagara Movement at Harpers Ferry," *The Voice of the Negro* 3 (1906): 408, 410; Katherine Mayo, interview with Henrietta Leary Evans, March 5, 1908, Box 12, John Brown–Oswald Villard Papers, Columbia University Rare Book and Manuscript Library; Daniel Murray to W. E. B. DuBois, Dec. 20, 1907, W. E. B. DuBois Papers, University of Massachusetts Amherst Archives; *Evening Star*, Aug. 14, 1908; *Washington Post*, Aug. 16, 1908; *Indianapolis Freeman*, Aug. 31, 1907.

3. *Presbyterian Banner* (Pittsburgh), Sept. 30, 1909; *Evening Star*, Dec. 13, 1908; March 27, May 1, 1910; Daniel Murray Papers, reels 1, 27; *Macon Telegraph*, Nov. 13, 1903; *Washington Post*, Dec. 20, 1908; *Baltimore Afro-American*, Jan. 30, 1909; *Washington Bee*, May 14, 1910.

15: Life's Work

1. Daniel Murray Papers, State Historical Society of Wisconsin, microfilm reels 1, 2; Daniel Murray Miscellaneous Personnel Files, Library of Congress Archives Manuscript Division, Library of Congress; *Evening Star*, Oct. 13, 1935.

2. Daniel Murray Papers, reel 27; *Cleveland Gazette*, Nov. 26, 1910; *Evening Star*, Oct. 13, 1935; *Washington Bee*, June 22, 1912; *Baltimore Afro-American*, April 9, Oct. 22, 1910; "Notes," *Journal of Negro History* 15 (1930): 384–86; *The Crisis* 16 (1918): 86; United States Official Register for 1909, 1917; *Annual Report of the Librarian of Congress* (Washington, DC: GPO, 1912), 13.

3. Daniel Murray Papers, reels 1, 2, 27; *Evening Star*, Oct. 13, 1935; *The Crisis* 5 (1912), 6; *Baltimore Afro-American*, July 27, 1912; Daniel Murray

to George Myers, Nov. 23, 1912, George A. Myers Papers, Ohio Historical Society, microfilm edition.

4. *Cleveland Gazette*, Jan. 27, Nov. 16, 1912; *Evening Star*, Sept. 30, 1911; Nov. 7, 1912; Daniel Murray Papers, reel 1; *Washington Bee*, June 18, 1910; April 13, 1912; *Washington Herald*, March 21, 1912.

5. Daniel Murray Papers, reels 1, 27; *Indianapolis Freeman*, Dec. 7, 1912; Dec. 12, 1914; *Washington Bee*, July 12, 1913; May 8, July 31, 1915; *Washington Post*, Sept. 22, 1913; Oct. 28, Dec. 7, 10, 1915; Jan. 14, 1916; Daniel Murray to George Myers, Nov. 4, 1915; *Washington Times*, May 8, 1916.

6. *Washington Bee*, June 8, 1912; Jan. 9, 1915; federal census data; Mara Cherkasky, " 'For Sale to Colored': Racial Change on S Street NW," *Washington History* 8 (1996–1997): 41, 43, 45, 47–50.

7. Eric S. Yellin, *Racism in the Service of the Nation: Government Workers and the Color Line in Woodrow Wilson's America* (Chapel Hill: University of North Carolina Press, 2013), 107–111, 159–162; Cleveland M. Green, "Prejudices and Empty Promises: Woodrow Wilson's Betrayal of the Negro, 1910–1919," *The Crisis* 87 (1980): 381–386; *Indianapolis Recorder*, June 12, 1909; *Washington Bee*, Sept. 9, 1916; Nov. 3, 1917; Jan. 24, 1920; NAACP Records, box C 280, Manuscript Division, Library of Congress; Stephen R. Fox, *The Guardian of Boston: William Monroe Trotter* (New York: Atheneum, 1970), 180–181; Daniel Murray to George Myers, Sept. 19, 1916.

8. *Washington Bee*, March 29, 1913; June 13, 1914; Daniel Murray Papers, reel 24; Mary Church Terrell, "What It Means to Be Colored in the Capital of the United States," *The Independent* 62 (1907), reprinted in *American Speeches: Political Oratory from Abraham Lincoln to Bill Clinton*, ed. Ted Widmer (New York: Library of America, 2006), 204–05, 208, 211–12; Neval H. Thomas, "The District of Columbia—a Paradise of Paradoxes," *The Messenger* 5 (1923), reprinted in *These "Colored" United States: African American Essays from the 1920s*, eds. Tom Lutz and Susanna Ashton (New Brunswick: Rutgers University Press, 1996), 79, 80; *Evening Star*, March 13, 1922; *Broad Ax* (Chicago), June 10, 17, 1922.

16: Ironic Fruits

1. Ralph W. Tyler, "Affairs at Washington," *The Colored American Magazine* 16 (1909): 229–30; Jacqueline M. Moore, *Leading the Race: The Transformation of the Black Elite in the Nation's Capital, 1880–1920* (Char

lottesville: University Press of Virginia, 1999), 156; *Baltimore Afro-American*, Oct. 29, 1910; *Indianapolis Recorder*, Dec. 3, 1910; *Washington Bee*, Feb. 18, May 13, Sept. 9, 1911; *Evening Star*, July 2, 1911; March 3, 1913; Daniel Murray Papers, State Historical Society of Wisconsin, microfilm reel 27; *Springfield* [Massachusetts] *Republican*, May 31, 1911; *Chicago Broad Ax*, Oct. 14, 1911; *The Crisis* 5 (1913): 296.

2. Daniel Murray Papers, reel 27; *Washington Bee*, March 13, 1905; Jan. 23, 1909; April 24, Dec. 28, 1915, Nov. 18, 1916; *Indianapolis Freeman*, Dec. 7, 1912; Feb. 1, 1913; Greater U Street Historic District, National Register of Historic Places, NPS, section 8, page 30; *Baltimore Afro-American*, Jan. 28, 1928; Willard Gatewood, *Aristocrats of Color: The Black Elite, 1880–1920* (Bloomington: Indiana University Press, 1990), 47; also see Elizabeth Dowling Taylor, *A Slave in the White House: Paul Jennings and the Madisons* (New York: St. Martin's Press, 2012).

3. Daniel Murray Papers, reel 2; *Washington Post*, Oct. 22, 1933; Bettye Gardner and Bettye Thomas, "The Cultural Impact of the Howard Theater on the Black Community," *Journal of Negro History* 55 (1970): 254–55; *Washington Bee*, Aug. 6, 1910; *Evening Star*, Feb. 23, 1915. Also see Michael Andrew Fitzpatrick, "Shaw, Washington's Premier Black Neighborhood: An Examination of the Origins and Development of a Black Business Movement, 1880–1920" (master's thesis, Brown University, 1987) and Blair A. Ruble, *Washington's U Street: A Biography* (Washington, DC: Woodrow Wilson Center Press, 2010).

4. *Indianapolis Freeman*, March 20, 1915; *Washington Bee*, Jan. 21, 1911; *Chicago Defender*, Oct. 2, Nov. 6, 1915; Daniel Murray Papers, reel 27; David Gilbert, *The Product of Our Souls: Ragtime, Race, and the Birth of the Manhattan Musical Marketplace* (Chapel Hill: University of North Carolina Press, 2015), 103–05, 156; Reid Badger, *A Life in Ragtime: A Biography of James Reese Europe* (New York: Oxford University Press, 1995), 132–33; *Washington Post*, Jan. 20, 2012.

5. Ralph L. Crowder, *John Edward Bruce: Politician, Journalist, and Self-Trained Historian of the African Diaspora* (New York: New York University Press, 2004), 91–92, 105–26; *Philadelphia Tribune*, Feb. 17, 1912; Daniel Murray Papers, reels 2, 27; Michael Benjamin, "A 'Colored Authors Collection' to Exhibit to the World and Educate a Race," in *Education and the Culture of Print in Modern America*, eds. Adam N. Nelson and John L. Randolph (Madison: University of Wisconsin Press, 2010),

51–52; Daniel Murray Miscellaneous Personnel Files, Library of Congress Archives Manuscript Division, Library of Congress; Jacqueline Goggin, *Carter G. Woodson: A Life in Black History* (Baton Rouge: Louisiana State University Press, 1993), 23, 31–36; *Baltimore Afro-American,* Jan. 2, 1915; *Bystander* (Des Moines, IA), Feb. 2, 1917; Elinor Des Verney Sinnette, W. Paul Coates, Thomas C. Battle, eds., *Black Bibliophiles and Collectors: Preservers of Black History* (Washington, DC: Howard University Press, 1990), 10–11; Charles L. Blockson,*"Damn Rare":* *The Memoirs of an African-American Bibliophile* (Tracy, CA: Quantum Leap Publisher, 1998), 236–37.

6. Charles Flint Kellogg, *NAACP: A History of the National Association for the Advancement of Colored People,* vol. 1 (Baltimore: Johns Hopkins University Press, 1967), 31, 119, 120–21, 124, 127, 134, 142–44, 293, 306; *Baltimore Afro-American,* March 16, 1912; *New York Age,* May 24, 1917; *Evening Star,* April 13, 1912; *Chicago Broad Ax,* May 2, 1914; *Appeal* (St. Paul, Minnesota), Oct. 9, 1915; Clarence G. Contee, "Butler R. Wilson and the Boston NAACP Branch," *The Crisis* 81 (1974): 347; Stephen R. Fox, *The Guardian of Boston: William Monroe Trotter* (New York: Atheneum, 1970), 190–91, 197.

7. Daniel Murray Papers, reel 2; Daniel Murray to George Myers, April 20, May 9, 1916, Ohio Historical Society, microfilm edition; *Indianapolis Freeman,* June 10, 1916; *Washington Bee,* June 24, 1916.

8. Daniel Murray to George Myers, April 20, Sept. 19, 1916; Daniel Murray Papers, reels 2, 27; *Washington Bee,* June 27, 1914; June 24, 1916; Harold Murray and Paul Murray alumni files, Cornell University Archives; Carol Kammen, *Part and Apart: The Black Experience at Cornell, 1865–1945* (Ithaca, NY: Cornell University Library, 2009), 14–15; Marjorie Lockett, "His Own Man," *Mexican-American Review* 9 (1971): 30; Federal census and Ithaca city directory data; Poppy Cannon, *A Gentle Knight: My Husband, Walter White* (New York: Rinehart and Company, 1952), 17.

9. Daniel Murray Papers, reels 2, 27; Daniel Evans Murray death certificate, record 233138, DC Archives; *Washington Post,* Nov. 24, 1916; Sept. 14, 2013, email communication with Woodlawn Cemetery recordkeeper Jan Fontaine; 2016 email communication with Mari Carmen Bondi Murray.

10. Daniel Murray Papers, reels 2, 27; George Henry Murray World

War I draft registration card, 1917, accessed at Ancestry.com; *Plain Dealer* (Cleveland, OH), Sept. 23, Dec. 8, 1917; Nina Mjagkij, *Loyalty in Time of Trial: The African American Experience During World War I* (Lanham, MD: Rowman and Littlefield, 2011), 54–61; *Chicago Defender*, April 7, 1917; Hal S. Chase, "Struggle for Equality: Fort Des Moines Training Camp for Colored Officers," *Pylon* 39 (1978): 297, 299, 303, 305–09.

11. *Washington Post*, March 1, 1918; Eric Ledell Smith, "Lillian Evanti: Washington's African-American Diva," *Washington History* 11 (1999): 26, 30–31; US passport application for Madrenne Murray, 1918, accessed at Ancestry.com; *New Journal and Guide* (Norfolk, VA), June 30, 1917; Harold B. Murray birth certificate, box 342, DC Archives; *Washington Bee*, Nov. 22, 1919; *Chicago Defender*, Oct. 12, 1918; *Washington Herald*, March 3, 1918.

12. *Evening Star*, Oct. 31, 1918; June 24, 1919; *Hearings Before the Select Committee of the U.S. Senate, S. RES. 310* (Washington, DC: GPO, 1920), 784–85, 1214–16, 1222–24; *Washington Bee*, May 3, 31, June 7, July 5, 1919; *Washington Times*, Feb. 1, 1921; *Savannah Tribune*, June 4, 1921.

17: New Negro/Old Cit

1. Cameron McWhirter, *Red Summer: The Summer of 1919 and the Awakening of Black America* (New York: Henry Holt, 2011), 98–110; Lloyd M. Abernathy, "The Washington Race War of July, 1919," *Maryland Historical Magazine* 58 (1963): 311–21; Sandra Fitzpatrick and Maria R. Goodwin, *The Guide to Black Washington* (New York: Hippocrene Books, 1999), 121; *Washington Post*, March 1, 1999; W. E. B. DuBois, "Returning Soldiers," *The Crisis* 18 (1919), 13.

2. Daniel Murray Papers, State Historical Society of Wisconsin, microfilm reels 2, 27; *Washington Bee*, Aug. 4, 1917; Sept. 20, 1919; March 13, 1920; *Hearings Before the Committee on Interstate and Foreign Commerce of the House of Representatives* (Washington, DC: GPO, 1919), 2011ff, 2037–38; *Charlotte* [North Carolina] *Observer*, Nov. 16, 1919; *Evening Star*, March 15, 1916; Daniel Murray to George Myers, Aug. 27, 1920, Ohio Historical Society, microfilm edition, Paul Murray World War I draft registration card, 1917–18, accessed at Ancestry.com; Paul Murray alumni files, Cornell University Archives; federal census data.

3. Daniel Murray Papers, reels 2, 27; *Evening Star*, March 30, May 9, 17,

1920; *Washington Herald*, March 31, May 30, June 2, 1920; *Washington Bee*, March 2, 12, 19, 1921; *Baltimore Afro-American*, Feb. 1, 1941.

4. *Indianapolis Recorder*, Dec. 3, 1910; *Washington Bee*, April 23, 1910; Jan. 11, 1913; July 4, 1914; *Baltimore Afro-American*, Dec. 3, 1910; *Chicago Broad Ax*, Oct. 14, 1911; *Indianapolis Freeman*, Oct. 14, 1911; Willard Gatewood, *Aristocrats of Color: The Black Elite, 1880–1920* (Bloomington: Indiana University Press, 1990), 204; Langston Hughes, *The Big Sea: An Autobiography* (New York: Thunder's Mouth Press, 1986), 206.

5. Daniel Murray Papers, reels 1, 27; *Pittsburgh Courier*, March 20, 1926; *Evening Star*, Oct. 13, 1935; Daniel Murray to George Myers, Nov. 23, 1912; Sept. 19, 1916; Aug. 27, 1920.

6. Marjorie Lockett, "His Own Man," *Mexican-American Review* 9 (1971): 29, 30; Daniel Murray Papers, reel 2; US passport application for Harold Murray, 1920, and passenger lists for Madrenne Murray, 1924, and Harold Murray, 1925, accessed at Ancestry.com; New York State census for 1925; Thomas Dyja, *Walter White: The Dilemma of Black Identity in America* (Chicago: Ivan R. Dee, 2008), 37, 42–43, 70–71; Carole Marks and Diana Edkins, *The Power of Pride: Stylemakers and Rulebreakers of the Harlem Renaissance* (New York: Crown Publishers, 1999), 40; Jervis Anderson, *This Was Harlem: A Cultural Portrait, 1900–1950* (New York: Farrar, Straus and Giroux, 1983), 343. In 1920, James Weldon Johnson was promoted from field secretary to executive secretary and White to assistant executive secretary; in 1931, White succeeded Johnson and served as NAACP executive secretary until 1955.

7. Ronald M. Johnson, "Those Who Stayed: Washington Black Writers of the 1920s," *Records of the Columbia Historical Society* 50 (1980): 485, 487, 490–99; Valerie Jean, "Georgia Douglas Johnson," *Beltway Poetry Quarterly* 4 (2003); Fitzpatrick and Goodwin, *Guide to Black Washington*, 158–59; Kim Roberts, "Langston Hughes in Washington, DC: Conflict and Class," *Beltway Poetry Quarterly* 12 (2011); Hughes, *The Big Sea*, 202–03, 205, 208–09, 216–17; Langston Hughes, "Our Wonderful Society: Washington," *Opportunity*, August 1927, 226; Eric Ledell Smith, "Lillian Evanti: Washington's African-American Diva," *Washington History* 11 (1999): 30, 32, 34.

8. Daniel Murray to George Myers, Oct. 9, 1915: Aug. 27, 1920; Daniel Murray Miscellaneous Personnel Files, Library of Congress Archives, Manuscript Division, Library of Congress; *Evening Star*, Jan. 2, 1926.

9. Federal census and Washington city directory data; Daniel Murray Papers, reels 2, 27; *Evening Star*, June 7, 1924; Dec. 7, 1959; Nathaniel Murray and Paul Murray alumni files, Cornell University Archives; Daniel Murray will, box 879, DC Archives; Paul Murray probate case file 80362, Probate Division, DC Courts.

10. *Colored American*, Feb. 1, 1902; Mary Church Terrell, "What It Means to Be Colored in the Capital of the United States," *The Independent* 62 (1907), reprinted in *American Speeches: Political Oratory from Abraham Lincoln to Bill Clinton*, ed. Ted Widmer (New York: Library of America, 2006), 206; Daniel Murray to George Myers, June 3, 1905; Daniel Murray, "Cyrus Field Adams," *The Colored American Magazine* 4 (1901): 149; Mark Schneider, "The Boston NAACP and the Decline of the Abolitionist Impulse," *Massachusetts Historical Review* 1 (1999): 101–02; Lawrence Otis Graham, *The Senator and the Socialite: The True Story of America's First Black Dynasty* (New York: HarperPerennial, 2006), 308–15; Mildred Fairchild, "The Negro in Oberlin" (master's thesis, Oberlin College, 1925), 62–63; Lockett, "His Own Man," 29–31; Smith, "Lillian Evanti," 36.

11. Daniel Murray Papers, reels 1, 27; *New York Amsterdam News*, Jan. 6, 1926; *Evening Star*, Aug. 6, 7, 1925; Jan. 2, 1926; *Washington Post*, Jan. 4, 1926; Daniel Murray death certificate (box 403) and will (box 879), DC Archives; *Annual Report of the Librarian of Congress* (Washington, DC: GPO, 1923), 111–12; Anna Murray to W. E. B. DuBois, March 24, 1926, W. E. B. DuBois Papers, University of Massachusetts Amherst Archives.

Epilogue

1. W. E. B. DuBois, *Black Reconstruction: An Essay Toward a History of the Past which Black Folk Played in the Attempt to Reconstruct Democracy in America, 1860–1880* (New York: Harcourt, Brace, 1935), 30; *Annual Report of the Librarian of Congress* (Washington, DC: GPO, 1926), 17; email communication with Cheryl Fox, Library of Congress Collections Specialist, Feb. 1, 2016; *Pittsburgh Courier*, March 20, 1926; http://memory.loc.gov/ammem/aap/aaphome.html; Daniel Murray Papers, State Historical Society of Wisconsin, microfilm reels 2, 4, 27; *Colored American*, Dec. 9, 1899; Elinor Des Verney Sinnette, *Arthur Alfonso Schomburg, Black Bibliophile and Collector: A Biography* (Detroit, MI: Wayne State University Press, 1989), 84; W. E. B. DuBois to Tuskegee Institute Library, May 5, 1936, Rayford W. Logan to

DuBois, June 19, 1937, Georgia Douglas Johnson to DuBois, Nov. 28, 1935, W. E. B. DuBois Papers, University of Massachusetts Amherst Archives; *Evening Star*, Oct. 13, 1935; Aug. 15, 1937; Julie Des Jardins, "Black Librarians and the Search for Women's Biography During the New Negro History Movement," *Organization of American Historians Magazine of History* 20 (2006): 17.

2. Jacqueline Goggin, *Carter G. Woodson: A Life in Black History* (Baton Rouge: Louisiana State University Press, 1993), 55, 69, 85; *New York Amsterdam News*, Dec. 29, 1926; see also Jonathan Fenderson, "Evolving Conceptions of Pan-American Scholarship: W. E. B. DuBois, Carter G. Woodson, and the 'Encyclopedia Africana,' 1909–1963," *Journal of African American History* 95 (2010): 71–91; Kwame Anthony Appiah and Henry Louis Gates, Jr., eds., *Africana: The Encyclopedia of the African and African American Experience* (New York: Basic Civitas Books, 1999).

3. *Evening Star*, June 7, 1935; Jan. 30, Aug. 15, 1937; Feb. 25, 1938; Feb. 6, 1939; Sept. 29, 1940; *Chicago Broad Ax*, Jan. 2, 1926; *Washington Post*, July 24, 1926; Sept. 24, 1928; *Baltimore Afro-American*, Oct. 9, 1926; July 19, Nov. 29, 1930; May 13, 1939; *Pittsburgh Courier*, Feb. 6, 1929; *New Journal and Guide* (Norfolk, VA), Dec. 6, 1930; *Chicago Daily Tribune*, Nov. 21, 1930; *New York Amsterdam News*, Nov. 12, 1930; Allan Keiler, *Marian Anderson: A Singer's Journey* (Urbana: University of Illinois Press, 2002), 192–95, 202, 207, 210–13.

4. Paul Murray probate case file 80362, Probate Division, DC Courts; Matthew Gambino, "These Strangers Within Our Gates: Race, Psychiatry and Mental Illness Among Black Americans at St. Elizabeths Hospital in Washington, DC, 1900–1940," *History of Psychiatry* 19 (2008): 388; Paul Murray alumni files, Cornell University Archives; Anna Evans Murray will, box 2411, DC Archives; Oberlin College Records for Anna Evans Murray; "The Observance of the Seventy-fifth Anniversary of Public Education for Negroes in the District of Columbia," *Negro History Bulletin* 3 (1939): 37; *Chicago Defender*, Oct. 25, 1941; *Evening Star*, Aug. 15, 1937; March 9, 1947; Sept. 26, 1950; May 6, 1955; Daniel Murray Papers, reel 27; email communication with Marco Murray Lasso, April 12, 2014; *Washington Post*, May 7, 8, 1955; *Baltimore Afro-American*, June 20, 1953; *Pittsburgh Courier*, Oct. 10, 1953.

5. Daniel Murray Papers, reel 27; *Chicago Defender*, March 10, 1928; Jan. 2, 1937; March 1, 1941; *Baltimore Afro-American*, Jan. 28, 1928; Sept. 5, 1931;

Feb. 6, 1932; Aug. 8, Dec. 12, 1936; *New Journal and Guide* (Norfolk, VA), May 5, 1934; *Evening Star*, March 18, 1934; Jan. 21, 1965; email communication with Marco Murray Lasso, April 12, 2014; Paul Murray probate case file 80362, Probate Division, DC Courts; *Pittsburgh Courier*, Dec. 19, 1936; Anna Evans Murray will, box 2411, DC Archives.

6. Daniel Murray Papers, reel 27; *New York Amsterdam News*, Feb. 15, 1941; *Baltimore Afro-American*, Feb. 14, 1942; Jan. 30, 1943; *Evening Star*, Dec. 7, 1959; Herman "Skip" Mason, Jr., *The Talented Tenth: The Founders and Presidents of Alpha* (Winter Park, FL: Four-G Publishers, 1999), 104, 119–22; *Ebony* 12 (1958): 58; *Los Angeles Times*, Dec. 9, 1959.

7. Marjorie Lockett, "His Own Man," *Mexican-American Review* 9 (1971): 29–31; Daniel Murray Papers, reel 27; *Pittsburgh Courier*, Aug. 31, 1940; *New York Amsterdam News*, April 29, 1944; *New York Age*, July 16, 1949; http://scalar.usc.edu/nehvectors/stakeman/marriage-divorce-and-remarriage; telephone and email communications with Marco Murray Lasso, Maria del Carmen Murray de Bondi, Mari Carmen Bondi Murray, and Gregory Lopez-Bondi, 2013–14, 2016; *Baltimore Afro-American*, Nov. 2, 1957; Eric Ledell Smith, "Lillian Evanti: Washington's African-American Diva," *Washington History* 11 (1999): 29, 35–36; *Washington Post*, May 8, 1996.

8. *Evening Star*, Dec. 13, 1965; email communication with Jonathan Nelson, Collections Development Archivist, State Historical Society of Wisconsin, April 30, 2014; Blair A. Ruble, *Washington's U Street: A Biography* (Washington, DC: Woodrow Wilson Center Press, 2010), 173–77, 241; *Washington Post*, Feb. 8, June 28, 1970; telephone interview with Jaqueline Kilkenny, Feb. 5, 2016; Harold Murray alumni files, Cornell University Archives; Smith, "Lillian Evanti," 26; telephone interview with Maria del Carmen Murray de Bondi, June 22, 2016.

9. W. E. B. DuBois, *The Souls of Black Folk* (Chicago: A.C. McClurg, 1903), 7; Emmanuel S. Nelson, ed., *African American Authors, 1745–1945: Bio-Bibliographical Critical Sourcebook* (Westport, CT: Greenwood, 2000), 408; *Washington Bee*, Aug. 4, 1917; Gerri Major with Doris E. Saunders, *Black Society* (Chicago: Johnson Publishing Company, 1976), 390; Alexander Walters, "The Afro-American Council and Its Work," *The Colored American Magazine* 11 (1906): 207; Rayford W. Logan, *The Betrayal of the Negro from Rutherford B. Hayes to Woodrow Wilson* (New York: Collier Books, 1954), 353; *Daily Progress* (Charlottesville, VA), July 1, 2016.

10. Daniel Murray Papers, reels 1, 22; William C. Welburn, "To 'Keep the Past in Lively Memory': William Carl Bolivar's Efforts to Preserve African American Cultural Heritage," *Libraries and the Cultural Record* 42 (2007): 168; Daniel Murray, "Struggling to Rise; Or the Handicaps of the Colored Race: Just and Unjust," *AME Church Review* 29 (1913), 253; DuBois, *The Souls of Black Folk*, 5; Eric Foner, *A Short History of Reconstruction* (New York: Harper and Row, 1990), 258.

Illustration Credits

Alpha Phi Alpha Fraternity, Inc.: 39

Author's collection: 2, 17, 24, 90

The Colored American Magazine: 46

Division of Rare and Manuscript Collections, Cornell University: 36, 38

Evans-Tibbs Collection, Anacostia Community Museum Archives, Smithsonian Institution: 9, 10, 13, 28, 29, 30, 31, 32, 33, 35, 64, 70, 71, 72, 73, 76, 77, 78, 79

Harpers Ferry National Historical Park: 25, 26, 27

Henderson-Francis Collection: 55

Library of Congress: 3, 4, 11, 14, 15, 16, 19, 20, 21, 51, 62, 63, 69, 74, 75

Manuscript, Archives, and Rare Book Library, Emory University: 68

Moorland-Spingarn Research Center, Howard University: 23

National Archives and Records Administration: 66, 67

Negro History Bulletin, Association for the Study of African American Life and History: 12, 37, 70, 71

New York Public Library: 40, 42, 43, 49, 52, 54, 57, 58, 59, 60

Oberlin College Archives: 5, 6, 7

Special Collections and University Archives, University of Massachusetts–Amherst: 22

The Voice of the Negro: 1, 41, 44, 47, 53, 56

West Virginia State Archives: 8

Wisconsin Historical Society: 34, 65

Index

About the Author

Elizabeth Dowling Taylor is the *New York Times* bestselling author of *A Slave in the White House: Paul Jennings and the Madisons.* She received her PhD from the University of California, Berkeley, and over a twenty-two-year career in museum education and research held the positions of Director of Interpretation at Thomas Jefferson's Monticello and Director of Education at James Madison's Montpelier. She is now an independent scholar and lecturer, and a fellow at the Virginia Foundation for the Humanities in Charlottesville, Virginia.